ARCHITECTURE OF MINOAN CRETE

ARCHITECTURE OF

UNIVERSITY OF TEXAS PRESS · AUSTIN

MINOAN CRETE

Constructing Identity in the Aegean Bronze Age

John C. McEnroe

To Catherine,
For your patience and good humor as, year after year, we climbed up the wrong sides of the mountains.

Printed in the United States of America
First edition, 2010

Requests for permission to reproduce material from this work should be sent to:
Permissions
University of Texas Press
P.O. Box 7819
Austin, TX 78713-7819
www.utexas.edu/utpress/about/bpermission.html

∞ The paper used in this book meets the minimum requirements of ANSI/NISO Z39.48-1992 (R1997) (Permanence of Paper).

Library of Congress Cataloging-in-Publication Data

McEnroe, John C.
Architecture of Minoan Crete : constructing identity in the Aegean Bronze Age / John C. McEnroe.
p. cm.
Includes bibliographical references and index.
ISBN 978-0-292-72193-7 (cloth : alk. paper)
1. Architecture, Minoan. 2. Architecture and society—Greece—Crete. I. Title. II. Title: Constructing identity in the Aegean Bronze Age.
NA267.M39 2010
722'.61—dc22 2009048479

This book has been supported by an endowment dedicated to classics and the ancient world and funded by the Areté Foundation; the Gladys Krieble Delmas Foundation; the Dougherty Foundation; the James R. Dougherty, Jr. Foundation; the Rachael and Ben Vaughan Foundation; and the National Endowment for the Humanities.

CONTENTS

PREFACE

THE PAST TWENTY years have been extraordinary in Minoan archaeology: G. Rethemiotakis discovered a new Palace at Galatas; the Shaws excavated monumental harbor facilities at Kommos; M. Tsipopoulou excavated fascinating buildings at Aghia Photia, Petras, Halasmenos, and elsewhere. In addition to these new projects, many excavations initiated at the beginning of the twentieth century have either continued or been revived, and much of Crete has been systematically surveyed. The Institute for Aegean Prehistory built a new research center in Pachyammos. Dozens of international conferences have provided opportunities for innovative scholarship. At a time when much of the rest of the academic world and particularly academic presses are financially threatened, new scholarly journals and monograph series have been launched in Belgium, Italy, Great Britain, Poland, Greece, and the United States.

One of the byproducts of the surge of scholarship has been increasing specialization. Excavators concentrate on specific sites, and surveyors focus on selected regions. Many scholars restrict themselves to particular periods (for example, Early Minoan, Middle Minoan, or Late Minoan III) or media (pottery, tombs, frescoes, or faience, for example). As a result, we have any number of excellent excavation reports and symposia papers, but no general synthesis. The primary goal of this book, therefore, is to provide the first overall history of Minoan houses, Palaces, tombs, and towns from the Neolithic period through LM IIIC. Placing things in the larger picture changes their appearance and their significance.

There are many ways to study architecture. One can study materials and techniques, as J. Shaw has so thoroughly done (*Minoan Architecture*). One can study changes in style, as most traditional architectural histories do. One can study function—how the buildings were used--as did most of the papers in two symposia organized by the Swedish Institute (Hägg and Marinatos 1987; Hägg 1997). Or one can focus on the relation between the house (an architectural unit) and the household (a social unit), as the recent STEGA conference did. In this book I shall consider all these issues in passing, but my primary concern is with the *meaning* of buildings.

Architecture does more than provide shelter. It is, perhaps first and foremost, a medium for conveying meanings. The thesis of this book is that architecture is one of the chief media through which humans shape their identities and present themselves to others. Through architecture we construct our identities as members of families, of communities, of particular social classes, and of regional, national, and international groups. (I discuss the concept of identity in more detail in Chapter 1.)

Only a small portion of this book is based on my own fieldwork. The recent flood of important, insightful scholarship has almost entirely reshaped the field. My role is to serve as a journalist, selecting, reporting, and synthesizing some of the most interesting stories in order to provide scholars who are not necessarily specialists in the Aegean Bronze Age with access to these ongoing conversations.

A Note on Conventional Terms

Over the course of its hundred-year history, Minoan archaeology has developed a unique terminology that has caused considerable confusion and disagreement. Some of the most commonly used terms—mostly coined by A. Evans—used to describe certain types of rooms ("lustral basins," "pillar crypts," "Throne Room," etc.) and buildings ("peak sanctuaries," "theatral areas," "villas," and, most problematically, "palaces") carry with them unwarranted implications. Resulting arguments over the function(s) of a "lustral basin" or a "villa" or a "palace" have literally filled volumes (Hägg and Marinatos 1987; Hägg 1997). Attempts to replace the traditional terms with more neutral language—"court-centered buildings" as opposed to "palaces," for example—have not had much success (Schoep 2002b, 18, for example). The problems arise when we interpret these terms as implying a set of functions. In this book I am concerned with problems of function only in passing. I shall use the traditional terms only to describe specific Minoan architectural forms, capitalizing them ("Lustral Basin" rather than "lustral basin," "Palace" rather than "palace," etc.) to signal their arbitrary, conventional nature. Thus in this book a Lustral Basin is a small, square, sunken room entered by descending a small stairway; whether or not it had anything to do with lustration is for others to debate. The conventional terms are defined in a glossary at the end of the book.

ACKNOWLEDGMENTS

For more than thirty years Joe and Maria Shaw have been my teachers, mentors, and friends. They not only opened the doors, but they pushed me through them. I owe them special thanks.

Over the years I have been fortunate to do archaeological fieldwork with a number of patient and encouraging colleagues, including Phil Betancourt, Giuliana Bianco, Costis Davaras, Jeremy Rutter, Vance Watrous, and Jim Wright. I am grateful for their friendship.

Although I have been studying Minoan architecture ever since I was attracted to it by Walter Graham's work decades ago, this book is a fundamentally new project, written in the spring of 2006 when I was an NEH Fellow at the American School of Classical Studies at Athens. I am grateful to Steve Tracy, the director, for welcoming me back to the school and to the National Endowment for the Humanities for making the semester possible. I could not have written this book anywhere other than the Blegen Library at the American School, whose resources, pleasant atmosphere, and collegiality made it possible.

While at the American School, I benefited from conversations with many scholars. I would particularly like to thank Leslie Day, Kevin Glowacki, and Nancy Klein of the American School for reading parts of my work, sharing unpublished material, and inspiring new thoughts. Charles Watkinson of the ASCSA Press was instrumental in this project from its conception. I deeply appreciate his encouragement. In Crete, I am grateful to Tom Brogan, director of the INSTAP Study Center.

I am indebted also to a number of colleagues from the international institutes in Athens. James Whitley, director of the British School of Archaeology, permitted me the use of the library at the school and provided me the opportunity to attend the Upper House Seminars. I am also grateful to Erik and Brigitta Hallager of the Danish Institute at Athens for allowing me to attend the Minoan Seminar, and to Anna Lucia D'Agata of the Italian School and Eleni Hatzaki of the British School for sharing their expertise. My basic understanding of Minoan architecture changed fundamentally that spring.

The students, my colleagues, and the administration at Hamilton College provide me with the perfect place to teach and learn. Financial support from Hamilton College and from the John and Anne Fischer Professorship in Fine Arts at Hamilton made my work in Greece possible. I thank Dean Joe Urgo for his support and Dr. Peter Fischer for his generosity to the college. Krista Siniscarco of the ITS department at Hamilton helped me set up a system for making the drawings and was always just a phone call away when I needed tech support.

This book is the product of a team effort. I am deeply indebted to Humanities Editor Jim Burr and his colleagues at the University of Texas Press. Nancy Bryan worked on the project as Assistant Marketing Manager. Manuscript Editor Lynne Chapman and freelance copyeditor Lawrence Kenney improved every page of my text. Lindsay Starr designed the book. I thank them for their expertise, enthusiasm, and thoughtful criticisms.

Finally, I would especially like to thank Jan Driessen of the Université catholique de Louvain, Dan Pullen of Florida State University, Jeremy Rutter of Dartmouth College, and Todd Whitelaw of the Institute of Archaeology, University College of London. Each read the entire manuscript and painstakingly offered advice, unpublished information, firm (but necessary) criticisms, and encouragement. They were extraordinarily generous with their time and their knowledge.

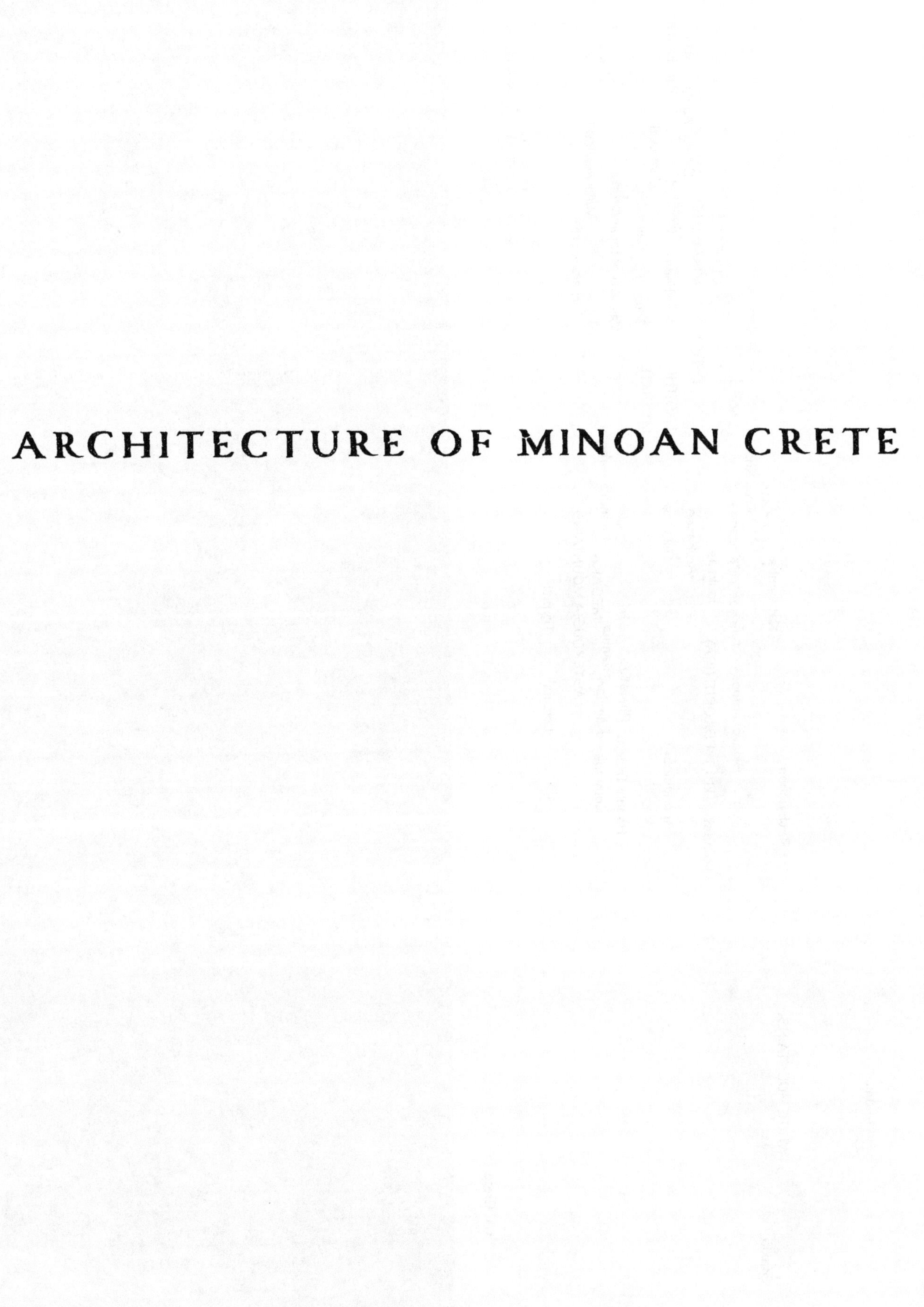

ARCHITECTURE OF MINOAN CRETE

Khania
WHITE MOUNTAINS
Sfakia
Rethymnon
Katsamba
Amnisos
Nirou Khani
Sklavokambos
Tylissos
Knossos
Malia
Monasteraki
PSILORITI (IDA)
Iouktas
Archanes
Galatas
Karphi
GULF OF
MIRABELLO
Apodoulou
LASITHI
MT. DIKTE
Pseira
Mochlos
Siteia
Aghia Photia
Palaikastro
Chamaizi
Gournia
Kavousi
Haghia Triada
Phaistos
Kommos
Kamilari
Kannia
MESARA
Khondro Viannou
Vasiliki
Monasteraki
Zakros
Makrygiallos
ASTEROUSIA MOUNTAINS
Myrtos
Hierapetra
Lebena
Trypiti
0
30 km

1.1. Crete.

The Land, the People, Identity

The Land

SEVENTY MILLION years ago, a slow-motion collision between the African and the European tectonic plates pushed a buckled ridge of land above the surface of the sea. Complex geological processes, including a nearly complete submergence, continued to shape the land for the next sixty-five million years. Three to four million years ago, in the middle Pliocene, the ridge reemerged as the largest island in the Aegean Sea (fig. 1.1).[1] Like a miniature continent, Crete has the entire range of Mediterranean topography condensed into a land mass ca. 250 km long and less than 60 km wide: snow-capped mountains, long beaches, inhospitable dry lands, fertile plains, bustling cities and large expanses of nearly inaccessible wilderness. Crete shares much with the surrounding continents of Europe, Asia, and Africa, but it also has much that is unique: of the approximately 1,650 species of plants known on the island, for example, about 160 are endemic.

A mountainous spine runs the length of the island. On the north the mountains give way to foothills, coastal plains, and large bays that provide deep harbors for modern ships. Historically most of the population has been concentrated along this coast. The large cities of Khania, Rethymnon, Herakleion, Haghios Nikolaos, and Siteia are here, along with most of the modern tourist developments. On the south the mountains descend so precipitously that habitation is limited to scattered coastal villages accessible mainly by boat. The single large town on the south coast is Hierapetra, located at the narrowest part of the island facing Africa.

The character of the landscape changes dramatically from west to east. The vast White Mountains dominate the western end of the island. On the north coast, the modern city of Khania was also an important Minoan city. East of Khania, the mountains turn into rolling hills before rising again to form Mt. Ida, Crete's tallest peak (2,456 m), located at the center of the island. The lush Amari valley, with the Minoan sites of Monasteraki and Apodoulou, runs along the western slopes of Mt. Ida. The eastern slopes of Mt. Ida descend into the fertile wine-growing land around Archanes. Here the highest promontory, Mt. Iouktas, overlooks the modern city of Herakleion and the Minoan city of Knossos.

Further to the south the Mesara plain, watered by the Ieropotomos River, has about two-thirds of the most arable soil on the island (ca. 40,485 ha) and once provided vast amounts of grain for export by the Roman administrators stationed in the Roman city of Gortyn.[2] The rugged Asterousia Mountains separate the Mesara from the south coast.

The Lasithi Mountains (Mt. Dikte) rise further to the east. Near the center of the range, at an elevation of ca. 850 m, is the Lasithi plateau, a large upland plain dotted with picturesque windmills. The coast to the north, near Malia, consists of long, flat beaches. East of the Lasithi Mountains the island narrows to only 12 km at the Isthmus of Hierapetra. The Thripti Mountains border the isthmus on the east and continue into the lower, barren mountains that extend to the east coast. Siteia is the main modern harbor in this part of the island. In the

Bronze Age, there were smaller harbors at Palaikastro and Zakros on the east coast.

Today a new national highway system makes it easy to get from one part of the island to another. In the Bronze Age the pace would have been slower, and walking times are more meaningful than the map. For example, the Minoan Palace at Phaistos is a little more than 40 km from the Minoan Palace at Knossos as the crow flies. The British archaeologist J. Pendlebury, a famously fast walker, writes that the trip takes about twelve hours on foot.[3] Athletic visitors using the E4 Hiking Trail can walk the length of the island in about ten days. Standing among the palms at Vai, on the sandy beach just north of Palaikastro, one can think back to the lush stands of chestnuts in the foothills south of Khania and reflect upon the extraordinary range of the island's topography and flora.

The fragmented and diverse nature of the landscape of Crete has always encouraged the development of distinctive regional cultures. Specific economic strategies, local festivals, and long-standing traditions give each part of Crete a distinct character of which its inhabitants are uniformly proud. Perhaps the best-known example of this regional identity is the area of Sfakia in the White Mountains of southwest Crete. Throughout Greece the men of Sfakia are regarded as fierce, independent, proud, cunning, and resistant to outside pressure. This stereotypical image of the Sfakiot is specifically tied to the rugged, isolated mountain environment, but, in a larger sense, it also embodies the way in which many Cretans picture their relation to the rest of Greece and to the world.

The People

In her book *Days in Africa* (1914), E. Bosanquet describes arriving in Khania on a boat from Marseilles and finding a fascinatingly complex city "of distinctly African flavour owing to its intercourse with the Cyrenaica." Looking around, she observed "an Arab from Benghazi," "remnants of a black serf population," "full-blooded Ethiopians in sacks," and "Arabs in flowing white from Cyrenaica." She speaks of memories of Saracen invaders and the recently departed Russian, French, and Italian soldiers who had been sent to establish peace in the newly independent island. The architecture included "Venetian galley houses" and "the Turkish Cemetery." In the harbor were "plenty of boats, Austrian, Italian or coasting Greek steamers."[4] The people, in other words, were as diverse as the topography: African, Asian, and European.

Homer also famously reported on the island's diversity:

> Crete is an island that lies in the middle
> Of the wine-dark sea, a fine, rich land
> With ninety cities swarming with people
> Who speak many different languages.
> There are Achaeans there and native Cretans,
> Cydonians, Pelasgians, and three tribes of Dorians.[5]

A. Evans thought that the Minoans were the product of several waves of immigration, first from southern Anatolia, with later additions from Libya and the Nile Valley, along with people of "Mediterranean stock." He associated nearly all the major cultural shifts in Minoan history with the arrival of peoples from outside the island.[6] While Evans based his interpretation on the grounds of similarities in artifacts, burial types, and linguistics, it is now possible to do genetic studies of population movements. A recent study using Y-chromosome haplotypes indicates that the earliest farmers in Crete had arrived from central Anatolia and that there were subsequent waves of immigration from Syria-Palestine and northwest Anatolia.[7]

Crete continued to have an ethnically diverse population under both the Venetians and the Ottomans, as S. McKee and M. Green have emphasized.[8] After Crete became an independent country in 1898, ethnic and cultural diversity, although still remarkable to Bosanquet, rapidly declined. Sizeable communities of Jews and Armenians left, and most of the so-called Turks, who were mainly Greek-speaking Moslems, emigrated even before the massive population exchanges between Greece and Asia Minor in 1923.[9] Today diversity is again on the rise as tourists visit from all over the world and growing numbers of people from other European Union countries, especially Great Britain and Germany, buy retirement houses.

Identity

A Google search of the words "archaeology" and "identity" results in 4,330,000 hits. In recent years, literature in anthropology, archaeology, and history has become filled with such phrases as "national identity," "ethnic identity," "gender identity," "the other," etc. The term "identity" is so ubiquitous that McKee has only half jokingly called for a moratorium on its use.[10] A major problem is that the term is not used consistently and is too seldom defined. In this book I shall follow the characterization recently provided by M. Diaz-Andreu, S. Lucy, A. Babić and D. Edwards.[11] I am primarily concerned with how individuals identify themselves with broader groups. As Diaz-Andreu and Lucy put it, "Identity, as we understand it, is inextricably linked to the sense of belonging. Through identity we perceive ourselves, and others see us, as belonging to certain groups and not to others. Being part of a group entails active engagement. Identity, therefore, is not a static thing, but a continual process."[12]

Personal or group identity is never singular, and multiple identities often overlap. M. Herzfeld offers a modern example of such fluidity in his study of the pseudonymous village of Glendi on the slopes of Mt. Ida. He describes what he terms the "concentric loyalties" of the Glendiot man: he is fiercely proud of his village, his region, Crete, and Greece.[13] Furthermore, Herzfeld notes, "*any* outsider—whether foreigner, non-Cretan, East Cretan, non-Rethymniot, lowlander, non-covillager (*ksenokhorianos*), non-kin, or more or less distant kin—is definitionally inferior."[14] Such concentric and overlapping identities, in other words, are defined in terms of oppositions: belonging and excluding are parts of the same process. We can transpose Herzfeld's notion of concentric loyalties back into the Bronze Age. In a multicultural island so topographically and demographically diverse as Crete, what did it mean to be a Knossian? a Herakleiot? a Minoan? The answers lie in much more than where a person happened to have been born.

In this book, I am interested in the role architecture plays in shaping, maintaining, and presenting identities and, in turn, how social notions of identity shape the buildings. I shall be concerned with different sorts of identity. Several of these, including household identity (generally that of a nuclear family), community identity (village or town), regional identity, ethnic identity, and island-wide Minoan identity, have to do with a sense of place: they are tied to the notions of home and belonging. Other kinds of identity make up additional layers of differentiation and assimilation. For example, Aegean archaeologists have long been concerned with the issue of social status—a person's location within a social hierarchy, both as self-proclaimed and as perceived. In this book we will see that architecture served as an eloquent, nuanced language for claiming a place in the larger social order. History also plays a role. How did the Minoans use buildings (tombs, Palaces, and houses) to declare a particular relation with the past? By echoing ancient forms Minoans could use buildings to assert their legitimacy and continuity; by ostentatiously breaking with local tradition, they could proclaim a broader Minoan, or even international, alliance.

Time, Chronology, and Historical Narratives

Like the various forms of identity, the perception of time (as opposed to the physics of time) is a social construction. For example, when R. Pashley traveled through Crete in 1834, he was surprised to find that the people of the island did not share his European sense of time and history. After speaking with a small group, he observed, "Not one knows the year, or has any idea of an *era*. They reckon neither by Christ nor Mohammed . . . but date all events one by another. Thus, in Crete, the year of the great earthquake; the time when Khadji Osmán Pashá was governor of Khaniá; the outbreaking of the Greek revolution; the peace of Khusein-bey; the war of Khadji Mikhali; and the final submission to the Egyptians are the principal epochs to which all the events of the last five and twenty years are referred."[15]

That local system of keeping track of events was intricately detailed, but it did without references to numerical chronologies and, more important, without the sense of unilinear direction Pashley expected. The Cretan perception of time in 1834 is an example of what J. McGlade calls "kairological," as opposed to chronological, time. This form of historical narrative describes time experientially and organizes it by reference to human-centered events.[16]

A. Evans constructed the chronological system used in Minoan archaeology. His division of the chronology into three main periods, Early Minoan (EM), Middle Minoan (MM), and Late Minoan (LM), is an example of what I. Hodder describes as the "classical beginning-middle-end narrative."[17] It was not a neutral sequence of dates, but a narrative with a story line that emphasized development, maturity, and decline, the climax coming in Evans's "New Era" at the end of the Middle Minoan period and the beginning of the Late. That story was, in turn, part of a larger Darwinian tale of universal progress.[18]

Today Evans's metanarratives are either critically deconstructed or politely ignored, but the basic framework of his chronological system is alive and well in two competing variations.[19] The more traditional, "lower" chronology as championed by P. Warren and V. Hankey is based primarily on cross-dating, that is, it uses the evidence of datable imports in Minoan contexts in conjunction with Minoan objects found in datable foreign contexts.[20] The second system, known as the "higher" chronology, relies more heavily on dendrochronology and radiocarbon dating. Using these two methods along with cross-dating, S. Manning proposes a modified version of the higher chronology.[21] There are a couple of significant differences between the resulting sets of dates. For example, Warren and Hankey place the beginning of the Early Minoan I period much earlier than Manning, making the Early Bronze Age longer. Recently, however, Warren has agreed that 3100/2900 might be a more appropriate beginning date for Early Minoan.[22] A second difference centers on the date of the Theran eruption. An increasing number of scholars now accept Manning's higher date of ca. 1628 BC, but the debate continues. The two systems are juxtaposed below.

Warren and Hankey 1989, 169	
EM I	3650/3500–3000/2900
EM II	2900–2300/2150
EM III	2300/2150–2160/2025
MM IA	2160/1979–20th c.
MM IB	19th c.
MM II	19th c.–1700/1650
MM IIIA	1700/1650–1640/1630
MM IIIB	1640/1630–1600
LM IA	1600/1580–1480
Theran Eruption ca. 1550–1530	
LM IB	1480–1425
LM II	1425–1390
LM IIIA1	1390–1370/60
LM IIIA2	1370/60–1340/30
LM IIIB	1340/30–1190 +–
LM IIIC	1190+–1070 +–

Manning 1995, 217	
EM I	3100/3000–2700/2650
EM IB/EM IIA	(2700)–2650
EM IIA	2650–2450/2350
EM IIB	2450/2350–2200/2150
EM III	2200/2150–2050/2000
MM IA	2050/2000–1925/1900
MM IB	1925/1900–1900/1875
MM II	1900/1875–1750/1720
MM IIIA(-B)	1750/1720–1700/1680
MM IIIB/LM IA	1700/1680–1675/1650
LM IA	1675/1650–1600/1550
Theran Eruption ca. 1628	
LM IB	1600/1550–1490/1470
LM II	1490/1470–1435/1405
LM IIIA1	1435/1405–1390/1370
LM IIIA2	1390/1370–1360/1325
LM IIIB	1360/1325–1200/1190
LM IIIC	[no dates given]

Because the main concern of this book has to do with broader architectural phases rather than with matters of specific dates, I use a very simple, broad system that corresponds roughly to Manning's modified high chronology (see table 1.1). Readers should translate the dates in this book into the system they think most appropriate.

Architectural History and Individualist Narratives

In writing an architectural history in the twenty-first century, what sort of historical narrative should one construct within that chronological framework? The grand Evansian model that describes a unilinear evolution from primitive hut to sophisticated palace to a final decadent squatter occupation no longer seems tenable.[23] In our nonlinear age, we are skeptical of the sweeping notions of progress and decline, and we are aware that things seem complicated, particular, and sometimes arbitrary.

Table 1.1.
Simplified System of Architectural Phases

Neolithic	Aceramic	ca. 7000–6000 BC
	EN I	ca. 6000–5000 BC
	EN II	ca. 5000–4500 BC
	MN/LN	ca. 4500–4000 BC
	LN/FN	ca. 4000–3000 BC
Early Prepalatial	EM I–EM IIB	ca. 3000–2200 BC
Late Prepalatial	EM III–MM IA	ca. 2200–1900 BC
Protopalatial	MM IB–MM IIB	ca. 1900–1750 BC
Neopalatial	MM III	ca. 1750–1700 BC
	LM IA	ca. 1700–1580 BC
	Thera Eruption late seventeenth century	
	LM IB	ca. 1580–1490 BC
Final Palatial	LM II–early LM IIIA2	ca. 1490–1360 BC
Postpalatial	LM IIIA2–LM IIIB	ca. 1360–1200 BC
LM IIIC	LM IIIC	ca. 1200–1100 BC

Recently Minoan scholars have been writing different narratives. Thanks to developments in the study of pottery and chronology, they are able to measure time in terms of a generation or two rather than in broad historical epochs, allowing them to understand the relationships among sites in much greater detail. They have learned that each of the major Minoan Palaces of the later Bronze Age had an individually distinctive history and that the relations between one Palace and another were likely to have been complex and changing. It is no longer sufficient to describe, as A. Evans did, the Neopalatial period as a unitary evolutionary stage, a New Era. That sort of label masks complicated interactions among the builders and their sponsors.

As Diaz-Andreu and Lucy point out, the growing interest in the topic of identity is part of an even larger shift in the field of archaeology. Rather than analyzing the past in terms of broad social processes, as the New Archaeology did in the 1970s, scholars today are examining not the general, but the individual. They are attempting to read competing multilinear, human-centered—one might say kairological—narratives that individual Minoans embodied in their buildings, and I propose to look here at the most interesting of these emerging stories.

Architecture and Social Identity in Neolithic Crete

CA. 7000–3000 BC

THE FOUR MILLENNIA from 7000 to 3000 BC saw the establishment of the first settlement at Knossos and ended in the Final Neolithic period. During this period Knossos became the most important settlement on the island and the basic forms and techniques of Minoan vernacular architecture were established.

Characterizing Neolithic

The earliest excavated remains in Crete date to the four-millennia-long Neolithic period.[1] Perhaps because of the immensity of the time involved, the Neolithic period in Crete is still generally understood in terms of broad, simplistic stereotypes.[2] It is traditionally assumed to have been a period that was both essentially timeless and classless, each household maintaining its own subsistence-level existence. In these respects, the Neolithic has been pictured as the antithesis of the Bronze Age. P. Tomkins recently put it as follows: Neolithic is seen as simple; Bronze Age is complex. Neolithic depends on domestic production; Bronze Age employs craft specialization. Neolithic is self-sufficient; Bronze Age is interdependent. Neolithic is conservative; Bronze Age is dynamic. In other words, Tomkins notes, Neolithic has traditionally been defined in terms of what it was *not*.[3]

Recently many of these assumptions have been challenged. Petrographic analysis of the Early Neolithic pottery at Knossos suggests that ceramic production is likely to have been more specialized than previously thought. For example, rather than having been entirely locally produced, at least some of the pottery found at Knossos had been imported from the Gulf of Mirabello region in eastern Crete, and some came from much more distant places.[4] This is one clear indication that each household was not a self-sufficient, totally independent economic unit, but that it was involved in exchange.[5] In addition, rather than having been a vast homogenous, timeless period the Neolithic period now appears to have been punctuated by moments of dynamic change.[6]

The Village and the House

In the Early Neolithic period at Knossos the two major elements of Cretan domestic architecture were already firmly established. One of these was the adoption of the hamlet (ten to one hundred people) or the village (one hundred to one thousand people) as the basic form of settlement, a pattern that characterized the Cretan countryside until relatively recently.[7] The second was the establishment of the individual house, almost certainly intended for a nuclear family, as the most common form of dwelling.

Cretan houses vary significantly from one place to another. Built of local materials, using local techniques, each settlement developed a unique character that helped to establish and maintain personal, family, and community identities.[8] Beyond the regional and local variations, however, there were some overall, island-wide architectural parameters.

In its most common form, the Cretan house is rectangular with a flat roof. The number of rooms, their size, and their appointments vary. The rectangular form of the houses made it relatively easy to build additions as the composition of the household altered. The house could also be made smaller by closing off a room or allowing it to fall into decay.

The basic building materials are rubble masonry, mud brick, rough timbers, branches, earth, and clay.[9] With the exception of timber in some parts of the island, all the building materials could have been gathered in the immediate vicinity of the building site.[10] The Cretan house was well suited to its climate. The thick walls and thick, flat roofs absorb the daytime heat, keeping the interior cool, and they radiate heat during the cooler nights.[11]

Despite later intrusions of features derived from foreign models such as ashlar masonry (Middle and Late Minoan), gabled and tiled roofs (classical), vaulted construction (Roman/Byzantine), and extensive woodwork (Ottoman), these natural materials have remained the basic stuff of Cretan houses from the establishment of the first permanent settlement at Knossos until their currently ongoing replacement by reinforced concrete.

J. Shaw's *Minoan Architecture: Materials and Techniques* examines Minoan construction in such depth that I need only review a few of the major points.[12] Typically the lower section of the walls, the socle, was of rubble (fig. 2.1). The size and kind of stones used vary according to local availability. The stones were generally laid in more or less horizontal courses. Walls were built simultaneously from the inside and outside in two "skins." Relatively large stones were used for the outer face of the wall, and the interstices of both faces were filled with earth and small stones. As this sort of construction tended to splay, it was important to insert a number of stones that were wide enough to nearly span the width of the wall to provide the necessary horizontal bonding. Later, wood was sometimes used in wall construction for this purpose. Occasionally walls were built to their entire height in rubble. More often in the Neolithic period, the stone socle course was relatively low and the upper wall was of mud brick (fig. 2.2).[13] One or both faces might be coated with mud plaster.

The roof was the most troublesome part of the house, requiring careful construction and frequent repairs. Thanks to a meticulous study of a fragment of a Late Bronze Age roof by J. Shaw and studies of the roofs of modern vernacular houses in Crete, we know quite a bit about their construction (fig. 2.3).[14] In traditional houses of present-day Crete, each part of the roof has a specific technical name. The development of this sort of specialized vocabulary is a way of assuring that the forms

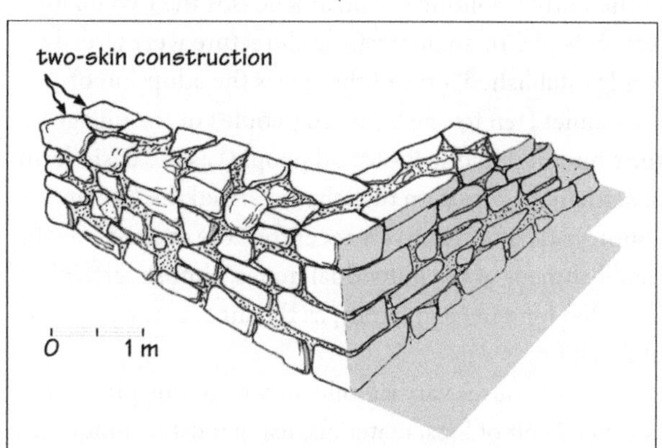

2.1. Reconstruction. Rubble wall.

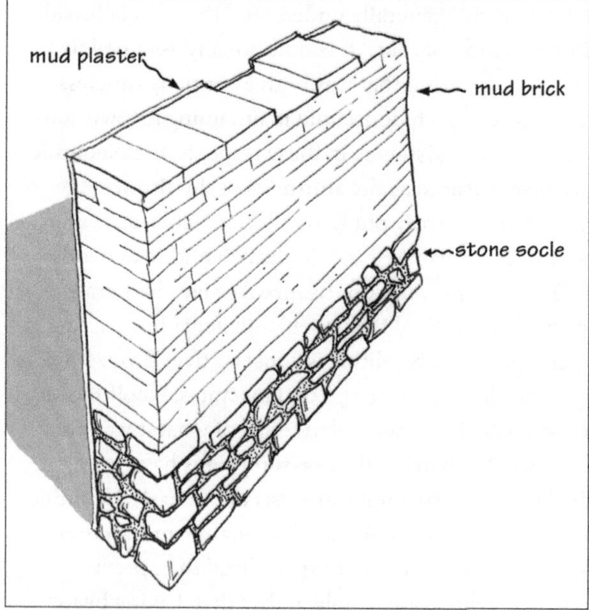

2.2. Reconstruction. Mud brick on rubble socle.

are standardized and that knowledge of the technique can be passed from one generation to another.[15]

When a roof was built over a large span, a single, massive beam was first laid across the width of the room, set into special niches at the tops of the walls. Next, wooden beams were laid across the main beam at right angles to it. Then a layer of small sticks and leaves was used to cover the gaps between the beams. Above them, a thick layer of earth was laid down, usually with a slight slope to allow for drainage. Finally, one or more layers of waterproof clay were applied and beaten with a special paddle called a *domatokopána*. The roof required yearly renewal, and every few years would have been completely replaced. As the roofs had to be built quickly, in recent times they were often done on Sundays or holidays (usually while the moon was waning, which was thought to help prevent leaks) and were the occasion for parties attended by friends and relatives.[16]

In addition to providing the primary source of shelter, the roof was the most important part of the house in other ways, affecting several aspects of the overall form of the building. The weight of the roof and its limited tensile strength dictated the possible spans and the sizes of rooms. Its flatness made it relatively easy to expand the houses by adding rooms as they were needed: the sloping lines of gabled roofs are much less adaptable. In the same way, the flat roof also allowed for houses to be built contiguously with their neighbors and enabled villages to take shape as clusters of bordering cells (see fig. 3.2). Perhaps more than any other single element, the flat roof determined the general appearance of Cretan villages.

Knossos

The major difficulty in dealing with the Neolithic architecture of Crete is that after more than a century of excavation only one settlement, Knossos, has been systematically excavated to any considerable extent (fig. 2.4). The key excavations were done by A. Evans in 1923–1924 and by J. Evans from 1957 through 1960 and in 1969–1970. In the past forty-five years no new excavations have significantly added to our understanding of the Neolithic architecture of Crete.[17]

Even at Knossos the evidence is limited. The site is essentially a tell—an artificial mound formed by centuries of occupation debris—with a Neolithic deposit up to 11 m thick. Unfortunately this deposit lies directly beneath the later Palace. The only places available for excavation were at the western edge of the Palace and beneath the Central Court. Within this restricted

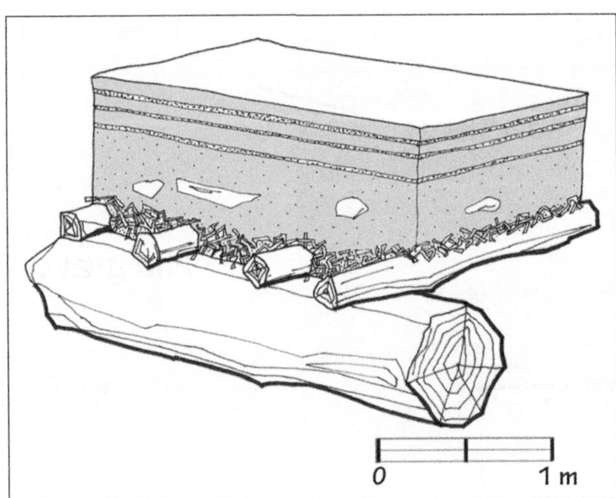

2.3. Construction of a flat roof.

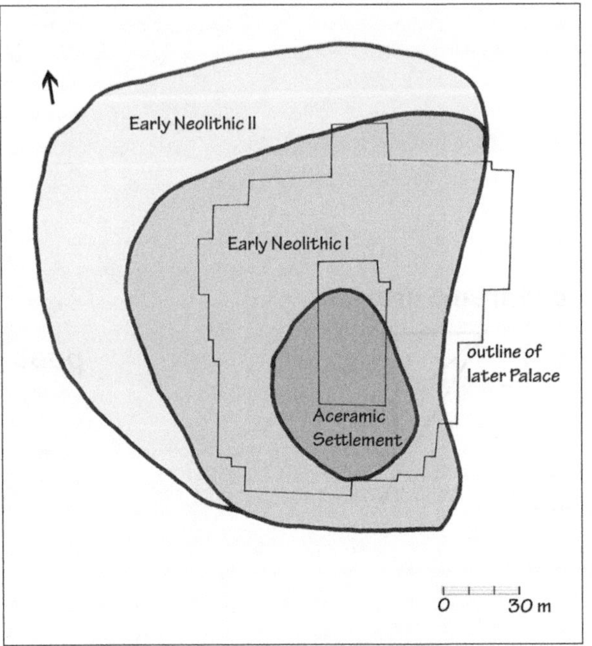

2.4. Plan. Early Neolithic Knossos. After J. Evans 1971, fig. 1.

framework, J. Evans was able to distinguish ten strata representing five major chronological phases from the earliest Aceramic settlement through the Final Neolithic period. J. Evans's chronology was recently confirmed by a new sounding in the Central Court.[18] Readers should note that the spans given for the various subphases of Neolithic in the following sections are only very rough approximations: we do not have clear beginning and end dates for these periods, only isolated radiocarbon dates that fall at points within the brackets suggested below. Similarly we do not have a series of buildings that can give us anything like a continuous architectural history: we have only fragments of a few buildings representing isolated glimpses of life at a handful of random moments in the four-millennia-long period.

Aceramic, 7000–6000 BC

It is not possible to reconstruct the overall shape of the earliest houses: only postholes and pits remain as footprints of the vanished buildings. The houses consisted of flimsy wattle-and-daub walls arranged around simple pits that served as hearths (fig. 2.5).

The construction technique is related to basketry, which may have been one of the main technologies in this community that did not use fired clay to produce pottery. A series of posts were first driven into the ground at intervals. Smaller branches were woven around the posts horizontally and the whole covered with mud daub (fig. 2.6). This kind of construction would have provided only a thin screen between the inhabitants and the outside world. It would have blocked the wind and provided shade and a degree of privacy, but it would not have been of much value against cold, excessive heat, or rain. These buildings may have been only seasonally occupied by a small group of perhaps twenty-five to fifty people.[19]

The people at Knossos had brought with them a complex mixed farming-livestock economy, growing a variety of crops and raising several kinds of animals. The surprising discovery of obsidian from the island of Melos points to early communication with other parts of the Aegean. Stone jewelry and baked-clay figurines may reflect more abstract thought. Yet the impermanence of the buildings suggested to the excavator that this earliest settlement might have been only a temporary camp. The most per-

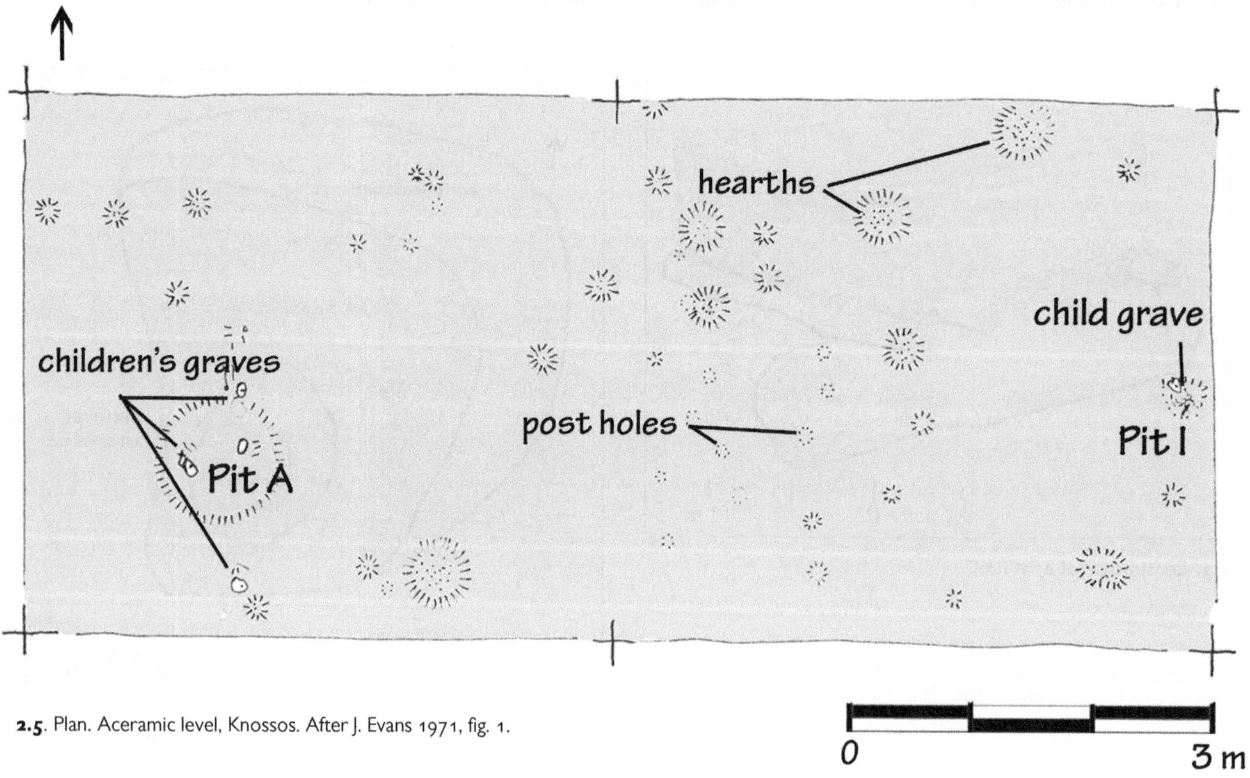

2.5. Plan. Aceramic level, Knossos. After J. Evans 1971, fig. 1.

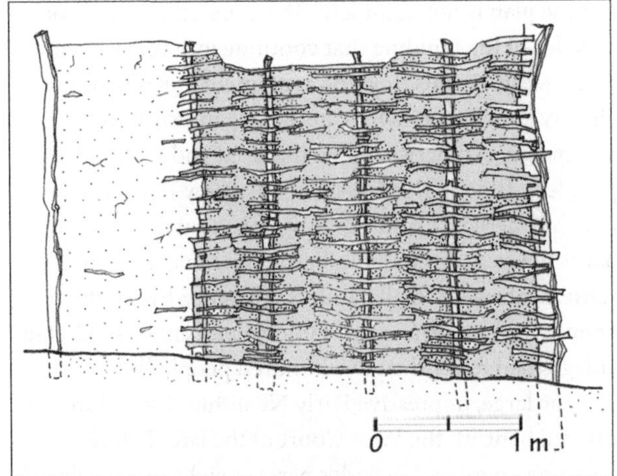

2.6. Reconstruction. Wattle-and-daub wall. After Theochares 1973, fig. 149.

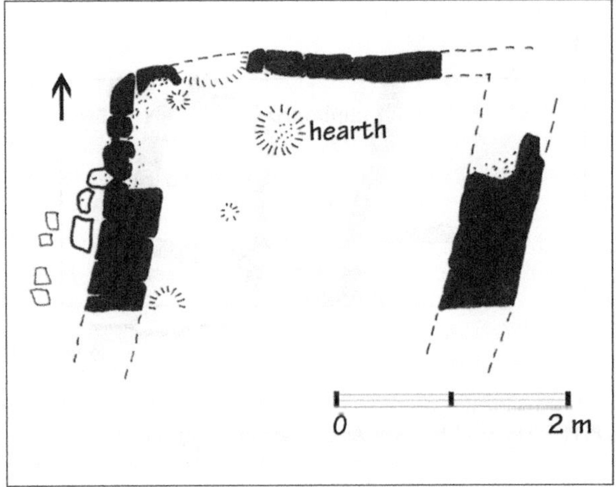

2.7. Plan. House E, Knossos. After J. Evans 1964, fig. 9.

manent features of the buildings were the seven shallow graves dug into the floors to hold the bodies of children.

The Early Neolithic Settlement 6000–5000

By the Early Neolithic period a permanent settlement was established at the site. From the small Aceramic camp, not much larger than the area of the Central Court of the later Palace, the settlement grew steadily over the course of the Early Neolithic period.

The buildings of this settlement are rectangular, and they were built to last. The walls were made from a variety of stones collected from the surrounding hills or from neighboring dilapidated buildings. Several walls included a number of discarded querns and mortars. The most important building material, however, was clay. This humble material has been associated with the establishment of permanent settlements throughout much of the ancient Near East.[20] At Knossos, most of the upper walls of the houses were of mud brick.[21] Baked bricks reported by the excavators, included randomly within rubble walls, were probably mud bricks taken from other buildings that had been destroyed by fire. Fragments of mud bearing the impressions of branches indicate that the flat roofs were already being constructed more or less by means of the technique described above (see fig. 2.3).

None of the plans of the buildings known from this period are complete. House E of the Early Neolithic I period is the earliest substantial building excavated at the site (fig. 2.7). Its walls vary in construction, probably as a result of a number of repairs and modifications. They were made of a variety of materials, including rubble, baked bricks, and worn-out stone tools. The plan of the building is unusual for Knossos. It appears to consist of a single rectangular room with a fire pit dug into the floor near the north wall.

House C (fig. 2.8), which belongs to a slightly later phase of the Early Neolithic I period, consists of several rooms. Its walls were of mud brick built on a flimsy rubble footing. The single line of stones may not have served as a proper foundation but was perhaps used simply to mark out the line of the walls. While not overly sturdy, the walls were surprisingly neat. Their interior faces were coated with a layer of mud plaster that was carefully finished to form a sharp angle with the floor. Inside the house a series of features established a fixed spatial order around which the household would have organized its movements. Near the centers of the rooms were a series of shallow depressions that served as small hearths. Not all were in use at the same time; rather, they were used for awhile and then filled with clay. Toward the north part of the building, a built triangular area served as a cupboard. Near another wall are traces of a domed clay oven. On the north, the two largest rooms open onto a paved area with a large cooking hole. In the plan, the building consists mainly of two rooms,

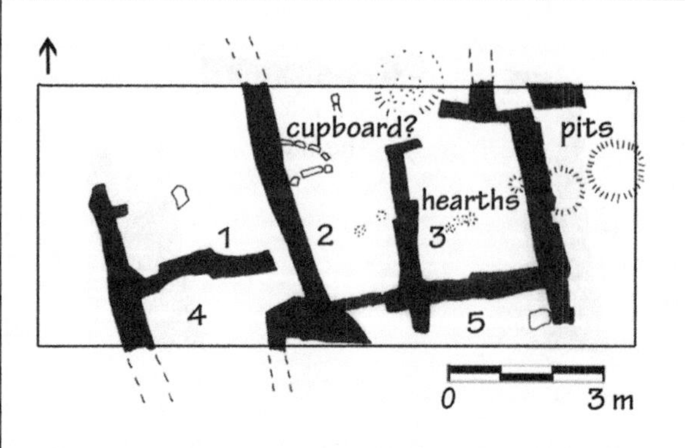

2.8. Plan. House C, Knossos. After J. Evans 1964, fig. 11.

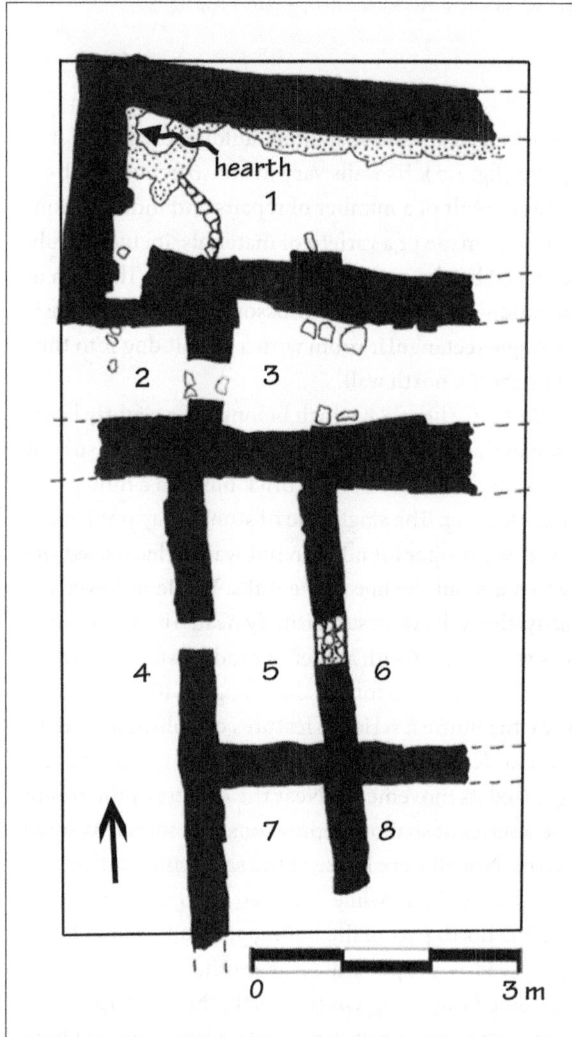

2.9. Plan. West Court House, Knossos. After Treuil 1983, fig. 128.

but the plan is not complete. There are other rooms on all sides of the building that continue into the unexcavated scarp. By this time the settlement at Knossos had already grown to some 2.5 hectares and may have had a population of between two hundred and six hundred people.[22] Though this is a small village by European or North American standards, it is not so small by the standards of Crete. Even in the Early Minoan period most settlements were small hamlets of twenty-five to thirty people, and as late as 1948 some 86 percent of all Cretan villages had fewer than five hundred people.[23]

The large, impressive Early Neolithic II structure excavated beneath the West Court of the later Palace covers some 50 m^2 and includes parts of eight rooms (fig. 2.9). Furthermore, the building continues beyond the limits of the excavation in all directions. The construction was much more regular than that of earlier periods. All the walls were of mud brick on stone socles. The socles all used the same basic two-skin technique. Especially large stones were carefully selected for the major points of stress, such as wall ends and around doorways. The plan is correspondingly regular. Most of the corners were laid out in right angles, and the doorways were centered on their walls and axially aligned. The building is extraordinary in that houses with more than three rooms do not appear elsewhere in the Aegean until the Early Bronze II period.[24]

Middle Neolithic-Late Neolithic, ca. 4500–4000 BC

The village at Knossos continued to grow into the later Neolithic period, reaching a population that C. Broodbank estimates to have been between five hundred and one thousand people.[25] There are corresponding changes in the buildings.

The Middle Neolithic House D, beneath the Central Court of the later Palace, appears to be a single-room structure measuring ca. 4 m by 4 m (fig. 2.10). This building is interesting primarily because of its construction and arrangement of interior features. As usual, the building was of mud brick on a stone socle, in this case preserved up to 1 m high. The interior faces of the walls and the floors were covered with plaster. In the north wall, adjacent to the entrance, the excavators identified two slots for timbers. They were uncertain whether the wooden beams inserted in these slots supported

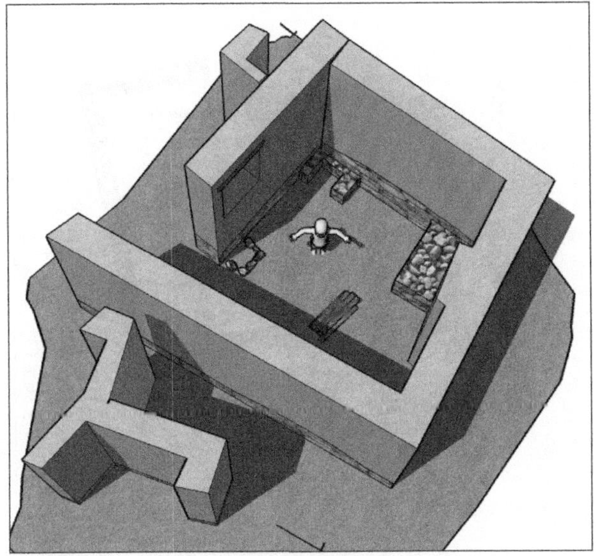

2.10. Reconstruction. Central Court, House D, Knossos. Based on J. Evans 1964, fig. 16.

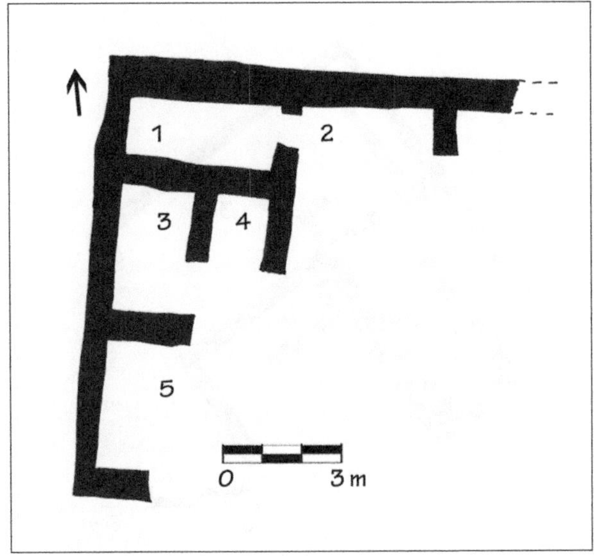

2.11. Plan. Great Middle Neolithic House, Knossos. After Zois 1973, fig. 18.

the wall or held the lintel of a window, as shown in the reconstruction. While the close pairing of window and door may appear unusual to our way of thinking, it has numerous parallels in later Minoan architecture (cf. fig. 6.13). At least in those later examples, the arrangement made for an economical use of wood, by allowing the intervening vertical timber and the upper lintel to serve double duty, framing both openings in the wall.

Near the center of the south wall, an internal pilaster projects slightly into the room. Similar features are common in Middle Neolithic Thessaly (Sesklo, Tsangli, Otzaki) and are known in Anatolia (Äan Hassan). All of the various interpretations are debatable: they might be internal buttresses (but would they work?); they could serve as space dividers (but was this their main function?); they might be intended to reduce the span of the room (but the spans were already small); among contiguous houses, they might be associated with entrances from above or upper-story rooms (but would this apply to Knossos?).[26] J. Driessen suggests another possibility, namely, that these features might have supported molded clay devices similar to the bucrania and relief figures at Çatal Hüyük.[27]

The arrangement of the other interior features of House D is simple and logical. The door is at one corner of the room. Near the center of the room is a hearth, providing the heat and light that shaped the surrounding space almost as clearly as the walls. The space immediately around the central hearth was kept clear, for it was in this zone, presumably, that the people of the house gathered for most of their household activities. Further back from the hearth, behind this busy space, a series of built features was aligned along the walls. These serve primarily to store the household goods in an orderly fashion. A roughly built cupboard stood beneath the window. A more substantial cupboard was built in the northeast corner. And in the southeast corner, at the furthest point from the door, a large raised platform forms a distinct subdivision of the interior. The exposed area directly in front of the door was left empty.

Just to the south of House D is the so-called Great House of the Middle Neolithic period (fig. 2.11). Although only about half of the building has been excavated, it is huge by Neolithic standards and large by any standards. Its five rooms cover over 100 m^2. Walls nearly a meter thick at the base would have allowed even for the construction of a second story.

Though unusual within the broader Aegean context, where most people were making use of much smaller two- and three-roomed structures, the Great House had several parallels in Crete. At Katsamba on the coast near modern Herakleion, S. Alexiou excavated a house that

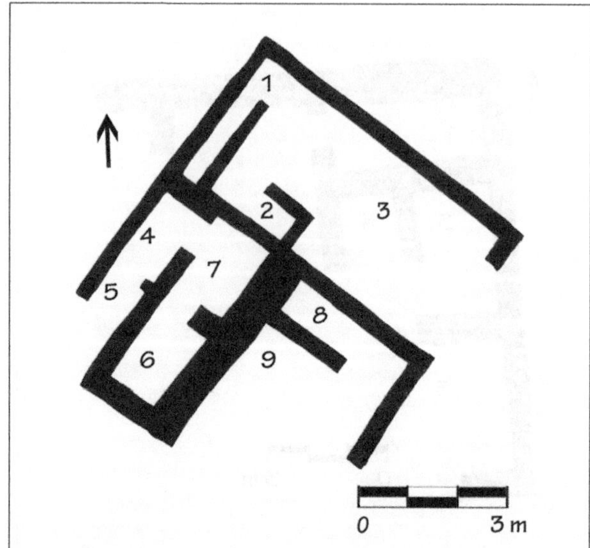

2.12. Plan. Middle Neolithic House, Katsamba. After Alexiou 1954, fig. 2.

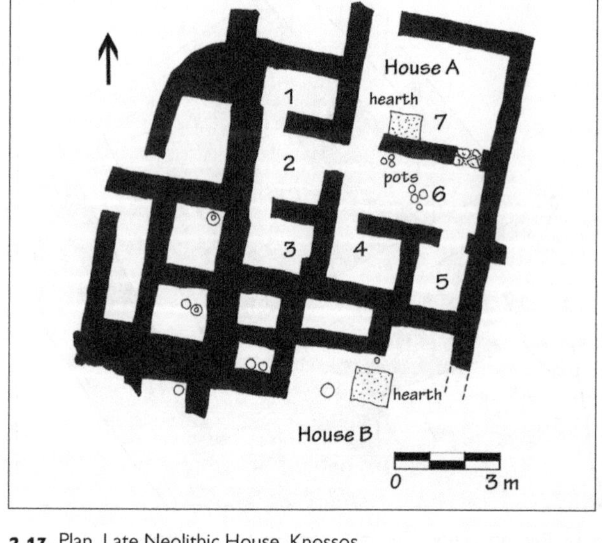

2.13. Plan. Late Neolithic House, Knossos. After *PM II*, fig. 8a.

he dated to the Middle Neolithic period but which may be Early Neolithic (fig. 2.12).[28] It was built with carefully squared angles and included nine rooms. Unexcavated walls and a small rock shelter used for burials suggest that the house was part of a small hamlet.

Late Neolithic-Final Neolithic, ca. 4000–3000 BC

The structures excavated by A. Evans beneath the Central Court of the Palace at Knossos immediately southwest of the Middle Neolithic Great House (see fig. 2.11) belong to the end of the Neolithic period (fig. 2.13).[29] Evans divided the complex into two houses, each centered on a large main room with a raised, rectangular hearth. In basic plan and construction, these houses are similar to those just considered. The major difference here is the use of a number of small, doorless spaces. These would be a familiar element in the architecture of Bronze Age Crete. They generally indicate the existence of upper-story rooms and were often, as here, used for storage. Other features of these buildings would also continue to be common in the houses of later Bronze Age Crete. These include the large size and number of rooms, the rectilinear layout, and the contiguous arrangement of the houses.

Other Sites

Only in the Late and particularly Final Neolithic were settlements widely established across other parts of the island.[30] This rapid growth was probably connected in part with a new wave of immigrants. The immigration may have created some tensions with the native population, as many of the new settlements, for example, the dramatic site at Monasteraki Katalimata, perched on the edge of Ha Gorge (see fig. 12.5), were located in defensible positions.[31] Architectural evidence, however, continues to be sparse. Of the 190 sites listed in T. Strasser's dissertation (1992), which covers the whole of the Neolithic period, 74 are caves, 120 are strays or surface finds, and only 6 are associated with architecture. The numbers have grown as a result of recent survey work, but the pattern remains the same.

At Phaistos, several walls, some with associated hearths, were found in test trenches beneath the later Palace in the area west of the Palace and at Chalara on the southeast slopes of the Palace hill. Because of the later buildings, no complete plans were recovered. The small (2.5 m diameter) circular structure described by L. Vagnetti may have been a storage building—perhaps a granary—rather than a house.[32] In the Asterousia Moun-

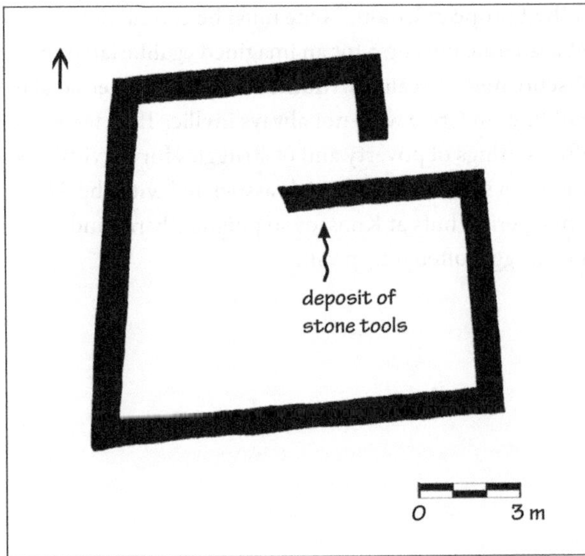

2.14. Plan. Final Neolithic building, Magasa. After Dawkins 1904–1905, fig. 2.

tains, Final Neolithic pottery has been found in association with several Early Minoan tholos tombs, but so far no tholos has been convincingly dated to this period.

Constructing the Identity of Cretan Architecture at Magasa

One other Neolithic structure that merits consideration is the small building at Magasa (near Palaikastro at the eastern end of the island), which probably dates to the Final Neolithic period (fig. 2.14).[33] Unusual in nature, the building consists of two very large rooms. A number of stone tools were found in the building (nineteen axes, four millstones, and obsidian bits), but otherwise it resembles a sheepfold more than the houses at Knossos. It is not even clear the building had a roof. The structure's rustic character is underscored by its association with a partially walled shallow cave or rock shelter located some 10 or 12 meters to the west.

Despite its simple form, for many years this odd little building had an undeservedly prominent position in the literature on Minoan architecture. In part, its notoriety stemmed from the fact that from its excavation in 1904 until 1923—the formative years of Minoan archaeology—it was the only Neolithic building known. A second factor had to do with its plan. D. Mackenzie used the Scots term "b'ut and b'en" to describe the layout.[34] After entering the small outer room (the "b'ut"), one was required to make a turn to enter the inner room. The term stuck because it seemed to describe something more significant than just this one building. With this catchy label, the building at Magasa came to be seen as the *Urform*—the essential core type—of all Minoan architecture from the later Lustral Basins to the Palaces themselves. To pick just one example, in his handbook on Greek architecture A. Lawrence writes, "The main interest of the house is its use of the 'but-and-ben' (Scots for 'out-and-in') method of planning which involves passing through the entire length of one room to enter another parallel with it. This habit persists in Crete throughout the Bronze Age—when the culture of the island is called Minoan (after the legendary King Minos of Cnossus)."[35] Thus the house at Magasa was interpreted as the archetype of the twisting, labyrinthine nature of Minoan buildings and of Minoan art in general. Furthermore, this circuitous essence of Minoan design was seen to contrast dramatically with the quintessentially linear, axial "megarons" of the Greek mainland, reflecting differences in the ethnic mentalities of the two cultures. The prominence of the idiosyncratic little hut, in other words, stemmed not from the building itself, but from its appropriation by early twentieth-century intellectuals to fit their belief that artworks or buildings could afford direct access to the zeitgeist of a period or a race.[36] As we shall see, traces of this Hegelian conceit crop up from time to time even in very recent scholarship.

Architecture and Changing Identities

A generation ago, J. du Boulay characterized the traditional Greek house in this way: "The house is not simply a place from which its members go out in the morning and to which they return at night; it is a sanctuary from the hostility of both nature and society, it is a monument to earlier generations who built it and lived in it and it is a cornucopia which is filled not just with fruits, but with the fruits of the family land gained by family toil."[37]

Today the various regional and local styles of vernacular houses in Crete are giving way to an international style of reinforced concrete buildings associated with the tourist economy. In 1990, I naively criticized this development as constituting a threat to the island's traditional identity.[38] From another point of view, however, the new concrete buildings, complete with heating, cooling, electricity, and telecommunications, can be seen as an integral part of a new Cretan identity. In the remarkably short span of two generations Cretans have dramatically transformed the island from what L. Allbaugh described in 1953 as a case study of an "underdeveloped" nation into a mainstream participant in the European Union.[39] One must be careful not to let academic nostalgia for an imagined egalitarian past obscure human realities. Modern and ancient vernacular buildings in Crete were not always idyllic. They were often settings of poverty and of struggles for survival. As the seven shallow child burials associated with the Aceramic period huts at Knossos so poignantly remind us, the struggle often was in vain.[40]

Local, Regional, and Ethnic Identities in Early Prepalatial Architecture

CA. 3000–2200 BC

During the Early Prepalatial period (EM I–EM IIB) the architectural landscape of Crete is characterized by tiny hamlets and communal tombs that vary according to regional and local traditions (fig. 3.1). Architecture was an essential means of constructing a sense of community among the living and maintaining a connection with earlier generations.

Myrtos and Household Identity

Myrtos, a small hamlet on the southern coast of Crete not far from modern Hierapetra, is the most informative EM site so far known (fig. 3.2). Since its exemplary excavation by P. Warren in 1968–1970 it has been the basis for all discussions of EM domestic architecture.[1]

Interpretations of the site have varied considerably. Initially Warren saw the settlement as a single unified building complex inhabited by an extended family or clan of 100–120 people. On the basis of a meticulous reexamination of the data a decade later, T. Whitelaw proposed an entirely different interpretation of the settlement.[2] His approach combined a careful study of the architectural phases with a study of the distribution of all the finds. Whitelaw found that the site broke down into five or six distinct areas and that each of these areas contained a more or less standard set of objects. On this basis, he proposed that the settlement consisted of a series of five or six independent units, each the dwelling of a nuclear family. The population of the entire hamlet, according to this view, would have been only about 25–30 people.

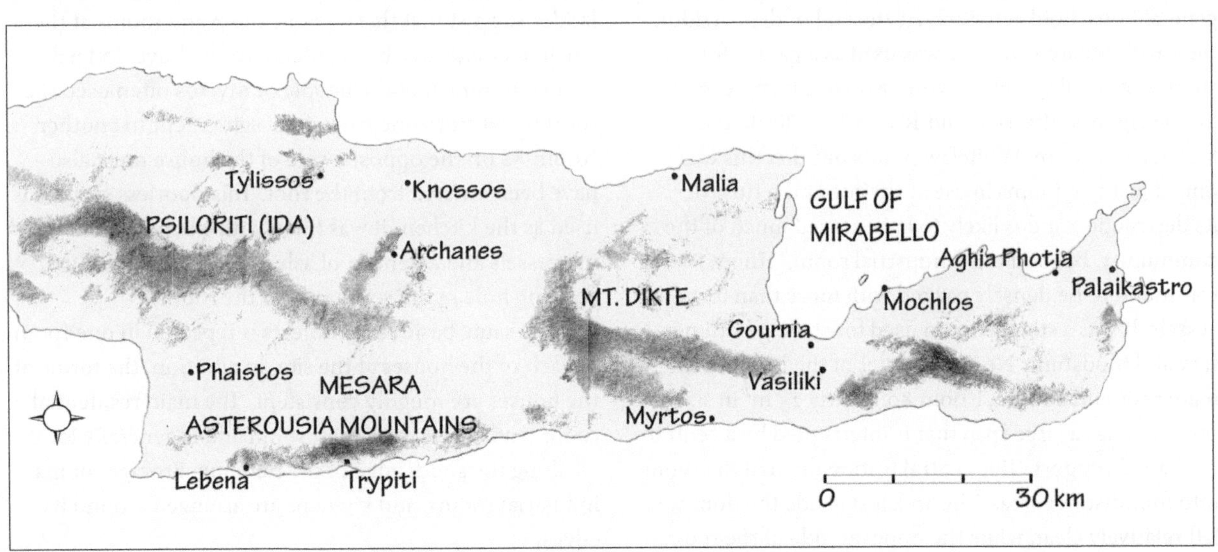

3.1. Sites discussed in chapter 3.

3.2. Plan. Myrtos. After Warren 1972, plan.

The South Central House is the best preserved of the houses at Myrtos (figs. 3.3, 3.4). The main entrance was from the north, into Room 74, a corridor that, to judge from the pottery found in it (an amphora, a pithos, a few small cups, bowls, and jars), was the site of a few general household activities. At the end of the corridor, the small, square Room 72 was used as a pantry for the storage of small vessels. Beyond a dogleg turn, several loomweights scattered about Room 81 indicate the location of a loom. Whitelaw points out that this was one of just two looms in use at the site at the time of its destruction and is likely to have served much of the community. Beyond this "industrial room," Room 82 was found to be densely packed with more than forty vessels. It was a storage room used for storing both pottery and foodstuffs. Near the center of the house is the main residential room, Room 80. Nearly 25 m^2 in size, the room has a large span that is interrupted by a central Π-shaped support. This central feature divided the room into four distinct areas. The area just inside the door was left relatively clear, while the opposite side of the room, against the south wall, was lined with some twenty storage vessels. A small cupboard and pot stand were built in the northwest corner of the room. To the east, Room 79 was used as a second pottery pantry. Traces of carbonized wood and what Warren took to be a support for a ladder suggest that this was one of several rooms at the site that could have been entered from above. Indeed, we can assume that the people of Myrtos often used the roofs to get from one part of the settlement to another. Room 88 on the opposite side of the house must also have been entered from the roof. This doorless space was used as the kitchen: it was fitted with a bench, and cooking vessels and a deposit of ashy fill were found near a cooking hole in the south part of the room.

The same basic set of objects is repeated in one room of each of the houses at the site. In addition, the forms of the houses are roughly consistent. The main residential room tends to be the largest room and is generally located along the south edge of the building. Storage rooms, industrial rooms, and kitchens are arranged around its edges.

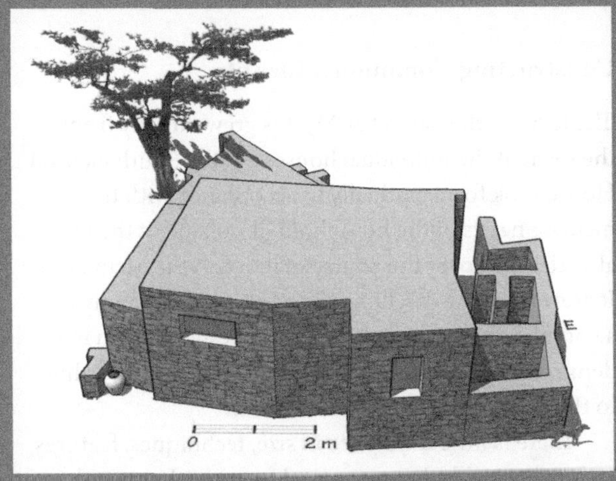

3.3. A restoration. South Central House, Myrtos. After Warren 1972, plan.

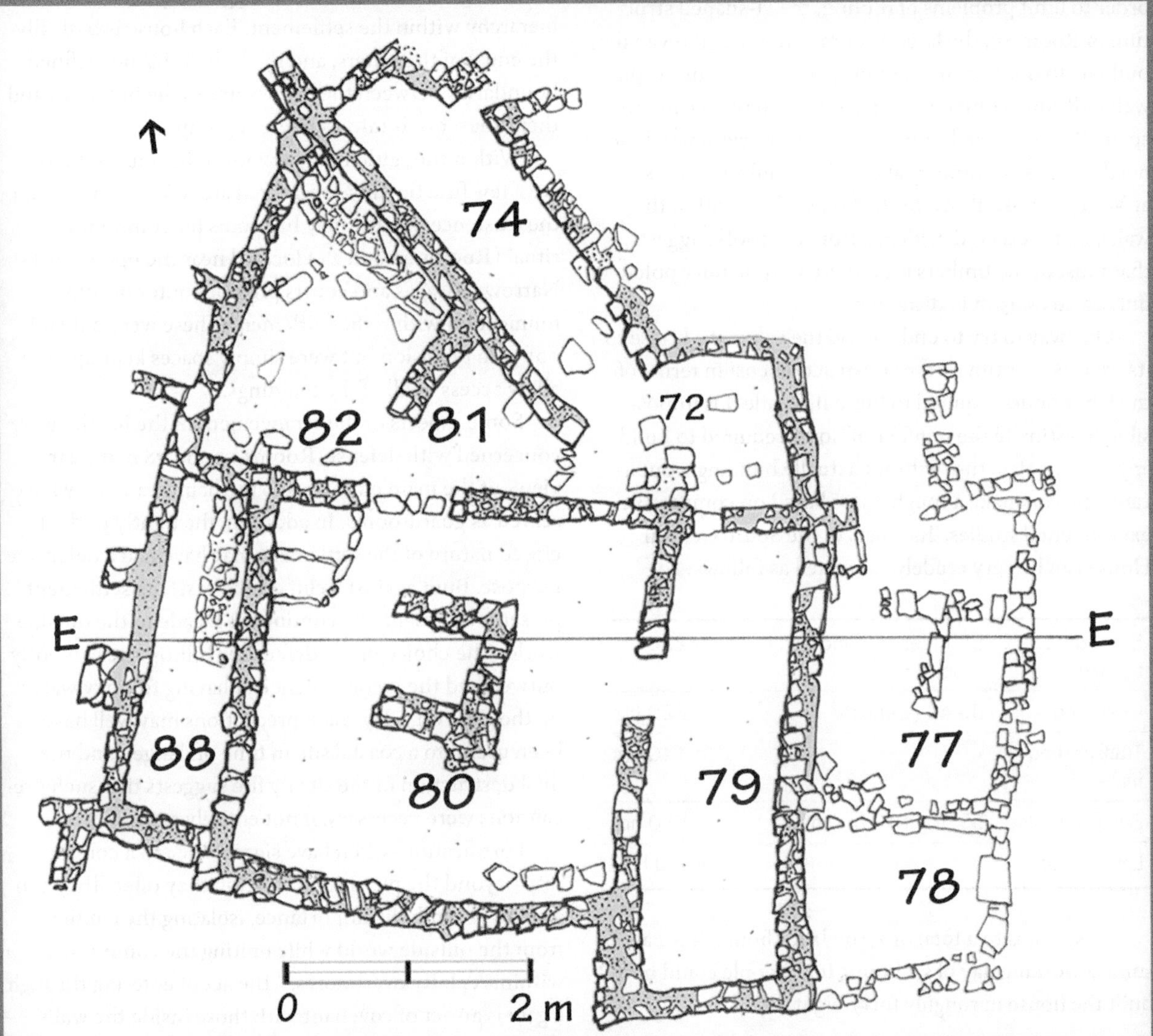

3.4. Plan. South Central House, Myrtos. After Warren 1972, plan.

The South Central House is about 110 m^2 in overall size, with ca. 70 m^2 of floor space. It was built primarily of uncut, but carefully selected limestone slabs placed in roughly horizontal courses. The eastern part of the house (Room 79) seems to have been built to its entire height in stone, while on the west (Room 88), well-preserved mud bricks suggest a different construction. Such differences in construction within a single house are partly due to the fact that the house was not built as a single project but took shape gradually in several phases. Traces of the incorporation of earlier phases are visible in Rooms 72, 79, and 82.

While most of the rooms are intentionally small in order to limit problems of roofing, the Π-shaped structure in Room 80, the largest room at the site, allowed the builders to limit the maximum span to ca. 2.5 m. A spur wall in Room 81 may also have served to reduce the roof span. The use of such supporting devices eliminated the need for massive timbers at the site. Unlike the houses at Vasiliki, those at Myrtos had no timbers within the walls, and preserved evidence from the roofs suggests that most of the timbers used there were slender poles, only ca. .03–.05 m in diameter.

One way to try to understand the value of a house to its users is to estimate the construction cost in terms of the labor hours required to build it. While it is impossible to estimate the number of hours required to build any ancient structure without actually building a duplicate, one can make a rough guess based on comparable experimental studies. The costs of the South Central House can be very crudely estimated as follows:

Excavating terrace	55 m^3 earth removed @ .25m^3/hr	= 220 hrs
Quarrying	55 m^3 @ 4hr/m^3	= 220 hrs
Transporting materials		= 140 hrs
Building walls	55 m^3 @ 10 hrs/m^3	= 550 hrs
Laying roof		= 30 hrs

This comes to a total of 1,160 labor hours. If we assume a working day of six hours, four people could have built the house in roughly forty-eight days.[3]

Constructing Community Identity

The form of the hamlet at Myrtos grew directly from the form of the individual houses. As the South Central House took form gradually in accordance with the immediate needs of the household, the shape of the village also changed over the course of its 150-year occupation. It grew from the dwelling of a single nuclear family to a complex of five or six houses. The resulting plan is a dense, concentrated cluster of cells arranged according to the contours of the site.

There is little difference in size, techniques, features, and quality of finds among the houses at the site. There is nothing, in other words, to suggest any sort of social hierarchy within the settlement. Each house is basically the equal of the others, and the lack of sharply defined boundaries between the houses unites the buildings and their households into a coherent group.

Within the settlement, as within the houses, there are a few functionally specialized areas. Whitelaw noted the existence of what may be rooms for community ritual (Rooms 46 and 21) located near the open courts. Narrow passages and courts provide routes of communication within the settlement. These were not laid out with precision but were simply spaces kept open to allow access to all of the buildings.

Some aspects of the arrangement of the hamlet were concerned with defense. Rooms 15 and 78 had clear views of the main entrances to the hamlet and may have served as guardrooms. In addition, the tightly packed, closed nature of the settlement may have had a defensive purpose. Built against a cliff on the east, the settlement presents an essentially continuous facade to the outside world. The choice of the defensible hilltop site evidently outweighed the inconvenience of having to carry water up the hill every day. Such precautions may well have been useful to a coastal site in time of danger, and the final destruction of the site by fire suggests that such precautions were necessary, if not entirely sufficient.

Fortifications often have significance to a community beyond the physical protection they offer. They can also be of symbolic importance, isolating the hamlet from the outside world while uniting the community within. As J. Rykwert notes, "The act of entering through a gate is an act of covenant with those inside the walls through which the gate leads."[4] This, he explains, is the real significance of security. If this hamlet is regarded as the architectural embodiment of a family's history through 150 years, such an affirmation of unity is particularly meaningful.

Vasiliki

Located on the Isthmus of Hierapetra, Vasiliki is not far from Myrtos, but its architecture is quite different (fig. 3.5).[5] The original excavator, R. Seager, was unable to decide whether the rooms he uncovered belonged to a single, large mansion or to several small, contiguous houses. Because of incomplete recording, much of Seager's information is now lost, and it is no longer possible to identify most of the activities associated with the individual rooms. Since the 1970s, excavations under the direction of A. Zois have helped to clarify many of the questions.

The site consists of a series of independent, contiguous houses constructed in several phases. The earliest buildings were built in EM IIA. These include Houses P, Q, X, the South Building (Rooms I, II, and III) and Building Y. These buildings were destroyed, and completely new structures, Building 43 and the Red House, went up in early EM IIB. The Red House was an impressively constructed house two stories high in places. L. V. Watrous was probably right when he recently suggested that the Red House actually consists of two separate buildings, one on the east (Rooms 39–42) and a second composed of Rooms 1–3, 6, and 13.[6] Each had its own set of storage magazines located on the lower terrace to the south (Rooms 15, 16, 33, 33a, and 35–38). There is a deep well in Room 39. At a later point in EM IIB the large but poorly constructed West House was built as an annex to the Red House. It was used mainly for storage and, to judge from the masses of loomweights, for weaving.

The Red House made use of several interesting techniques. The walls are made of small rubble and mud and are up to .65 m thick. They were strengthened with horizontal timbers ca. 0.1 m thick that were laid along the face of the wall and at irregular intervals transversely through it. There was no use of vertical timbers.[7] The walls of the upper story may have been entirely of mud brick.

The Red House takes its name from its distinctive plaster. This was applied in stages. The first layer was about .05 m thick and consisted of clay mixed with lime

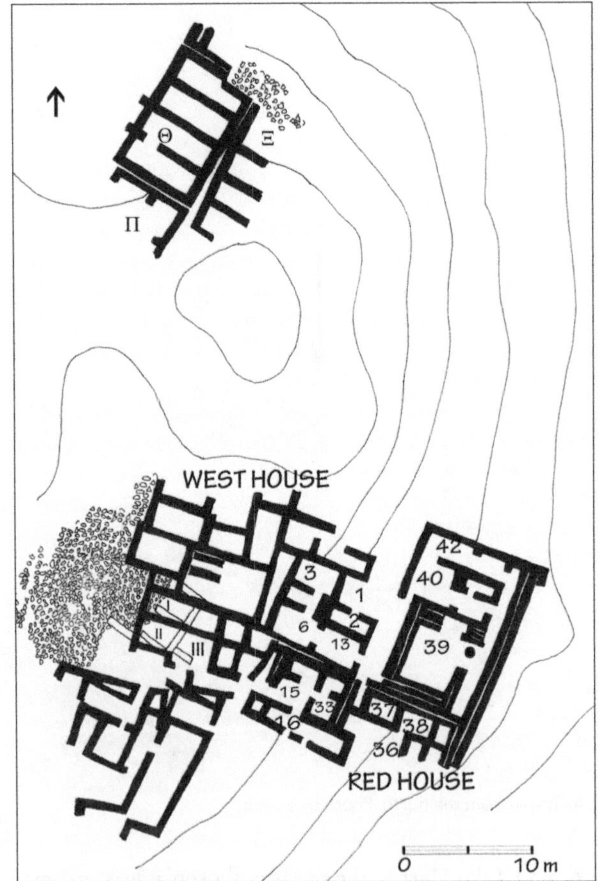

3.5. Plan. Vasiliki. After Zois 1979, fig. 2.

and straw, with added potsherds and pebbles. Over this was applied a thin layer of much finer clay that was painted red and polished.[8]

In plan, the Red House is quite different from the South Central House at Myrtos. Similarly, just as each EM village seems to have developed its own house plans, each site also used a unique set of materials and techniques, and, as a comparison of the Red House and the cruder West House shows, the techniques changed over time. The uniqueness of the construction methods is our best indication that the houses were built by local workers.

Trypiti

The tiny hamlet of Trypiti offers another example of a unique, site-specific style of domestic architecture (figs.

3.6. Trypiti from the north. Photo by author.

3.6, 3.7). Like Myrtos, the site was chosen at least in part for defensive purposes. The houses were built on the top of a small natural acropolis about 800 m from the sea. The settlement was gradually built over the course of the EM II–EM III/MM IA periods. An earlier (EM I) tholos tomb was excavated on a lower hilltop to the east of the settlement.[9]

The settlement is divided into two parts by a narrow east-west court. To the north of the court are three houses, each with a large main room with a central hearth and stone cupboards. On the sides of the main rooms are one or more storage rooms. The area south of the court is more difficult to figure out because it is the result of several different construction phases. At least four large main rooms representing four individual houses can be distinguished. This makes a total of about six or seven houses in the hamlet, about the same number as at Myrtos, and a similar total population of about thirty to thirty-five people. The rectilinear layouts and the massive construction of the buildings, however, are strikingly different.

The overall picture one gets from these settlements is that each is small, unique, and, for the most part, self-sustaining. The defensive positions of Myrtos and Trypiti suggest that the villagers were concerned about the possibility of being attacked. That does not mean, of course, that the hamlets were totally isolated.

Researchers had long assumed that each Early Minoan site produced all of its own pottery, but petrographic studies of ceramics have shown that a considerable amount of pottery was produced at a few sites and distributed around the island.[10] Aghios Onouphrios ware, for example, was made at a few sites in the Mesara, while Vasiliki ware may have been produced at only one or two places near Vasiliki.

One other kind of artifact suggests an unexpected form of transregional familiarity: pavement games, small stone slabs carved with rows or circles of small depressions. The slabs are generally located in public areas, often near entrances or intersections. They have been labeled *kernoi* by some and explained as having had a religious function. Others, including A. Evans,

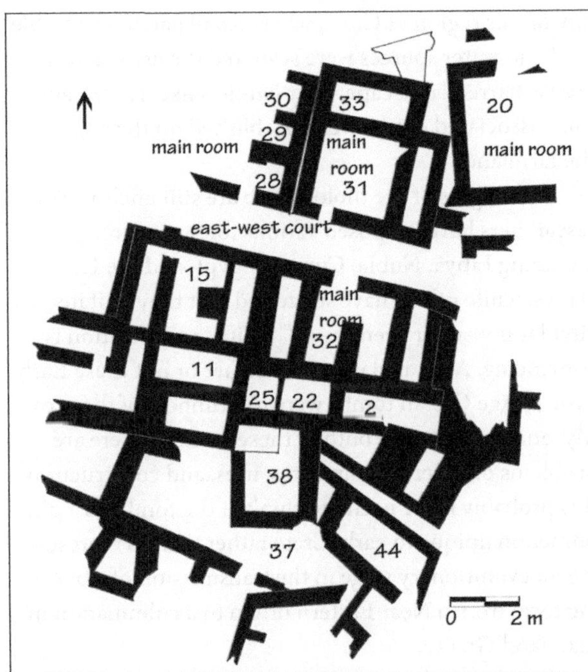

3.7. Plan. Settlement at Trypiti. After Watrous 1994, fig. 7.

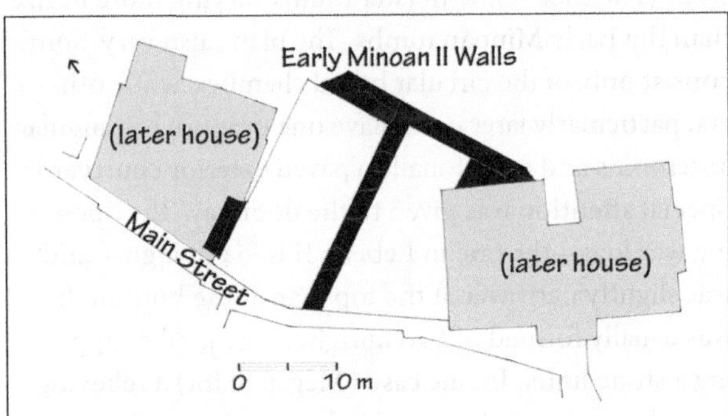

3.8. Plan. Monumental building, Palaikastro. After Dawkins 1904–1905, plan X.

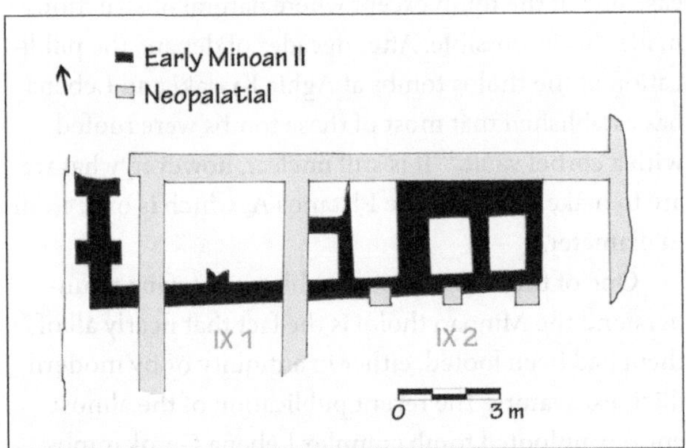

3.9. Plan. EM II building, Malia. After Pelon 1993, fig. 3.

regarded them as having been the Minoan equivalent of board games such as Chinese checkers. N. Hillbom has recently completed an exhaustive statistical analysis of 167 examples, taking into consideration such factors as the number and arrangement of the holes, location, date, etc. He concludes that with the exception of a handful of monumental examples from Malia, they were first and foremost games.[11] The games were being played at Myrtos (six examples), Vasiliki (twenty-one examples), and Trypiti (at least one example). Knowledge of the rules, perhaps along with an awareness of what Hillbom calls "the connection between gaming and religion, divination and fortune-telling, luck and destiny," may have been something else these tiny settlements had in common.[12]

Monumental Architecture in the Early Prepalatial Period?

The image we now have of early Prepalatial Crete is dominated by tiny, largely independent hamlets. It may be that this picture is seriously incomplete. Here and there we find hints that there may have also been much larger-scale buildings. In Block X at Palaikastro, for example, the excavators found traces of what appeared to be an enormous building below later constructions (fig. 3.8). Although fragments of only six walls were uncovered, if they connect to form a single building, as they appear to do, it would cover more than 600 m^2 and have walls nearly 2 m thick.[13]

There are also very large EM II remains beneath the Salle à Piliers and the West Magazines of the Neopalatial Palace at Malia (fig. 3.9).[14] While O. Pelon and I. Schoep are inclined to view these walls as belonging to some sort of predecessor of the later Palace, it is not clear how the walls related to one another. They do appear, however, to be quite different from the village architecture described above.[15]

In a forthcoming article, J. Driessen will lay out the evidence for the widespread existence of monumental architecture in the EM II period, citing examples at Knossos and Tylissos in addition to those mentioned here.[16] Unfortunately, none of these massive structures has been thoroughly excavated, so we know little about them beyond the tantalizing fact that they exist.

Tholos Tombs

The excavated tholos tomb below the settlement at Trypiti (visible in figure 3.6) predated the houses. However, this was not the only tholos tomb at the site. S. Alexiou located two tholos tombs in 1967, one of which was later excavated by A. Vasilakis. In addition, on the basis of the size of the settlement, K. Branigan estimates that a total of about four tholos tombs would have been built over the course of the settlement's occupation. It is quite likely, then, that anytime one looked down the east slope of Trypiti during the Early Bronze Age, one would have seen two or three circular tombs with corbel vaults projecting above the surrounding fields.[17]

Tholos tombs served as communal graves for families for an almost unimaginably long time, often as much as eight or nine centuries. The tombs were typically visible from the settlement and would have seemed a familiar, almost permanent part of the landscape. The relation between the tombs and the settlement was a meaningful one. The visibility of the tombs linked the living families with their dead ancestors, and the tombs also served as visible intermediaries between the village and the land on which it depended. As J. Murphy puts it, "The presence of the dead in the landscape is a continuum which marks and parallels the perpetuation of the living in the landscape. The act of maintaining these tombs and their visual effect on the landscape mark and legitimize the related community's right to act as guardians of restricted resources in the vicinity."[18]

There are about ninety known tholos tombs. While they continued to be built into the time of the first Palaces, they were primarily a Prepalatial phenomenon. They were also associated with a particular region. The earliest circular tombs are concentrated on the flanks of the Asterousia Mountains along the southern edge of the Mesara plain. They continued to be the major, perhaps the only, form of tomb used in this area for at least a millennium. Gradually they spread to the rest of the Mesara and by the Middle Bronze Age isolated examples appear as far east as Myrsini (near Mochlos) and Aghia Photia (near Siteia). As the form spread, the significance of the tholos shifted (see Chapter 4).

The greatest concentration of tholoi was in its original home in the Asterousia Mountains. Their density in this part of the island is tied to the inhospitable topography of this region of Crete, where small patches of arable land and water sources were scattered through an otherwise barren landscape. Tiny hamlets like Trypiti and their associated tombs were established on the edges of the farmland.[19]

The origins of the tholos tomb are still unclear. Some researchers have proposed various foreign sources, including Libya, Nubia, Cyprus, Egypt, and the Cyclades, while others have suggested that they imitate circular houses or even caves.[20] Neither proposition is convincing. A parallel issue is whether or not these Early Bronze Age Cretan tombs were forerunners of the great Mycenaean tholoi. In both of these matters, there are problems of differences in dates, uses, and construction. It is probably more useful to think of the tombs as a phenomenon unique to early Crete rather than as representing an evolutionary stage in the transmission of a building form from a Near Eastern origin to a culmination in mainland Greece.

The Cretan tholos tombs vary in size from an interior diameter of less than 2.5 m (Apesokari) to larger than 13 m (Platanos A), with later tombs varying more in size than the Early Minoan tombs. The plans also vary. Some consist only of the circular burial chamber, while others, particularly later ones, have one or more rectangular anterooms and occasionally a paved exterior courtyard. Special attention was given to the doorway. The opening was low—the one in Lebena II is .64 m high—and was slightly narrower at the top than at the bottom. It was usually formed of two upright stone jambs supporting a stone lintel. In one case (Megali Skini) a relieving triangle was located above the door, and sometimes the lintel slab was thickened in the center, at the point of maximum stress. Doorways were generally on the east side of the tomb except where natural obstructions made this impossible. After decades of debate, the publication of the tholos tombs at Aghia Kyriaki and Lebena has established that most of these tombs were roofed with a corbel vault.[21] It is still unclear, however, what we are to make of tombs like Platanos A, which is over 13 m in diameter.

One of the most serious problems in trying to understand the Minoan tholoi is the fact that nearly all of them had been looted, either in antiquity or by modern illicit excavators. The recent publication of the almost entirely unlooted tomb complex Lebena Gerokampos

3.10. Tholos, Lebena Gerokampos II from the southwest. Photo by author.

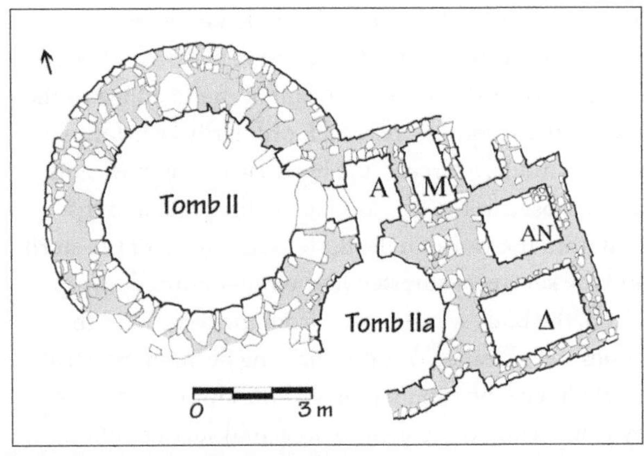

3.11. Plan. Tholos, Lebena Gerokampos II. After Alexiou and Warren 2004, fig. 12.

II and IIa is therefore welcome (figs. 3.10, 3.11).[22] Like many tholoi, this complex was in continual use for more than one thousand years, during which it underwent several changes. Alexiou and Warren identify four main architectural phases.[23] The tholos of Tomb II was built in Phase 1 (EM I). Its inner diameter was 5.00–5.15 m, and its walls were 1.90 m thick. In Phase 2 (EM IIA) a second, smaller tholos, Tomb IIa, was added, perhaps by a new branch of the family. In Phase 3 two rectangular outer chambers were built: Room Δ was built as an ossuary to contain secondary burials, while Room AN was filled with the cups, bowls, and jugs from the meals that accompanied the reinterment. Phase 4 was in MM IA or until the MM IA–MM IB transition. By this time the main burial chambers had apparently been filled and went out of use, and two more rectangular chambers were added. Like the earlier outer rooms, one of these chambers, Room A, served for secondary burials, while the other, Room M, held the pottery that was offered following the funerary meal.

The human remains from Lebena Gerokampos have not yet been published, but information from other sites tells us something about who used these tombs. The number of burials in a tomb varies from 157 in Koumasa A to 850 in Platanos B, but the raw numbers are not in themselves especially informative, as they have to be measured against the length of time the tomb was in use. Branigan, using a formula developed by J. Bintliff that holds that a nuclear family of five will contribute twenty bodies per century to a tomb, concluded that most Minoan tholoi had been used by two to four nuclear families.[24]

Tombs and Ritual

It is possible to reconstruct the outlines of the funerary rites at Lebena Gerokampos. Probably only one or two people would have dragged the body through the low doorway; they carried lamps—the underside of the lintel was blackened from smoke—to light the way. Other mourners would have remained outside. To judge from the remains of olive pits and animal bones, food offerings were placed near the corpse along with some personal effects the deceased had probably used during his or her lifetime. Other objects like miniature vases and stone vases were apparently made specifically for the tomb. Alexiou pointed to a small slab feature on the northwest side of the chamber of Tomb II, and he suggested it might have marked the burial of the founder of the tomb. Otherwise most of those interred were provided with essentially the same set of equipment, with no obvious distinctions of social status.

On the basis of ethnographic comparisons, Murphy has tried to understand what the funerary rites might reveal about larger issues of Minoan ontology.[25] As in modern rural Greece, the burial process had three stages. After initial preparation in the village, the body was brought to the tomb and laid in the grave with a small number of objects: at this stage the corpse, still belonging to the world of the flesh, depended on material goods for survival. Outside the tomb, mourners shared food, drink, and conversation and began to adjust to the loss. In the second stage, which ordinarily lasts for five years in modern Greece, the body lay in the tomb and decomposed as the deceased made the gradual transition from the world of the flesh to the world of the spirit and the survivors adjusted to their loss. After decomposition, the body was removed from the tomb, and the bones were cleaned of any remaining flesh. In modern rural Greece the exhumation is done almost exclusively by women and is the focus of a second set of public funerary rites. Similar rites might explain the pottery placed in Rooms M and AN at Lebena Gerokampos. After this stage, the major period of mourning ended. The deceased now belonged to the world of the ancestors, and the bones could be reinterred without any material offerings.

Murphy's close reading of the tholos tombs provides new insight into the issue of community identity in the Early Bronze Age. Her recognition of the interdependence of the villages of the living with the communal tombs of their ancestors and her reconstruction of the rituals that tied them together show that the notion of a community is much more than a matter of physical proximity. It depends on active community participation.[26]

House Tombs

While tholos tombs were rooted in the Mesara, another form of communal tomb, a form H. Hawes called a house tomb, was used at sites such as Archanes, Gournia, Pyrgos-Myrtos, Mochlos, Palaikastro, Vasiliki, and Zakros in the northern and eastern parts of the island.[27] The earliest house tombs date to EM II, that is, more than three hundred years later than the earliest tholos tombs. House tombs were a major form of burial during the Prepalatial period and continued to be used sporadically into the Neopalatial period. J. Soles divides house tombs into four basic types: the first has one room; the second has two rooms; the third is a compound structure with more than two rooms; and the final type is a monumental version of the house tomb that develops only in EM III–MM IA (see fig. 4.14).

Tomb Complex IV, V, VI at the west slope of the small islet of Mochlos is an example of Sole's compound type (fig. 3.12).[28] The building was dramatically placed at the edge of a cliff dropping precipitously to the sea on the west. Natural bedrock ledges fixed its boundaries on the north and east, and, unlike the generally east-facing tholoi, the bedrock contours also determined the tomb's orientation. Originally the building consisted of just two rooms, IV and VI, built in EM IIA. Room V was added later, probably within EM II. A paved court in front of the tomb marked the area as a special precinct. A raised platform near the southeast corner of the building may have served as an altar.

Burial procedures, as Soles reconstructs them, were similar to the three-step programs of the tholoi. When Tomb IV, V, VI was in its original two-room state, the body would have been initially laid out in Room IV. Cups with food offerings, personal belongings, and objects made especially for the grave were placed around it. The tomb was then closed, and the body left to decompose. After the requisite time, the tomb was reopened, and the bones—with special attention given to the skulls—were placed in Room VI. The process was repeated over the course of several centuries, making it necessary at some point to add a second ossuary chamber, Room V.[29] Using calculations similar to those of Branigan and Bintliff, Soles concluded that the house tombs, like the tholoi, were intended for the use of a group slightly larger than a single nuclear family.[30]

In other ways, however, the house tombs were different from the tholoi. The tholoi were ordinarily built either individually or in groups of two or three. They were placed in more or less prominent positions within view of the tiny settlements with which they were associated. The house tombs resemble houses in overall shape, and in addition their densely packed, sometimes contiguous arrangement reiterated the layout of the EM village in the manner of a genuine necropolis, or City of the Dead. Moreover the house tombs, though above ground and visible, were not in plain view of the houses of the living. The tombs at Mochlos, for example, were tucked into craggy cleavages in the bedrock on the seaward side of the islet, invisible from the houses on the calmer harbor on the southern slope. Unlike the tholoi, house tombs did not serve as the physical and conceptual link between the village and the landscape. At Mochlos, Gournia, Malia, and Archanes the living families provided houses for their dead but placed them largely out of sight.

Aghia Photia

In addition to tholos tombs and house tombs, there were several other forms of burials in EM Crete: burials in rock clefts, caves, rock shelters, cist graves, and pit graves. In 1971 C. Davaras added a completely new type—new to Crete at any rate—when he began to excavate a cemetery at Aghia Photia on the coast near modern Siteia in East Crete.[31] Ultimately he excavated 263 tombs, most of which were built in a form remarkably similar to the tombs at Ano Kouphonisi in the Cyclades.[32] All the graves date to the late EM I period.

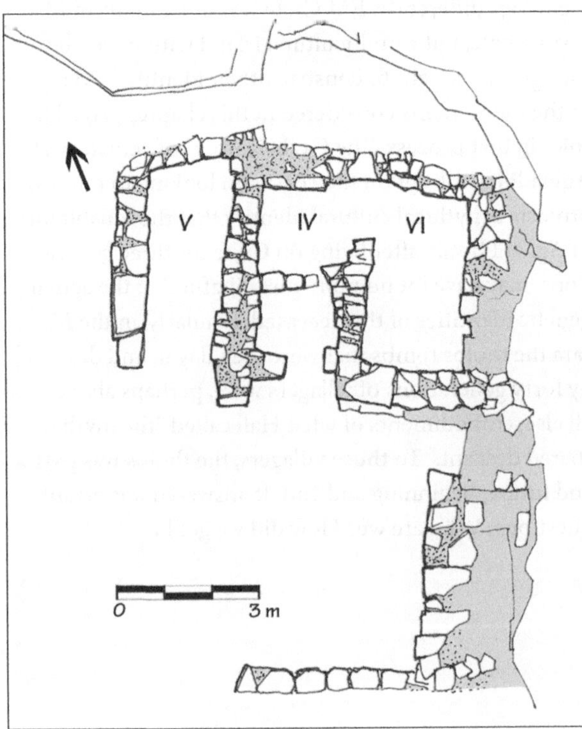

3.12. Plan. Tomb Complex IV, V, VI, Mochlos. After Soles 1992, fig. 20.

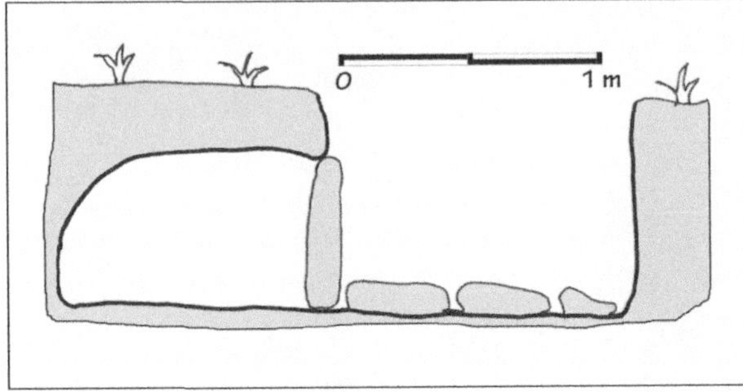

3.13. Section. Tomb 218, Aghia Photia. After Davaras and Betancourt 2004, fig 493.

Tomb 218 is a good example (fig. 3.13).[33] The tomb was made by digging a hole ca. .80 m deep into the soft *kouskouras* bedrock. A second chamber for the burial was then excavated on the south side, and slabs were placed on the floor of the antechamber. The entrance to the tomb faced downhill toward the sea. Two bodies were placed in the tomb. (Whether or not this happened in a single event is unclear.) Five vessels and sixteen obsidian blades were placed in the burial chamber, the door was sealed, and the antechamber was filled with rocks. The tombs contained from one to thirteen bodies. That some tombs, Tomb 163, for example, had two strata of burials indicates that at least some of the tombs were occasionally opened to receive more burials.

The burial process in these tombs was entirely different from that in the communal tholoi and house tombs. There was no exhumation or reburial of the cleaned bones. There is no evidence of marking the funeral by toasting or dining, as at Lebena, for example. There were no outside altars (like the one at Mochlos IV, V, VI) and no other indication of the later veneration of the dead. Rather the corpse was shut in the burial chamber and the anteroom was filled, as if, C. Davaras and P. Betancourt write, "from a fear that the ghost of the deceased may escape to harm the living."[34]

The dramatic differences in architectural form and burial process are tied to another issue: of the masses of pottery found in the cemetery, all but a small percentage are stylistically distinctive. A petrographic analysis by P. Day, D. Wilson, and E. Kiriatzi identified most of the pottery from Aghia Photia as Cycladic rather than Minoan. The vast majority of the pottery belongs to the Kampos Group, and it is particularly close to the pottery from Ano Kouphonisi.[35] Considering the duration of the cemetery's use and the number of burials, Day, Wilson, and Kiriatzi estimate that the cemetery would have served a village of about fifteen families (seventy-five people) and was perhaps the predecessor of the later Prepalatial fortified settlement located about 150 m to the west (see fig. 4.3). While a settlement of seventy-five people is tiny by modern standards, it is nearly three times the size of the estimated population of EM II Myrtos. The community, however, did not stay for very long. Who were they? How did they get there?[36]

Ethnic Identity in Crete

Recent scholarship has established that ethnic identity has no fixed biological or geographical boundaries.[37] It is a social construction subject to variation and change, and it is often difficult to characterize. J. M. Hall points out that it is not a matter of genetics: DNA does not determine cultural characteristics. Nor is ethnic identity simply a matter of language or religion.[38] Yet it can be defined. For Hall, an ethnic group must have one key characteristic: "Above all else . . . it must be the *myth of shared descent* which ranks paramount among the features that distinguish ethnic from other social groups" (italics added).[39] Actual descent matters much less than the self-defining mythic belief among a group of people that they have descended from a common origin.

In their study of the pottery from the cemetery at Aghia Photia (subtitled "Burying Ethnicity in the Cemetery at Aghia Photia, Siteias") Day, Wilson, and Kiriatzi raise a number of intriguing questions.[40] Within that context, for example, what is foreign and what is native? Is the 10 percent of the pottery we routinely regard as Minoan, which had been brought to the site from as far away as the Mesara, to be considered native, while the 90 percent of the pottery that is called Cycladic is to be considered somehow foreign? Does the island of Crete, by virtue of its geographical independence, naturally define cultural boundaries? or might we more meaningfully see Aghia Photia as having been, for a century or so, part of a different sea-oriented cultural zone that included the Cyclades? The same scholars provocatively ask, "Has our use of the cultural term 'Minoan' to label all settlement in EBA Crete hindered our ability to identify cultural and/or ethnic diversity within the island at this time?"[41]

With these questions in mind, if we look again at Myrtos, Vasiliki, Mochlos, Trypiti, and Lebena—and if we temporarily suspend our notion of Minoan—we may see things differently. EM Crete was not a uniform Minoan whole, but a multicultural island within which various groups sought to construct their identities. Many of the monuments considered in this chapter played key roles in that process. The Cycladic form of cemetery at Aghia Photia, built on the coast and looking to the sea, projects a mythical cultural identity that the inhabitants of Aghia Photia, after living on Crete for three generations, may have found more meaningful that the actual genetic identities of the deceased. Similarly, in the Mesara the tholos tombs that were seen day in and day out by forty generations of villagers were, perhaps above all else, embodiments of what Hall called "the myth of shared descent." To those villagers, the tholos was past and future, beginning and end. It answered important questions: Who are we? How did we get here?

Palace at Phaistos from the northwest. Photo by author.

Aerial photo, Knossos. © Yann Arthus-Bertrand/CORBIS.

West Magazines, Knossos. ©

Hall of Colonnades, Knossos.

Queen's Megaron, Knossos. © Roger Wood/CORBIS.

Grand Staircase, Knossos. © Roger Wood/CORBIS.

Throne Room, Knossos. © Gail Mooney/CORBIS.

Gournia from the east. Photo by author.

Architectural Experiments and Hierarchical Identity in Late Prepalatial Architecture

CA. 2200–1900 BC

THE THREE-CENTURY period from 2200 to 1900 BC (EM III–MM IA) is often overlooked in Minoan archaeology. The unusual architecture of these centuries includes monumental tombs, fortifications, new construction techniques, and the development of a city whose extraordinary size was without precedent on Crete (fig. 4.1).

Chronological Complexity

Despite (or perhaps because of) a great deal of research, the period EM III–MM IA looks more complex today than it did a generation ago. For many years clear deposits of EM III material had been so rarely excavated that some scholars questioned whether it actually existed as a period, or whether the pottery labeled EM III was simply a regional style contemporary with MM IA.[1] In 1994 L. V. Watrous wrote, "The hard truth is that we know next to nothing about Crete during the EM III period."[2] Today the situation is less obscure. We know that EM III was in fact a distinct period that lasted for at least a century, but there are still problems.[3] Not only does EM III continue without a break into MM IA, but nearly all the EM III–MM IA houses and tombs discussed in this chapter continued to be used in MM IB and MM II as well.[4]

Hierarchical Identities in Funerary Architecture

In general, most of the basic Early Prepalatial forms of funerary architecture continue into the Late Prepalatial

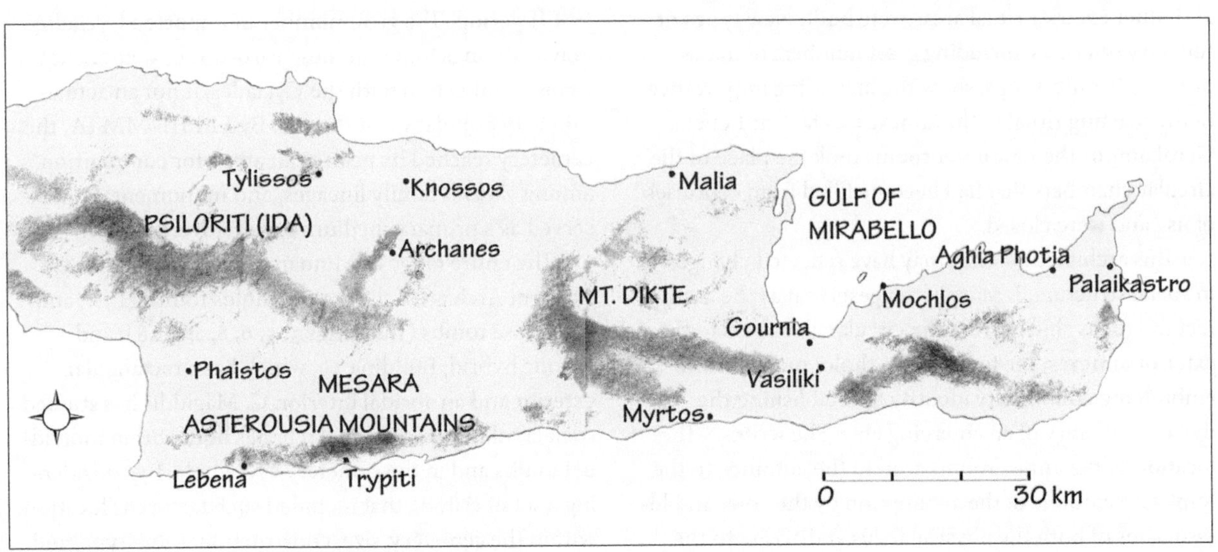

4.1. Sites discussed in chapter 4.

period. At Mochlos, for example, most of the house tombs constructed in EM II continued to be used in EM III. Fewer continued into MM IA, by which time Mochlos, dependent on Cycladic trade, seems to have been losing ground to agriculturally based sites such as Malia.[5]

In the Mesara, the use of tholoi continued. Of the sixty-five datable tholos tombs in K. Branigan's gazetteer, only eleven went out of use after EM II. Another eleven, many of which were built in places far beyond the southern edge of the Mesara, were new constructions in the Middle Minoan period. These were the exceptions, however. The vast majority of EM I–EM II tholos tombs—forty-three in Branigan's list—continued to be used into MM IA and beyond.

This is not to say there were no changes. As in the case of the Lebena Gerokampos tholoi, there were both architectural additions and changes in funerary customs. The first outer chambers were added in EM IIB or EM III, and a second pair of outer chambers was added in MM IA (see fig. 3.11). These outer chambers reflect a growing concern for the rituals associated with the secondary burials.

The tholoi at Lebena Gerokampos were not unusual in this respect. Across much of the island there were significant changes in the ways tholoi were used. One important change was the introduction of individual burials in pithoi and larnakes within these formerly communal ossuaries.[6] There was an increase in the size of many new tombs and in the costliness of the grave goods associated with them. At many sites new annexes and other exterior ritual areas were built. New types of funerary offerings, including great numbers of mass-produced conical cups, show the increasing importance of the toasting ritual in the annexes. In fact, at Lebena Gerokampos the new outer rooms took the place of the circular chambers that had become filled from centuries of use and were closed.

This architectural shift may have reflected changes in social structure. J. Murphy suggests that as the architectural focus shifted from the circular chambers to the exterior annexes, the focus of the tholoi moved from embodying community identity to establishing the dynastic identity of an emerging elite. She writes, "The location of the annex-rooms around the entrance to the tombs is symbolic of the assumption by the chief and his associates of both the physical focus and access to the ancestors. In this way the chief can legitimately act as the intermediary between the ancestors and the people."[7]

Ever since the publication of S. Xanthoudides's *Vaulted Tombs of the Mesara* in 1924, tholos tombs have been cited as the classic example of a regional style. Recently M. Relaki has brought new life to the issue by showing that regional identity was not simply a matter of geographical distribution but a complex process that changed over time. From their earliest appearances in tiny remote valleys of the Asterousia Mountains, the tholoi began to expand toward the Mesara plain and eventually reached Phaistos and Haghia Triada on the north side of the plain. Relaki interprets the spread of the tholos to areas beyond its homeland not to the widespread adoption of the subsistence lifestyle of the tiny EM Asterousian hamlets but to competition for authority that needed to appear deeply rooted and legitimate.[8] During the early part of the following Protopalatial period the little mountain hamlets would be abandoned, the population would shift to a relatively few urban centers, and the first Palaces would be built.[9]

Phourni Archanes

Nowhere is the use of monumental funerary architecture as a means of ostentatious display of social status more marked than at Phourni Archanes, located in what is today the rich wine-producing country a few kilometers south of Knossos (fig. 4.2).[10] The cemetery had a long history. Its earliest tombs, such as Tholos E, date to the EM II period. The great number of imported Cycladic grave offerings found in these early tombs demonstrate a close connection with the Cyclades, if not an actual minority population at the site. By EM III–MM IA, the cemetery reached its peak as an arena for competition among various family lineages, and monumental tombs served as a primary medium of self-advertisement.

The entire range of Minoan tomb types is found at Phourni Archanes: cist graves, tholos tombs (E, B, and G), house tombs (Buildings 3, 5, 6, 8, and 18), and a unique hybrid, Building 19, which has a rectangular exterior and an apsidal interior. C. Magiddis has studied social ranking at Phourni Archanes both within individual tombs and in the cemetery as a whole. By considering a set of criteria that included such factors as location within the cemetery, size, construction, tomb type, and

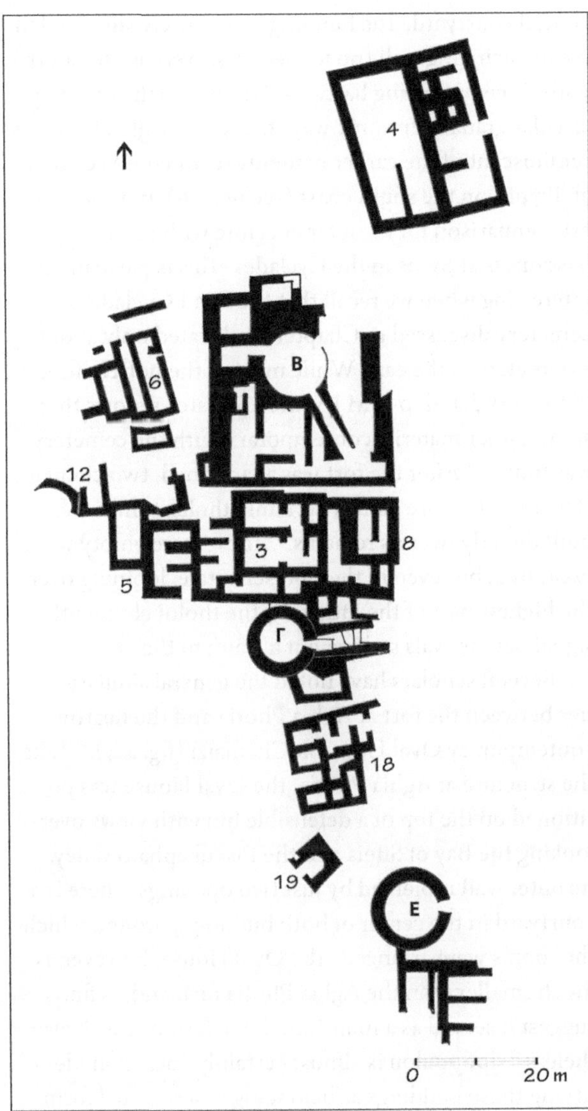

4.2. Plan. Phourni, Archanes. After I. and E. Sakellarakis 1991, p. 67, fig. 40.

grave goods, he concludes that the Phourni cemetery represents the development of an advanced social hierarchy at a moment just prior to the beginning of the first Palatial period.[11] In particular, because of its prominent location, combination of house tomb and tholos forms, and monumental two-story construction, Magiddis identifies Tomb B as the tomb of an elite family line. These tombs, in other words, did not simply commemorate the dead, but primarily served the living whose power was largely rooted in their proclaimed ancestry.

Peak Sanctuaries

Peak sanctuaries are among the most distinctive features of the landscape of Bronze Age Crete.[12] In their earliest stages they were simple affairs: an open space at or near the peak of a prominent mountain. Only in the Neopalatial period would some become monumentalized with architecture. The sites were carefully selected for their visibility from the surrounding landscape and from other peak sanctuaries. Views of the sites would have been especially spectacular when seen from a distance at night lit by blazing bonfires, remains of which have been found in several excavations. Some of the most prominent peak sanctuaries, such as those at Iouktas and Kophinas, were visible to a wide populated area and served as regional shrines. Others were probably of purely local interest. In all cases they seem to have served as places for the rural people who visited them to practice their popular religion by presenting votive offerings representing their most fundamental concerns: clay statuettes of animals for their prosperity and figures of humans or of human limbs for their personal well-being.

It has generally been thought that, as A. Peatfield put it, "in strictly chronological terms peak sanctuaries are limited to the Palace period—no Palaces, no peak sanctuaries."[13] The thinking was that the organizational power needed to establish such a homogeneous and widespread network of sanctuaries would have been tied to the emerging central authorities of the first Palaces. In turn, the rural sanctuaries would have served to reinforce the political authority of the emerging urban centers.[14] However, it now seems that the Late Prepalatial (EM III–MM IA) was the crucial period for the establishment of these mountaintop sanctuaries, and a few of them (Atsipadhes, Iouktas, and Petsophas) may have been founded even earlier.[15] In other words, the peak sanctuaries preceded the major period of the first Palaces. D. Haggis has suggested, therefore, that the peak sanctuaries may have played a role in the establishment of regional, as opposed to purely local, cultural identities and thus laid some of the groundwork for the development of the Palaces.[16] Similarly, J. Driessen and C. Macdonald propose that they had been initially the sites of popular cults and that their role was only gradually appropriated by the Palaces.[17]

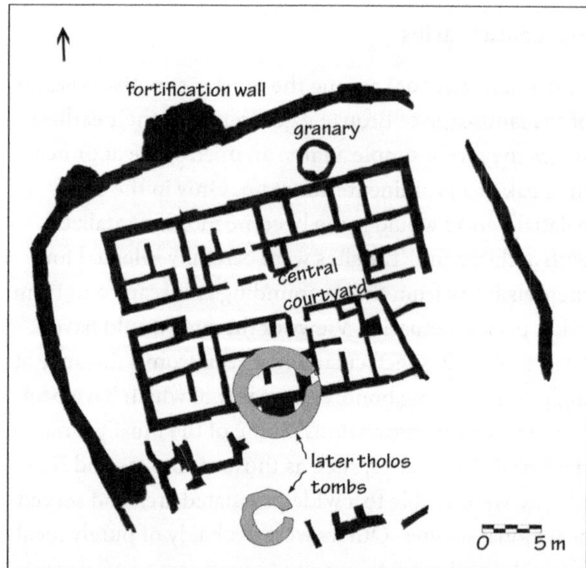

4.3. Plan, Aghia Photia. After Tsipopoulou 1999, pl. XXVIII.

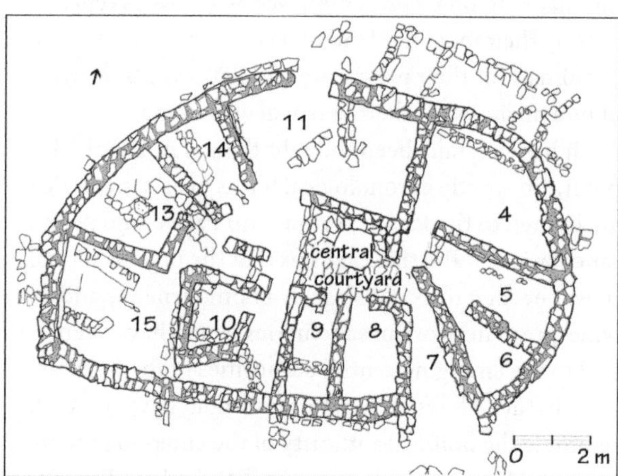

4.4. Plan. Oval House, Chamaizi. Based on Myers 1985, p. 22.

Aghia Photia, Chamaizi, and Petras

One of the strangest developments of this entire rather strange period was the establishment of a cluster of three defensible settlements in the area around modern Siteia. These sites, Aghia Photia, Chamaizi, and Petras, overlap in date and appear to constitute a unique regional phenomenon. The most interesting of the three is the fascinating site that M. Tsipopoulou excavated on the coast at Aghia Photia (fig. 4.3).[18] This settlement consists of an impressively rectilinear building ca. 18 m by 27.5 m with more than thirty rooms arranged around a small central courtyard. The building was entirely surrounded by an encircling wall (no longer preserved on the south) with three projecting bastions. On the north is a small circular granary. In some ways the fort at Aghia Photia is reminiscent of the earlier naturally fortified EM citadel at Trypiti on the south coast (see fig. 3.6), but the closest comparison for its outer enceinte with projecting bastions is at Syros in the Cyclades. This is particularly interesting when we recall that the EM I Cycladicizing cemetery discussed in Chapter 3 is located only about 150 meters to the east. While most of the pottery found in the fort dated to MM IA, the excavator reports that some earlier material contemporary with the cemetery was found.[19] After the fort was abandoned, two circular structures that are almost certainly tholos tombs were built directly over its remains.[20] These were empty when excavated, but even in their present state, looming over the highest part of the little fort, the tholoi eloquently signal new arrivals staking out a claim to the area.

Several scholars have noted the general similarities between the fort at Aghia Photia and the nearby contemporary Oval House at Chamaizi (fig. 4.4).[21] Like the structure at Aghia Photia, the Oval House was positioned on the top of a defensible hill with views overlooking the Bay of Siteia and the Piskokephalo valley. Its outer wall is pierced by just two openings. There is a courtyard in the center of both buildings, around which the rooms were arranged. The Oval House, however, is much smaller than the Aghia Photia fort, and its finds suggest it served as a multifunctional farmhouse. Nevertheless Tsipopoulou is almost certainly correct in identifying these buildings as belonging to a regional form specific to the area around modern Siteia.[22]

In addition to these two unusual buildings, a third fortified building designed around a small central courtyard is located at nearby Petras. The earliest Protopalatial phase of the fortified building at Petras dates to about the time Chamaizi was destroyed (see fig. 8.15). These three buildings are within a few kilometers of each other. They constitute a specific regional or local type that seems to have begun in the tradition of Cycladic forts and eventually adopted Minoanizing features such as worked-stone column bases and ashlar masonry. Because the Neopalatial phase of the building at Petras has been identified as a mini-Palace, I shall return to it in the discussion of Neopalatial Palaces in Chapter 8.

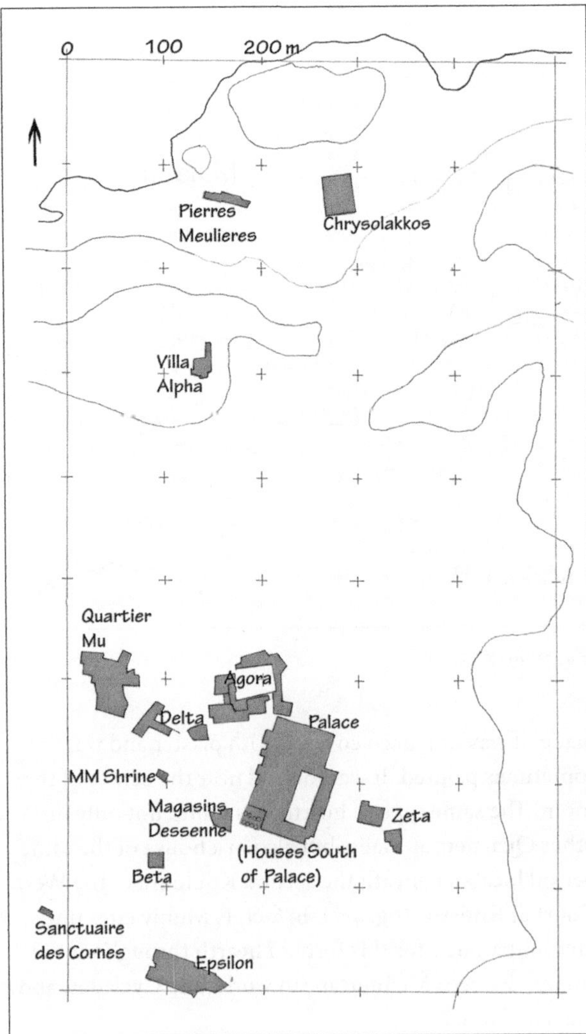

4.5. Plan. MM Malia. After Pelon 1992, plan 1.

The EM III–MM IA City of Malia

So far we have seen a number of interesting phenomena underway in various parts of Crete during the EM III–MM IA period, including the experimentation with new forms of monumental tombs, the individualization of burials, and the introduction of peak sanctuaries. We have seen nothing, however, to prepare us for the extraordinary developments that took place in Malia during this period.

First, some qualifications: our knowledge of Malia during this period, in fact during the whole of the Bronze Age, is literally patchy because of the excavators' decision to excavate in isolated, widely scattered areas ("Quartiers") rather than in a continuous broad swath as at, for example, Zakros. This means we cannot know what existed in the vast expanses of unexcavated land around the Quartiers. Second, chronology is a problem here, as at so many sites during this period. Most of the excavators stress that there is no evident distinction between EM III and MM IA at the site and that they are best regarded as a single continuous period, even if this makes for some imprecision.[23]

Despite these limitations, we can get some notion of the vastness of EM III MM IA Malia if we compare the plans of the tiny Early Prepalatial settlement at Myrtos (see fig. 3.2) with the map of Malia (fig. 4.5). The comparison is difficult at first because the scale is so dramatically different. It helps to realize that the entire settlement at Myrtos is almost precisely the same size as the small buildings immediately south of the later Palace at Malia (fig. 4.6). In this period Malia, a nascent city, was exponentially larger than any settlement discussed up to this point.

Malia: The Buildings South of the Later Palace

The buildings excavated along the south edge of the later Palace at Malia resemble the earlier structures at Myrtos in some ways. As at Myrtos, the individual houses here have no defined exterior perimeters. As at the earlier site, much of the irregularity resulted from continuous decay, additions, repairs, and alterations made over several generations, spanning the ceramic phases EM III–MM II. The numerous double walls, butted walls, overlapping walls, collapsed rooms, and shifts in orientation testify to the complexity of the history of the area. That complexity makes it difficult to determine even how many houses there are in the group. The original excavators and, more recently, H. van Effenterre divided the area into three houses, A, B and C, as indicated on the plan.[24] Within the buildings a few distinct types of rooms could be recognized on the basis of form, relative location, and built features.

The excavators found a distinctive form of hearth in several rooms. Unlike the mixture of types at Myrtos, here the hearth is standardized. It is circular, ca. .65–.86 m in diameter with a central, deeper circular depression and sometimes a raised outer border. It was usually

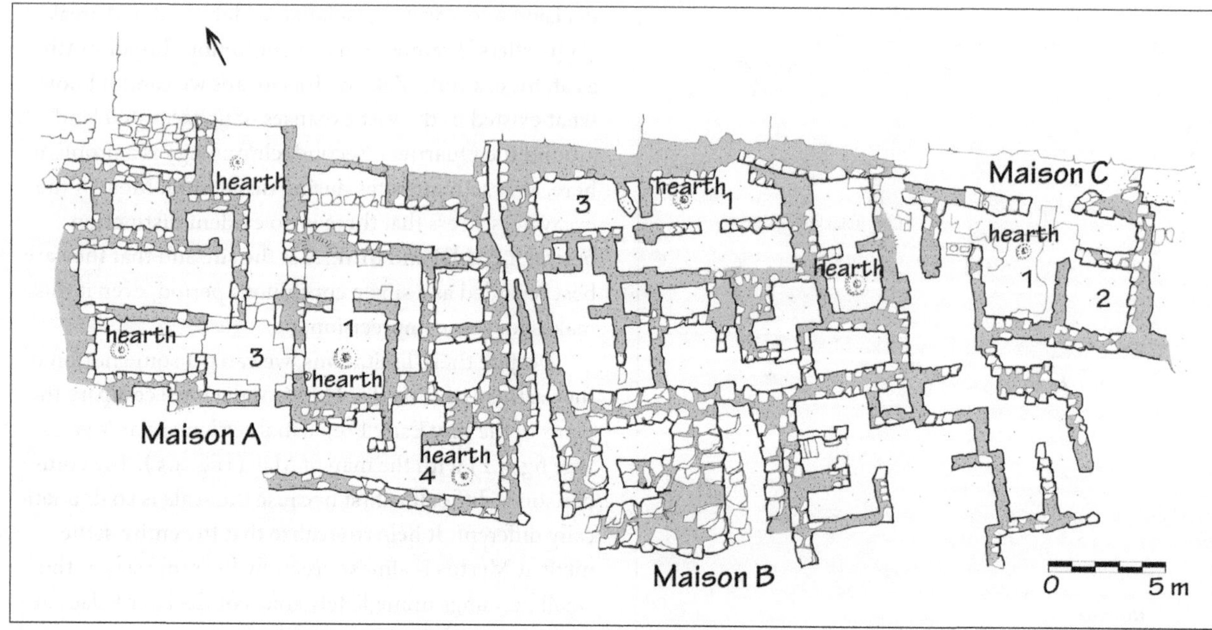

4.6. Plan. MM IA buildings south of Palace, Malia. After Chapouthier and Demargne 1942, plan II.

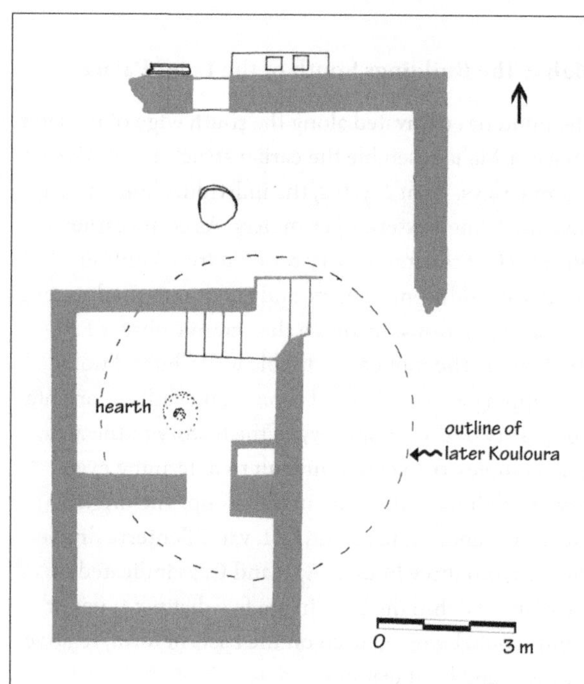

4.7. Plan. House under Kouloura 2, Knossos. After H. and J. Pendlebury 1929–1930, fig. 2.

made of clay or stucco covered with plaster and was sometimes painted. It was located near the center of the room. The same type of hearth was found not only in other Quartiers at Malia, but also in a house of the same period located beneath the second Kouloura of the West Court at Knossos (fig. 4.7). In fact, P. Muhly cites numerous parallels for this form of hearth throughout the ancient Eastern Mediterranean world, the Cyclades, and the mainland.[25]

The presence of this hearth allowed F. Chapouthier, P. Demargne, and van Effenterre to identify a number of main living rooms among the buildings south of the Palace. These include Rooms 1, 3, 4, and 5 in Maison A, Rooms 1 and 5 in Maison B, and Room 1 in Maison C. These main rooms are generally rectangular and can be entered by either one or two doors. When there is a single door, it is located on the shorter wall of the rectangle. Beyond the door, the main room is preceded by a vestibule, often fitted with benches. Most of the other rooms are doorless spaces.

If all of the rooms with hearths were used for more or less the same range of activities, as seems likely, it may be necessary to divide this building complex into more than three houses. For example, does Maison A have four main rooms? or does this group of rooms represent

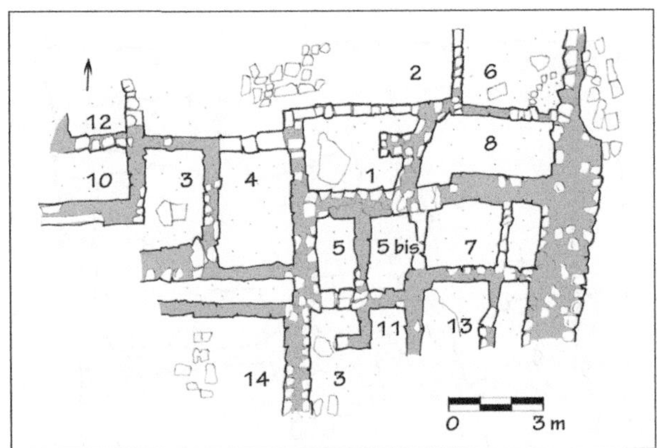

4.8. Plan. Quartier Gamma, section excavated in 1924, Malia.

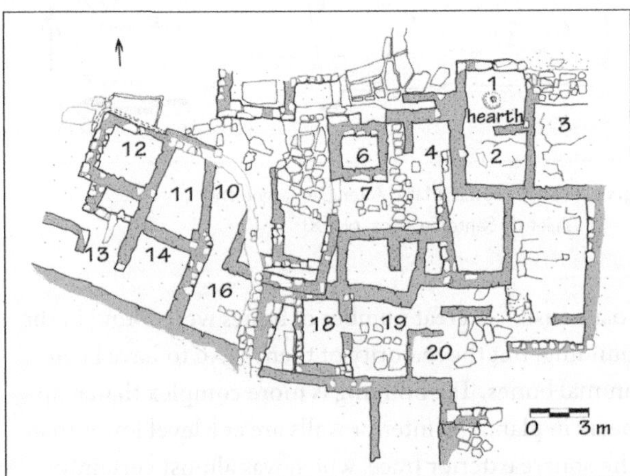

4.9. Plan. Quartier Gamma, section excavated in 1931, Malia. After Demargne and Gallet de Santerre 1953, pl. LXII.

parts of four houses? The size of the complex also suggests that some further divisions might be made. The overall area measures some 675 m^2. As presently defined, Maisons A and B are huge. Dividing the area into six parts (the number of hearths and main rooms) yields houses of a size more common in Minoan architecture. Yet the situation is unclear. A convincing solution would require a careful correlation of architectural details with the distribution of the artifacts of the sort T. Whitelaw provided for Myrtos.

Another Maliote feature is the so-called *auge*, a carefully cut block of sandstone with two depressions incised into the top. It sometimes has additional mortices at the edges to support a wooden framework. It is almost always found built into a rubble wall, rather like a thick threshold. About forty of these objects have been found at Malia—there is one northwest of Room 1 in Maison C—and they are found at no other site. At Malia, the auges have a long history, lasting through the LM I period. Various functions have been suggested for these objects, including supports for looms and feeding troughs for animals.[26] The auges may not have had a single function, but they serve as a reminder that, even as Minoan architecture became more uniform throughout the island over the course of the Bronze Age, purely local traditions were still important.

Quartiers Gamma, Theta, Zeta Gamma, and Beta

The excavators at Malia have found Late Prepalatial architectural remains across much of the site. Quartier Gamma was excavated in two campaigns. The rooms uncovered in 1924 are shown in figure 4.8, and those dug in 1931 are shown in figure 4.9.[27] In general terms, the area is similar to the rooms south of the later Palace in most important ways. This complex also represents many years of alternating disintegration and accumulation, resulting in a confused tangle of rooms.

Circular hearths of the now-familiar sort may help to distinguish some of the main rooms and hint at divisions among the houses. Rooms 1, 2, and 3 at the east end of the 1931 plan (see fig. 4.9) may represent one residential unit. Room 1 has a terra cotta hearth, while Room 3, containing two auges and several querns, may have had an industrial function. Rooms 12–14 at the west end of the Quartier may form a similar group, Rooms 10 and 11 being later additions.

Quartier Theta (fig. 4.10) resembles Quartier Gamma in a number of respects.[28] This too is an incompletely excavated set of rooms that spans a number of phases from EM III through MM III (the plan shows the second phase, MM IB). The plan appears to represent parts of two houses separated by a central passageway. The rooms continue into the unexcavated scarp on all sides.

The excavators of Maison Beta were uncertain about its role in the community (fig. 4.11).[29] H. van Effenterre proposed that the building was a rectangular house tomb similar to Chrysolakkos. Its location near the center of the town, however, makes that unlikely; J. Soles is probably correct in identifying the walls as belonging

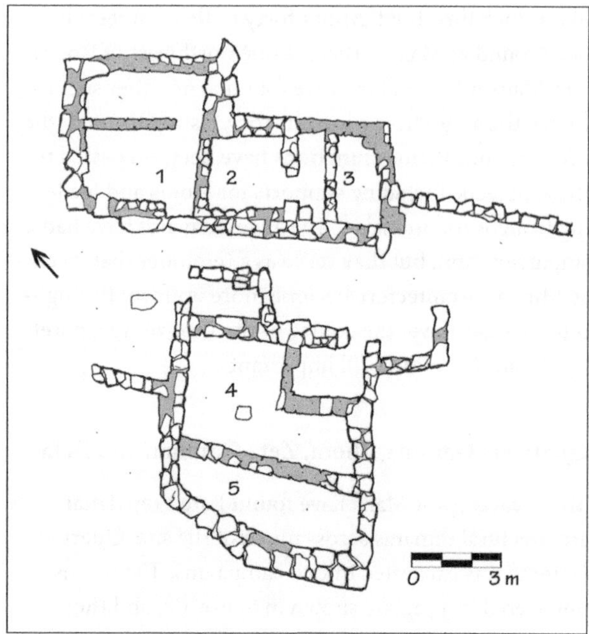

4.10. Plan. Quartier Theta. After H. and M. van Effenterre 1976, pl. 30.

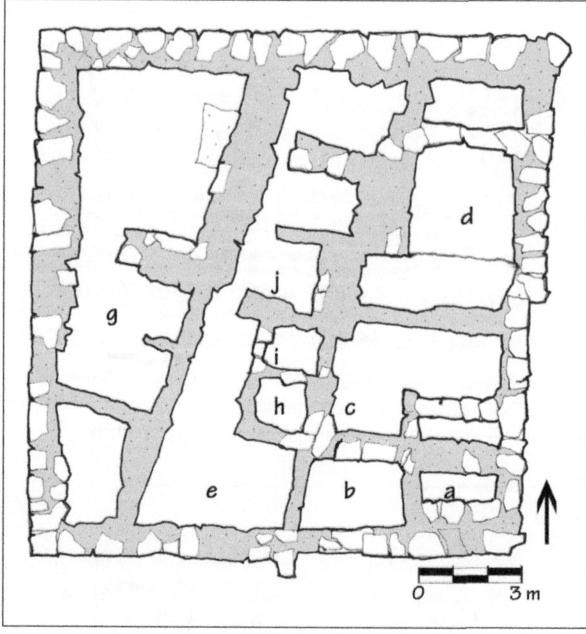

4.11. Plan. Maison B, Malia. After Demargne and Gallet de Santerre 1953, pl. LXI.

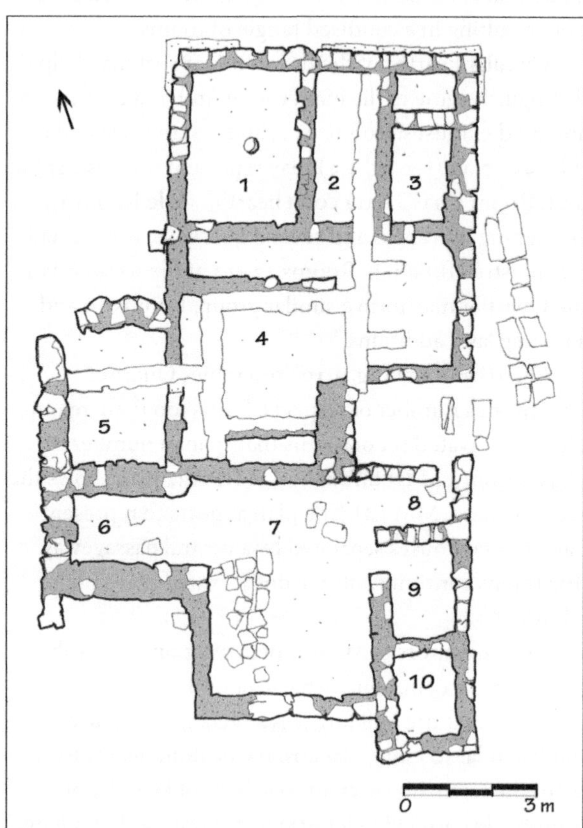

4.12. Plan. Quartier Zeta Gamma, Malia. After Deshayes and Dessenne 1959, plan IV.

to a house.[30] A great number of bones were found in the building, but the majority of them seem to have been animal bones. The building is more complex than it appears in plan. The interior walls are at a level lower than the square exterior trace, which was almost certainly added at a later date. The original plan of the building would have differed considerably from that shown here.

Several phases of the complex Zeta Gamma (fig. 4.12), located east of the Palace, are contemporary with those of Building Alpha, also called Villa Alpha (see below). Zeta Gamma shares with that complex also its general rectilinear arrangement and its location near a stretch of the town wall.

Villa Alpha

Villa Alpha may be the most extraordinary building of the period (fig. 4.13).[31] This large complex of rooms is located about 350 m north of the site of the Palace. Its rooms were built against the western face of the massive city wall that enclosed at least part of the settlement from the early part of the Minoan period.

The complex consists of some thirty-five rooms and measures nearly 500 m² in overall area (not including

4.13. Plan. Villa Alpha, Malia. After Demargne and Gallet de Santerre 1953, pl. LX.

the large paved court on the north). On three sides the building continues even further into the unexcavated scarp. Furthermore, stairways and the numerous doorless spaces indicate that much of the building also had a second story, which, to judge by the kinds of objects fallen into Rooms 1, 2, and 9, were of considerable importance.

While it is not absolutely certain that all the rooms belong to a single house, it does appear that many of the main walls were constructed as a single project. The major north-south and east-west walls that divide the site into a regular grid did not result from the sort of piecemeal approach that we have seen in Minoan architecture up to this point.

In its enormous scale—a scale only occasionally approached in domestic architecture even during the Neopalatial period—the building is without precedent. The regularity of the building's plan is also unusual. Previously, such rectilinear design had appeared only on a much smaller scale at such sites as Vasiliki (see fig. 3.5) and Trypiti (see fig. 3.7). Technically sophisticated individual features, such as the ashlar pillar, correspond with the grand scale and geometrically arranged plan.

A major difficulty in dealing with this building is that it was occupied over several periods. The excavators dated the building to the early part of the Middle Minoan period. Most of the finds published from the building date from MM II through MM IIIB. In its main phase, the building was a contemporary of the even more impressive structures of Quartier Mu (see Chapter 6) and of the latest phases of the buildings south of the Palace and those of Quartier Gamma.

Monumental Funerary Architecture at Chrysolakkos

While the date of the earliest construction in Quartier Alpha remains uncertain, there are parallels for its large size, regular plan, and careful construction from Malia as early as EM III. The nearby cemetery at Chrysolakkos (fig. 4.14) is a traditional rectangular ossuary, or house tomb, enlarged to monumental scale: it is nearly five times the size of the large House Tomb 3 at Archanes.[32] In its present form, the building dates to MM I.[33] It has around forty remaining chambers—originally there may have been twice as many—and covers an area of nearly

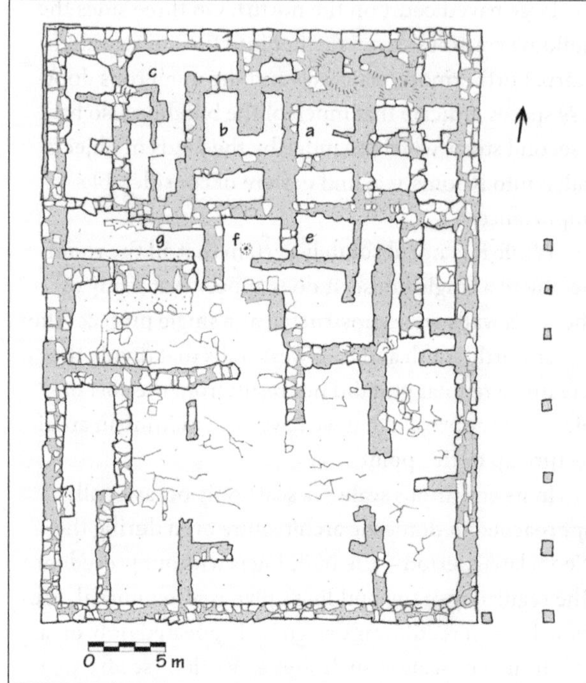

4.14. Plan. Chrysolakkos, Malia. After Demargne 1945, pl. XXXVIII.

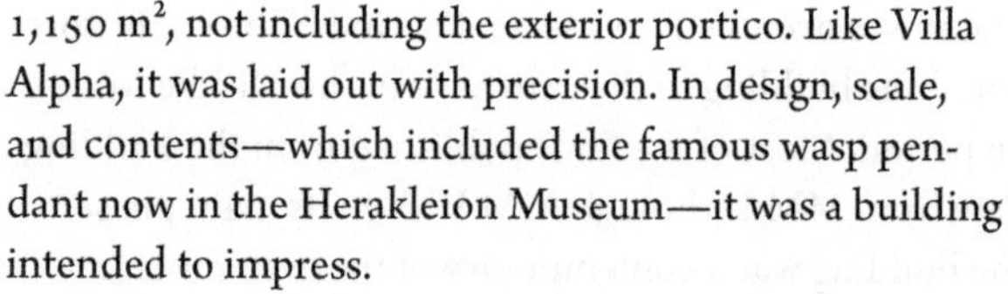

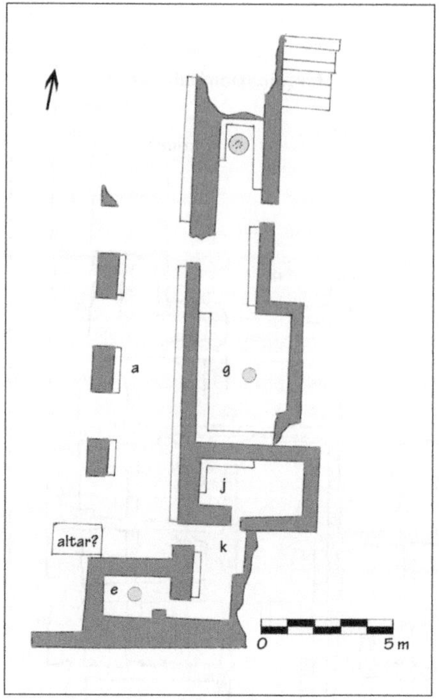

4.15. Plan. Building east of Chrysolakkos, Malia. After H. van Effenterre 1980, fig. 230.

1,150 m^2, not including the exterior portico. Like Villa Alpha, it was laid out with precision. In design, scale, and contents—which included the famous wasp pendant now in the Herakleion Museum—it was a building intended to impress.

The outer wall of the building at Chrysolakkos is the earliest example of orthostate construction known on the island.[34] In this technique, a ground-level course of ashlar blocks with drilled mortices supported a horizontal beam and rubble superstructure. The cuttings in the blocks show that they had been reused from an even earlier (EM III?) structure. In J. Shaw's view, this building "may be the earliest monumental architecture of cut stone in Crete or, for that matter, in Greece."[35]

A Mortuary Chapel at Malia?

The large Chrysolakkos tomb was built over the remains of an earlier building just to the east (fig. 4.15).[36] The purpose of the building is unclear. Its proximity to the monumental Chrysolakkos house tomb has generally led to the assumption that this building represented the remains of its predecessor. No human remains were found, and Muhly has suggested that the building was purely domestic.[37] Indeed the building has several of the features we have seen in the EM III–MM IA houses at Malia. It has a circular terra cotta hearth with a central depression in Room H and several rooms lined with the same sort of plaster-covered benches found in the buildings south of the Palace. However, in the southwest corner of the preserved section of the building, there is a monumental version of a *kernos* and a raised platform that Soles identifies as an altar like that of House Tomb II at Gournia. A series of rounded capping stones found scattered about the area may have belonged to a mud brick wall that framed the courtyard. Watrous has pointed out that the best parallel for this construction technique is from Egypt and suggests that the building resembles the corridor chapels associated with Egyptian *mastabas*. While architectural similarity is not particularly convincing by itself, Watrous also notes that the pointed-bottom cups found in the building are a shape not found in Crete but common in Egypt.[38]

New Construction Techniques

The EM III–MM IA buildings at Malia employ a remarkably consistent set of features and techniques. The builders made extensive use of plastic materials like clay, plaster, and stucco to cover walls, to make benches, and to form bins and hearths. This thick coating concealed the underlying rubble masonry and gave the interiors of the rooms a molded, uniform appearance. The repetition of standardized rooms with central hearths marks a new level of planning consistency. But most striking about these constructions at Malia is the new sense of monumentality we see, above all at Chrysolakkos.

In the same period, the first ashlar masonry was introduced at Chrysolakkos in Malia and in the Monolithic Pillar Basement at Knossos.[39] The use of cut ashlar masonry, along with the tools that the technique requires, including bronze saws to trim block edges and drills for the mortices, implies the existence of at least part-time specialist builders and toolmakers.

Soon thereafter, with the establishment of the first Palaces, what had begun as a few limited innovations would blossom into revolutions in building technology and in the construction industry. Precisely the same techniques of elaborate plaster and stucco work covering walls, floors, and benches combined with ashlar masonry would be characteristic of the elaborate buildings of Quartier Mu at Malia (see figs. 6.15–6.17) and of the first Palaces at Malia, Phaistos, and Knossos.

These were not small-scale buildings designed and built by the families who used them. These were monumental structures built to assert and maintain the power of the people who had ordered their construction. Architecture had begun to serve in the construction of a new kind of hierarchical social identity.

Summary: The City of Malia

The EM III–MM IA constructions at Malia represent a town or a small city on a scale entirely different from anything seen before in Crete. As we saw in Chapter 2, Myrtos was a typical EM II hamlet of about twenty-five to thirty people. At Malia, excavated EM III–MM IA remains are scattered throughout most of the thirty-six hectares covered by the Neopalatial city. Applying Whitelaw's calculations to EM III–MM IA Malia, one would come up with an estimated population of several thousand people.[40] Malia was extraordinary, so extraordinary, in fact, that it raises a difficult but unavoidable question.

Was the First Minoan Palace Built in EM III–MM IA?

How, when, and where the Minoans came to build the first Palaces in Crete is one of the long-standing questions in the discipline. I will return to this issue in Chapter 5, but this is a good place to briefly outline the architectural evidence for the existence of Minoan Palaces before MM IB, the date to which the first Palaces have been traditionally assigned. The evidence is incomplete but suggestive.

First, at Knossos there is a large terrace wall located partly under the northwest corner of the current west facade of the Palace that is dated to EM III (fig. 4.16).[41] This is a large wall made in a distinctive style of roughly dressed rectangular blocks shaped like large shoe boxes.[42] Soundings against the west walls of Magazines XI, XII, and XIV revealed sections of the same wall associated with EM III–MM IA pottery.[43] Today, visitors to the site generally overlook this wall, though it is quite visible. Where it runs east-west below the later Palace facade, a section of the wall is preserved to a height of nearly 2 m (fig. 4.17). More significantly, this wall represents only a small part of a grand undertaking. Here, at the heart of the settlement, much of the hill was leveled and a terrace, as massive in scale as the corresponding section of the later Palace, was constructed. This terrace represented an enormous investment of time and labor. Unfortunately whatever stood on this terrace was replaced by the later Palace construction.

The terrace wall is the most enticing clue that a monumental building was constructed on the palace site in EM III. A few other clues are scattered around the site. The strange Hypogaeum at Knossos (fig. 4.18), a vast underground storage chamber cut from the soft bedrock and furnished with a spiral stairway, should probably be assigned to this period.[44] The Monolithic Pillar Basement, which was incorporated into the later Palace, was built in MM IA.[45] Something significant was happening in three quite distant parts of the Palace site at this early date, but the relations among them are unclear.

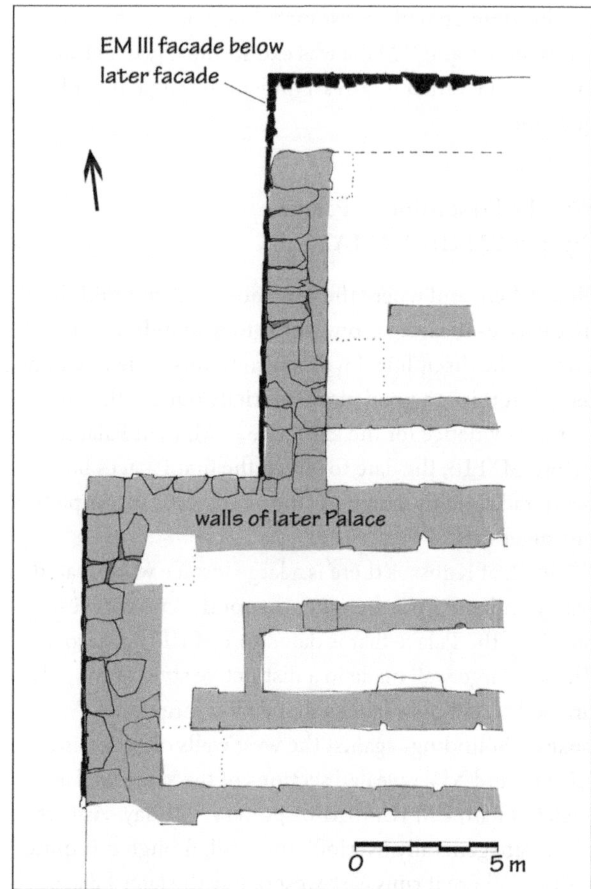

4.16. Plan. EM III facade, Palace at Knossos. After Graham 1987, fig. 158.

4.17. EM III facade, Palace at Knossos. Photo by author.

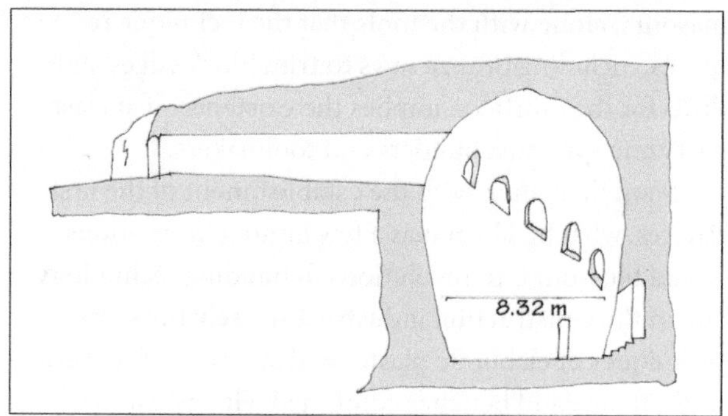

4.18. Restored section. Hypogaeum, Knossos. After *PM I*, fig. 74.

At Malia the evidence of an early palace is only slightly better. At least part of the street system with its characteristic raised walkways was laid out in MM IA.[46] The date of the first Palace is more problematic. Although I. Schoep has recently accepted the existence of an EM III–MM IA Palace at Malia as an established fact, the situation is not settled.[47] It is further complicated by a basic disagreement among the excavators: van Effenterre categorically denies the possibility of a Palace in EM III–MM IA.[48] On the other hand, O. Pelon, who has been conducting soundings within the later Palace for many years, claims to have found not only evidence of an EM III–MM IA Palace, but also substantial remains of an EM II predecessor.[49] J.-Cl. Poursat, the excavator of the adjacent MM II Quartier Mu, says the evidence is too scant to be certain.[50]

Pelon's evidence comes mainly from two areas. First, in his reexcavation of the Northwest Quarter of the Palace, where Chapouthier had found two elaborate bronze ceremonial swords in 1936, Pelon found some EM III–MM IA sherds along with the MM II floor deposit. He reasonably dated the destruction to MM II but went on to presume that the earlier material meant that the first Palace had been constructed over the course of MM IA.[51] Second, a sounding below Room IV 7 revealed a short section of an early wall along with what Pelon described as a "foundation deposit." This consisted of a complete EM III–MM IA "tea pot" set into a small construction of upright slabs built against the wall. Unfortunately the wall fragment itself is isolated and not clearly related to any other contemporary walls. While the evidence is scattered, Pelon has definitively shown that the remains of the first Palace at Malia are much more extensive than most scholars had realized and that something major was going on as early as EM III–MM IA. This is confirmed by the contemporaneous building activity that was spread across this surprisingly vast settlement.

How Did the First Minoan Palace Come into Being?

A. Evans considered the more or less simultaneous appearance of the first Palaces at Knossos, Phaistos, and Malia to have been largely the result of eastern influence. While he was careful to point out the importance that purely local elements played in the process, he believed that the basic concept of a Palace had probably been imported. In fact, to Evans the overall historical significance of Minoan Crete was the crucial role it played in the transmission of high culture from the eastern "Cradle of Civilization" to Europe.[52]

In the 1970s, partly in reaction to A. Evans's diffusionist *ex oriente lux* model, a new generation of scholars, including C. Renfrew, K. Branigan, and P. Warren, saw the Palaces as the end products of a series of interacting local social and economic processes that had been underway throughout the Early Bronze Age, but that only fully meshed at the beginning of the Protopalatial period.[53] Branigan and Warren saw most of the essential elements of the later Palaces already present in the EM buildings at Myrtos and Vasiliki.

Most scholars would now agree that at least the general idea of a monumental Palace, along with the general notion of writing and record keeping, was inspired by Near Eastern or Egyptian models or both.[54] What has changed since the time of A. Evans, however, is that experts have acquired a new appreciation of the complexity of the issue. As we shall see in the next chapter, J. Cherry saw the first Palaces as the products of a sudden cultural revolution.[55] Today scholars are gradually deconstructing the assumption that there was a single, monolithic event. No two sites shared precisely the same history, and the underlying social processes are likely to have been intricate and multilinear.[56] The extraordinary EM III–MM IA buildings at Malia not only embody that complexity, but also encourage one to question the assumption that the first Minoan Palace had to have been built at Knossos. Malia is at least as likely a candidate.

5.1. Palace at Phaistos from the northwest. Photo by author.

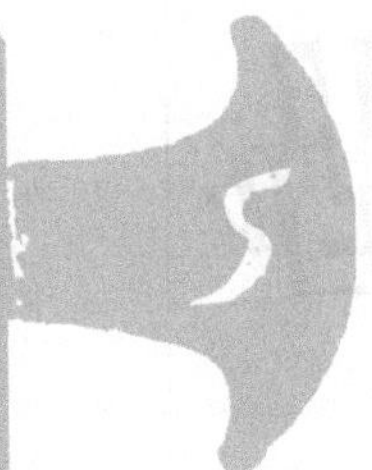

The First Palaces and the Construction of Power

CA. 1900–1750 BC

THE PROTOPALATIAL period (MM IB–MM IIB) lasted from ca. 1900 to 1750 BC, about 150 years. Over the course of this period the construction of the first Minoan Palaces at Phaistos, Knossos, and Malia transformed the island's history.

The Early Palace at Phaistos

To someone approaching from the Mesara plain, the immense Palace at Phaistos, perched on the end of a ridge, would have been visible from a considerable distance.[1] To one coming from the opposite direction, the Timbaki plain to the northwest, the first view of the Palace would have been different (fig. 5.1)—it would have appeared more suddenly, stretching out below the path that crossed the top of the ridge—but the immediate effect would have been much the same: here was a building whose enormous size, elaborate techniques, geometrical design, and gleaming surfaces dramatically set it apart from its surroundings. It was a building that dominated the ridge, dwarfed the surrounding houses, and dazzled the nineteenth-century-BC visitor with its magnificence. Nothing quite like it had ever been seen in this part of the island.

To modern eyes, conditioned by the inflated architectural scale of the twenty-first century AD, the enormity of this building is apt to be lost. Although it was built in several phases, by the end of the Protopalatial period, it covered some 9000 m^2, nearly nine times the area of the entire EM village at Myrtos. When one stood in front of the Palace for the first time, however, the only scale that would have mattered was the relationship between the vast building and oneself. Most buildings, up to this point, had been made to correspond to the immediate needs of the individual person and family. Their scale was correspondingly intimate and immediately comprehensible. Even if their plans and interiors were sometimes complex, these were buildings whose overall form could be taken in at a single glance. The Palace at Phaistos was different. Its monumental scale aimed to overwhelm.

Another way by which the scale of the building can be measured is by the amount of labor required to build it.[2] Although the work was spread out over several generations, the eventual size of the building demanded a cumulative effort unprecedented in earlier periods. Along the west side of the Palace, the sloping ground had to be leveled by cutting three immense terraces. Hundreds of tons of earth were removed, each worker excavating only about one cubic meter per day. Building materials had to be collected and brought to the site. Most of the walls were of rounded limestone cobbles and boulders that were collected on the site. Larger blocks of limestone for the ashlar masonry might also have been quarried from the slope immediately southwest of the Palace facade. Chunks of harder, gray limestone—called *siderópetra* (iron stone) locally—may have been brought from the nearby town of Peri. Gypsum, to be used for pavements and dado courses, probably came from the quarry southwest of the Palace that was filled in by the excavators in 1900.[3]

Building walls of rubble masonry that were to rise three stories on a sloping site was a formidable job. The builders were timid engineers and built all the walls

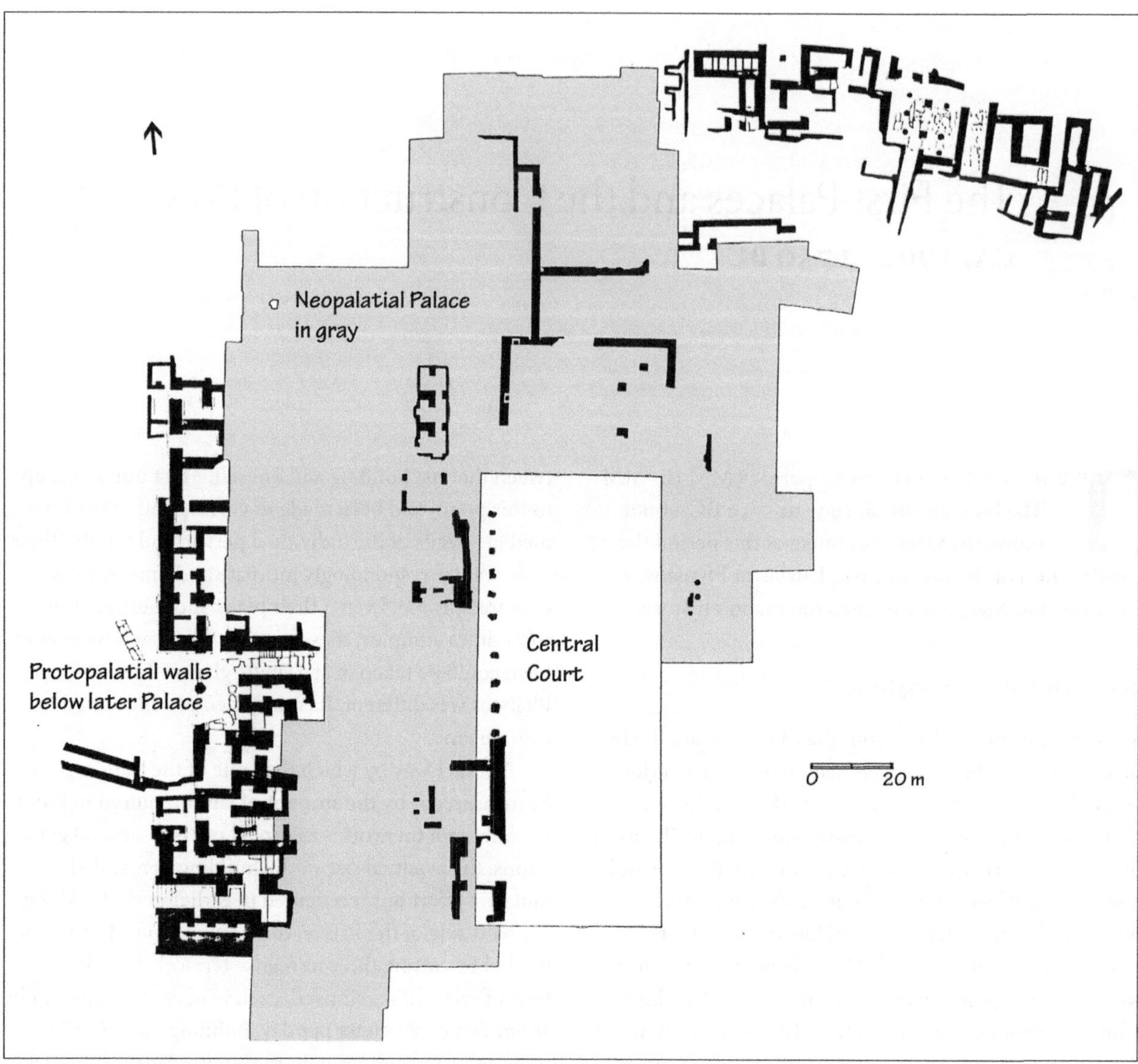

5.2. Plan. Protopalatial Palace at Phaistos. After Levi 1976, plan B.

thicker than they had to be. They were particularly concerned about the southwest angle of the Palace, which was not only one of the major external angles of the building, but also the lowest part of the Palace and therefore crucial in countering the outward thrust of the building. Here the walls were especially massive—up to 2.80 m thick in places (figs. 5.2–5.4). While the walls in the rest of the old Palace were less thick, care was taken throughout to counteract the downhill thrust of the building. Thus all the major walls of the ground stories run east-west, at right angles to the slope. Thinner walls and openings such as doors and windows were oriented north-south, where less support was needed. On upper stories, where there was less thrust, the doors could go in the opposite direction. On the ground floor, however, where support was literally fundamental, the builders had to keep even the yet-to-be-built third story in mind.

Trees had to be felled and the timber transported to the site. Most logs were left unfinished and, possibly after their ends were burned to prevent rot, were set into slots left in the walls.[4] Layers of smaller twigs, stones, and earth were placed on top, much as for a roof. A few

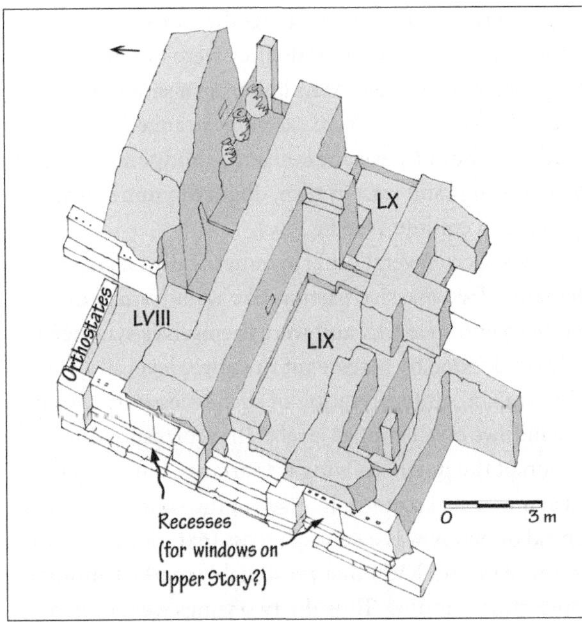

5.3. Reconstruction. West wing, Palace at Phaistos. After Levi 1976, pl. N.

5.4. West facade, Palace at Phaistos, from the northwest. Photo by author.

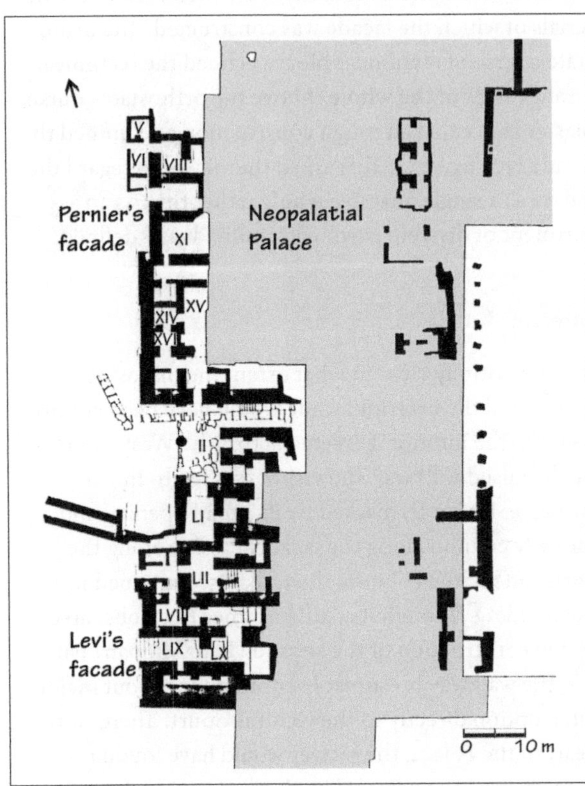

5.5. Plan. West wing, Protopalatial Palace at Phaistos. After Levi 1976, plan B.

floor surfaces were especially elaborate, being paved with limestone (Room LIX) or gypsum (Room LIII), and some were even frescoed in patterns that may have imitated woven carpets. Walls were also commonly plastered and painted and occasionally lined with gypsum dadoes. Benches were commonly built at the foot of the walls and niches provided places to rest small vessels.

The most elaborate technique was confined to the outer facade, where it could be seen by all (figs. 5.4, 5.5). Around the foot of the entire length of the facade, a *krepidoma,* or leveling course, of cut ashlar blocks supported a course of orthostates, massive, well-cut blocks set on edge.[5] On the tops of the orthostates, a series of rectangular mortices were used to hold horizontal timbers in place by means of a series of tenons. These timbers, unlike those used in the floors and roofs, would have required sophisticated carpentry, as would the windows, which were almost certainly located on the upper stories above the recesses that can be seen in the facade.[6] A similar technique had been tried earlier at Chrysolakkos, but what appeared there was a tentative experiment using very hard stone. Here the technique was applied to softer limestone, which continued to be preferred for fine ashlar masonry.

In materials and techniques, the Palace represents a revolution in Minoan architecture. The building would have demanded specialized builders working with completely new tools. J. Shaw describes in detail the new kit of bronze tools that included double-axes, adzes, axe-adzes, picks, sledgehammers, saws, drills, and chisels.[7] The production of the tools implies the availability of skilled toolmakers.

The changes in building technology were paralleled in other areas. Seal cutters found the tools and the means to work hard stones. Potters began to produce eggshell-thin Kamares ware. Even the system of writing that developed during this period is directly reflected in the architecture. A series of pictographic masons' marks were carved on the ashlar blocks of several parts of the Palace here and at Knossos and Malia.[8]

Monumental Architecture

The Palace at Phaistos was built by a small army of construction workers organized by an efficient administration. Its plan no longer grew from specifically local traditions but corresponded to the plans of the slightly earlier Palaces at Knossos and Malia. An island-wide palatial style began to form a unifying veneer over the multifarious local and regional forms that continued to constitute the mass of Minoan architecture.

In works of monumental architecture such as the Palace at Phaistos, artificiality and abstraction dominate the randomness of the natural surroundings. Other Minoan buildings, including even those built around the edges of the Palace, took their setting as a given limitation and were arranged according to the contours of the site. For the Old Palace at Phaistos, an arbitrary N-S-E-W orientation was imposed on the site, and much of the ridge was completely reshaped and geometrically ordered to accommodate it. Outside the west facade, the main facade of the building, this regularization of the ridge took the form of an apron of broad, flat, paved courtyards ascending in three stages from south to north, completely restructuring the natural slope.

Artificial geometry of a surprisingly complex sort continues through both major levels of the west facade of the building. Although the two wings were constructed so that the ground floor of the northern terrace was level with the floor of the third story of the southern wing, the two wings operated together through most of the Middle Minoan period. They were not mirror images of one another, extending from a single symmetrical axis, yet they were carefully arranged. The main entrance, Room II, was located at the midpoint between the two wings and was, in turn, divided symmetrically by a central column (see fig. 5.5).

There were several other symmetrically balanced elements. Two massive bastion-like walls framed the southern entrance LIX and were themselves symmetrically subdivided by recesses at the lower level and, if J. W. Graham's interpretation of such recesses is correct, by windows on the upper levels.[9] The corresponding section of the northern wing was arranged in a different symmetrical pattern. In place of the southern wing's central doorway was a central recess (exterior facade of Rooms XIV and XVI) that presumably marked another upper-story window. Thus the two wings were united not by a simple bilateral symmetry, but by a more complicated and varying rhythm of alternating projections and recesses.[10]

That geometrical regularity extended even to the materials of which the facade was constructed. The orthostate course of rectilinear blocks echoed the rectilinear arrangement of the whole. Above the orthostate course, plaster concealed all rough construction and unified the facade (see fig. 5.3). This asked the viewer to regard the Palace as a single, massive whole rather than as an assortment of discrete parts, each individually defined.

Interior

It is not entirely clear to what extent the imposing impression of the exterior facade would have been continued into the interior. Directed across the West Court by the raised walkway, the visitor was led to the major entrance, Room II, marked by its broad opening and the only column along the facade. Passing along the north side of the column, the walkway continued into the building. Though its path has since been obscured by the construction of the second (Late Minoan) Palace, the walkway presumably continued without major interruption directly to the Central Court. There, at the heart of the Palace, the viewer would have found the monumentality promised by the facade. As J. Driessen has recently phrased it, the Central Court was the heart of the Palace, a "constructed landscape" that served as the site of ritual performances that "were the first unifying and integrative actions that bound society together and made Minoans out of them."[11] The vast rectangular paved court was framed, at least on its west side, by a line of over twelve large columns. The screen of vertical columns, the essence of geometrical regularity, masked the complexities of the rooms behind.

At least five other entrances led into the Palace from the West Court. If the visitor were to have entered by any of these, the impression of the Palace would have been quite different. The intricate web of tiny rooms beyond these doors was the antithesis of the imposing facade, intimate rather than intimidating. Most of the rooms were tiny. In fact, many of the spaces were smaller than the walls that frame them. Experienced in three dimensions, most of the spaces would have appeared as tiny, low, dark cavities that appeared to be hollowed out of the mass of the building.

Many of the spaces were made even closer by the benches that line the walls. Niches hollowed into the walls above the benches—cavities within cavities—usually contained vessels and nourishment (see fig. 5.3). These benches and niches were an integral part of the architecture. They were covered with a thick layer of plaster of the sort used for the EM III–MM IA buildings at Malia. Here too the plaster formed a smooth surface that continued over the ceiling, walls, and benches, covering the separate parts of the room with a single, organic skin. Within this kind of space, one's usual categorical divisions into ceilings, walls, and furniture seem nearly as arbitrary as they would if applied to the similar continuous surfaces of a cave.

Probably few Minoan viewers wandered through many of the rooms: Minoans are likely to have gone to the rooms where their business took them. But if they had for some reason toured the building, they would have found that communication among the rooms was complex. Seldom were more than three chambers aligned. Ninety-degree changes of direction were common, and there were several 180-degree turns (from Room LVIII to Room LX, for example). Shifts among various levels and stories were also common, and the visitor would have found that many of the rooms connected by east-west passages on the ground floors shifted to north-south passages on the second floor. There was no distinct direction to be followed, and at least in this part of the Palace there was no sense of beginning and end, no sense of progressing toward a focal point. The complex, irregular, unstable interior, in other words, contrasts with the massive, imposing, unified, stable, and regular west facade.

Neither the Minoan builders nor the Minoan visitors are likely to have thought of the first Palace at Phaistos in the purely formal terms just given; nevertheless we can be reasonably certain that the basic elements of scale, unity, symmetry, mathematical regularity, and abstract geometry would have been noticed. One does not build such a building thoughtlessly nor look at it without thinking.

Activities

It is surprisingly difficult to identify many of the activities conducted in the western rooms of the Palace. Although many of the rooms were found to be packed with objects and have been meticulously reported, it is still not entirely clear what each of the spaces was used for or how they related to one another within the larger Palace. However impressive the remains, only a fragment of the building is preserved.[12]

Some of the rooms can be described in purely architectural terms: Room III was a corridor, and Rooms II, L, LVI, LVII, and LIX were vestibules. A number of rooms were used for storing pottery, including XXVII, XXVIII, LI (upper), LV (upper and lower), LXI, LXIII, LXV, and LXVI. Room LVIII (upper and lower) was apparently used for the storage of agricultural produce. Rooms XIX and XX were used for food preparation, as were Rooms V–IX. This latter group of rooms, which opens onto the West Court immediately next to the Theatral Area, has been defined as a shrine largely on the basis of a rectangular terra cotta "offering table" set into the floor.[13] P. Muhly, however, has shown that there is no compelling reason to identify the complex as having been used for religious purposes. Its doorway from the west was a secondary one that was largely closed off from the West Court by the time of its final, Protopalatial use. The real orientation of the room was toward the unknown rooms to the east, which were buried beneath the Neopalatial Palace. The offering table is actually a hearth of the sort found in various domestic and pos-

5.6. Arthur Evans. Corbis.

sibly religious structures in MM IA Malia (see above), in MM II Quartier Mu, and in what may be an independent shrine at Malia. This form of hearth, in other words, is not in and of itself sufficient reason to define a room as a shrine.[14]

The Old Palace at Phaistos is the major source of information concerning the architecture of the early Palaces. It was neither the largest nor the earliest of the Minoan Palaces, for by this time Palaces had already been built at both Malia and Knossos.

The First Palace at Knossos

At Knossos the Middle Minoan builders leveled much of the top of the hill and built a Palace that stretched over some 14,000 m^2, a building nearly half again as large as the Palace at Phaistos. Excavated by Arthur Evans in the first decade of the twentieth century, the Palace at Knossos is the central monument of Minoan archaeology.

The site had been well known long before Evans began his excavations.[15] In the winter of 1878–1879 Minos Kalokairinos excavated in what turned out to be the west wing of the Palace. Some of his finds were published and were widely known. Others, including the American diplomat W. J. Stillman, M. Joubin of the French School, J. Myres of the British School, and even H. Schliemann, had expressed an interest in excavating the site. By 1894 Evans had begun to purchase the site, but it was only with the more stable political situation that accompanied the independence of Crete in 1898 that excavation became feasible. With the encouragement of J. Hazzidakis, founder of the Herakleion Museum, and the invaluable assistance of D. Mackenzie, Evans began excavating on March 23, 1900, and the work proceeded quickly. By the end of the 1902 season, all the major lines of the Palace had been determined, and within the next few years the major points of Evans's interpretation of the site (and of Minoan civilization) were established.

When Evans began at Knossos, he took upon himself the job not just of excavating a building, but also of uncovering the sources of the most enduring myths in European history: the story of Minos, the Minotaur, and the Labyrinth (fig. 5.6). As he excavated Evans found images of bulls all over the Palace, some with graceful youths leaping over their backs. It remained only to explain the origin of the labyrinth. Evans accepted the etymology of the term "labyrinth" proposed by P. Kretschmer and A. Fick.[16] They identified the word as pre-Greek (as its "nth" ending shows), and they held that it derived from the Carian *labrys*, meaning axe, citing, among other examples, the Carian Zeus Labraundos, who was depicted holding a double axe. The etymology was questioned at the time and continues to be debated, but for Evans it opened another series of suggestive parallels. Here, Evans decided, was the significance of the Double Axe signs carved on the pillars and walls of the Palace. The Labyrinth was literally the house of the Double Axe. A few other interesting bits of information have come up since Evans. The back of a clay tablet from Pylos (Cn 1287) depicts a labyrinth pattern, apparently the doodle of an idle scribe. And a tablet from Knossos (Gg 702) mentions as a deity "da-pu2-ri-to-jo po-ti-ni-ja," the Mistress of the Labyrinth.[17]

At Phaistos much of the earlier Palace had been

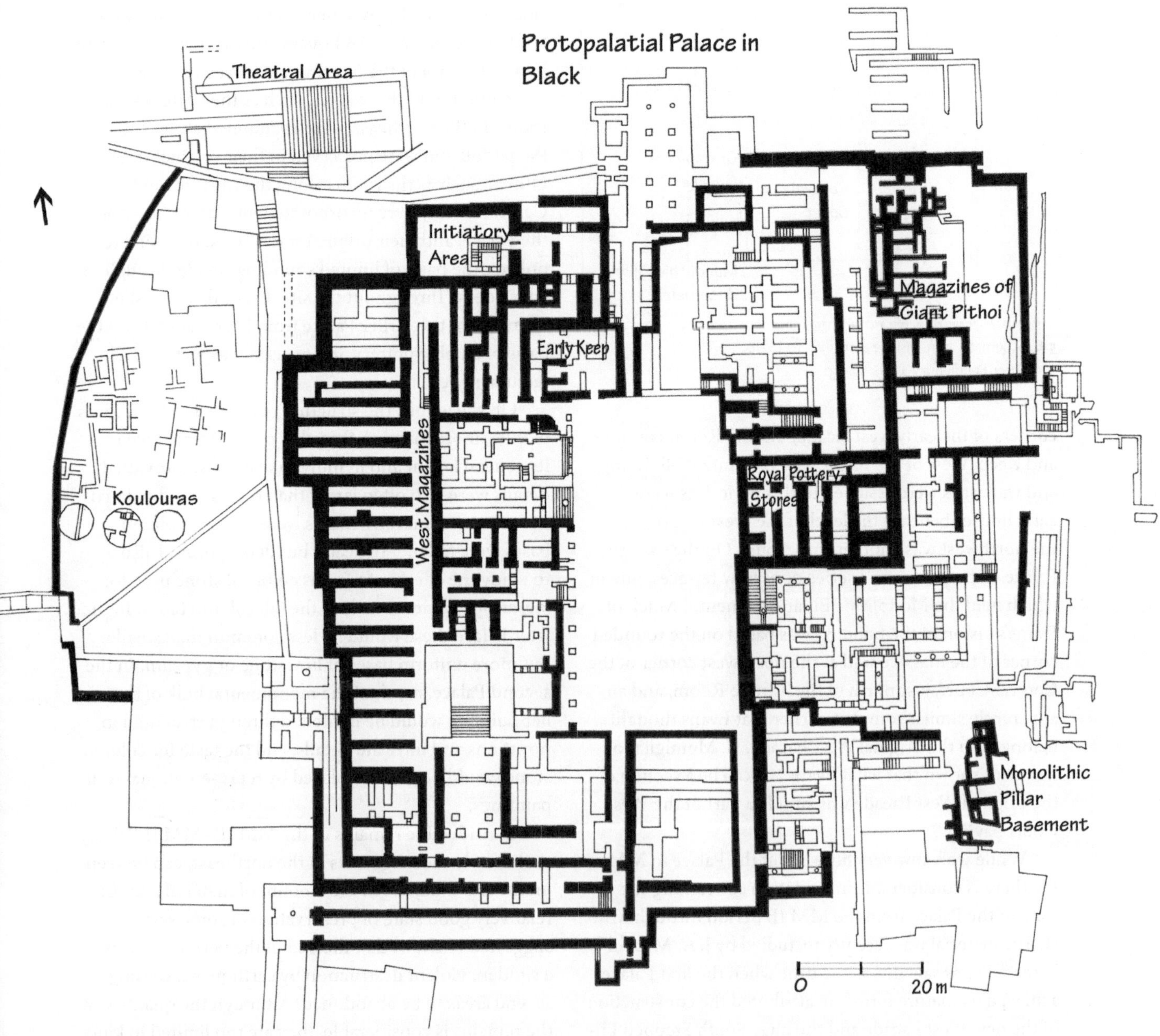

5.7. Plan. Protopalatial Palace at Knossos. After Macgillivray 1994, fig. 2.

encased in a cement-like fill and preserved nearly intact beneath the western edges of the later Palace. At Knossos, however, most of the early Palace was incorporated into or covered by the later building (fig. 5.7). Evidence is more limited, more scattered, and more complex than at Phaistos.

Evans dated the original construction of the first Palace to MM IA. As indicated in the diagrammatic plan, he saw this early formative stage of the building as the time when the Palace began to coalesce from a series of independent parts that he called insulae (fig. 5.8). To this period, he thought, belonged the rounded

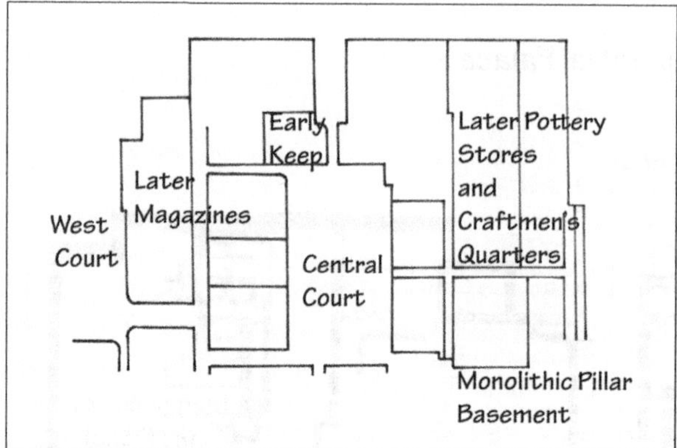

5.8. Schematic plan. Insulae according to Evans. After Pendlebury 1939, fig. 13.

corners of the early west facade, Throne Room complex, and Keep. West of the Palace, the Enceinte Wall, Ramp, and walkways were assigned to this period, as were the early houses beneath the level of the West Court. On the northwest was another early court. On the east, the Palace sloped down in a series of narrow terraces, one of which held the Monolithic Pillar Basement.[18] Much of Evans's vision of the building was based on the rounded corner of the massive wall at the northwest corner of the Central Court, just north of the Throne Room, and an apparently similar rounded corner that Evans thought belonged to the original West Facade. N. Momigliano has since shown that what Evans took to be a section of the original West Facade was simply a part of the West Court paving.[19]

While we know very little about the Palace in MM IA, there is considerable information concerning the state of the Palace from the MM IB period through MM II. The material was recently restudied by J. A. MacGillivray.[20] Evans saw this as the time when the first Palace achieved its mature form. He attributed the construction of the new West Facade and the huge South Stepped Entrance to the early part of the period (MM IB). In MM II came the consolidation of the basic lines of the Palace plan: the original West Porch and West Magazines were built. To the north, the Keep was covered with a floor, and the Initiatory Area built. In the northeast were the Royal Pottery Stores and the Magazines of the Giant Pithoi. A great terrace was supposedly cut along the east side of the Palace, and several of the huge storm drains below the later Residential Quarter were laid out. Outside the Palace, the pavement of the West Court was extended over the MM IA houses and the Koulouras were built. The level of the Northwest Court was raised.

A number of these areas, such as the pottery storage rooms in the northeast, were abandoned at the end of the period and were preserved in their original states. Others, such as the rooms along the west side of the Central Court, were incorporated into later phases of the Palace, and their original states could be estimated only on the basis of limited soundings made through the later floors. Throughout the site, Evans distinguished elements of the earlier Palace from later elements on the basis of datable pottery and of certain aspects of architectural style.

On the whole, the structure of the earlier Palace was bulkier, more massive, than that of the later Palace in its general layout and in individual details. Individual details were also often larger than their second-palatial counterparts: masons' marks were larger;[21] column bases were taller.[22] The early builders appeared also to enjoy the effects of various colors of stone used for *mosaiko* pavements and for the tall column bases. In the later Palace these would be less common than smaller but more uniform bases of limestone or gypsum. In the second Palace, much of the monumental bulk of the earlier building would be lightened through structural innovations and intricate details, and the taste for colored stone would be partly replaced by representational wall paintings.

Considerable remains of the MM IB–MM II Palace, particularly the magazines in the northeast, can be seen on the site today. Both the amount of material and the relatively good state of preservation of some sections suggested to Evans that the end of the period came as a sudden, violent destruction by earthquake, causing several areas to be abandoned. Although the quantity of the remains is considerable, they are too limited in kind to provide an accurate picture of the general character of the building. None of the important public or residential rooms remain, only storage rooms and industrial areas.

Malia

The excavators at Malia, as we saw in Chapter 4, are divided over the nature, date, and even the existence of a Protopalatial Palace at the site. H. van Effenterre, the

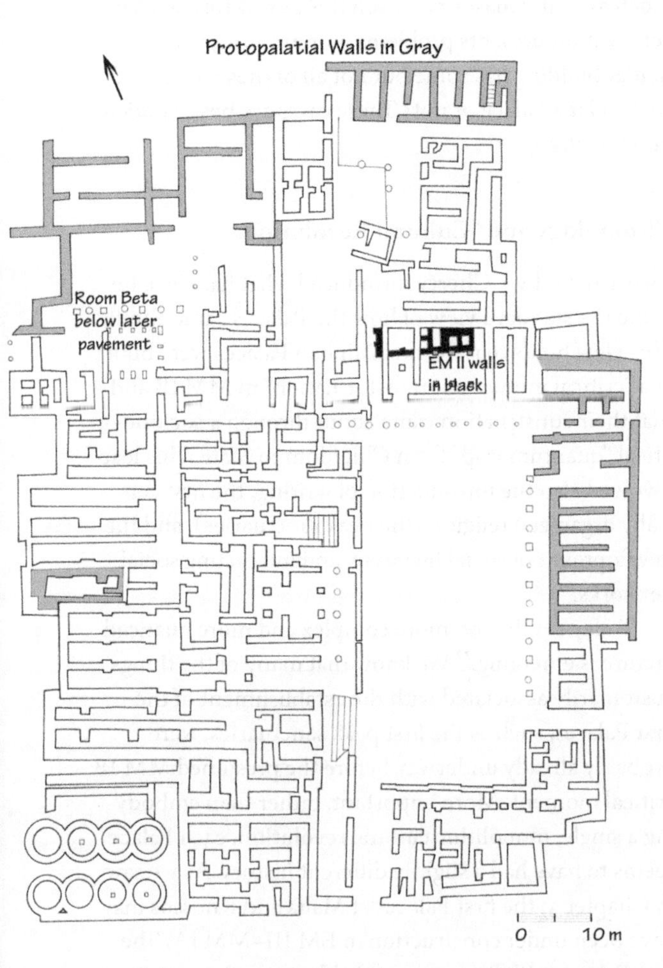

5.9. Plan. Protopalatial Palace at Malia.
After H. van Effenterre 1980, fig. 54.

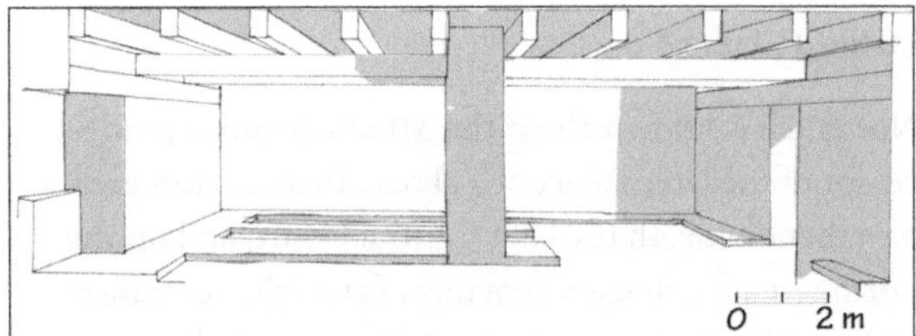

5.10. Reconstruction. Room Beta, Palace at Malia.
After Pelon 1983, fig. 18.

excavator of the so-called Agora and the Crypte Hypostyle, insists that no true Palace existed at the site until the Neopalatial period. Instead, he proposes, a series of separate monumental buildings, including those he excavated, each with a specific range of social, political, religious, and economic functions, operated in concert as a sort of "nebuleuse palatiale."[23] J.-Cl. Poursat, the excavator of the important Protopalatial Quartier Mu, disagrees adamantly with van Effenterre's notion. Poursat holds that the town and the Palace developed in concert at more or less the same time.[24] O. Pelon has conducted excavations within the Palace and has shown that there are remains of the early Palace almost everywhere beneath the later Palace (fig. 5.9).[25] Despite these disagreements, we know more about the first Palace at Malia than is ordinarily assumed.[26]

The clearest evidence of the first Palace is from the northwestern area, where F. Chapouthier had found two well-known ceremonial swords in 1936. Supplementary excavations by Chapouthier after World War II and by Pelon in the 1980s established that this part of the Palace belonged to the Protopalatial period. Room Beta, where the swords were found, was a storage room of a very distinctive form. Raised stucco platforms ran around all the walls and down the center of the room. These would have held a series of storage vessels. So-called collector vases were set into the floor to catch liquids spilled from the storage vessels. Essentially the same technique was used in the East Magazines, which also were constructed during the Protopalatial period.[27] There is less evidence for the date of the North Magazines, but they probably also date to the Protopalatial period and, like the East Magazines, continued in use into the Neopalatial period (fig. 5.10).

The same sort of magazines with raised plaster platforms arranged around the walls and with sunken floor features were also used in Quartier Mu (see figs. 6.15–6.17), the Magazines Dessenne southwest of the Palace (see fig. 6.14), and the Hypostyle Crypt (see fig. 6.11). All these structures are broadly contemporary and belong to one phase or another of the Protopalatial period. Their heavy use of clay and lime plaster to cover floors and raised platforms and benches is a direct development from the similar features so widely used in Malia during the preceding EM III–MM IA period in, for example, the possible shrine east of Chrysolakkos (see fig. 4.15) and in the rooms with the hearths south of the Palace (see fig. 4.6). The thick application of plaster over walls, floors, and benches is also one of the chief characteristics of the first Palace at Phaistos (see fig. 5.3).

Other Palaces?

Not much is known about the Middle Minoan predecessor of the later Palace at Zakros. There was an earlier pavement beneath the later Central Court, and on the northeast are extensive remains of an earlier entrance system. Ongoing excavations at Monasteraki have revealed extensive sections of a Protopalatial administrative center. The architecture at the site, however, is not comparable to that at Phaistos, Knossos, or Malia. In south central Crete, the earliest of the monumental harbor buildings at Kommos was constructed during the Protopalatial period, and at Petras there are extensive Protopalatial remains beneath the Neopalatial building (see Chapter 8).

What Is a Minoan Palace?

Although the term "Palace" is widely used and deeply ingrained in Minoan archaeology, Driessen has remarked that the term has been used to describe a number of quite different things and that there is no consensus on what the term signifies.[28] The debate usually centers on the presumed functions of the buildings.[29] Evans assumed that the buildings known as Palaces had several roles, including royal residences, administrative centers, economic centers, manufacturing centers, and cult centers. Over the years, each of those functions has been called into question. For example, I. Schoep notes, "The use of the term Palace carries with it a whole host of perhaps unhelpful baggage, which consciously or unconsciously encourages interpretation of the 'Palace' as the residence of a royal elite, occupying supreme position within a hierarchical social and political structure"; she suggests using the more neutral term "court-centered building" instead.[30] The problem, however, comes not from the architectural label one applies, but from making unwarranted assumptions about how the Palaces were used. In this book I use the word "Palaces" (capitalized to signal its arbitrariness) not to imply a range of functions but to refer to a group of buildings that share a set of formal elements. These include monumental scale, specific sets of rooms (such as Residential Quarters and magazines) arranged around a large, rectangular central court, specific structural features (such as pier-and-door partitions and light wells), and constructional elements (such as ashlar masonry). Even this purely formal characterization presents problems. For example, if a particular building has some but not all of these features do we label it a Palace or not? These cases are best handled individually.

Chronology and "Cultural Revolution"

Two articles by J. Cherry introduced what has since become the standard view of how the Palaces came about. This view holds that the first Minoan Palaces were built at a "critical moment of transformation" in MM IB and that their construction came about through a sociopolitical "quantum leap" from Chiefdom to State. This leap involved also the introduction of writing, the first centrally organized religion (the peak sanctuaries), and the development of social hierarchy and interacting social networks.[31]

Today a different, more complex and more nuanced picture is emerging.[32] We know that many of the things customarily associated with the establishment of the first Palaces, such as the first peak sanctuaries, were probably already underway before the presumed MM IB critical moment. More important, rather than embodying a single, monolithic cultural revolution, each Palace seems to have had a slightly different history. As we saw in Chapter 3, the first Palaces at Malia and Knossos may have been under construction in EM III–MM IA. The first Palace at Phaistos was probably begun later and was built over a long period of time. The southern part (the section excavated by D. Levi) was begun in MM IB, and the northern section (excavated by L. Pernier) was added in MM II. The buildings at all three sites probably experienced a number of significant changes over the course of the 150-year Protopalatial period.

The understanding of the relation between the first Palaces and the presumed sociopolitical revolution is also changing. In her "cart-before-the-horse" model, Dabney views the construction of the first Palaces not as the product of a new state-level society, but as one of the central factors in bringing about the social transformation. The vast amount of labor, organization, and resources required for their construction might well have triggered the necessary political reorganization rather than the other way around.[33] In this view, the formation of the state might have been a rather long process, one

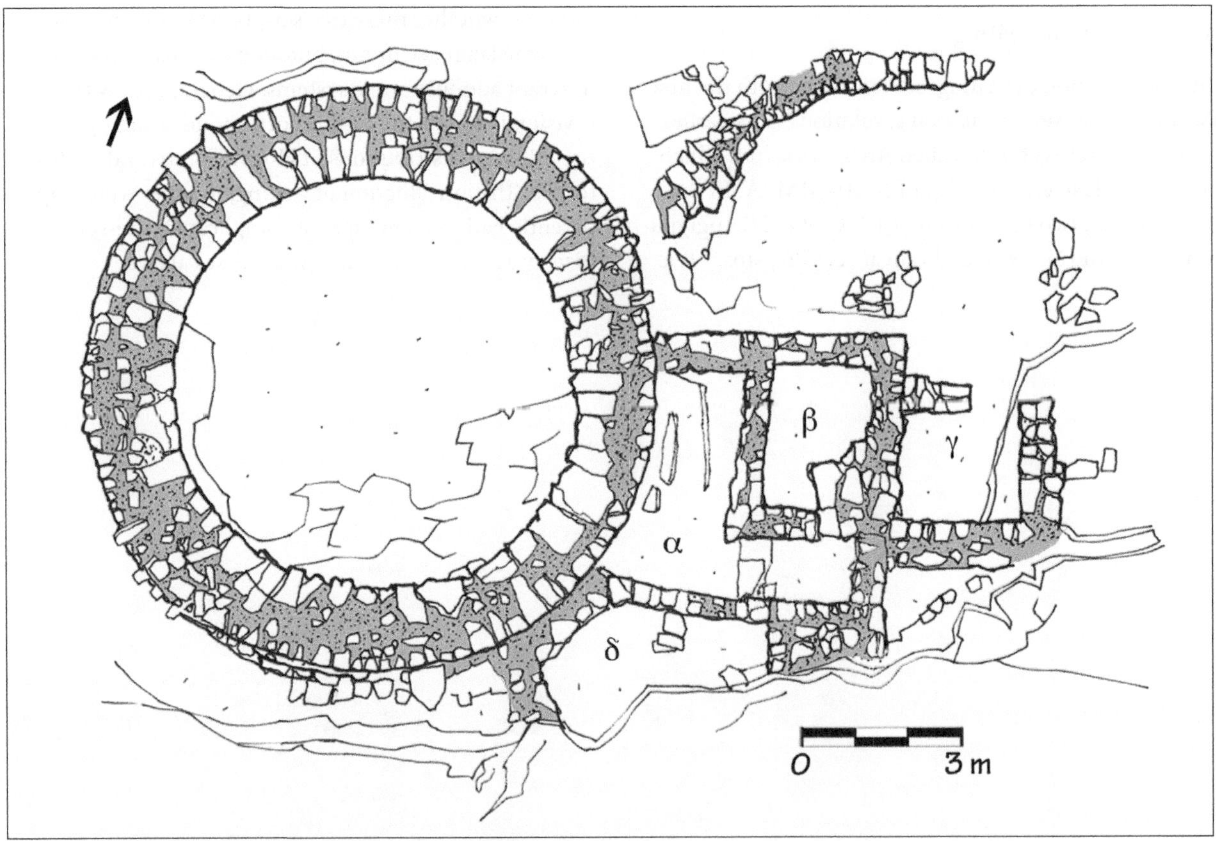

5.11. Plan. Tholos Tomb, Kamilari. After Di Vita and La Regina 1984, fig. 309.

involving decisions and adjustments as the construction proceeded, rather than a quantum leap. It also likely happened at slightly different times and at different paces at each of the palatial sites.

In many ways the first Palace at Phaistos was the culmination of this long complicated process as it synthesized various elements that were introduced elsewhere. Its general layout—a monumental building arranged around a central court—followed earlier designs at Knossos and Malia. Many of its construction techniques also appear to have been imported in a fully developed state. The use of orthostates for the facades and the use of thick layers of lime and clay plaster slathered over interior walls, floors, and benches echoed techniques that, as we have seen, were first used in EM III–MM IA Malia.

The people who had the Palace at Phaistos built also drew on a millennium-old tradition of the Mesara. The grand tholos tomb at nearby Kamilari (fig. 5.11) was almost certainly associated with the Palace.[34] It was constructed at the same time (MM IB) and was used through the entire Protopalatial period. Even later, in the Neopalatial and Final Palatial periods, people continued to visit it. We saw in Chapter 4 that, as the traditional Mesara tholos grew in size and spread beyond its original home in the Asterousia Mountains, its significance shifted from being a monument bound with the identity of the community to a monument that helped to establish and maintain dynastic legitimacy and authority. In a way the Kamilari tholos encapsulates the entire new architectural era at Phaistos. By adopting message-laden plans, techniques, and scale from a variety of sources, those who caused these buildings to be built had created a new architectural language whose message was unavoidably clear. In J. Rykwert's words, "What we call 'monumental' architecture is first of all the expression of power."[35]

A Postscript on Writing

The introduction of writing is often linked with the first Palaces in a presumed cultural revolution.[36] The earliest writing in Crete is the so-called Archanes script, which appears exclusively on seals in EM III–MM IA. In the early Palaces, two scripts were used: Cretan Hieroglyphic at Malia and Knossos and Linear A at Phaistos.[37] It is not clear whether these two scripts were used to write the same language or not, but they were used in quite different administrative systems. Geographically the division between the scripts corresponds roughly with the different distributions of House Tombs and tholos tombs. The introduction of writing, in other words, apparently had the same sort of complicated, site-specific history as the construction of the first Palaces.

The Protopalatial City and Urban Identity

CA. 1900–1750 BC

As IMPRESSIVE as the first Palaces at Malia, Knossos, and Phaistos were, they were components in much grander architectural programs. Entire cities and towns with courts, streets, and areas for community interaction were planned and built at the same time. This explosion of civic architecture would never be equaled again in Bronze Age Crete. With this urban transformation came the establishment of a new Minoan identity.[1]

West Courts

C. Palyvou has remarked that architecture is not just about buildings. It can also be about the "un-built" and about places that are neither quite one nor the other. As she puts it, "Each pair of opposites (built/un-built, outdoor/indoor, exterior/interior, open/closed, open air/sheltered) defines a spectrum of intermediate situations. In Minoan architecture those spectrums are very rich in nuances."[2] Palyvou also notes that just as there are gradations between the built and the unbuilt, so the concepts of public and private involve varying degrees.

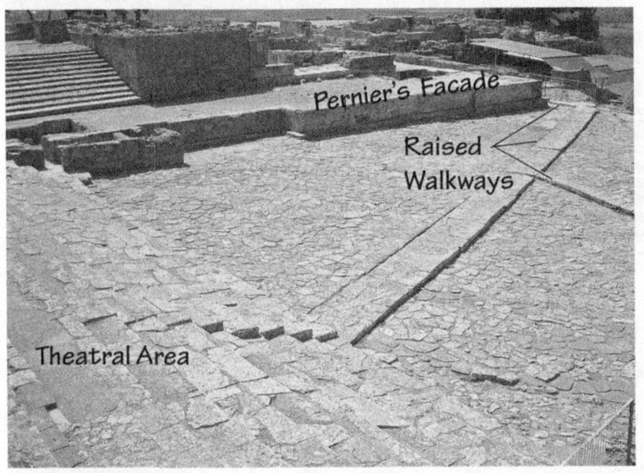

6.1. West Court at Phaistos. Photo by author.

Immediately west of each of the three Palaces at Phaistos, Knossos, and Malia, for example, a large, paved open area conventionally called the West Court (fig. 6.1) was constructed at the juncture of the town and the Palace. To the extent that the Palaces had a front facade, it was the one facing the West Court with its imposing masonry and upper-story windows.

At all three sites, the stone pavements of the West Courts are crossed at various angles by raised walkways—a quintessential feature of Minoan cities. The walkways probably had some practical value, providing dry footing in the rain and helping to direct visitors' movements through the courts. On occasion the walkways could be put to ceremonial use, as the later example in the Corridor of the Processions in the Neopalatial Palace at Knossos suggests. Palyvou points out that the raised walkways also have formal significance. Their white, rectilinear slabs contrast with the surrounding "crazy" paving; their diagonal directions counter the vertical and horizontal grid of the Palatial facade, and, most significant, at key entrances they continue from the exterior public court into the interior of the Palace. Palyvou writes, "They penetrate the building compound in a symbolic manner, as if the town is invading the Palace."[3]

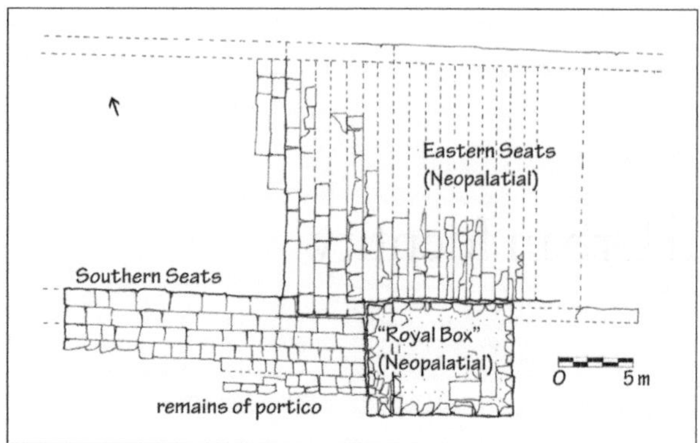

6.2. Plan. Theatral Area, Knossos. After *PM II*, fig. 362.

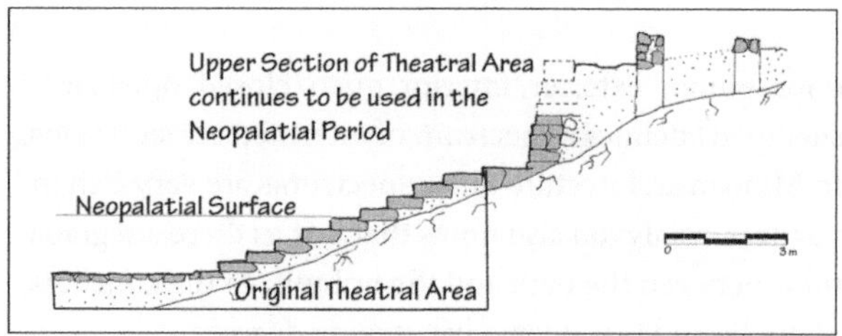

6.3. Section. Theatral Area, Phaistos. After Pernier 1935, fig. 79.

Theatral Areas

The north borders of the West Courts at Phaistos and Knossos are formed by a so-called Theatral Area, rows of low risers that provided seating for spectators. The final form of the Theatral Area at Knossos dates to the Late Minoan period, but supplementary excavations carried out by A. Evans in 1913 showed that much of the structure had been originally laid out at the time of the first Palace (fig. 6.2 and see also fig. 9.39).[4] Streets entered the area from the north, northeast, and west. Under the eastern (LM) bank of seats, Evans found that the original court continued about 10 m further to the east. The most important surviving feature of the original Theatral Area is the south bank of seats. Parts of six tiers, higher and more massive that those of the later eastern flight, remain. A stepped walkway, 3.17 m wide, ascends southward toward the West Court and the main entrance to the Palace, dividing the bank of seats into halves. Only five bases remain of a screen of pillars or portico that originally ran across the top of the bank of seats.

6.4. Theatral Area, Phaistos. Photo by author.

The Theatral Area at Phaistos is essentially similar in form, and, with modifications, it too continued to be used through the Second Palatial period (figs. 6.3, 6.4).[5] Originally it consisted of a courtyard with nine rows of seats, the topmost being slightly deeper than the others. The original back wall (the southernmost of the two back walls shown on the plan) was punctuated with a series of setbacks. The seats at Phaistos, like those at Knossos, were divided by a walkway that turns obliquely when it meets the lowest step. The western end of the Theatral Area was much destroyed by erosion and later construction, but in the bedrock, at the level of the lowest steps, the excavators noted four circular cuttings that may have been for columns supporting a pavilion corresponding to the portico on the south side of the Knossos Theatral Area. The two areas are also alike in that at both, rustic *kernoi* of the sort we saw at several EM sites were hammered into some of the seats. These were almost certainly pavement games to help the spectators pass the time (see Chapter 2).[6]

Although the name Theatral Area suggests consensus on the point, the purposes of these structures have been debated. Some have seen them as the settings for various sorts of performances, thinking of the dancing women depicted in the Miniature Fresco and the later tradition of the dancing floor that Daidalos built for Ariadne. Evans thought their main function was for the reception of ceremonial processions that approached the Palaces by the major streets that fed into the Theatral Areas. Whether or not he was correct, his interpretation called attention to the prominent locations of the Theatral Areas. At both sites they were located at the juncture of the main streets and the main approaches to the Palaces, and they formed an important nexus within the city. Others have also noted their prominent positions but proposed different functions. For example, W. McDonald and S. Damiani Indelicato suggested they were used for political assemblies.[7]

The excavators proposed a similar political interpretation for the Agora at Malia (fig. 6.5).[8] The Agora

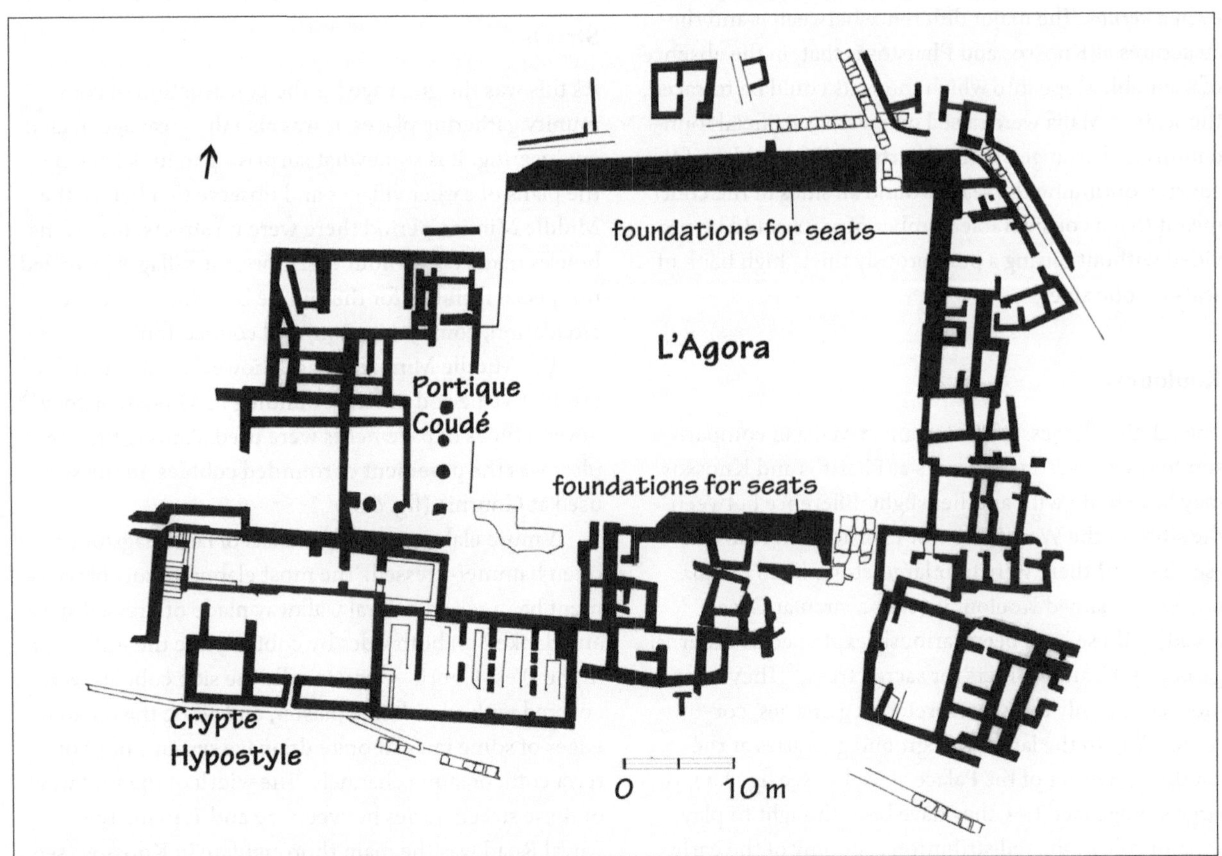

6.5. Plan. Agora, Malia. After H. and M. van Effenterre 1969, plan I.

consists of a large (29.10 m × 39.80 m), rectangular courtyard surrounded by massive foundations that originally supported banks of seats. The banks of seats were originally faced with a course of orthostates, at three points interrupted by stairways that led up to the seats. Behind the seats on the east and south, groups of irregular rooms were accumulating by the MM III period. A rustic kernos with twenty-three depressions is located at the Porte des Magasins. At the southwest corner of the Agora is the Hypostyle Crypt and immediately north of the crypt is the Portique Coudé, an L-shaped portico reminiscent of the porticoes at the Theatral Areas of the other Palatial sites. These porticoes were apparently essential parts of the Theatral Areas. Formally, they were the only emphatically vertical elements in these complexes. They helped to raise the otherwise basically two-dimensional theatral courts into three-dimensional relief, defining them as distinct spaces.

The Agora at Malia had all the requisite components of the Theatral Areas: location at the juncture of streets immediately north of the West Court seats, portico, and even a *kernos*. The major difference between it and the structures at Knossos and Phaistos is that, in the absence of a suitable slope into which the seats could be terraced, the seats at Malia were raised on massive artificial foundations and arranged around parts of all four sides of the court. Continuing the seats around all sides of the court meant that a considerable number of seats could be provided without raising a ponderously thick, high bank of seats on one side.

Koulouras

The relative flatness of the terrain at Malia in comparison to the terraced west fronts at Phaistos and Knossos may have to do with another slight difference between the sites. In the West Courts of Phaistos and Knossos (see fig. 5.7) there were four large, stone-lined circular pits Evans named Koulouras (after a circular Greek bread).[9] These have been variously explained as cisterns, garbage pits, and planters for sacred trees.[10] They have most commonly been interpreted as granaries, corresponding to the later aboveground granaries at the southwest corner of the Palace at Malia (see fig. 8.4). As large storage facilities, they have been thought to play a major role in the redistribution economy of the early Palaces.[11] T. Strasser, however, has recently shown that they could not have functioned as granaries. He revives Evans's idea that they were instead "blind wells" for the disposal of water.[12] From an architectural point of view this makes a great deal of sense.[13] Anyone who has visited a shopping mall will have noticed the large catchment basins built to receive the runoff from the mall roof and parking lots. The architects at Knossos and Phaistos might have foreseen a similar problem with drainage from the roofs of the Palaces and the expanses of paved areas. Because the site at Malia was more level and more expansive the water could be expected to run off without being captured on relatively confined terraces. If this interpretation of the Koulouras is correct, they should be linked categorically not with the economy and the magazines inside the Palace, but with civil engineering and the walkways outside the Palace. In any case, they did not last long: the Koulouras at Phaistos and the two western Koulouras at Knossos were paved over in MM III for the construction of the second Palaces.[14]

Streets

As this was the great age for the construction of community gathering places, it was also the great age of civil engineering. It is somewhat surprising to look back on the plans of earlier villages and observe that before the Middle Minoan period there were no streets. Just as the houses made do without corridors, the villages provided no special facilities for the simple but crucial needs of circulation, communication, and connection.

The Middle Minoan period, however, was the most productive period of street building in Minoan history.[15] Several types of pavements were used. Among the simplest was the pavement of rounded cobbles, of the sort used at Gournia (fig. 6.6).

A more elaborate type consists of large flagstones, often hammer-dressed. The most elaborate sort of pavement has a raised central walkway made of dressed slabs and flanked on both sides by cobbles, like the walkways in the West Courts. Occasionally the side cobbles were covered with a hard lime plaster, and along the outside edges of some ran elaborate drainage systems built of terra cotta or stone channels. The width of the walkways of these streets varies between .70 and 1.40 m. The Royal Road was the main thoroughfare in Knossos (see

6.6. Street at Gournia. Photo by author.

6.7. Royal Road, Knossos, from east. Photo by author.

6.8. Reconstruction. Viaduct at Knossos. After *PM II*, fig. 46.

fig. 6.7). It led toward the Palace from the west, originally passing in front of the Theatral Area, through which one could proceed to the West Court. Smaller constructions that provided seating for spectators, called viewing stands by the excavator, overlooked the Royal Road near its west end.[16]

A major road led to the Palace from the south. After passing through the site of the later Caravanserai (see fig. 9.37), the monumental, corbel-vaulted Viaduct carried the road across the Vlychia ravine (fig. 6.8). Unfortunately, the street on the north side of the ravine disappears.

Defensible Sites

The street systems of all the major Palatial cities and smaller villages (Gournia, Kommos, Palaikastro, and Pseira) were built in this period. These streets, with occasional repaving, continued to be used through the Neopalatial period until most of the sites were abandoned.

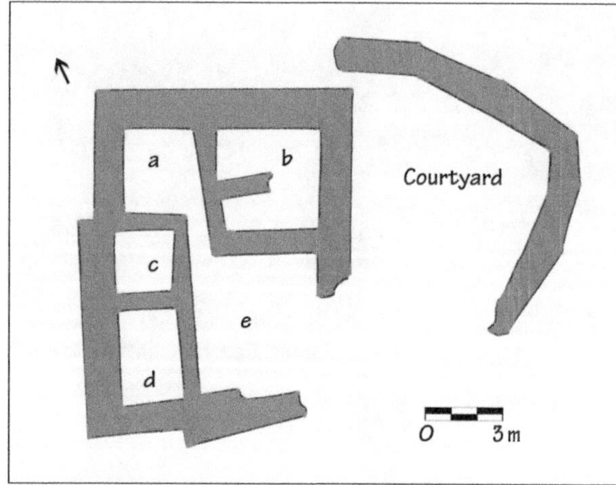

6.9. Plan. Guard house at Zakros. After Chrysolakki 1999, pl. VII B.

At least in the eastern end of the island a network of roads was built to connect the various towns.[17] A number of small buildings built along the roads have been called guard houses (fig. 6.9). However, these may have been simple farm buildings, as L. V. Watrous suggests, a function that many continued to serve during later periods.[18] If the small buildings were in fact guard houses (a term introduced by Evans), they would signal that the transformations taking place in Crete during the Protopalatial period were probably not entirely peaceful affairs.

The occupation in MM II of several remote and nearly inaccessible defensible sites, including the extraordinary site at Monasteraki Katalimata on the cliff of the Ha Gorge (see fig. 12.4), might also indicate tensions among the various regional centers.[19] The sections of MM fortification walls that have been excavated at Malia (see fig. 4.13), Petras, and Pyrgos-Myrtos may also be tied to intersite rivalry and insecurity.

6.10. Hypostyle Crypt, Malia from the west. Photo by author.

The Hypostyle Crypt at Malia

As Palyvou noted, the distinction between public and private is seldom a matter of absolutes; it is a matter of degree. Streets, roads, and open areas like the West Courts were primarily public, while the Agora at Malia,

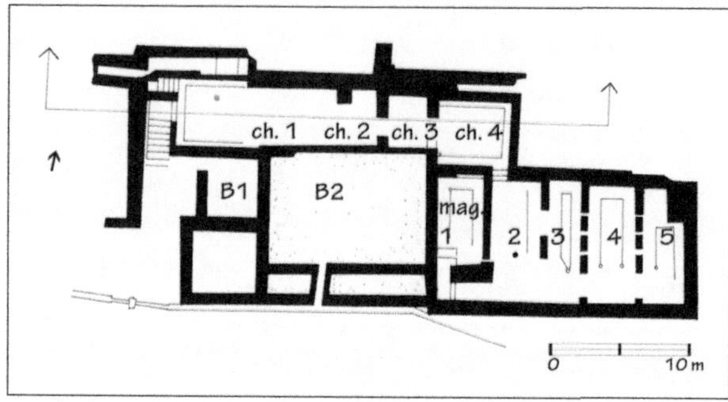

6.11. Plan. Hypostyle Crypt, Malia. After H. and M. van Effenterre 1969, plan I.

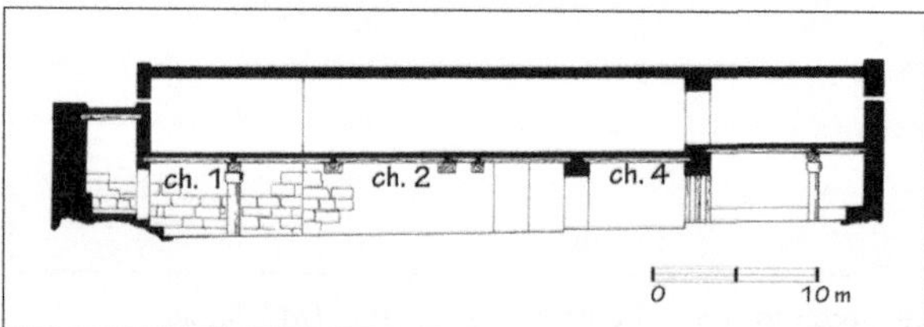

6.12. Restored section. Hypostyle Crypt, Malia. After Amouretti 1970, section 2.

which could be closed off, might be considered semipublic.[20] Immediately adjacent to the Agora, the Hypostyle Crypt further blurs the public/private boundary (figs. 6.10–6.12). Its prominent position near the center of the city, adjacent to the Agora and the West Court outside the Palace, certainly had public visibility. On the other hand, most of the surviving parts of the building were underground, basement rooms. The building did, however, have a second, perhaps more accessible story, probably entered from the Agora via the Portique Coudé.

The construction of the Hypostyle Crypt is similar to that of Quartier Mu (see below) and to the first Palaces. The building includes coursed ashlar masonry, columns, and the thick plaster so characteristic of the period. In the doorway that leads into the room in the northeast corner of the building, impressions of the original woodwork frames are preserved around the door and window openings. The pairing of door and window conserved materials by requiring some of the timbers to serve double duty (fig. 6.13). This arrangement of beams has close parallels in the carpentry of the Second Palatial period.

The purpose of the building is unclear. On the basis of its impressive quality, its prominent location, and its analogy with classical Greece, the excavators proposed that it served a town council. A larger citizens' assembly was presumed to have met in the adjacent Agora.[21] Others have proposed a commercial function. Much of the basement level of the building was used for storage. Its magazines resemble not only those in the Palace, but also those in Quartier Mu and the Magasins Dessenne (fig. 6.14).

The distribution of large storage facilities among several buildings in the center of the city is an interesting phenomenon. Since the 1980s, it has been widely assumed that Palaces were the key components in an economic system that involved the collection, storage, and redistribution of surplus goods.[22] As I. Schoep has shown, at Malia that economic role was probably filled by a number of facilities, confusing the lines between public and private and between Palace and non-Palace.[23]

The Hypostyle Crypt has no close parallels at the other Palatial centers. A building south of the modern tourist pavilion at Phaistos may have been similar in general terms, but its fragmentary state prohibits detailed comparison. Although more distant from the Palace, it may have been situated along one of the main approaches. Its construction is not as elaborate as that of the crypt—it has no coursed ashlar or columns—but it is more substantial and more rectilinear than the MM houses at the site.

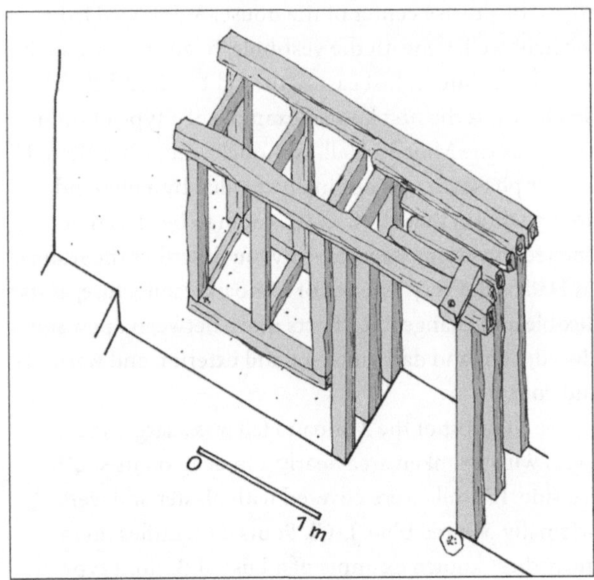

6.13. Restored doorway. Hypostyle Crypt, Malia. After Amouretti 1970, fig. 3.

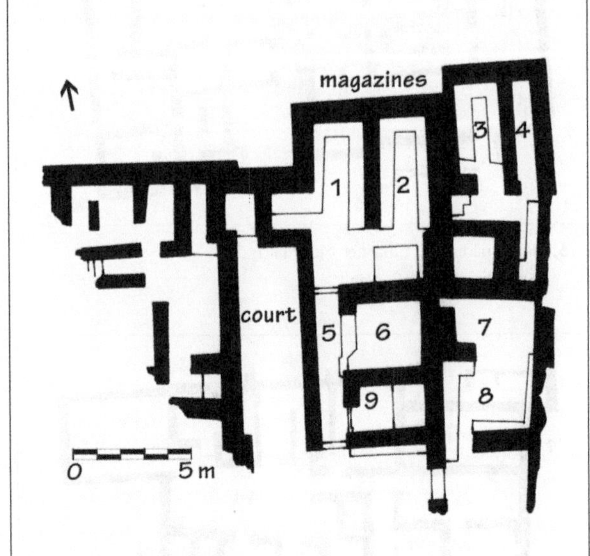

6.14. Plan. Magasins Dessenne. After H. van Effenterre 1980, fig. 300.

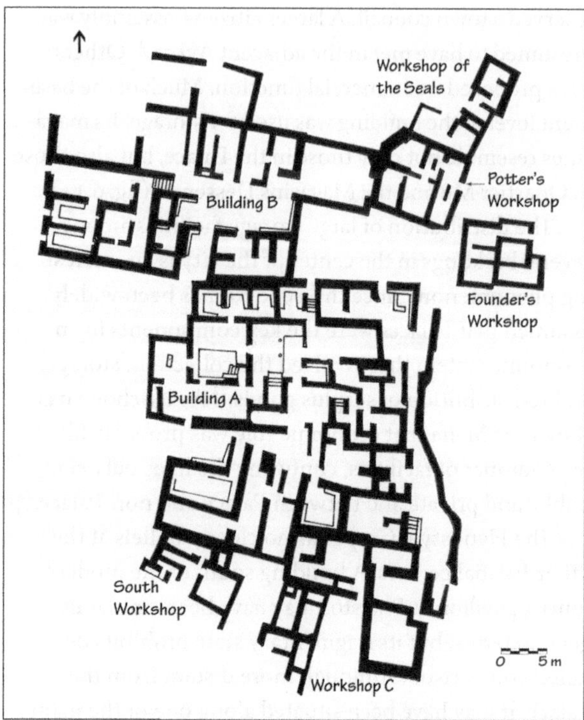

6.15. Plan. Quartier Mu, Malia. After Poursat 1992, plan.

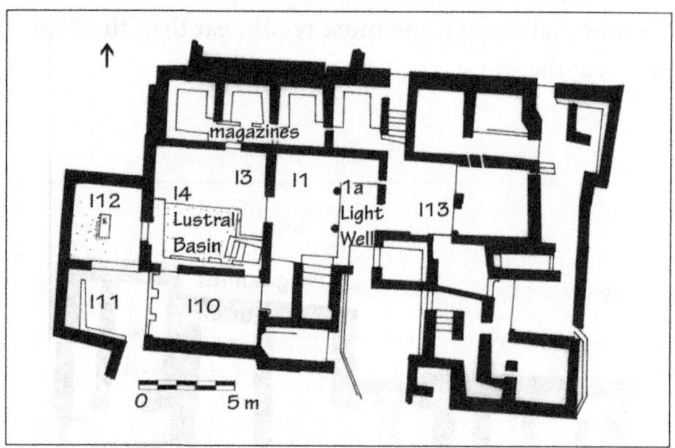

6.16. Plan. Building A, Quartier Mu, Malia. After Poursat 1978, plan I.

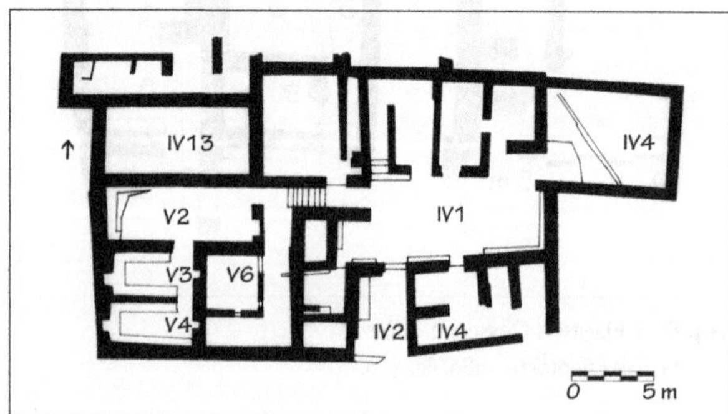

6.17. Plan. Building B, Quartier Mu, Malia. After Poursat 1978, plan I.

Quartier Mu at Malia

The line between public and nonpublic gets even fuzzier at Quartier Mu (figs. 6.15–6.17).[24] With the exception of the Palaces, Building A of Quartier Mu is the grandest structure known from the Protopalatial period. The building was among the largest of the period (ca. 450 m2 in its original state and ca. 800 m^2 after the extension was added). Also distinctive are its elaborate use of coursed ashlar masonry and the regularity and formality of its design. Several of its rooms anticipate forms that would become standard in Neopalatial Palaces and Villas. The grand suite of main residential rooms in Building A gives the best indication of what the missing Residential Quarters of the first Palaces looked like.

The original entrance to Building A, later obstructed by the construction of the extension to the south, was near the center of the south wall. The door opened onto a vestibule, the intermediary space between the public exterior and the private domain of the house. From the vestibule, one had a choice of turning to the right and ascending the stairs to the second floor or continuing straight ahead toward the main ground-story rooms. In the northwest corner were storage magazines, their walls surrounded with raised platforms. Just beyond the vestibule was a light well with two columns on its west side, providing light and ventilation where it was most needed, in the precise center of the house. A drain led from the light well, beneath the vestibule, to an area originally outside the house. Just east of the light well and closely tied to it was the first known example of a type of room known as the Minoan Hall. Although somewhat altered in later phases, it was originally divided by a pier-and-door partition that allowed the room to be closed or opened to varying degrees. Palyvou describes the Minoan Hall as the very essence of Minoan architecture, as its flexible and changeable effects move between open and closed, light and dark, interior and exterior, and warm and cool.[25]

To the west of the Minoan Hall was a large, square room with a sunken area nearly 2 m deep on its southern side. Its walls were covered with plaster and were originally painted blue. J.-Cl. Poursat identifies this as the earliest known example of a Lustral Basin, a type of room that would also become standard in the Neopalatial Palaces and that has been variously interpreted as either a shrine or a bath. The Lustral Basin was entered from the large room in the southwest corner of the house. G. Gesell and W.-D. Niemeier have suggested that the Lustral Basin formed a religious complex with Room I12 just to the west.[26] This room, a later addition built against the original ashlar facade, was furnished with a fixed rectangular hearth with a circular depression, which the excavators label an altar and compare with those known from the contemporary shrine at Malia and the Palace at Phaistos. P. Muhly has shown, however, that the religious nature of these hearths and therefore of this room is far from certain.[27]

At a later date within MM II a large extension was added to the south side of the building, doubling its size. This extension was not quite so rectilinear as the original construction, at least on the ground story, and most of its major rooms may have been on the upper story. A stairway opening onto the street on the east led directly to these upper rooms, and a second stairway linked the vestibule of Building A with the upper rooms of Building C. The plan of this part of the complex was partly obscured in the southernmost section by MM III constructions.

Building B of Quartier Mu, which may have been built somewhat earlier, is similar to Building A in most major respects (see fig. 6.17). They shared the same grand size (570 m^2), overall proportions (ca. 4:7), and elaborate techniques. More important, they were similar in design. Both have specialized provisions for a variety of activities on the ground floors, including living, storage, industries, and religion. Each of these activities was conducted in a room of distinctive form, and each of those rooms was located in a specific part of the house. In the center of the building was a light well. Near the light well was the main room of the house, the Hall. Around the Hall were arranged the magazines, industrial rooms, stairs, and various other rooms. In both houses the main entrance was through a vestibule with a bench, which was located near the center of the south facade of the building. Such consistency predicates a systematic approach to design that distinguishes these buildings from earlier houses as much as their size and technique do.

Artisans' Quarters

The grand houses of Quartier Mu were found with most of the original contents, including a great variety of luxury items in stone, terra cotta, and metal. Many of these were produced in the neighboring Artisans' Quarters.[28] These quarters served as the combined workshops and living areas of the crafts makers. One was occupied by a family of seal engravers, the second by a family of potters, and the third by a family of metalworkers. Except for the specialized workshops in the upper stories, these buildings are identical to ordinary houses of the period.

The close association of the Artisans' Quarters with the large houses of Quartier Mu has interesting economic implications. Many of the objects made in the artisans' houses were intended for use in Houses A and B. Other objects probably filtered through Houses A and B of Quartier Mu for wider distribution, in exchange for which their capacious magazines may have been filled with agricultural produce. The artisan families may have been dependents of the people who lived in the neighboring mansions.[29] Thus, the residents of Quartier Mu and the Artisans' Quarters seem to have played an economic role that complemented that of the Palace.[30]

Public Shrines

For many years, archaeologists thought that Minoan religion was conducted in Palaces, houses, and rural sanctuaries. The existence of specialized urban public shrines was seriously doubted.[31] A growing body of evidence from various parts of the Aegean, however, has encouraged a reassessment of the information. Public shrines are now clearly attested at Phylakopi, Keos, and Mycenae and are important in Postpalatial Crete. While the Palaces were almost certainly the most important ceremonial centers in the Protopalatial and Neopalatial periods, a few specialized shrines were also built. The clearest example is the small shrine building excavated at Malia (fig. 6.18).[32] The building is simple in plan. A door leads to the central room, which appears to have served as an entrance to the other two rooms. The west room was used for storage. The eastern room was the shrine proper. In the center of the room was a rectangular clay hearth with a circular depression, similar to those found in Quartier Mu and the Palace at Phaistos. While the hearth alone is not sufficient to define a building or a room as a shrine, here there were other finds, including portable offering tables, many lamps and lamp stands, animal figurines, a triton shell, and a small stone object that may be a miniature set of horns of consecration.

The nearby Sanctuary of the Horns (fig. 6.19) likely dates to this period also. This small building was entered

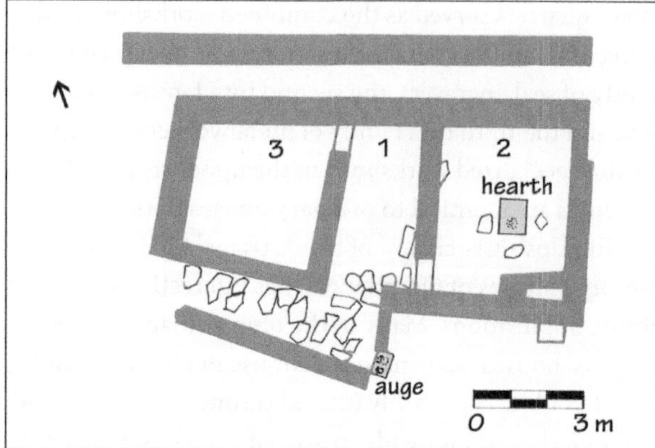

6.18. Plan. MM II shrine, Malia. After Poursat 1966, fig. 3.

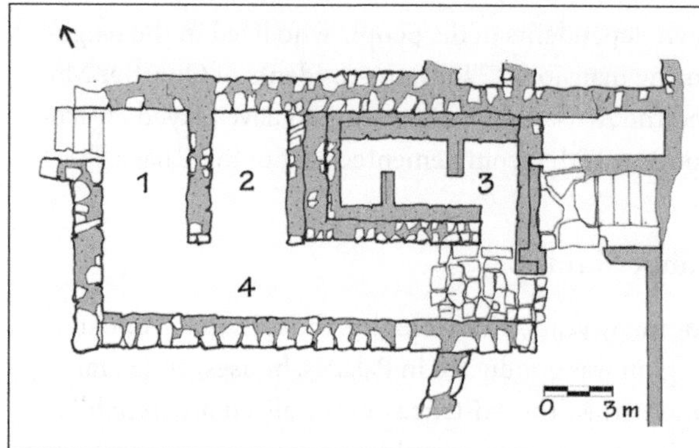

6.19. Plan. Sanctuaire des Cornes, Malia. After Daux 1957, fig. 15 *bis*.

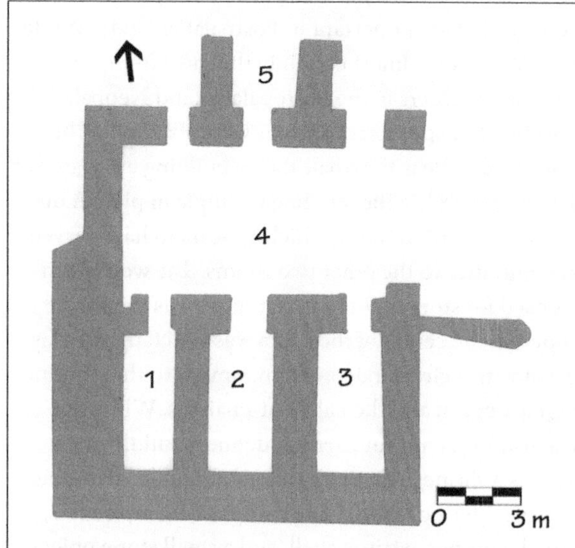

6.20. Plan. Sanctuary, Anemospilia. After Rutkowski 1986, fig. 310.

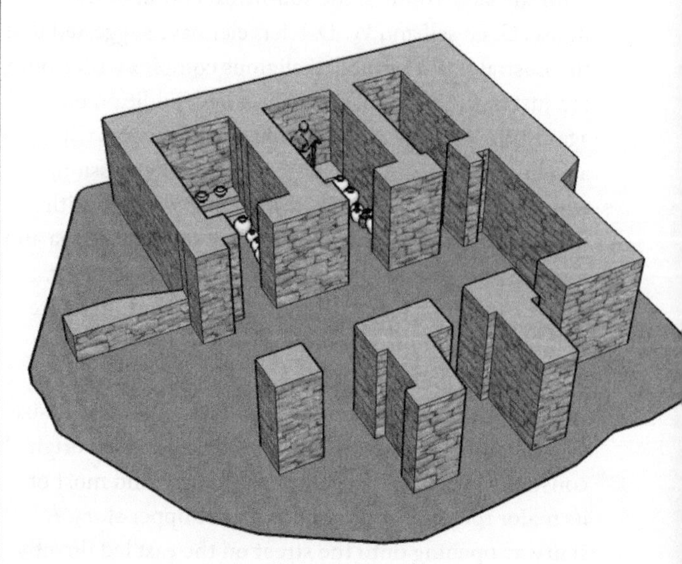

6.21. Reconstruction. Sanctuary, Anemospilia. After Rutkowski 1986, fig. 311.

by stairways on the east and on the west. Like the MM II sanctuary, it was divided into three interior spaces. The main room was subdivided on the east by plaster partitions. The horns after which the building was named were not standard Horns of Consecration, but single plaster cones that may or may not represent stylized horns.[33]

One of the most interesting chapters in the history of Minoan archaeology began in 1979 with excavations at a rural place called Anemospilia on the slopes of Mt. Iouktas just outside Archanes. Excavations that season and in 1981 uncovered part of a building dating to the MM IIB–MM III period (figs. 6.20, 6.21). The excavated portion of the building is centered on a broad central corridor. At least three partially excavated rooms extend to the north. On the south is a row of three rooms arranged like storage rooms. In the eastern room, a number of pots were arranged around the walls and placed on the raised platform at the end of the room. In the central room there were more pots and a set of clay feet that, according to the excavators, belonged to a large cult statue. In the western room, a human body and a bronze blade (or spearhead) were found on a central platform. Two more skeletons were found on the floor of the room and a fourth in the corridor to the north.

From this evidence the excavators reconstructed a ritual involving human sacrifice.[34] Like the other three bodies found in the building, however, the purported sacrificial victim may have been a casualty of the earthquake that destroyed the building.

Other Sites

D. Levi excavated parts of three Protopalatial houses in the West Court at Phaistos, and L. Platon excavated a large part of a similar building immediately east of the Palace at Zakros.[35] Outside the major Palatial centers the earliest phases of the rural buildings at Pera Galini, Chamalevri, Apesokari, Prasa, and Riza Achladion belong to the Protopalatial period, but no complete house plans were recovered. In the Amari Valley ongoing excavations at the important site of Monasteraki and nearby Apodoulou promise important new information.[36]

The Urban Matrix and the Emerging Minoan Identity

The history of architecture generally focuses on the study of buildings. As Palyvou notes, this is not adequate in the case of Minoan architecture, whose essence is the interrelation of indoor and outdoor space. Just as individual buildings interweave closed rooms with open light wells and courts, in the larger urban matrix Minoan builders similarly integrate the masses of buildings with significant open spaces.[37] To neglect the spaces between the buildings at Malia, for example, would be to neglect the fabric that tied the city together: the streets, walkways, courts, and public gathering places. It would also overlook the enormous investment that went into both the construction of these public facilities and their maintenance and programming.[38]

The same can be said for the social and political organization of the city. Rather than having been concentrated exclusively in the Palaces, civic functions like surplus storage, religion, and administration were apparently spread through various public, semipublic, and private facilities.[39] Neither spatially nor socially did the Palace stand in isolation. The Palace and the city were interdependent. And if, as I noted at the end of the last chapter, the construction of the first Palace at Malia was the expression of power, the city provided the resources for that power and shared its benefits.[40]

The emerging cities at Malia, Knossos, and Phaistos shared a distinctive new urban form marked by a specific set of characteristics: Minoan Palaces, West Courts, paved streets with walkways, Theatral Areas (at Knossos and Phaistos), Koulouras (at Knossos and Phaistos), etc. Even if relations among (and perhaps within) the various towns and cities continued to be contentious and competitive—as the number of defensible sites suggests—a common architectural language was beginning to emerge. This new architectural language marks the beginning of a specifically Minoan identity.

7.1. Aerial photo, Knossos. © Yann Arthus-Bertrand/Corbis.

The Second Palace at Knossos and the Reconstruction of Minoan Identity

CA. 1750–1490 BC

BETWEEN MM III and LM IB (ca. 1750–1490 BC) the Second Palace at Knossos became the grandest monument in the history of Minoan Crete. Centuries later Evans used this monument to define the Minoans.

Viewing the Palace

Today a cursory tour of the Palace at Knossos requires about an hour (figs. 7.1–7.9). What the visitor sees represents—not including the modern restorations—several centuries of sporadic construction. What the Minoan visitor to the site would have seen at any one moment in the Late Bronze Age would have been quite different. The building would have stood to its complete height with all of its decorations and furnishings—alive with the sounds and the movement of people. Yet, ironically, most Minoan visitors would probably have seen less of the Palace than the modern tourist. What they would have seen would have depended on who they were and what specific business had brought them to the Palace. The Palace seen by visiting dignitaries was different from that inhabited by craft workers, pilgrims, slaves, and scribes. The public Palace that staged official or ritual celebrations was not the same as the private chambers. Lacking a guidebook with numbered plan, Bronze Age visitors depended on the people of the Palace and on the form of the building itself to guide them to their objectives.

As in the Protopalatial period, so in the Neopalatial most of the major streets of Knossos fed into the West Court. From here the visitor attained the first close and direct view of the Palace (see fig. 7.3). The west facade was appropriately elaborate: huge, well-dressed orthostates stood above a projecting base course called a krepidoma; broad windows opened into the upper story that floated above the lower.[1]

After its size and careful construction, two other aspects of the Palace would have dominated the visitor's early impressions. The first was the irregular massing of the building. The Palace did not appear as a single, unified entity but displayed evidence of having been built as a series of discrete structural blocks. The blocks were arranged in a series of projecting and recessing facades. Across the top of the building, the rooflines also shifted levels with the constituent blocks. No single linear boundary defined the building in any direction. At least on the west, houses further obstructed the view of the facade. As a result, the visitor cannot take the entire building in from any single viewpoint, as one can a classical temple or a Renaissance villa. To see the building, one must move around it, and with every movement the appearance changes.

The second major aspect the visitor would notice is the predominant horizontal expanse of the building. The Palace was a broad, low, sprawling structure seated firmly on the ground rather than aspiring toward the sky. It extended across the surface of the hill so far that no clear ends—which were concealed behind projecting angles—to the building could be seen. Its size was impossible to judge. The builders emphasized the horizontality of the building by arranging most of the major elements of the facade horizontally. The krepidoma, the orthostates, the upper masonry, and even a hypothetical

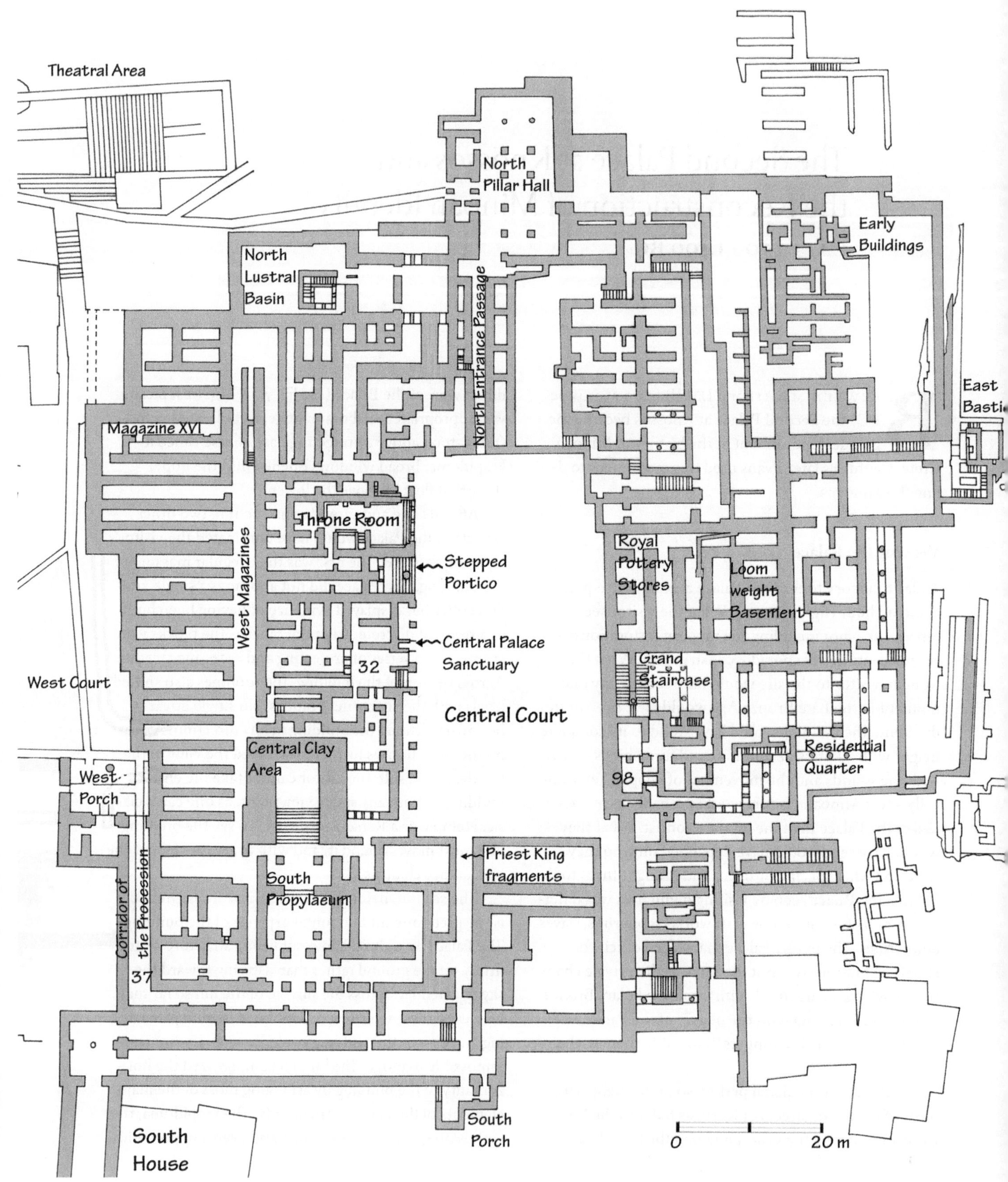

7.2. Plan. Palace at Knossos. After Pendlebury 1954, plan.

7.3. West facade, Palace at Knossos. Photo by author.

row of upper-story windows were all arranged in horizontal bands reinforcing the dominant direction of the building.

Few verticals countered those bands. Keeping the building from being entirely horizontal, a series of recesses ran from the ground floor through the upper story, where they held windows. The locations of the recesses in the centers of the projecting blocks of the building also had the effect of calling attention to the individual components of the building and helping to divide its vastness into smaller, visually comprehensible components. The positioning of stable, symmetrical elements such as these recesses within an overall shifting asymmetrical design is also a recurring design strategy in the interior of the building, where the dynamic balance between what H. Frankfurt called "arrest and movement" contributed to the kinetic effect of the building.[2]

Even before reaching the Palace, the visitor had been prepared for the shifting rhythm of motion and stillness. All the approaches to the Palace were punctuated by a series of architectural pauses marked by changes in direction, changes in level, or sometimes by actual structures, such as the Theatral Area or the Caravanserai (see fig. 9.37). Inside the Palace, the sequential arrangement continued, as the builders distributed a series of stage-like focal points along the main passages.

The West Porch

A raised walkway conducted the visitor across the West Court to the West Porch, a main entrance to the Palace. Here the builders combined several architectural elements to create a temporary focal point for the visitor. A single massive column, ca. 1.20 m in base diameter and perhaps 6 m tall, stood in the center of the broad opening of the entrance.[3] Probably even from the outside the visitor would have seen that the interior of the West Porch was decorated with the image most intimately associated with Knossos, a painting of a bull. More eloquently than a lettered sign, the painting introduced the visitor to the building and its legends. The West Porch also provided a spatial introduction to the Palace. As

7.4. South Propylaeum, Palace at Knossos, from the southeast. Photo by author.

J. Driessen puts it, "Following the walkways through the West Courts and entering the complex implies a transition from one world, open to the view of the public, to another, hermetically closed off. The narrowness of the pathway to follow, with a funnel effect at the entrance, implies a line-up of individuals and a selection process."[4] The West Porch was both reception area and filter.

The Corridor of the Procession, South Propylaeum, and the South-North Corridor

From the half-light of the entrance porch, the walkway continued into the darker Corridor of the Procession, where the visitor fell into step with the painted figures of the procession fresco. The figures led first to the south and then—the route is no longer preserved above the level of basement foundations—to the east. Another turn to the north would bring the visitor to the South Propylaeum, a spacious room fitted with massive pillars and columns arranged symmetrically. This room was much altered in LM III and today is largely the result of A. Evans's restoration (see fig. 7.4). In contrast to the corridor, the South Propylaeum would have been flooded with light coming through the unroofed area above its columns. Here, apparently, the procession fresco stopped.

Continuing through the South Propylaeum, the visitor, according to Evans, could have proceeded to the important rooms of the upper Piano Nobile by means of a monumental stairway. Evidence of that stairway is, however, extraordinarily slight. This part of the site Evans called the Central Clay Area. It was almost entirely empty save for the foundations of a later rectangular structure variously interpreted as a Mycenaean building or a classical temple.

A second route along the Corridor of the Procession is also poorly preserved. According to Evans, the Corridor of the Procession made its way eastward over the South Terrace Basements before turning north in the South-North Corridor, passing through a small pavilion on its way toward the Central Court. The life-size relief fresco of the "Priest King" (restored from fragments that actually belonged to several figures) was found in the area. Evans proposed that the relief fresco had originally been on the wall near the entrance to the Central Court, where it would have formed a complement to the Bull Relief in the North Entrance Passage on the opposite side of the Central Court.[5]

The Central Court

After the narrow confines of the twisting, dark corridor, the broad, brilliant Central Court offered sudden expansion and release. As Driessen recently remarked, "The Central Court of a Minoan Palace is not a simple step en route . . . but indeed, the *final* destination of this circulation pattern."[6] It was without doubt the dominant element in the building. Of the four facades along the Central Court only that along the west side is sufficiently preserved today to provide much indication of the original appearance. In plan, the facade appears basically unified behind a screen of columns and pillars. In restored elevation, however, the impression of a unified facade quickly breaks down into a series of independent elements, each calling attention to itself and competing for the visitor's attention.

The Facades of the Central Court

On the north end of the west facade of the Central Court were the four doors through which one stepped down into the Throne Room complex, probably one of the most important ceremonial areas in the Palace.[7] Inside, the Anteroom and the Throne Room proper repeated the same major forms on their northern walls. In both these rooms, central seats, or thrones, were symmetrically flanked by benches. The symmetrical pattern was reinforced in the Final Palatial period by the painted griffons that heraldically flanked the seat (see fig. 10.1). Much of the opposite side of the room was taken up with a Lustral Basin.

South of the Throne Room complex was the Stepped Portico, the major opening in the facade (see fig. 10.3). A broad flight of stairs, its roof supported by a column as large as that of the West Porch, led up to the important rooms on the Piano Nobile. Here, figures of a Procession Fresco regrouped to guide the visitor up the stairs. However many other ways there were to reach the Piano Nobile, this surely was a major one, combining and reiterating all the major elements of the West Porch, South Propylaeum, and the conjectural Stairway 22. The Stepped Portico was a relatively late addition, constructed only in the Final Palatial Period.[8]

Further to the south, in the dead center of the west facade of the Central Court, Evans restored the tiny facade known as the Tripartite Shrine. Evans's reconstruction was based in large part on a feature in the Grandstand Fresco (see fig. 10.3).[9] In Evans's reconstruction, the small size of the facade was made up for by its ornateness, with pairs of small columns used on each of its flanking wings. Unfortunately, the architectural evidence for the Tripartite Shrine is slight, and the rooms behind it are completely unrelated to the symmetry of the facade. If it existed at all, this little facade would resemble the false architecture of theatrical scenery.

The rooms behind Evans's Tripartite Shrine comprise what is called the Central Palace Sanctuary.[10] This complex consists of the Lobby of the Stone Seat, the Vat Room, the Great Pithos Room, the Temple Repositories, and the East and West Pillar Crypts. Thanks to a recent study by M. Panagiotaki we know that these rooms underwent a series of significant architectural changes over the course of the Neopalatial and Final Palatial periods.[11]

Following Evans, many scholars have seen this area as the religious heart of the Palace.[12] The Temple Repositories were found filled with pottery and a range of remarkable objects such as the famous faience Snake Goddesses now in the Herakleion Museum. Evans and

7.5. Mason's mark, Knossos. © Elio Cid/Corbis.

others interpreted the East and West Pillar Crypts as places for chthonic worship. According to him, the pillars, incised with the sacred sign of the Double Axe (see fig. 7.5), were aniconic embodiments of the deity.[13]

For other scholars, the religious function of these rooms is far from clear. For example, the pillars were structural, not simply symbolic. In addition, as D. J. I. Begg recently demonstrated, the incised Double Axes were probably masons' marks, signifying the work of various teams of masons.[14] It is not even certain the rooms were used for rituals. Their main function—and the function of what Evans labeled the Temple Repositories—was storage.[15] The Central Palace Sanctuary, in other words, may be a misnomer. In her painstaking reexamination of the Central Palace Sanctuary (or CPS), Panagiotaki concludes, "Taking into account Renfrew's criteria for determining the recognition of a religious area, there is nothing in the CPS to declare a cult activity."[16] On the other hand, P. Rehak and J. Younger note that costly objects like those found stored in the so-called Temple Repositories and the corresponding set of prestige items found in the Treasury of the Shrine (Room XXV) at Zakros might have been brought out only on ceremonial occasions for temporary display, as happened in Egypt and the Near East. This, they suggest, might explain why so few permanent religious and ceremonial areas have been identified.[17] In this regard it is useful to recall E. Hallager's suggestion that the Lobby of the Stone Seat, located in a key position between the Central Court and the Magazines, was used to provide bureaucratic oversight of the West Magazines and for occasional celebrations (see no. 32 in fig. 7.2).[18] This is a reminder that religious activities may have been sporadic rather than ongoing, and the distinction between sacred and secular may have been indistinct.

The southernmost section of the Central Court facade is usually restored as a series of pillars, of which one pillar base was found *in situ*. The pillars formed a shallow portico masking the rooms behind. Those rooms, centered around the Room of the Chariot Tablets, are poorly preserved and stratigraphically complex. Driessen has tried to untangle their history.[19]

J. Shaw and A. Lowe have recently proposed that a similar pillared portico ran along much of the east facade of the Central Court. When Evans excavated in the southeast corner of the Central Court he found that the area had been eroded to a depth of 2 m below its original level, erasing nearly all traces of the original facade. While J. Shaw's and Lowe's proposal is largely hypothetical, by straightening the line of the facade and narrowing the proportions of the Central Court, it has the advantage of bringing Knossos more into line with what we know of the other Palaces.[20]

Other Entrances

The North Entrance system was the second important entrance into the court from outside the building. Although the exterior facade has been lost, one can assume it would have been dramatically marked. The entrance system itself was less convoluted than that from the West Porch but equally impressive. From the entrance vestibule, one entered the great North Pillar Hall, which gave on to the narrow North Entrance Passage, and this gradually ascended toward the Central Court. At some time during the course of the Neopalatial period, the North Entrance Passage was made narrower by the construction of the East and West Bastions.[21] The resulting narrow corridor was probably unroofed, like a steep-sided ravine, contrasting both with the covered space of the North Pillar Hall to the north and with the vast open expanse of the Central Court to the south. The upper-story wall of the West Bastion, echoing that of the West Porch, was decorated with the emblematic bull in plaster relief (see fig. 7.6).

7.6. North Entrance Passage, Palace at Knossos. Photo by author.

7.7. West Magazines, Knossos. © Roger Wood/Corbis.

There were at least two more entrances to the Palace, the South Porch and the East Bastion, but both of these were small, unconnected with the main streets of the city, and probably intended for private communication. They were well constructed, particularly the East Bastion, with its elaborate drainage system. Unlike the main entrances, these were not concerned with affording visitors a dramatic presentation of the Palace. J. W. Graham has suggested that another entrance led into Magazine XVI. Like the corresponding entrances at Malia and Phaistos, this would have served the magazines. Unfortunately the walls of this part of the Palace are poorly preserved. There is even less evidence for the stepped entrance to the Piano Nobile that Evans imagined here.[22]

The Quarters

Much of the western part of the Palace was given over to storage magazines (see fig. 7.7). Each magazine held up to thirty huge storage jars (pithoi), each with an average capacity of ca. 590 liters. The total capacity of the pithoi may have approached a quarter of a million liters.[23] In addition to the pithoi, the magazines, except for numbers 1, 2, 14, 15, 16, and 18, were equipped with a series of ninety-three carefully constructed subfloor cists, their walls and covers carefully fitted with stone slabs and sometimes lined with lead. Another series of these cists ran the length of the Long Corridor, and, as we have seen, there was a great deal of additional storage in the adjacent Central Palace Sanctuary.

Both Evans and Graham thought that the most important rooms of the Palace were located on the Piano Nobile, the upper floor above the west wing.[24] Nothing of these rooms remained *in situ*, but both scholars attempted hypothetical reconstructions of the plan based on the layout of the ground-floor rooms, especially thick or buttressed ground-floor walls, and the location of window recesses along the west facade (see fig. 7.8). On the evidence of the objects found fallen into the ground-floor rooms (which at Knossos date to the Final Palatial period) and of comparison with finds from other Palaces, Begg suggests that these upper-story rooms were also used for more mundane purposes, including storage and manufacture.[25]

The northeastern part of the Palace seems traditionally to have been the service quarter of the Palace,

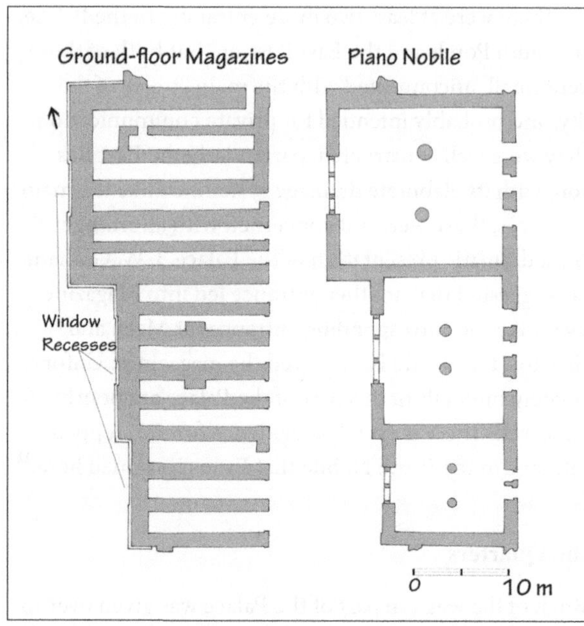

7.8. Plan. Piano Nobile according to Graham. After *PoC*, fig. 85.

providing sufficient storage for the day-to-day operation of the Palace and facilities for various Palace industries. Evans thought that by the Late Bronze Age much of the area was no longer in use. In a recent reexamination of the evidence, however, K. Christakis has shown that both the Royal Pottery Stores and the Magazine of the Medallion Pithoi were operational in LM I.[26] Only basement rooms are preserved further south, but basing himself on the plan of the basement rooms and the fragments of frescoes fallen into them, Evans pictured a Great East Hall above the Royal Pottery Stores and the Loomweight Basement. This large room would have been entered by steps leading up from the Central Court.

Further to the south, the Residential Quarter is one of the primary monuments of Minoan architecture (see fig. 7.9).[27] Its main ground-story room (at a level two stories below the level of the Central Court) Evans named the Hall of the Double Axes (see fig. 10.7), after the masons' marks cut into the wall of the adjacent light well. The hall received light from three directions. On

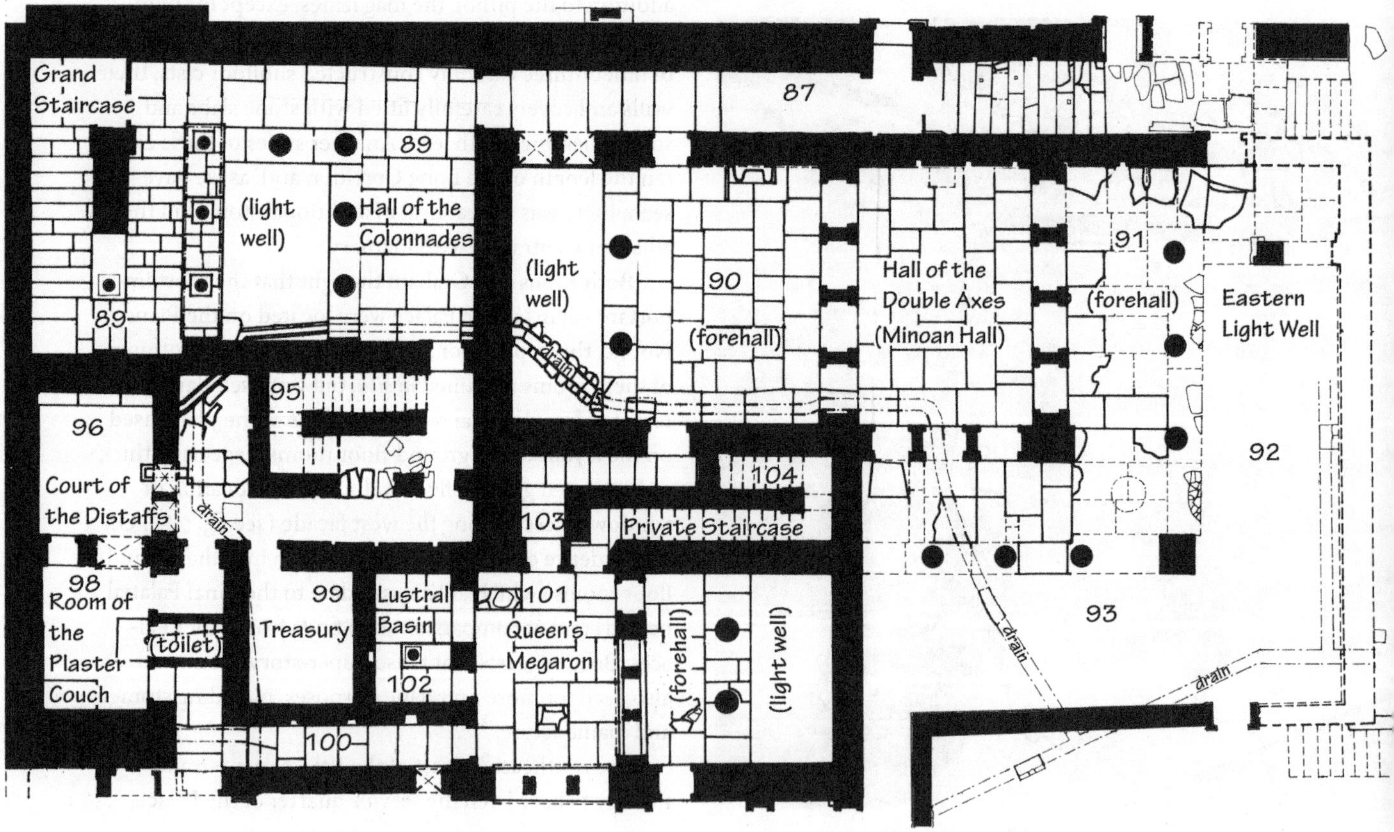

7.9. Plan. Residential Quarter. After Hood and Taylor 1981, Plan.

7.10. Grand Staircase, Palace at Knossos.
© Vanni Archive/Corbis.

the west was a light well, while on the east and south an L-shaped colonnade overlooked the Kairatos Valley. The shape of the colonnade was echoed in the L-shaped pier-and-door partition that defined this section of the hall and joined the pier-and-door partition that separated the center of the hall from the light well on the west. The partitions gave the space great flexibility: screen walls could enclose the space; the room could be entirely opened to the sheltered portico and light well; one or two sides could be opened or partly opened. There were innumerable possible variations that could be adjusted to the season, temperature, time of day, and social context.

To the south of the Hall of the Double Axes was a more private room that Evans called the Queen's Megaron and Graham called the Women's Hall—my guess is that it served as a bedroom (see fig. 10.6). It could be reached through the corridor from the Hall of the Double Axes or from the stairway from the upper floors. It was basically similar in form to the hall, though smaller and simpler. There were light wells on two sides, each bordered by pier-and-door partitions. On the west was a room Evans interpreted as a bath, which originally was a Lustral Basin whose floor was raised at some relatively late point in the Neopalatial period. Behind this room were storage rooms, another small stairway, and a toilet that was connected with the main storm drains of the Palace.

The main entrance to the Residential Quarter from the Central Court was by means of the Grand Staircase, which Evans excavated with difficulty and restored with care (fig. 7.10). It was constructed with an impressive light well and provided a grandiose entrance to the two stories of the Residential Quarter that were located below the level of the Central Court and to the one story that stood above it. On each of these levels, apparently much the same group of rooms was repeated.

There have been various interpretations of the Residential Quarters, including some that insist they were not residential at all but religious.[28] At the other end of the spectrum, Graham described the palaces in largely secular (and anachronistically modernist) terms: "The considerable degree of urbane elegance reached by this society is revealed in their domestic architecture. From the spacious and commodious design of the living quarters of the Palaces and better houses, often adorned with alabaster veneering and plaster walls painted with scenes from nature or court ceremonial, provided with bathrooms and toilets and with ingenious devices to secure adequate lighting and looking out through columned porticoes upon terraced and beautiful landscapes, it is clear that the Cretans aimed at comfortable living."[29] Probably neither extreme does justice to the complexity of these buildings.

Chronology

More than a century after Evans's initial excavations, there is still uncertainty over the dating of the Neopalatial Palace. Most of the difficulty comes neither from inefficiency on the part of the excavators nor bias of later historical revisionists, but is inherent in the building itself. The huge Palace was in the process of continual change for more than six centuries. It suffered periodic destructions by earthquakes followed by ambitious campaigns to level the ruins and construct large areas *ex novo*. But these were only the major events in an ongoing, seldom stable dialogue between decay and renovation. We do not have a clear history of the Palace because its history was never clear.

There are two main opinions as to when the Second Palace was begun. Evans thought that it was initially constructed in MM IIIA, following the destruction in MM IIB of the earlier Palace by earthquake. In his reexamination of the pottery, J. A. MacGillivray supports this position.[30] C. Macdonald, on the other hand, regards MM IIIA as the final phase of the Protopalatial period and dates the construction of the new Palace to MM IIIB.[31] One of the underlying problems is that there is little certainty about the MM III period in general. Particularly with the chronological system I use here, MM III was approximately a fifty-year period only, and, as W.-D. Niemeier and G. Walberg have noted, it is difficult to distinguish two distinct subphases based on the pottery style.[32] The only absolute certainty is that at least some parts of the new Palace were built in MM III.

There was also a serious disruption within the Neopalatial period, perhaps to be associated with the Thera seismic events in MM IIIB–LM IA and the subsequent eruption in LM IA. Macdonald divides the Neopalatial Palace into two main phases, the MM IIIB "New Palace" and the LM IA "Frescoed Palace."[33] To the first he attributes the overall layout of the new building, characterized by "austere monumentality." Macdonald says that much of the Palace was rebuilt in LM IA with lighter, thinner but more stable walls. At this time the west facade of the Central Court was moved east, making the Central Court narrower; the South Propylaeum and the North Entrance Passage were made narrower, and the newly plastered walls were painted with frescoes; the Temple Repositories were closed; and the Central Palace Sanctuary was rearranged.[34] Macdonald also proposes a third, LM IB phase of the Palace that he names the "Ruined Palace." Very little was found in the Palace that dated to this period, suggesting to Macdonald that the building was largely abandoned. As we shall see in Chapter 10, the lack of LM IB material is more likely due to the extensive rebuilding of the Palace in the Final Palatial period.

The New Architecture

The Second Palace at Knossos marked a second revolution in Minoan building techniques. One way to see the change is by comparing the construction of the Residential Quarter at Knossos (see fig. 7.9) with the southwestern section of the Old Palace at Phaistos (see fig. 5.3). The two are not precisely comparable. Important differences in function almost certainly affected their forms. Nevertheless both areas were faced with the same fundamental structural problem, namely, the construction of a three-story building on a steeply terraced slope. Probably the first difference one notices is that Knossos made much more use of labor-intensive techniques. There is more dressed masonry, for example, and it was cut to a greater variety of shapes (slabs, blocks, column bases, jamb bases) and used for a greater variety of purposes (floors, steps, dadoes, stylobates, cornices, balustrades, and walls).[35] The dadoes, floor slabs, steps, and orthostates at Phaistos are limited in comparison.

Even more important than the new uses of dressed masonry was a new approach to the use of wood. Beams in the new Palace were much more massive and carefully milled. Carpentry skills had changed even more than masonry skills. Wooden beams were also put to a greater range of uses. At Phaistos, wood was limited to roof beams, windows, and door frames, a few columns, and horizontal timbers. The builders of the Second Palace at Knossos also used wood for vertical timbers, half-timber construction, long architraves, columns, pillars, and pier-and-door partitions. The new system placed increasing emphasis on engineering finesse and less on brute mass.[36] Even the new techniques of wall construction affected the plans of the Palaces. The new walls, more vertical and thinner, meant that the architects could draw the outer traces of the buildings in, so that at both Knossos and Phaistos the new Palaces had much smaller footprints than their sprawling Protopalatial predecessors.

The Neopalatial walls in the Residential Quarter were coated with a new kind of plaster with a much higher lime content than the plaster used earlier.[37] Because the walls were stronger, the plaster could be much finer and more brittle than the thick, mostly clay plaster that had been used to consolidate Protopalatial walls. At Knossos this fine plaster was often painted with representational frescoes. Unlike the occasional geometric designs used on the walls and floors at Phaistos, which served to decorate and confirm the surfaces to which they were applied, the effect of illusionistic, representational frescoes was to visually dissolve the plane of the wall, creating the illusion of a three-dimensional space that continued beyond the pictorial plane. Relief frescoes, molded out from their walls, were even more effective in confusing the space of the painting with the space of the viewer, as in fact viewer and image shared the same architectural space.

The combined result of all these changes was a building entirely different in character from the earlier, Middle Minoan structure. Walls could be thinner without sacrificing strength. Spaces—even those on the ground floor—could be expansive. Rooms no longer had to be tiny cavities hollowed out of the mass of the walls, and walls became partitions around space. In many cases, walls were eliminated entirely and replaced by colonnades or, that most Minoan of devices, the pier-and-door partition, which, like a folding screen, allowed borders to be formed and dissolved at will. New variety became possible, in features, in shapes of spaces, in relations among spaces, and in lighting. The ultimate example of the architectural revolution is the Grand Staircase. It was so strong that it remained nearly complete when Evans excavated it, yet it appears to consist as much of air as of masonry. It effortlessly descended three stories, keeping one side open to the daylight of the light well all the way. It is the antithesis of the bulky mass at Phaistos.

Evans's Reconstructions

Today nearly every guidebook to Crete contains some allusion to the controversial nature of Evans's reconstructions. The reconstructions have also been the subject of a number of recent scholarly studies.[38] Not all the reconstructions in the Palace are the same. In 1927 Evans divided them into three phases, "marked respectively by the use of wooden supports, of iron girders, and of ferro-concrete." Evans initially defended the reconstructions as necessary for the preservation of the site and for continued excavation.[39] Shortly after making that statement, however, Evans undertook another campaign of reconstruction. This phase of the reconstructions, above all the work done between 1928 and 1930 with the assistance of the architect Piet de Jong and the artist Emile Gilliéron *fils*, had little to do with conservation. Instead it was among the earliest attempts to construct a historical heritage site.

The late 1920s and early 1930s were an exciting time for archaeology. Spurred in part by the "Tutmania" that swept through Europe and the United States following Howard Carter's discovery of King Tutankhamun's tomb in 1922, archaeology became enormously popular. New periodicals were launched, and old periodicals expanded their coverage of antiquity.[40] Knossos was back in the news for the first time in decades and was reaching a new audience. It was to this audience that Evans addressed his new reconstructions. In an interview with a French periodical in 1933, Evans explained the restorations not as necessary for preservation but "for the education of the public."[41] Evans's new concrete displays were carefully distributed through all four corners of the site—the South Propylaeum (see fig. 7.4), the North Entrance Passage (see fig. 7.6), the Residential Quarter (see fig. 7.9), and the Throne Room (see fig. 10.1)—assuring that each area had a visual focal point. A small gallery displaying reproductions of the frescoes was built in the Piano Nobile. To criticize the Evans constructions—or those at more or less contemporary Colonial Williamsburg in Virginia or Greenfield Village in Michigan—as historically inaccurate not only involves an enormous understatement, but it misses the point: these were fundamentally new kinds of institutions, addressing a new constituency. Those constituencies have continued to grow. Knossos is now the second-most-visited site in Greece, with more than six hundred thousand visitors per year. To accommodate these huge crowds Evans's reconstructions underwent a major conservation program in 1996–1998.[42]

Evans's reconstructions have greatly shaped our perceptions of the Minoans. But this is not due to the reinforced concrete at the site alone. More subtly, the language Evans developed to describe the buildings (and which I have used throughout this chapter)—phrases like "Throne Room," "Queen's Megaron," "Lustral Basin," "Temple Repositories," "Piano Nobile," "Pillar Crypt," not to mention the term "Minoan"—are laden with implied meanings, and yet they are irrevocably embedded in the discipline. We cannot write about, speak about, or think about so-called Minoan identity except in Evans's terms.

8 Comparing the Neopalatial Palaces

CA. 1750–1490 BC

RATHER THAN considering the functions of the Palaces, I want to discuss in this chapter matters of form. From this point of view, the five known Minoan Palaces—Knossos, Phaistos, Malia, Galatos, and Zakros (fig. 8.1)[1]—reveal a fascinating balance between consistency and individuality.

Chronological Complexity

The Neopalatial period was nearly twice as long as the Protopalatial period. It lasted from about 1750 BC until the violent wave of destructions that swept the island at the end of LM IB ca. 1490 BC. Of all Minoan history, this was the period about which scholars thought they knew the most. That confidence was seriously challenged by the publication in 1997 of the landmark study *Troubled Island* by J. Driessen and C. Macdonald.[2] The book's main thesis is that the LM IB period, traditionally regarded as the high point of Minoan power and culture, was instead a time of turmoil and decline in the wake of the eruption of the Theran volcano. Driessen and Macdonald painstakingly reviewed masses of evidence from all the known sites of this period and tried to demonstrate how each was diminished during the sixteenth century BC, apparently as they attempted to recover from the political and economic upheaval caused by the volcano eruption while at the same time trying (ultimately in vain) to forestall the wave of destructions that would sweep the already weakened island in 1490 BC.

As we shall see in Chapter 9, some thirteen years after its publication *Troubled Island* no longer seems to paint an accurate picture of most of LM I Crete. Never-

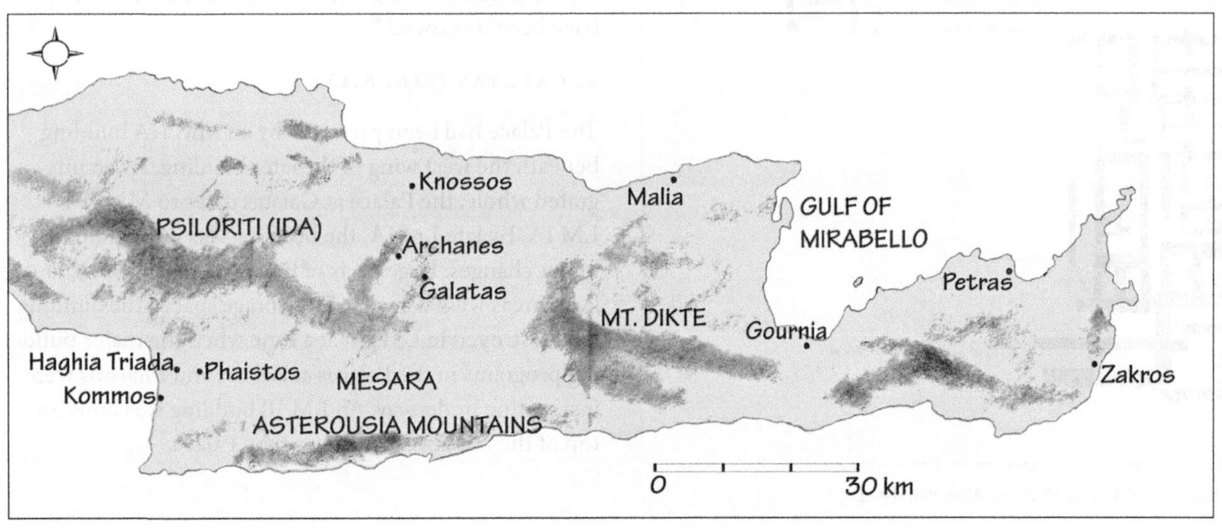

8.1. Sites discussed in chapter 8.

theless, the book brought about two permanent changes to the discipline. First, Driessen's and Macdonald's research, in combination with subsequent studies taking up their challenge, resulted in a much more sophisticated and precise understanding of Late Bronze Age chronology. Second, scholars are now much more aware that this long period was a time of ongoing social, economic, political, and architectural complexity, a time which can no longer be regarded as a single, monolithic Neopalatial period: each of the major Palaces experienced a different series of events.

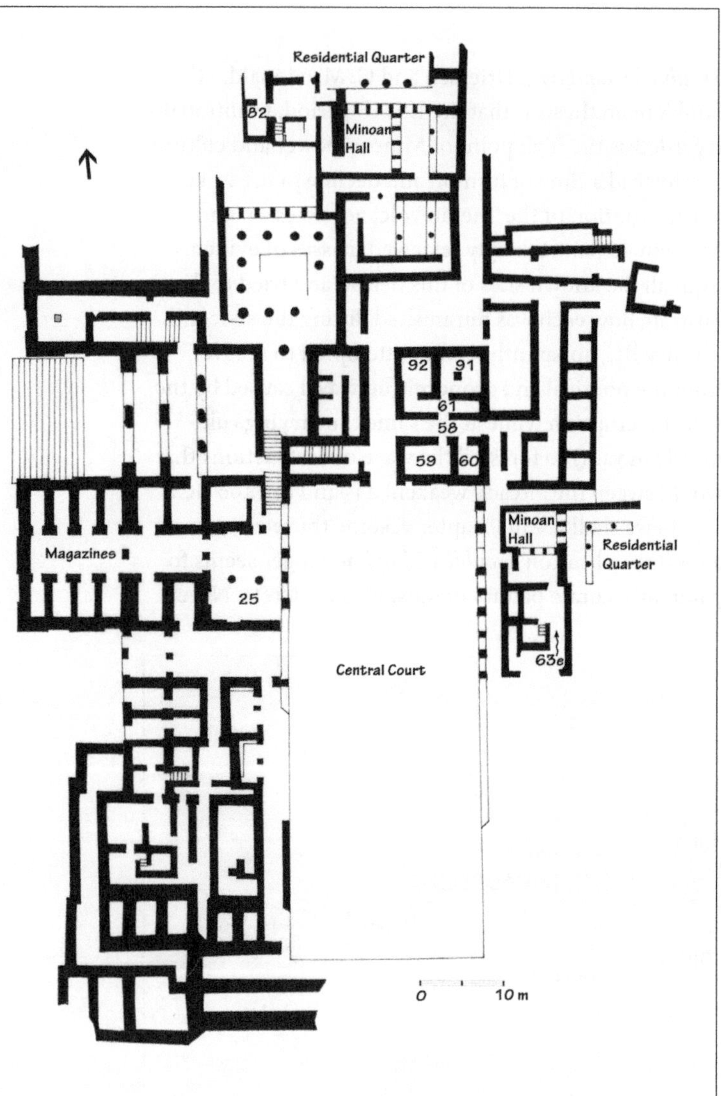

8.2. Plan. Palace at Phaistos. After *PoC*, fig. 4.

Chronology of the Five Palaces

1. KNOSSOS

The Second Palace at Knossos was built in MM III. It underwent a series of major alterations in LM IA, after which the picture is unclear. As we shall see in Chapter 10, the Palace was almost totally rebuilt in the Final Palatial period.

2. PHAISTOS (FIG. 8.2)

The First Palace at Phaistos was destroyed at the end of MM IIB. F. Carinci says there was a limited attempt at rebuilding in MM III (D. Levi's Phase III), but that this effort was aborted, and in MM IIIB–early LM IA the Palace was largely abandoned.[3] The major construction of the Second Palace dates to mature (presumably post-Thera eruption) LM IA and continued into LM IB, contemporary with the Palace at Zakros. At the end of LM IB, the Palace at Phaistos, like that at Malia (but unlike that at Zakros) was emptied of its contents and destroyed by fire.

3. MALIA (FIGS. 8.3, 8.4)

An isolated MM III wall beneath the later Residential Quarter may represent the first attempt to build a second Palace at Malia.[4] The main period of the Palace was probably LM IA, with a second phase of repairs and alterations in LM IA–LM IB.[5] The Palace was almost empty when it was excavated, so there is not much evidence for the date of its destruction. The generally accepted date is LM IB, when much of the town seems to have been destroyed.[6]

4. GALATAS (FIG. 8.5)

The Palace had been preceded by an MM IIA building beneath the west wing of the later building. As an integrated whole, the Palace at Galatas dates to MM IIIB–LM IA. By late LM IA, the building was undergoing major changes: large parts of the Palace lay in ruins, and large areas were converted to storage space. The building was destroyed in LM IA, at a time when the major building programs in the Palaces at Zakros and Phaistos were just getting underway. An LM IB building was built on top of the northwest section of the Palace.[7]

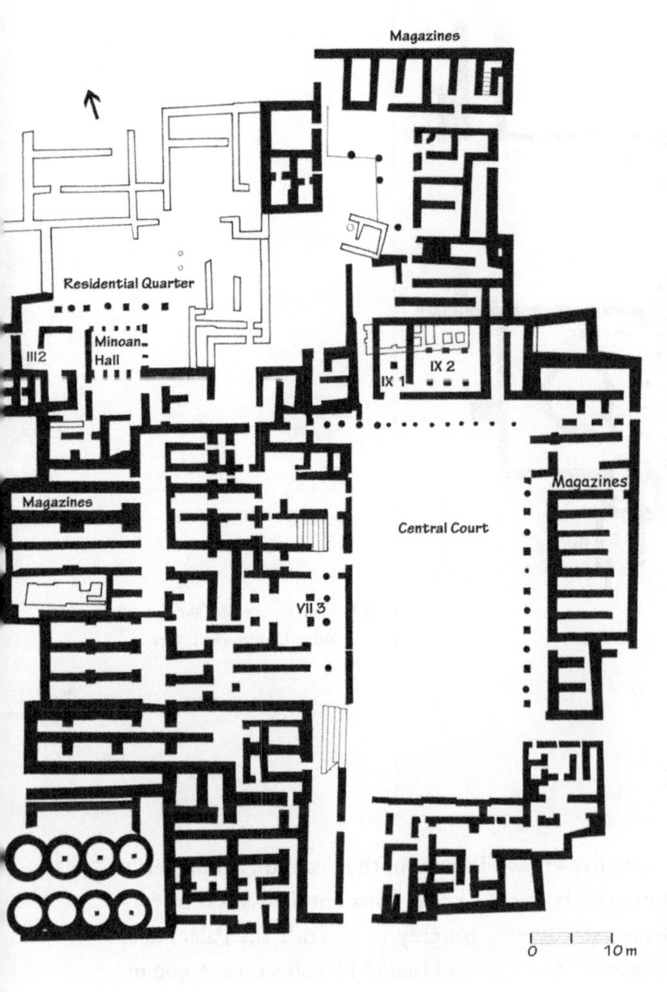

8.3. Plan. Palace at Malia. After H. van Effenterre 1980, fig. 313.

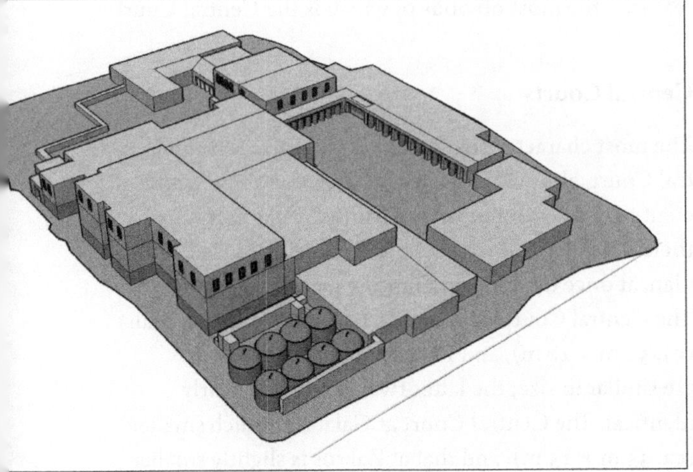

8.4. Reconstruction. Palace at Malia. After *PoC*, fig. 58.

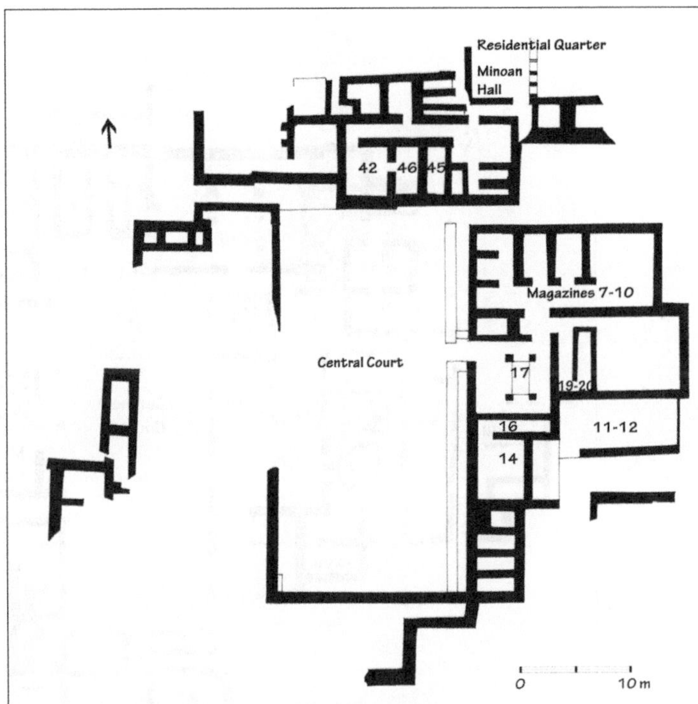

8.5. Plan. Palace at Galatas. After Rethemiotakis 2002, pl. XII.

5. ZAKROS (FIG. 8.6)

While some MM IIIB–early LM IA material has been found in the east and south wings at Zakros, the main construction of the Palace dates to mature LM IA and continued into LM IB. The Palace was destroyed by fire in LM IB with most of its contents in place. The south wing of the Palace may have gone out of use at a somewhat earlier point in LM I.[8]

Comparing the Forms of the Palaces

In 1962 J. W. Graham published the first edition of *The Palaces of Crete*, drawing on a series of studies he published in the *American Journal of Archaeology* beginning in 1956. It was not the first analysis of the architecture of the Minoan Palaces, but it was the first to place primary emphasis on comparison rather than on individual descriptions of the buildings. Instead of diversity of detail, Graham focuses on similarities, shared components, and correspondences among the Palaces in an attempt to understand the body of principles that underlies Minoan architecture.[9] I follow that approach here.

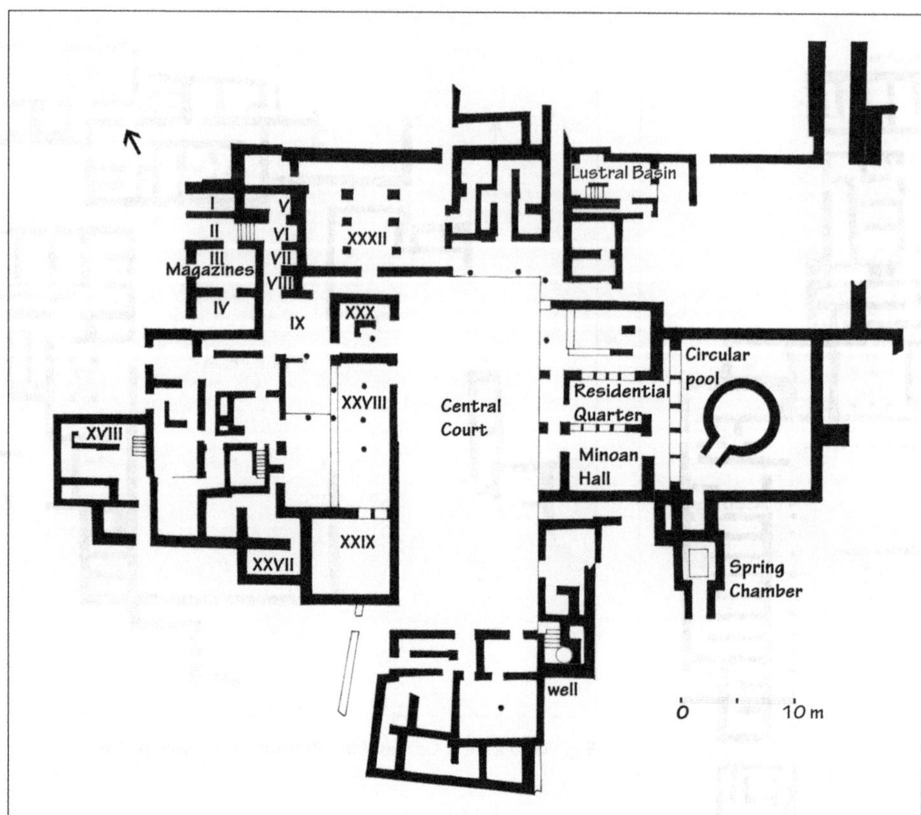

8.6. Plan. Palace at Zakros. After Platon 1971, p. 102.

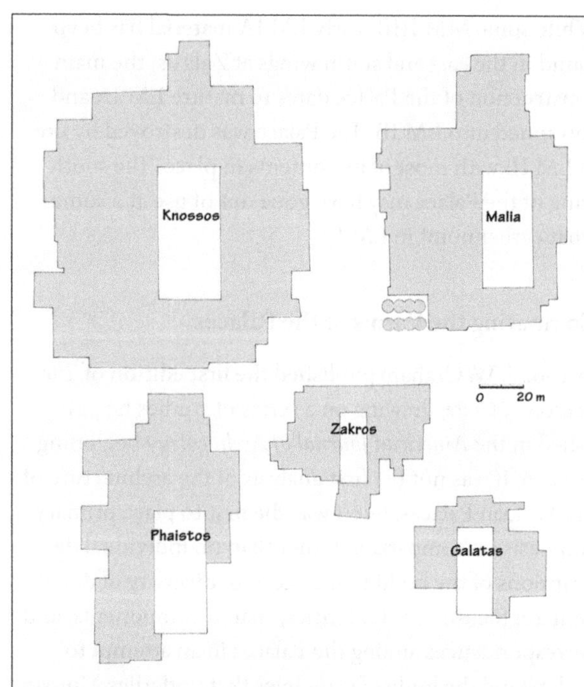

8.7. Plans of Neoplatial Palaces to scale. After Palyvou 2002, pl. LVI.

The five known Palaces of the Second Palatial period differ in scale (fig. 8.7). The Palace at Knossos is by far the largest, covering roughly 13,000 m^2. The Palace at Malia is ca. 7,500 m^2 and that at Phaistos is ca. 6,500 m^2. Galatas and Zakros are much smaller, ca. 4,000 m^2 and 3,500 m^2, respectively. In terms of overall design, however, the five buildings share a number of important features, the most obvious of which is the Central Court.

Central Courts

The most characteristic feature of the Palaces is the Central Court, although a Central Court alone is not sufficient to define a building as a Minoan Palace. It is nevertheless, as Graham writes, "the organizing nucleus of the plan, at once dividing and uniting parts of the Palace."[10] The Central Courts at Knossos (ca. 53 m × 28 m), Malia (ca. 51 m × 22 m), and Phaistos (ca. 51 m × 22 m) are similar in size; the latter two, in fact, are nearly identical. The Central Court at Galatas is much smaller (ca. 35 m × 15 m), and that at Zakros is slightly smaller

8.8. Central Court, Palace at Phaistos. Photo by author.

still (ca. 30 m × 12 m). While the Central Courts vary considerably in size, they share the same approximate proportions, roughly 2:1.[11] The Central Courts also share a roughly similar north-south orientation, although the axis at Zakros is more than 37 degrees east of true north-south.[12] The orientation of the Palaces has been explained in a number of ways. Some have opted for practical explanations, suggesting that the proportions and direction of the Central Courts were chosen to provide maximum sunlight to the facades bordering on the court.[13] J. Shaw, on the other hand, suggests that the direction of the Central Courts was based on an orientation in the strict sense of the term: the determining factor was the desire to have the important rooms along the west facade of the courts oriented toward the rising sun.[14]

At all five Palaces special attention was given to the facades surrounding the Central Court. At Malia porticoes ran along the north and east facades. The eastern portico consisted of alternating columns and pillars, and both could apparently be closed off by low wooden balustrades. The west side provided formal openings to the cult rooms, and, as at Knossos, a broad stairway led to the Piano Nobile.

Porticoes also fronted the east and west facades of the Central Court at Phaistos. But it is the north facade here that is of particular interest. This is one of the most elegant compositions in Minoan architecture (fig. 8.8). The wide central doorway is symmetrically flanked by half columns, which are in turn framed by niches, and these are framed by recesses and second-story windows—all with Mt. Ida as dramatic background.

Even the facades of the much smaller court at Zakros were given special attention. Every element has a specific reason for being where it is. The column and the pillar on the east side are good examples (see fig. 8.6). Seen from one point of view, they stand before the centers of the two main blocks of the east wing. Seen along the length of the facade, the pillar and column align themselves to form a straight facade. Two more columns continue the effect around the north end. And on the west side, two narrow doors flank a wide central door, the tripartite symmetry concealing the asymmetrical disposition of spaces beyond.

G. Rethemiotakis suggests that the design of the ashlar north facade at Galatas was changed over the course of its construction (see fig. 8.5).[15] Originally the intention seems to have been to have two recesses flanking a projecting central section. In the end, however, the architects apparently decided to substitute a small portico for the western recess. Five windows along this facade opened onto the Central Court, two on the right, one in the central section, and two more in the back wall of the portico. A second portico ran the length of the east facade and probably supported balconies on the upper floor. Unfortunately the west wing of the Palace is not well preserved.

At all five Palaces the Central Court facades were composed of the same basic elements, and all aimed at creating similarly splendid effects. They also had the same roles to play in the Palaces. They were to frame the Central Courts, announce the presence of the important rooms behind, and, at the same time, conceal the actual complexity of those rooms. The narrow porticoes behind the colonnades provided covered passageways connecting one end of the Palace to the other. On the ground floor they offered shade and shelter, and on the upper floor they probably supported balconies and balustrades.[16] Even though the Central Court facades had similar roles, however, no two Palaces treated them in precisely the same way.

Magazines

During the Neopalatial period the storage magazines provide the clearest information about the important economic and administrative functions of the Palaces. Each Palace was a center for the collection of agricultural produce from the surrounding region. The magazines provided the capacity for the Palaces to operate effectively within the larger Minoan economic system.[17] The magazines were self-contained units, and most were kept removed from other parts of the Palace. Residential Quarters, in particular, were placed as far from the magazines as possible. The magazines were structurally related to the rooms on the upper story. The closeness of their walls made them the perfect supports for the larger upper-story rooms (see fig. 7.9).

Most storage magazines were similar in form to those at Knossos: long, low, dimly illuminated rooms arranged in rows and having a common entrance corridor. They tend to be located on the west sides of the Palaces, where they would have been most accessible to the streets and roads that fed into the west courts; at Malia, however, they were placed around three sides of the Palace, and those at Galatas are on the east.

At Malia the west magazines closely resemble the magazines at Knossos. The magazines on the north and the east had probably originally been built in the Protopalatial period and continued in use.

The magazines at Phaistos were arranged somewhat differently. They open from a wide east-west passage and run parallel to the main exterior facade. The arrangement allowed the builders to divide the relatively small space into ten individual units.

At Zakros (Rooms I–VIII) and at Galatas (Rooms 7–10) the magazines were also grouped in a separate block. They were much smaller than the magazines at the other Palaces and in both cases were placed so that they would be readily accessible to dining facilities.

West Wings

Based largely on what Evans found at Knossos—although, as we saw in Chapter 7, the evidence there is more ambivalent than is usually admitted—it has been generally assumed that the west wings contained the main cult rooms of all the Palaces.[18] In his study of the Central Palace Sanctuary at Knossos, E. Hallager proposed that the Lobby of the Stone Seat (no. 32 in fig. 7.2) served as a control point for materials going into and out of the magazines. On appropriate occasions like the annual harvest, the room might take on related ceremonial functions.[19] On the basis of the room's pivotal position controlling access between the Central Court and the magazines, Hallager identified contextually similar rooms at Phaistos (Room 25), Malia (Room VII3), and Zakros (Room IX). At Galatas the large Pillar Hall (Room 17) is in an equivalent position.

Reception Halls

In the Palaces at Knossos, Malia, and Phaistos many important rooms, those Graham calls Reception Halls, may have been located on the Piano Nobile of the west wing. Nothing of these rooms survived *in situ*. Evans and Graham have dealt with the problems of restoring them on the basis of information acquired from the ground stories.[20]

One of the many ways that Zakros differs from the other Palaces of the period is that it had some of these important Reception Halls on the ground story.[21] Here was tangible evidence for the forms of these rooms and basic confirmation for the proposals of Evans and Graham. For the first time, the relative scale and elegance of the rooms were indisputably clear.

The excavator, N. Platon, divided these spaces into two major parts. The south room (Room XXIX) he thought was used for formal and ritual dining. A sizeable room (ca. 6 m × 7 m), it was decorated with a rosette frieze in plaster relief running around all four walls. The floor was divided into two rows of rectangles formed by raised plaster borders. The material set within these borders (carpets? wooden inlays?) has left no trace. Platon called the northern section of this area the Hall of Ceremonies (Room XXVIII), regarding it as a single space, ca. 10 m × 12 m. Although there are no interior partition walls, the Hall of Ceremonies consists of five component spaces. In the northwest corner is a light well paved with flagstones and bordered on three sides by columns. It was the central light source for the entire western wing of the Palace. The other four subspaces were distinguished from one another by columns, different sources of light, distinct floor patterns, and, to judge from poorly preserved remains, differing wall decorations. The northeastern area was itself subdivided into two discrete areas. That on the north operated as vestibule to the complex and as corridor leading to the light well. A column and the beginning of the plaster borders on the floor mark the beginning of the second space to the south. Large double windows opening onto the Central Court supplied the southern sections with their own source of direct light from the east, supplementing the borrowed light from the light well on the north. Divisions within the Hall of the Ceremonies were effected more through subtle implications than through solid architectural barriers. The space could be perceived and presumably could have operated as a whole or it could be seen as five or six distinct spaces. To judge from the stairs, at least part of the plan was repeated on the upper story.

Rethemiotakis found evidence of a similar situation in the east wing at Galatas (see fig. 8.5).[22] On the ground floor both the Pillar Hall (Room 17) and the Columnar Hall (Room 14) were used for ceremonial dining. These rooms were convenient to the large kitchen (Room 11–12) and to the storage magazines (Rooms 7–10). Stairways in Rooms 16 and 19–20 led to more dining facilities on the upper story. Rethemiotakis suggests that these upper rooms joined balconies and verandas that overlooked the Central Court and the vista to the east.

If these rooms at Zakros and Galatas were ceremonial dining rooms, which, particularly at Galatas, seems to have been the case, what is one to do with the series of rooms that Graham called Banquet Rooms?[23] Graham noticed that on the north sides of the Central Courts at Knossos (the North Pillar Hall), Malia (Rooms IX1–IX2), Phaistos (Rooms 58–61, 91–92), and Zakros (Room XXXII) there were rectangular rooms or blocks of rooms whose ground-floor plans suggested they supported large upper-story rooms with two rows of interior columns. The fact that Graham had defined this form before the Palace at Zakros was excavated seemed to confirm his idea. His identification of the room as a Banquet Hall was based largely on a comparison with banquet halls in some Egyptian palaces and was supported by a bit of artifactual evidence. Graham's Banquet Halls are formally similar to one another, though it is anybody's guess as to what they were used for. With a bit of wishful thinking, one could imagine a corresponding room above Rooms 42, 45, and 46 at Galatas, although the location of the setback in the facade complicates the matter.

Residential Quarters

The Residential Quarters at Malia, Phaistos, Galatas, and Zakros, like those at Knossos, were among the best-built parts of the buildings, if on much smaller scales.[24] The monumental Residential Quarter at Knossos repeated essentially the same plan on three stories terraced into the slope on the east side of the Palace. The Residential Quarters at Phaistos and Malia probably had two stories, and Zakros and Galatas probably only one. Aside from the differences in size the Residential Quarters were remarkably similar. All were composed of the same set of rooms, incorporated similar features, and made use of the same sorts of intricate details.

All Residential Quarters had some storage space, though the size and relative location of the closets varied. Corridors and stairways were used to provide communication from one area to another. At the innermost part of the Residential Quarters, furthest from the point of entry, was a suite of rooms consisting of a Lustral Basin and a room that, at Knossos, Evans called the Queen's Megaron and Graham renamed the Women's Hall. Often a toilet was located nearby.[25] There is no convincing evidence that the Queen's Megaron was intended primarily for women. Its secluded position would also be appropriate for a bedroom.

The major room in each of these complexes was the Minoan Hall. This was the largest room and was defined at Knossos and Phaistos North on two sides and at Phaistos East, Malia, and Zakros, on three sides by pier-and-door partitions, allowing it to be almost completely opened to surrounding spaces. One side of the Minoan Hall generally opened onto the forehall, which in turn opened onto a light well. One or more of the other sides of the Minoan Hall opened onto a colonnaded portico facing a court. In every case the hall received light and air from at least two and usually three sides—a remarkable achievement given the structural limitations of stone masonry.

The courts onto which the halls opened provided not only light and ventilation, but also the best views in the Palace. At Knossos and Phaistos they overlook valleys. At Malia, the court may have overlooked a garden and was arranged to catch the sea breeze from the north. At Zakros, since the Palace was situated in a low valley, no spectacular views were available. As if to make up for this unavoidable shortcoming, the court onto which the hall opened was fitted with a private bathing pool.

The views afforded by the Residential Quarters may have influenced their locations within the Palaces. They were not positioned with reference to a specific compass bearing. None were on the south sides of the Central Courts or on the west, which was taken up with ceremonial rooms, but they otherwise ranged around all sides of the Central Court: northwest (Malia), north (Phaistos North), northeast and east (Zakros), east (Phaistos East), and southeast (Knossos). They were generally removed from the public courts, magazines, and Reception Halls and placed in relatively secluded sections of the Palace. Usually a single door provided access. Within the Residential Quarters, rooms became increasingly private as one moved from the entrance through the hall to the innermost suite of Queen's Megaron and Lustral Basin.

Only a fragment of the Residential Quarter at Galatas is preserved, but it is sufficient to assure us that it was similar to the others: it has a clearly defined Minoan Hall with light well, forehall, and hall; it makes use of the same carefully cut bases for the pier-and-door partition; and it was situated to take full advantage of the view and to be removed from the bustle of the rest of the Palace.

Design and Measurement

One of the major aims of Graham's *Palaces of Crete* was to counter the then-prevalent conception that Minoan architecture, in contrast to Egyptian architecture and classical Greek architecture, consisted of essentially disorganized, senseless, "labyrinthine" agglomerations. Where others saw chaos, Graham saw order. Looking at the Palace at Phaistos, for example, he saw various dimensions being repeated, and, reckoning that the major sections of the Palace might have been laid out in round numbers of a standard unit of measurement, he concluded that the Minoan architects had used a unit of 30.36 cm that he called the Minoan foot (fig. 8.9). Tests at the Palace at Zakros, which was not excavated until after Graham had proposed his Minoan foot, appeared to support his hypothesis.[26] Several years later J. Cherry submitted Graham's published figures to a statistical test. He found that while the measurements were, in fact, quantal, that is, did correspond to *some* unit of measurement, the preferred quantum (or Minoan foot) was 46.8 cm.[27]

In 1983 D. Preziosi proposed that the Minoan Palaces had been laid out not with a simple linear unit of measure, but according to a grid module (fig. 8.10).[28] Thus the approximately 2:1 proportions of the Central Courts were to be seen as half of the original square module, the other half of which defined a line of the west magazines.

One problem with both Graham's and Preziosi's proposals is that they are both products of "paper architecture," largely two-dimensional schemata that can be fitted to the actual three-dimensional topography only with difficulty and take even less notice of the fourth dimension, time. The Palace at Knossos, for example, was

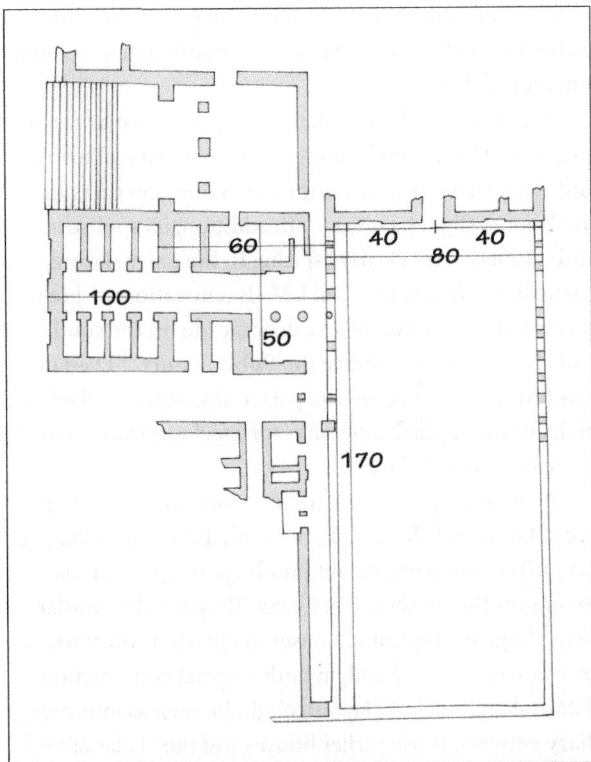

8.9. Design of Palace at Phaistos according to Graham's Minoan foot. After *PoC*, fig. 144.

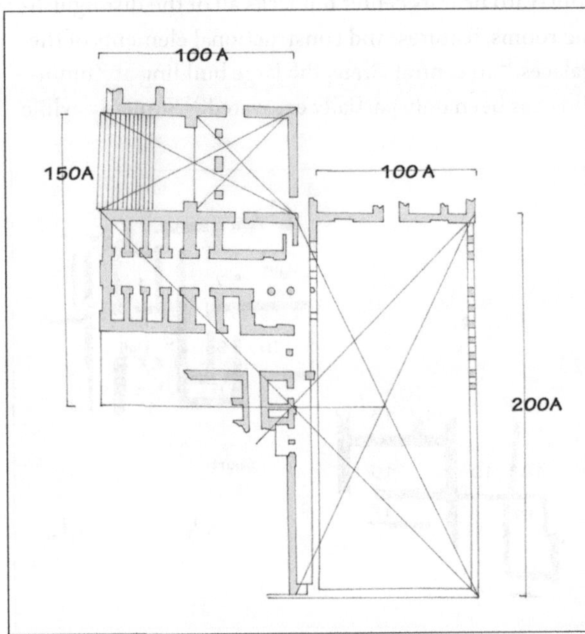

8.10. Design of Palace at Phaistos according to Preziosi's module. After Preziosi 1983, figs. IV.30.B and IV.30.C.

under sporadic construction for a millennium. At what points would the geometrical design have been applied?

Preziosi himself recently pointed out another problem. The search for the Minoan unit of measure or module, while centered on trying to understand how the buildings were actually constructed in antiquity, is in addition an issue grounded in the traditions of modernist scholarship: identifying the unit of measure was presumed to be equivalent to the discovery of "a mark of conceptual sophistication no less significant than the discovery of the systems of writing in Bronze Age Crete."[29] Within this context, to understand the unit of measure was to understand the fundamental principles of Minoan design, and having access to those principles meant having access to the Minoan mind and conceptual worldview. Within the actual context of Knossos, however, the Palace was the result of innumerable decisions, compromises, innovations, mistakes, and corrections. While some linear unit or units of measure were almost certainly employed along the way, they cannot encapsulate the mentality of generations of builders.

Are There Other Minoan Palaces?

Before considering the question of whether or not there are other Minoan Palaces, I will explain again how I am using the term "Palace."[30] First, I do not use the term to imply a standard of architectural quality or social importance: in fact, the five known Palaces vary in quality and importance (however one defines those terms). Second, as noted in Chapter 4, I am not using the term "Palace" to refer to a set of functions, such as economic center or religious center or administrative center. Neopalatial Palaces may have served these and other functions, but so did many other buildings. I am using the term "Palace" to refer only to an architectural form that is identifiable on the basis of its scale, plan, set of rooms, and certain structural features and techniques. As we have seen in this chapter, while each of the Palaces at Knossos, Phaistos, Galatas, Zakros, and Malia is unique, they share a specific set of characteristics, such as Central Courts with articulated court facades, formal rooms in the west wing, magazines, Residential Quarters with Minoan Halls, Queen's Megarons, Lustral Basins, light wells, and architectural features, such as pier-and-door partitions and columns. Even this highly arbitrary archi-

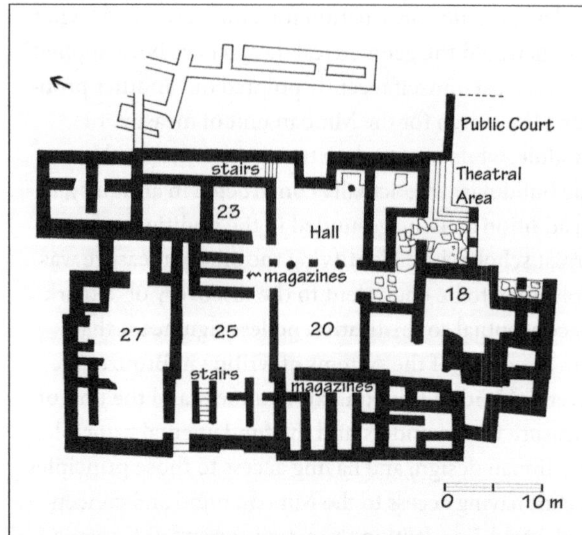

8.11. Plan. So-called Palace at Gournia. After *Gournia*, plan.

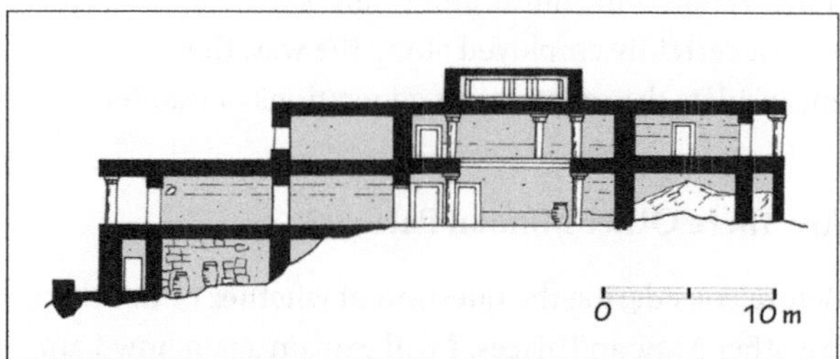

8.12. Restored section. So-called Palace, Gournia. After Soles 1979, p. 13, fig. 3.

tectural definition leaves a number of gray areas, as the distinction between "Palatial" and "non-Palatial" is often a matter of degree.

For example, the so-called palace at Gournia was the largest and best-built building in the Neopalatial town, and it may have served many of the same functions as the Palaces (figs. 8.11, 8.12). In addition, its sponsors and builders were clearly aspiring to the palatial form, particularly during the final LM IB renovations, which involved the addition of an ashlar facade on the south and an attempt to embrace the Public Court.[31] Even in this final form, however, the palace at Gournia lacked many of the sophisticated masonry techniques seen in more canonical Palaces.

In many respects the building most similar to the palace at Gournia is Maison E, the Little Palace at Malia (fig. 8.13). These two important buildings are quite similar to one another in several respects. They are also similar to the large Protopalatial houses in Quartier Mu at Malia (see figs. 6.15–6.17) and, in both original construction date and architectural layout, might be seen as intermediary between those earlier houses and the "Palatializing" houses of the later part of the Neopalatial period.

Several other Neopalatial buildings have also been described as palaces. A house at Makrygiallos has a small courtyard near its center but lacks all of the distinguishing rooms, features, and constructional elements of the Palaces.[32] In central Crete, the large building at Zominthos has been only partially excavated.[33] Similarly, while

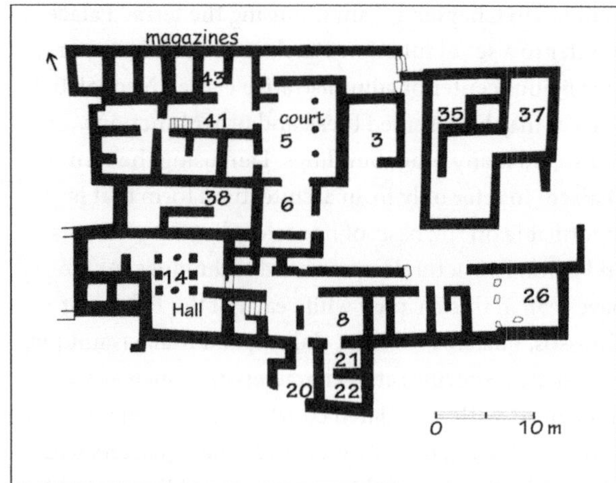

8.13. Plan. Maison E, Malia. After Deshayes and Dessenne 1959, plate 7.

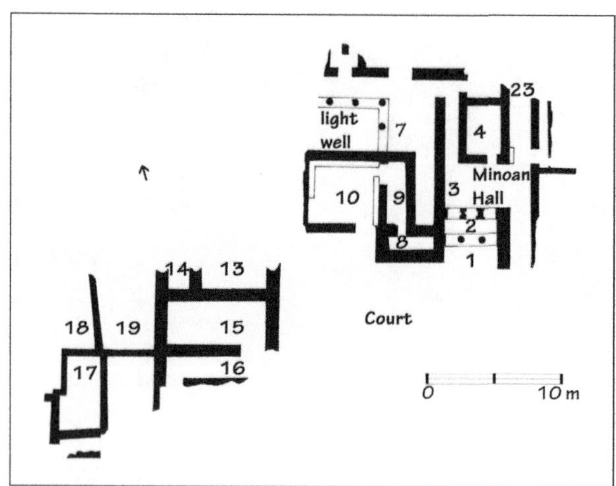

8.14. Plan. Archanes Tourkogeitonia. After Sakellarakis and Sapouna-Sakellaraki 1997, p. 79, drawing 6.

the part of the building excavated at Tourkogeitonia in Archanes includes a grand canonical Minoan Hall that might well belong to a Minoan Palace, most of the building lies under the modern town, and its overall plan is unknown (fig. 8.14).[34]

In a recent discussion of Petras (fig. 8.15), M. Tsipopoulou expresses the hope that scholars will stop using the term "Palace" to describe Minoan buildings. The term not only carries with it a number of powerful implications, but also fails to describe the complexity of buildings (like the one at Petras) that do not fall neatly into modern categories.[35] She acknowledges that Petras may seem atypical when compared to the other Palaces—for example, its Central Court is tiny, only 6 m × 13 m in LM IA and reduced to 4.9 m × 12 m in LM IB. But, she explains, one of the factors involved is that much of the building was laid out during the Protopalatial period. She also notes that conditions in this relatively isolated part of the island were decidedly different from those in the expansive plains of central Crete and in a separate study argues that Petras needs also to be approached within a regional framework.[36] She argues that over the years Petras had a complex relationship with the nearby MM IA fortified site at Aghia Photia (see fig. 4.3) and the MM IA defensible site at Chamaizi (see fig. 4.4). The fortifications at those sites suggest to Tsipopoulou that the relationship between the coastal fort at Aghia Photia and the more inland farming site at Chamaizi had been contentious, and the establishment of the first major building at Petras in MM IIA, after the destruction of Aghia Photia in MM IA, represented a shift of power in the region. She concludes, "Thus it is possible that Aghia Photia provided, to a certain extent and after a chronological hiatus, a model for Petras."[37] Certainly not all of the features at Petras are regional or provincial. The building makes use of the same kind of ashlar masonry, cut jamb bases, dovetail clamps and masons' marks seen in the most sophisticated Neopalatial buildings. Clearly the builders were in part emulating the island-wide Minoan Palatial style. On the other hand, much of the building is also deeply rooted in a distinctively local tradition.

Unique historical circumstances and complicated local and regional relationships were also involved in Building T at the harbor site of Kommos (fig. 8.16).[38] Building T was designed as a monumental rectangle. The north facade is one of the most impressive walls in Minoan architecture. It was built in a single straight line over 55 m long with coursed ashlar blocks rising above massive orthostates and a projecting krepidoma.

The interior of the building is extraordinarily simple. The rooms are arranged around a large (28.64 m × 39.10 m) court. The east wing consists of a series of eight long (ca. 31.5 m) galleries, each nearly 4 m wide. The north and south sides are framed by stoas. Whether or not the building had a west wing is debatable: if such a wing existed it has been washed away by the sea. Therein lies the problem in understanding the building.

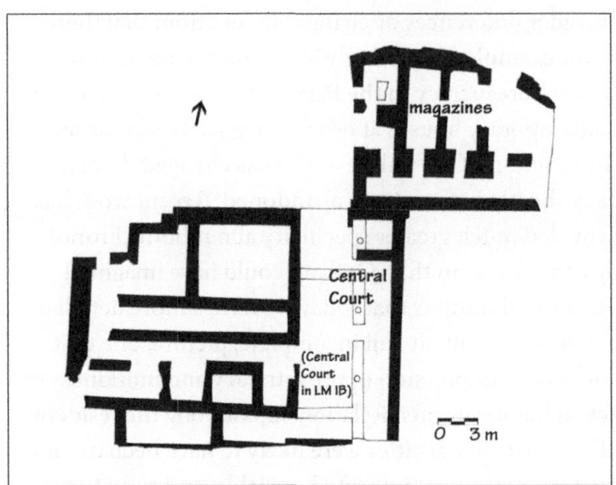

8.15. Plan. Petras. After Tsipopoulou 1999, pl. CXC.

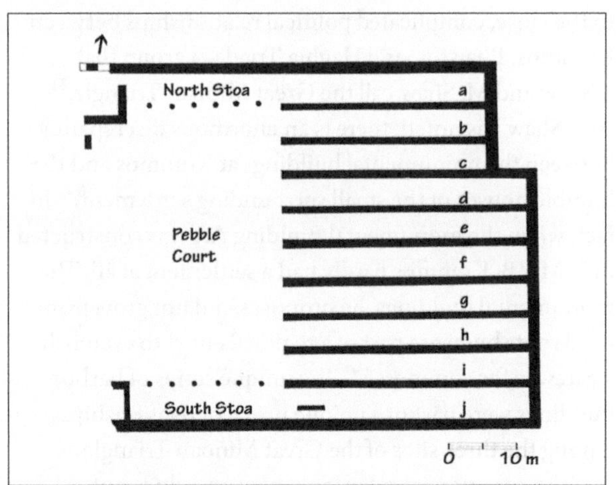

8.16. Plan. Building T, Kommos. After J. Shaw and M. Shaw, 2006 pl. 1.7.

J. Shaw notes that Building T has many things in common with the Palaces, including its rectilinear layout, its orientation, the existence of wings around a court, and features such as pier-and-door partitions and ashlar masonry. But he also notes a number of differences: the straight facades without any characteristic setbacks or recesses, the unusual depth of the stoas, the unusual proportions of the court, the lack of entrances, and the extraordinary size of the east galleries.[39]

As at Petras, it may be that the unique character of Building T is grounded in local history and a complex network of regional ties. Building T was not the first monumental building on the site. It had been preceded by Building AA, built in MM IIB, on a very similar plan. Building T was in turn followed by another monumental structure, Building P, in LM IIIA2 (see fig. 11.4). This later building consists of a series of six long galleries and an administrative building (Building N); it had no west wing. Building P was probably a shed used for the storage of ships during the winter. D. Puglisi suggests a similar function for Buildings AA and T.[40] There are scrappy remains of several other Minoan ship sheds, including examples at Nirou Khani, Amnisos, Poros, and Gournia, but these are not so monumental or so long-lived: the sequence of harbor buildings at Kommos was built and rebuilt over the course of six centuries.[41]

How did such a monumental and enduring facility come to be built at Kommos? In part it had to do with natural resources: a suitably sheltered harbor site, the availability of water, etc. But it was probably also related to the close, complicated political relationships between Kommos, Phaistos, and Haghia Triada, a group that J. Shaw and M. Shaw call the Great Minoan Triangle.[42] As J. Shaw has noted, there is an enormous discrepancy between the monumental buildings at Kommos and the humble houses of the small surrounding settlement.[43] In fact, when the monumental Building AA was constructed in MM IIB, Kommos hardly had a settlement at all. The monumental buildings, he proposes, did not grow from local roots but were part of a regional effort to establish a gateway for commerce.[44] The unique series of harbor buildings were part of a unique nexus of relationships among the three sites of the Great Minoan Triangle.

The commercial role alone, however, does not explain the extraordinary monumentality of the harbor facilities at Kommos. In addition to their workaday functions, these buildings constituted a grand seaside facade for the entire Great Minoan Triangle. For merchants, sailors, and emissaries arriving from other parts of Crete or from around the Mediterranean these buildings presented an identity of authority, tradition, and internationalism. Over time that identity became sacred. By the late eleventh century BC, a sanctuary with strong Phoenician and Egyptian ties was established on the site of the Bronze Age harbor buildings. For more than a thousand years until it was finally abandoned around AD 150, Kommos served as a cosmopolitan safe haven for visiting merchants and pilgrims.[45]

Complexity and Contention

More than forty years after its initial publication, Graham's *Palaces of Crete* remains the starting point for discussion of the Minoan Palaces. Yet there are many things his book did not attempt to do. For example, Graham felt that at the time he was writing, "We are not, I think, ready at present to attempt to trace the evolution of Minoan architecture and to relate it closely to the political or social history of the period."[46] He had little notion then of how complex the issues were: that each Palace had a unique history; that some Palaces (Phaistos and Zakros) were only begun as others (Galatas and the building at Petras) were being dramatically reduced in size; that each Palace underwent significant changes over time. Similarly, Graham did not attempt to consider differences or changes in function: that there is, for example, surprisingly less evidence for administrative bureaucracy in the Palace at Phaistos than in the contemporary houses at nearby Haghia Triada; or that the function of the Palace at Galatas changed dramatically shortly before it was abandoned. Recent work has provided much greater specificity about both chronology and function than Graham could have imagined. The overall result is that today we have a more detailed and nuanced, albeit still incomplete, picture, one that conveys an impression of the intricacy and murkiness of actual human events. Relationships among the residents of the Neopalatial cities were likely to have been not homogeneous, but complicated, variable, and sometimes contentious.

9 Houses and Towns in the Neopalatial Period

CA. 1750–1490 BC

Some societies invest heavily in tombs, others in temples or cathedrals, and still others in sports stadiums and museums. During the Neopalatial period, Minoans invested in domestic architecture (fig. 9.1). Houses range from the magnificent mansions at Knossos to the modest houses of artisans and farmers. The investment came to a halt when the houses and towns and the intricate social network that linked them were violently destroyed at the end of LM IB, bringing an end to the period that Evans called the New Era.

The Evidence

More than 60 Neopalatial sites have been excavated, and we have the remains of more than 320 houses.[1] Given the extensive literature on the architecture of this period, including J. Driessen's and C. Macdonald's useful "Gazetteer of Neopalatial Sites," I need not discuss these buildings individually but instead shall look at a number of examples.[2]

Although the number of excavated houses is large, the evidence is uneven. It includes a number of partially excavated buildings, fragments of several buildings that have been published as single structures, and buildings that originally had been constructed in the Protopalatial period and continued in use. Incomplete excavations have led to a number of misconceptions. For example, many of the excavated houses are frequently described in the literature as villas, a term that, at least in English, implies a country house.[3] Most, if not all, of those buildings were not isolated structures but belonged to larger, as yet unexcavated settlements. To avoid confusion, I will discuss only buildings that have been completely excavated and published in substantial detail.

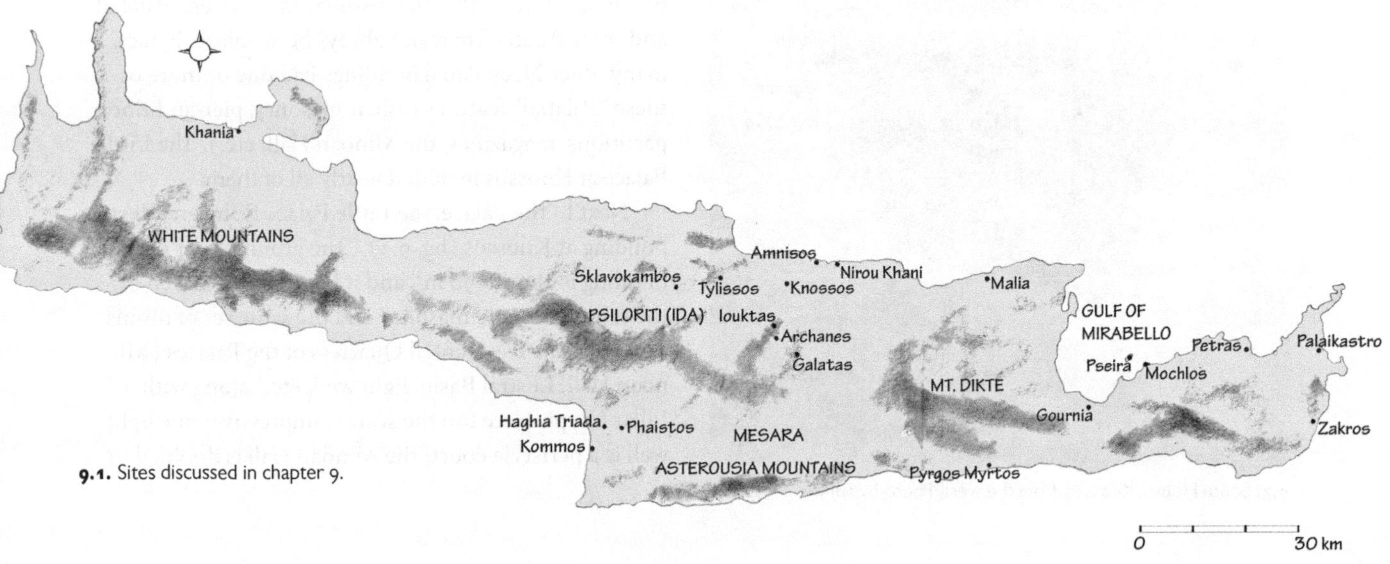

9.1. Sites discussed in chapter 9.

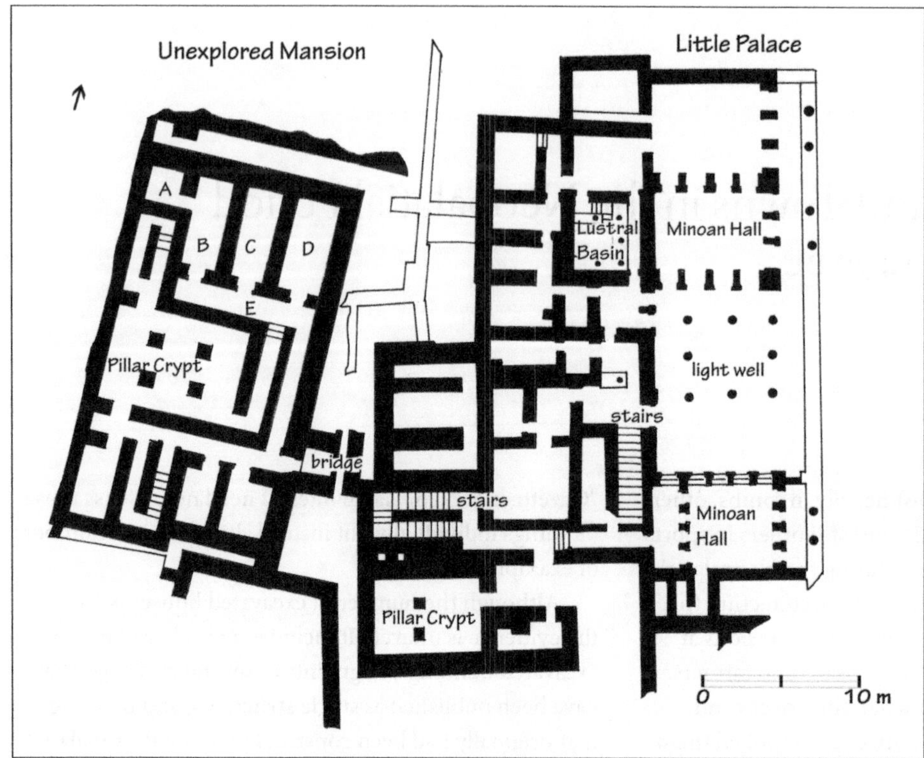

9.2. Plan. Little Palace and Unexplored Mansion, Knossos. After Popham et al. 1984, plan.

9.3. South House, Knossos, from the west. Photo by author.

The Architectural Continuum

In Chapter 8, I compared the five Neopalatial Palaces with several other buildings that incorporated some "Palatial" features but lacked others. For example, there are no standard Residential Quarters at Petras or in Building T at Kommos. On the other hand, while the so-called palace at Gournia has a version of the Residential Quarter, it does not have a Central Court. These buildings indicate that the distinction between "Palatial" and "non-Palatial" may not always be absolute. In fact, many other Neopalatial buildings had one or more of these "Palatial" features (ashlar masonry, pier-and-door partitions, magazines, the Minoan Hall, etc.). The Little Palace at Knossos included nearly all of them.

Next to the Palace, the Little Palace is the grandest building at Knossos (fig. 9.2).[4] The ground floor of the building is about 990 m^2, and it incorporates much of the same elaborate masonry and the same set of rooms we saw in the Residential Quarters of the Palaces (Minoan Hall, Lustral Basin, light well, etc.) along with a Pillar Crypt. Here too the scale is impressive: one light well is a peristyle court; the Minoan Hall is doubled in

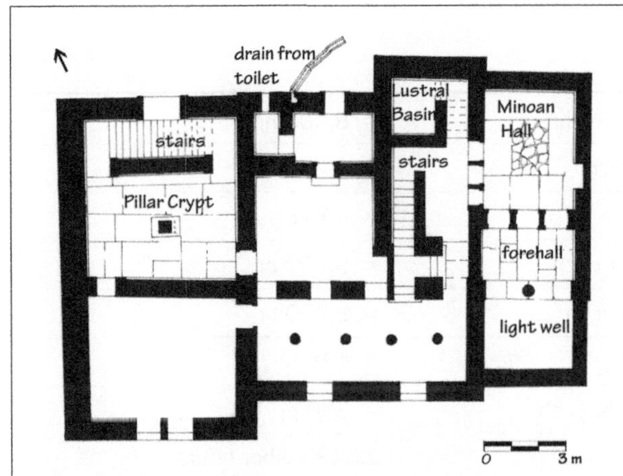

9.4. Plan. South House, Knossos. After *PM II*, fig. 208.

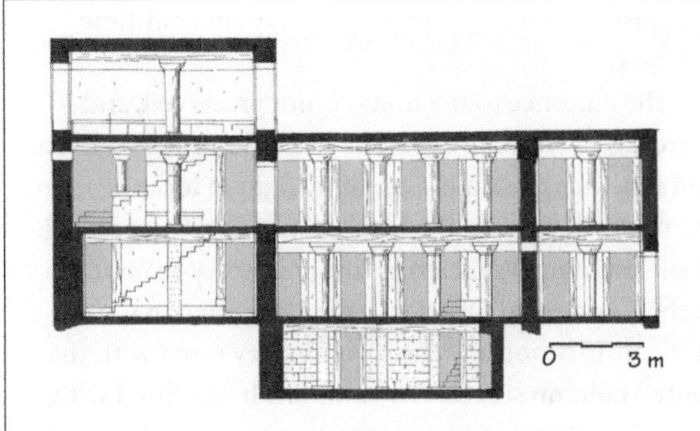

9.5. Section. South House, Knossos. After *PM II*, fig. 208.

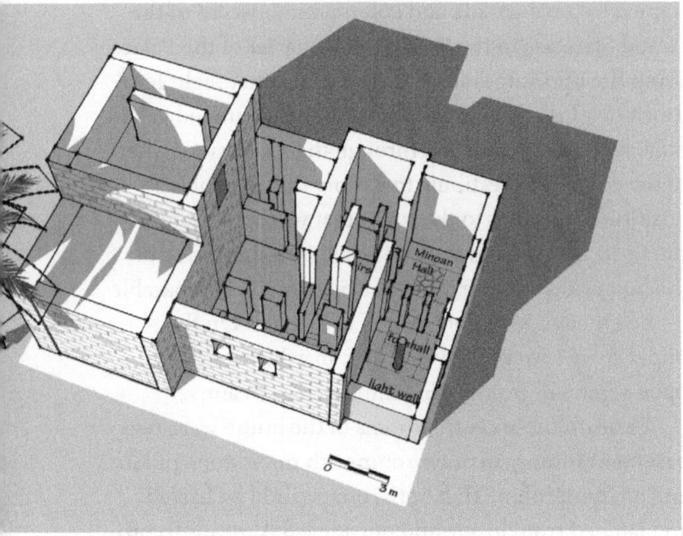

9.6. Reconstruction. South House, Knossos.

plan with two main rooms illuminated by light wells on two sides, like the Hall of the Double Axes in the Palace; the Pillar Crypt has two pillars.

A bridge connects the Little Palace with the so-called Unexplored Mansion, another impressive building that is neither unexplored nor a mansion, if that term implies a residential function. The Unexplored Mansion lacks the distinctive Minoan Hall, Lustral Basin, and light well characteristic of the Residential Quarters. If it was not a mansion, what was it? The excavator of the building argued that the Unexplored Mansion duplicated many of the (primarily religious) functions of the Little Palace.[5] A few years later, J. Poblome and C. Dumon argued convincingly that the Unexplored Mansion had been originally built as a storage and industrial annex to the Little Palace, in the same way that Building B at Tylissos was built as an annex to House A.[6] The Little Palace and the Unexplored Mansion taken together as part of the same complex have a total area of about 1,450 m^2, or roughly half the size of the Palaces at Galatas and Zakros. The only reason that the Little Palace does not qualify as a Palace in my terms is that it lacks a Central Court.

The South House at Knossos

Other houses at Knossos also emulated the Residential Quarters of the Palaces. It is significant that they do so on the ground floor. In more modest houses of the period, the main living quarters were on the upper story. Placing the Minoan Hall on the ground made it accessible to visitors, suggesting that perhaps, as in later Roman houses, an important function of this kind of house was the reception of visitors and clients. A similar arrangement is found much earlier in Building A at Quartier Mu in Malia, a building that had already incorporated many of the same features (Minoan Hall, Lustral Basin, and light well) in the MM II period. As I. Schoep has recently noted, the Malia example means it is not entirely clear whether this set of rooms originated in the Palaces and was then imitated in the houses, or, vice versa, it was initially a monumental domestic form that was then adopted in the Residential Quarters of the Palaces.[7] By the Neopalatial period it is common to both.

The South House at Knossos was built as part of a series of major constructions along the southern borders of the Palace (figs. 9.3–9.6).[8] To form a level terrace

Table 9.1.
Labor Hours Required for South House at Knossos

Excavating terrace	2,000 m^3 earth	@ .25 m^3/hr	= 8,000 hr
Quarrying	320 m^3 stone	@ 4 hr/m^3	= 1,280 hr
Transporting materials			= 450 hr
Dressing block	2,400 blocks	@ 4 hr each	= 9.600 hr
Building walls	320 m^3	@ 10 hr/m^3	= 3,200 hr
Laying roofs	225 m^2		= 125 hr
Plastering	14 rooms	@ 20 hr each	= 280 hr
TOTAL			22,485 labor hours

for the house, a huge cutting was made into the slope, infringing upon the foundations of the Stepped Portico and the original South Corridor of the Palace. A. Evans collected sherds from within the walls that date the original construction of the building to MM III B–LM IA.

Like the Palaces and many other houses of this period, the South House underwent a series of modifications during the course of its history. The Lustral Basin was filled, and a new floor and new wall paneling were added. The stairway south of the Lustral Basin was modified. In addition, Driessen has suggested that the Minoan Hall and light well that form the eastern unit of the house were added only during the LM IA period.[9] The South House was destroyed in LM IA. Unlike many other houses at Knossos, it was never reoccupied.[10]

The South House was impressively constructed of coursed ashlar masonry on the north and east sides. Inner walls of the ground story were rubble coated with painted plaster. Many of the walls on the upper stories were of mud brick, to judge from the amount of clay that A. Evans reported finding collapsed into the lower rooms. Most of the rooms had dadoes of gypsum slabs, and several also had corresponding gypsum floor panels. The building made use of an extravagant number of wooden columns, stone pillars, and pier-and-door partitions. No labor was spared. Even in the basement some of the doorjambs were entirely of cut gypsum rather than of the more usual wood-on-gypsum bases.

The techniques employed by the builders were not only impressive, but also quite costly in terms of labor hours (see table 9.1). Assuming a workday of about six hours, building this structure in a four-month building season would have required thirty-one full-time laborers.[11]

The entrance to the house is not preserved, and there has been some debate as to its location.[12] A. Evans and Driessen are almost certainly right in locating it on the upper floor from the higher terrace on the west side of the building. We see similar upper-story entrances in the Residential Quarter of the Palace and in several of the nearby houses. The second-story room with the central column served as a vestibule. It was fitted with a bench and provided access to the rest of the house. In the northwest corner of the room, a stairway led up to the rooftop terrace. The west end of the stairway was framed by a balustrade and column reminiscent of the Grand Staircase in the Residential Quarter of the Palace. From the opposite side of the room, another flight led down to a Pillar Crypt just beneath the columned vestibule. A third doorway led through the southeast corner of the columned vestibule to a room that occupies a position equivalent to the room that was associated with the Lustral Basin and toilet. Tucked into the center of the house, these three rooms formed a suite comparable to the Queen's Megaron suite in the Palace. On the upper story (not preserved) there may have been an open verandah overlooking the Vlychia stream.

Beneath these central rooms of the house were two basement rooms, an outer room with three stone pillars and an inner room. That both rooms could be barred and latched from inside and outside led A. Evans to propose that the inner room, with its hoard of bronze tools,

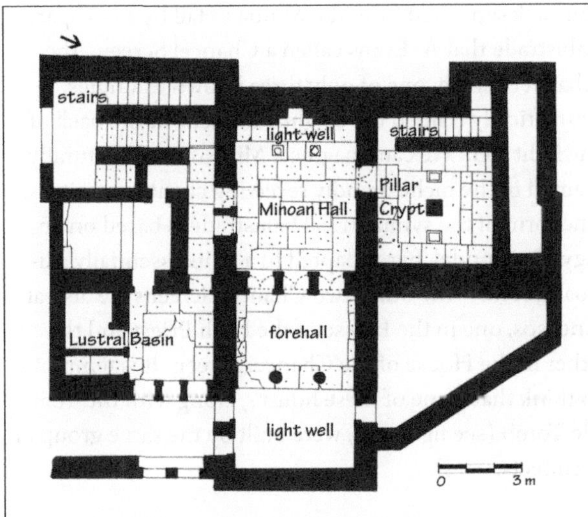

9.7. Plan. Royal Villa, Knossos. After *PM II*, fig. 225.

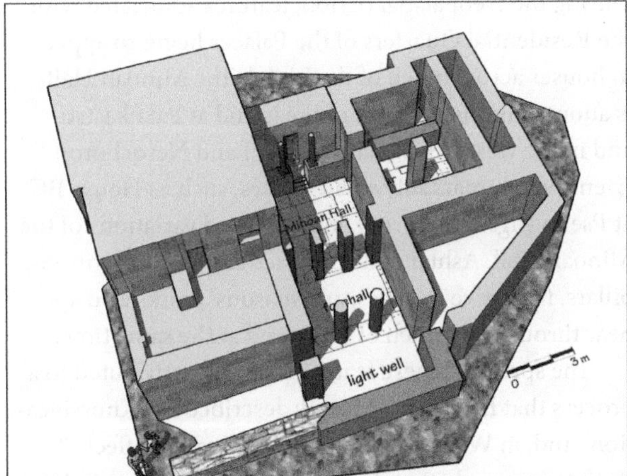

9.8. Reconstruction. Royal Villa, Knossos. After *PM II*, fig. 225.

9.9. Reconstruction. Minoan Hall in the Royal Villa, Knossos. After *PM II*, fig. 232.

was also equipped with a trapdoor from the room above. These rooms were used for storage, but, as is the case in several other houses adjacent to the Palace at Knossos, there were no storage magazines. This may mean that the residents of these houses depended on the Palace for supplies.

Along the east side of the house is the set of rooms which most clearly characterizes this type of house, the Minoan Hall consisting of an unroofed light well, a hall, and a forehall that intermediates between the two. The house might have had a secondary entrance from the lower terrace level into the light well, though the poor preservation of this part of the building means that any restoration is conjectural.

The builders of the South House used the new building technology that we saw in the Residential Quarter of the Palace. Columns, pillars, and pier-and-door partitions frequently replaced the dead mass of walls. Communication within the house was open, and windows and light wells flooded the house with light and air. In all these things, the South House is a direct product of the second architectural revolution.

The Royal Villa at Knossos

Houses like the South House share another characteristic with the Palaces, namely, the cultivation of individuality and variety. Even when using the same materials, the same techniques, and the same set of rooms and when building at the same site in topographically similar plots, builders contrived to make each building distinct. For example, at the Royal Villa (figs. 9.7–9.11)[13] the Minoan Hall–light well complex occupies the center rather than, as at the South House, one side of the house. It is flanked by two sets of rooms. On the north is a Pillar Crypt and stairway similar to those of the South House. On the south is the suite consisting of an inner room and Lustral Basin.

The forms of the rooms also differ from their counterparts in the South House. The elaborate three-part stairway in the southwest corner of the house has no close parallels anywhere. It capitalized on the house's terraced setting and provided access to the second and third stories independently. The Minoan Hall is also different. Not only is it entered through a light well, but it also has a second, much narrower light well at

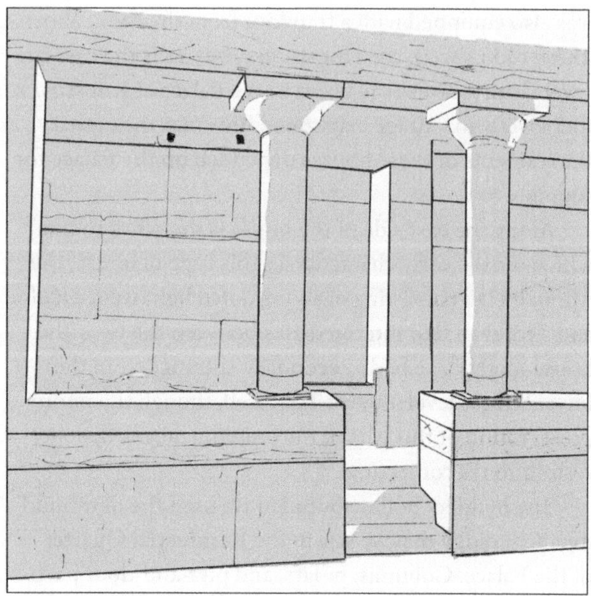

9.10. Reconstruction. Chancel Screen in the Royal Villa, Knossos.

9.11. Reconstruction. Pillar Crypt in the Royal Villa, Knossos. After *PM II*, fig. 235.

the back separated from the Minoan Hall by a two-part balustrade that A. Evans called a Chancel Screen. The Chancel Screen, one of only three known examples, dramatically framed the brightly lit niche at the back of the light well. We can imagine a Minoan architecturally framed in the niche grandly receiving clients or visitors. The form of the symmetrical balustrade is based on an Egyptian model, here adapted to a quintessentially Minoan room.[14] The other two Chancel Screens are also at Knossos, one in the House of the High Priest and the other in the House of the Chancel Screen. It is tempting to think that some of these houses, along with the Temple Tomb (see fig. 9.38), were built by the same group of architects.

The Extent of Palatialization

During the Neopalatial period, features associated with the Residential Quarters of the Palaces begin to appear in houses across much of the island. The Minoan Hall is adopted in the east end of the island at Palaikastro and in the west at Khania (fig. 9.12) and Nerochorou.[15] Even some remarkably small houses, such as House BC at Pseira (figs. 9.13, 9.14), incorporated variations of the Minoan Hall. Ashlar masonry, pier-and-door partitions, pillars, figurative frescoes, and masons' marks also appear throughout much of the island at the same time.

The spread of these features has been attributed to a process that has been variously described as "Knossification" and, in Wiener's phrase, the "Versailles effect."[16] Both terms imply that during the Neopalatial period builders around the island were imitating architectural forms associated with the Palace at Knossos. Not clear, however, is whether the process involved direct imitation of Knossian forms or the indirect emulation of forms through more local intermediaries like the Palaces at Malia and Phaistos. Neither is it clear whether or not the motivations behind the process remained the same throughout the Neopalatial period: what may have started for one set of reasons (social competition, for example) may later have been adopted for other purposes (the expression of Knossian control). Because of these ambiguities, I shall use the more general (but no less awkward) term "Palatialization" to describe the process.

While Palatializing houses had a broad geographical distribution, they were few in number. There are five

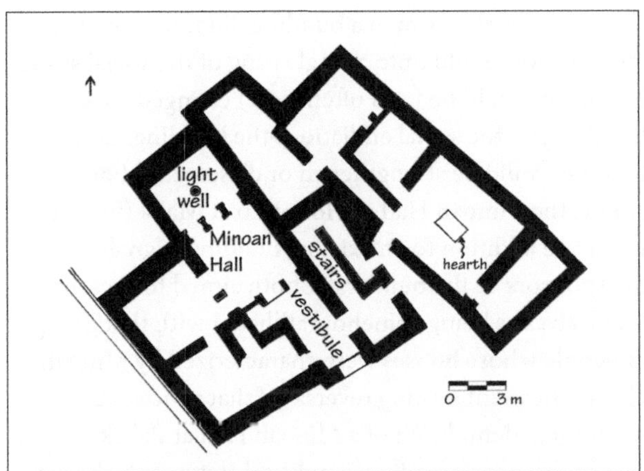

9.12. Plan. Neopalatial House, Kastelli, Khania. After E. Hallager 1990, fig. 1.

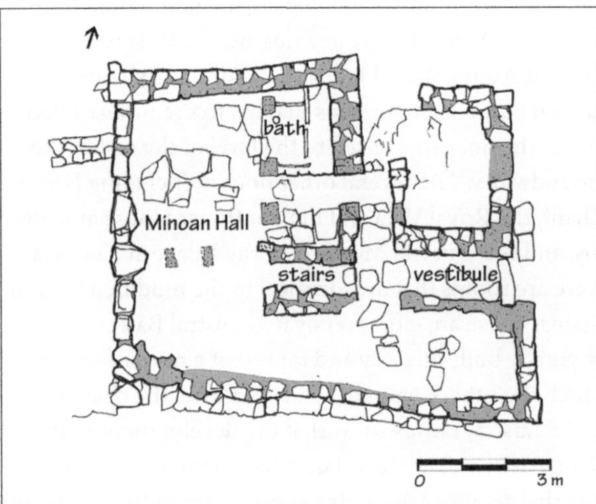

9.13. Plan. House BC, Pseira. After McEnroe 2001, fig. 39.

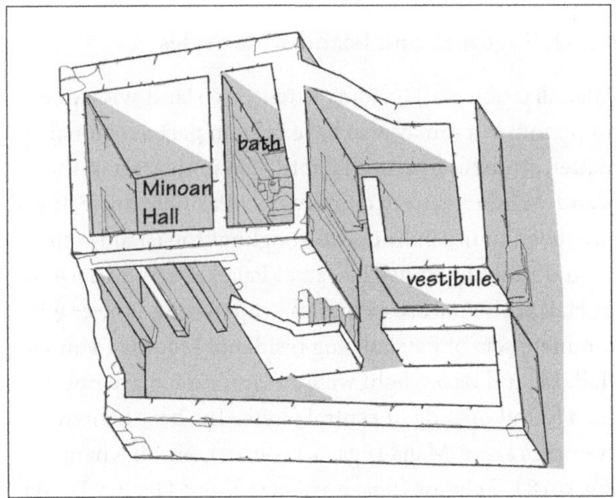

9.14. Reconstruction. House BC, Pseira. After McEnroe 2001, fig. 27.

Palaces and about two dozen Palatializing houses, less than 10 percent of the total number of excavated houses. The vast majority of houses had no Palatializing features. On the other hand, every town that has had reasonably large areas excavated (Knossos, Phaistos, Malia, Haghia Triada, Gournia, Mochlos, Pseira, Palaikastro, and Zakros) had at least one Palatializing building. Presumably every Minoan was aware of the phenomenon.

The Date of Palatialization

In 1982 Driessen posed an important rhetorical question: "The Minoan Hall in Domestic Architecture on Crete: to be in Vogue in Late Minoan IA?"[17] This article was perhaps the first attempt to date the process of Palatialization, a phenomenon Driessen assigned to LM IA. Driessen and Macdonald investigated this process more thoroughly in 1997 and came to the conclusion that the process of emulating Palatial forms reached its peak in LM IA and dramatically declined over the course of LM IB.[18]

The decline was not universal, however. During LM IB builders added the ashlar facade to the so-called Palace at Gournia and perhaps endeavored to incorporate (or "Centralize") the Public Court. Recently J. Soles described a similar process at Mochlos in LM IB.[19] Similarly, the major constructions of the Palaces at Zakros and Phaistos also date to late LM IA and LM IB. In other words, while the Palatializing process may have begun in LM IA, it continued during LM IB at sites in various parts of the island.

Palatialization and Social Identity

Driessen and Macdonald explained that the process of Palatialization was not simply a matter of being fashionable. Its cost in human and material resources indicates that monumental architecture was first and foremost the expression of power, wealth, and authority.[20] For the elite sponsors that built them, monumental Minoan buildings were a primary means of establishing and maintaining a place in the larger political and economic order—a proclamation and display of social identity. On the other hand, there is no consensus as to how the political and economic order was organized.

One view, held by A. Evans and more recently reiterated by P. Warren and P. Betancourt, sees this as a top-down hierarchical ranking with Knossos in political control of the entire island.[21] In contrast to this hierarchical model, another interpretation would explain the potential relationships between the houses and the Palaces as being more complex and subject to change.[22] Rather than having been imposed from a central authority, the pattern might reflect competitive social climbing. By emulating the Palaces, the elite owners of monumental Minoan houses might even have been encroaching upon Palatial social and economic prerogatives.[23]

This second approach, anticipated by J. Cherry years ago, suits the evidence better, even though (or perhaps because) it involves greater complexity.[24] Unlike the Final Palatial period, when the bureaucratic administration of most of the island was for a brief time in the hands of the Knossos regime, there is no clear evidence that this was the case in the Neopalatial period. In the Neopalatial period, the Linear A economic administration was distributed among a variety of sites, and the interactions among them are likely to have been complicated and subject to change. For example, political and economic relationships among Haghia Triada, Kommos, and Phaistos shifted several times over the course of the long Neopalatial period.[25]

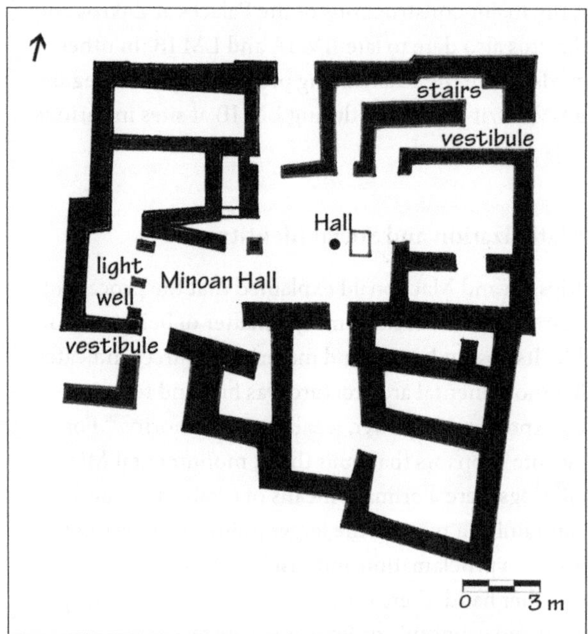

9.15. Plan. House Zb, Malia. After Deshayes and Dessenne 1959, pl. 3.

Similarly, the form of a building did not permanently lock the household onto a single rung of the social scale, for houses could be (and often were) changed. With the changes, the social affiliations the buildings aimed to imply could be strengthened or dissolved.[26] For example, the Minoan Hall in House Zb at Malia (fig. 9.15) was a late addition to an existing building, signaling that the sponsors or the builders or both aimed to present themselves as being somehow affiliated with that group of people whose houses were characterized by Minoan Halls.[27] In an interesting reversal of that process, the intentional demolition of a Minoan Hall at Palaikastro was, in Driessen's reading, a political statement: the erasure of an undesired Knossian symbol.[28]

Lustral Basins are another example of ongoing building renovations. In several houses, including the Little Palace, the South House at Knossos, the Villa of the Lilies at Amnisos, and Houses A and C at Tylissos, the sunken basins and the steps that led to them were filled in and the floor was raised to the level of the rest of the ground story.[29] At several other houses, including Nirou Khani, the Royal Villa and the Southeast House at Knossos, and the Queen's Megaron in the Palace at Knossos, there are rooms that are identical to the modified Lustral Basins. These are either renovated Lustral Basins or were originally built this way and represent a newer form to which the others aspired.[30] In either case, the changes in the Lustral Basins show that the development of the Neopalatial architectural language was an evolving process that required the active engagement of the residents and their builders.

Local, Regional, and Island-wide Styles

Palatialization was, to some extent, an island-wide phenomenon, but it may also have been in part a regional matter, stronger in central Crete than in the rest of the island. While a variety of individual Palatializing features have been found in houses throughout the island—the Lustral Basin in House B 1-22 at Palaikastro and a Minoan Hall at Khania are examples—up to now, houses with complete sets of Palatializing residential rooms (Minoan Hall, Lustral Basin, light well, Pillar Crypt) have not been found outside of central Crete. The best-known examples are at Malia (figs. 9.15–9.17), Nirou Khani (fig. 9.18), Tylissos (figs. 9.19–9.21), and Haghia Triada (figs. 9.22, 9.23).[31]

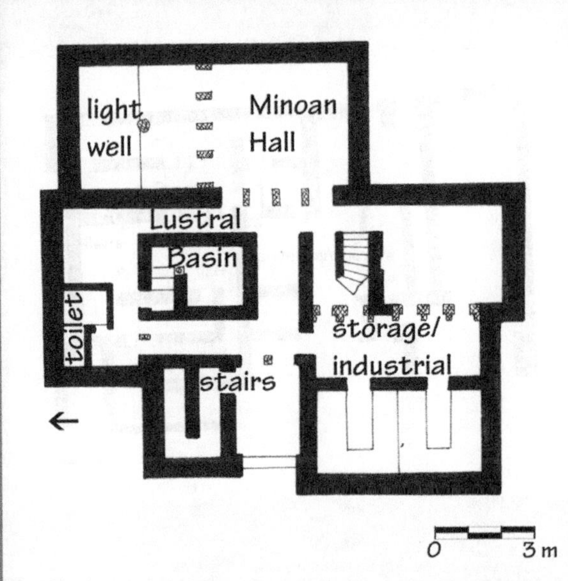

9.16. Plan. House Da, Malia. After Demargne and Gallet de Santerre 1953, pl. LXV.

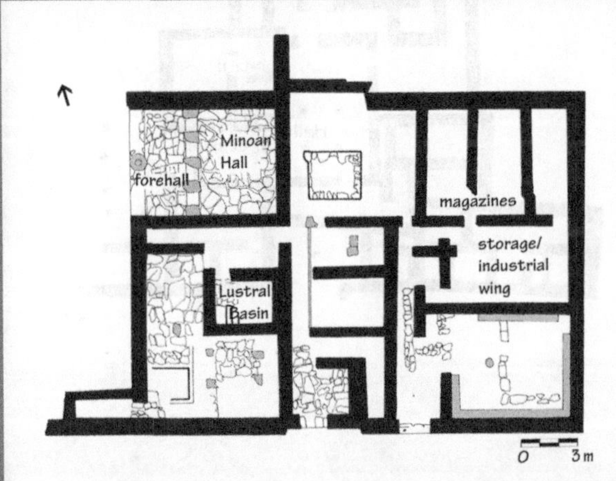

9.17. House Za, Malia. After Demargne and Gallet de Santerre 1953, pl. LXVI.

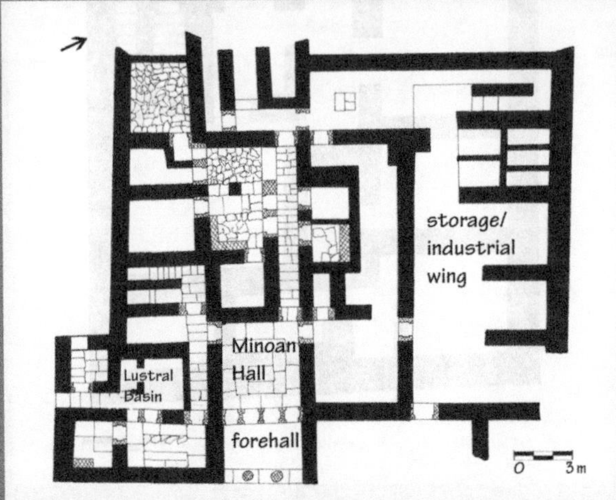

9.18. Plan. Nirou Khani. After *PoC*, fig. 31.

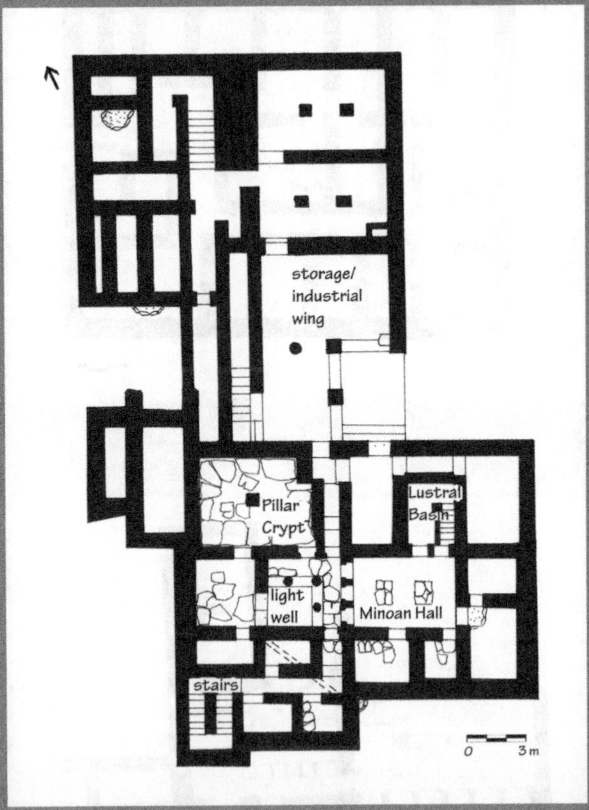

9.19. Plan. House A, Tylissos. After Hazzidakis 1934, Pl. 6.

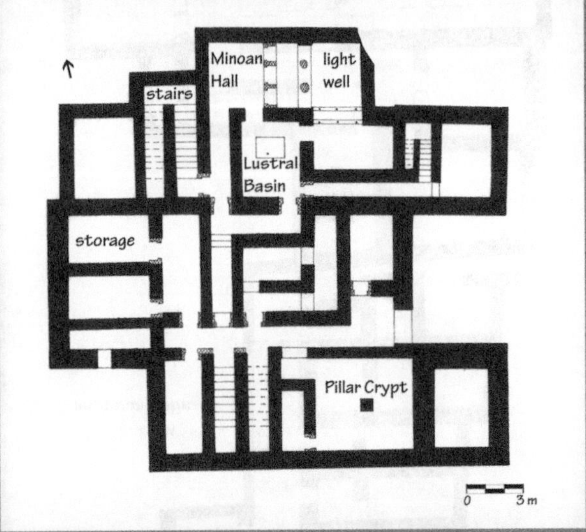

9.20. Plan. House C, Tylissos. After Hazzidakis 1934, Pl. 6.

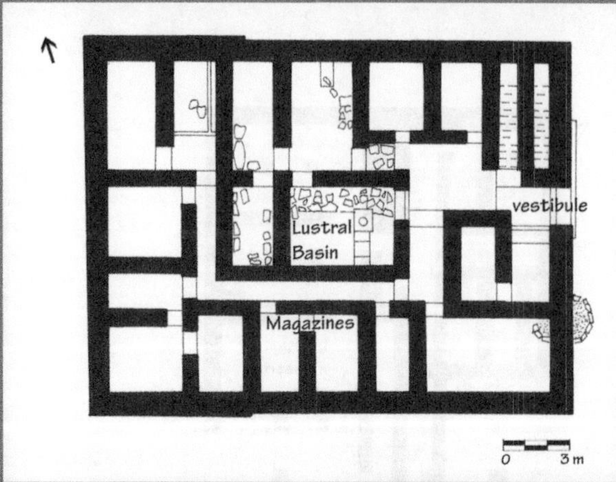

9.21. Plan. House B, Tylissos. After Hazzidakis 1934, Pl. 6.

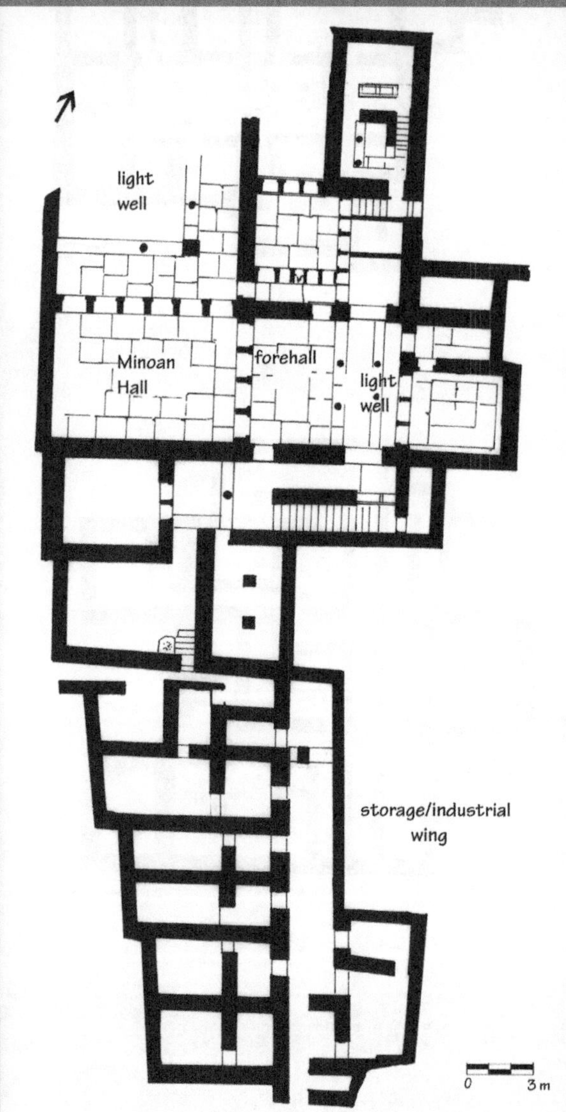

9.22. Plan. House A, Haghia Triada. After Di Vita and La Regina 1984, fig. 230.

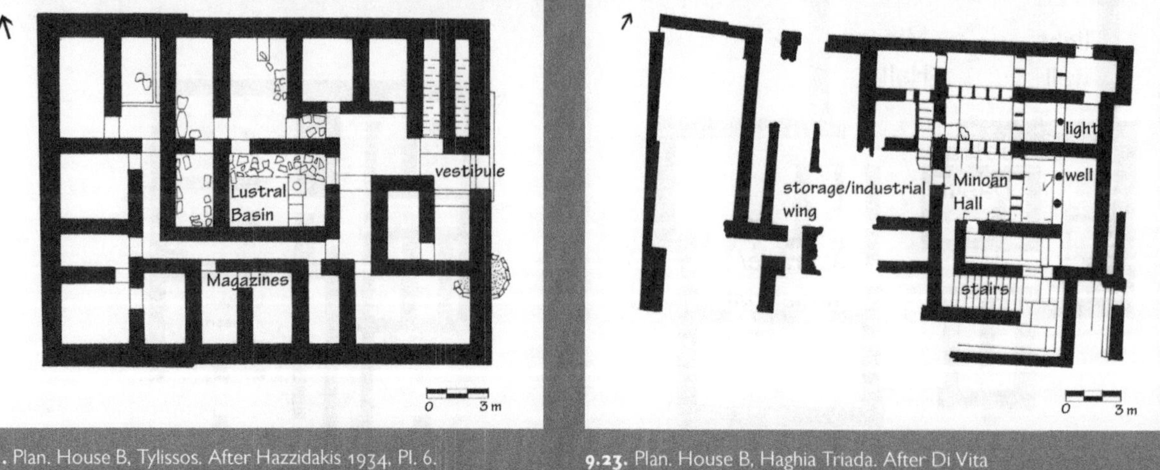

9.23. Plan. House B, Haghia Triada. After Di Vita and La Regina 1984, fig. 230.

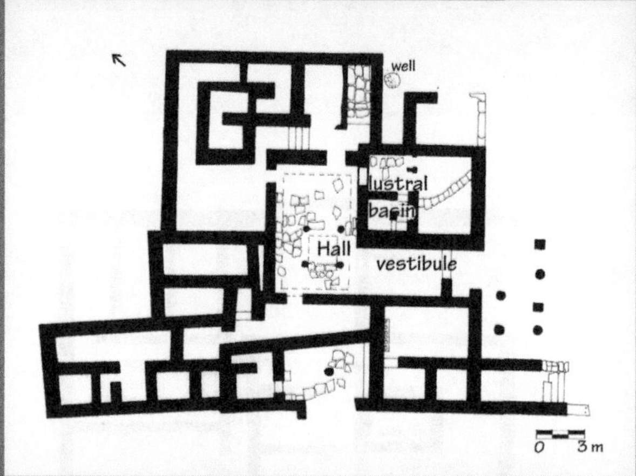

9.24. Plan. House B 1–22, Palaikastro. After Bosanquet 1901–1902, pl. XX.

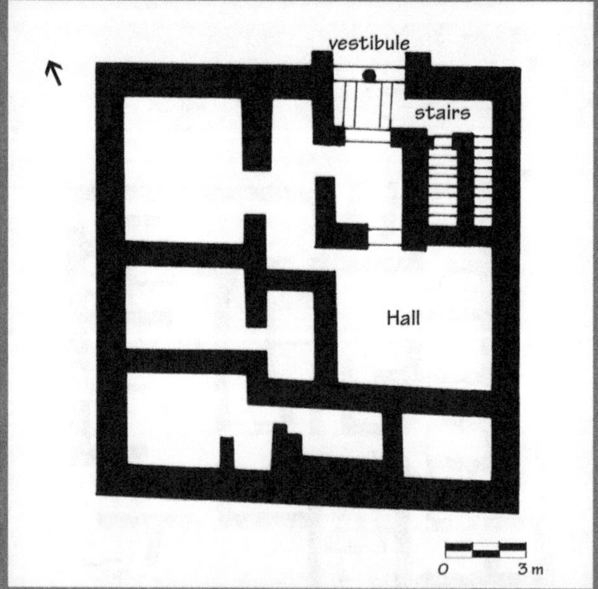

9.25. Plan. House G, Zakros. After Hogarth 1900–1901, p. 138, fig. C.

Even these houses are different from the houses built next to the Palace at Knossos in that they had separate wings devoted to agricultural storage and industry. In most cases a single door connects the storage and industrial wing with the main body of the house; the wings were built of rubble and mud brick and lacked the elaborate features of the residential wings.

Pithoi found in the magazines of the service quarters were used primarily for the storage of agricultural produce. They were also used for various specialized industries, as shown by the finds in House Za at Malia and House A at Tylissos.[32] Sometimes costly goods and records were also stored in these wings. For example, a stock of copper ingots and Linear A tablets was found in the east service quarters of House A at Haghia Triada. More often, however, expensive metal was kept in storage closets of the residential wings. Many storage and industrial wings had second stories (Tylissos A, Tylissos C, Little Palace, Malia Da), while others had only a single story (Nirou Khani, Malia Za). In a few cases, large houses were associated with separate storage and industrial annexes. Building B at Tylissos (see fig. 9.21), for example, was attached to House A by means of a bridge in the same way that the Unexplored Mansion was attached to the Little Palace at Knossos.

Purely local (as opposed to regional) traditions also continued to play a major role in this period. House B 1-22 at Palaikastro is a good example (fig. 9.24). In the center of the building, the largest room is what Driessen calls a Palaikastro Hall (or PKH).[33] Unlike the familiar Minoan Hall, with its pier-and-door partition and light well, the Palaikastro Hall has a sunken square area framed by four columns, rather like the later Roman *impluvium*. Other examples of this unique feature have been found in blocks Gamma, Delta, and Sigma at Palaikastro, but at no other sites.

The houses at nearby Zakros were different from the Palaikastro houses. House G (fig. 9.25) is a good example. As L. Platon has noted, the large Zakros houses are characterized by their remarkably square plans.[34]

9.26. Gournia from the east. Photo by author.

They are entered by a large vestibule which gave access to rooms used for service, storage, and industry on the ground floor and, by means of a stairway, to the living quarters on the upper story. These houses, along with smaller houses and supplementary structures, formed the basic matrix of the town before the new, Knossian Palace was inserted into their midst.[35]

Gournia

From 1901 through 1904 H. Boyd (and, later, H. Hawes) conducted one of the earliest American excavations in Crete at Gournia on the Isthmus of Hierapetra (figs. 9.26–9.30).[36] More than a century later it is still the site that gives visitors the best impression of life in a typical Minoan village. The main part of the town was built over the top of a low ridge. Already sizeable in the Protopalatial period, by the Neopalatial period it covered about 4 hectares and had a population of perhaps fourteen hundred people.[37]

Boyd and her team excavated more than forty substantial houses. Most of the Gournia houses were about 80–100 m² in total ground-floor area. These houses were larger than their recent Cretan counterparts (see fig. 9.28). In 1948 the average floor space (not including the thicknesses of the walls) of houses in villages was

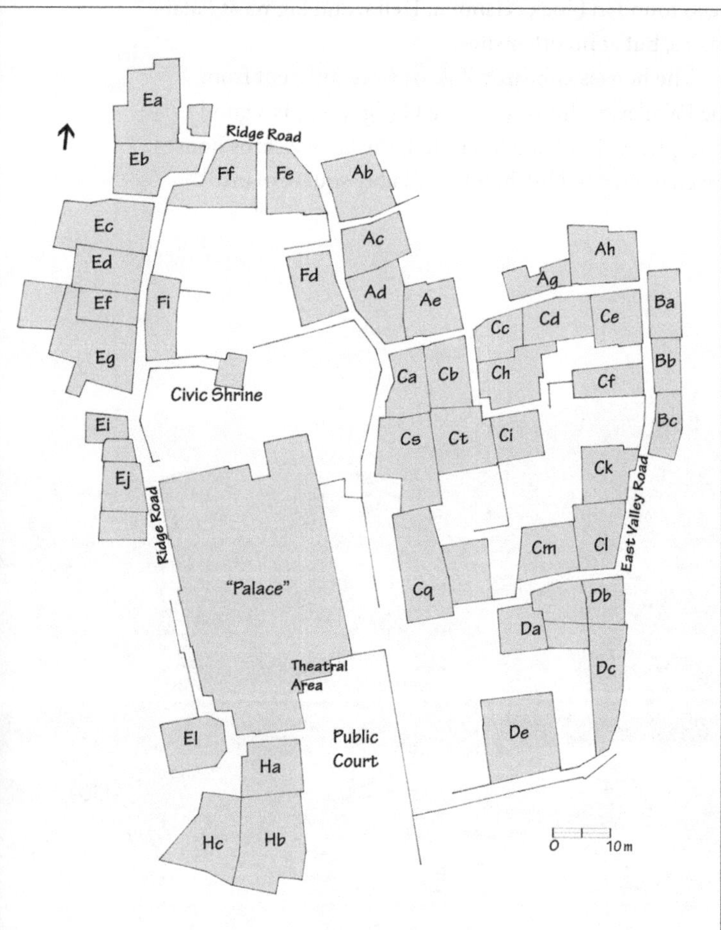

9.27. Gournia. After *Gournia*, plan.

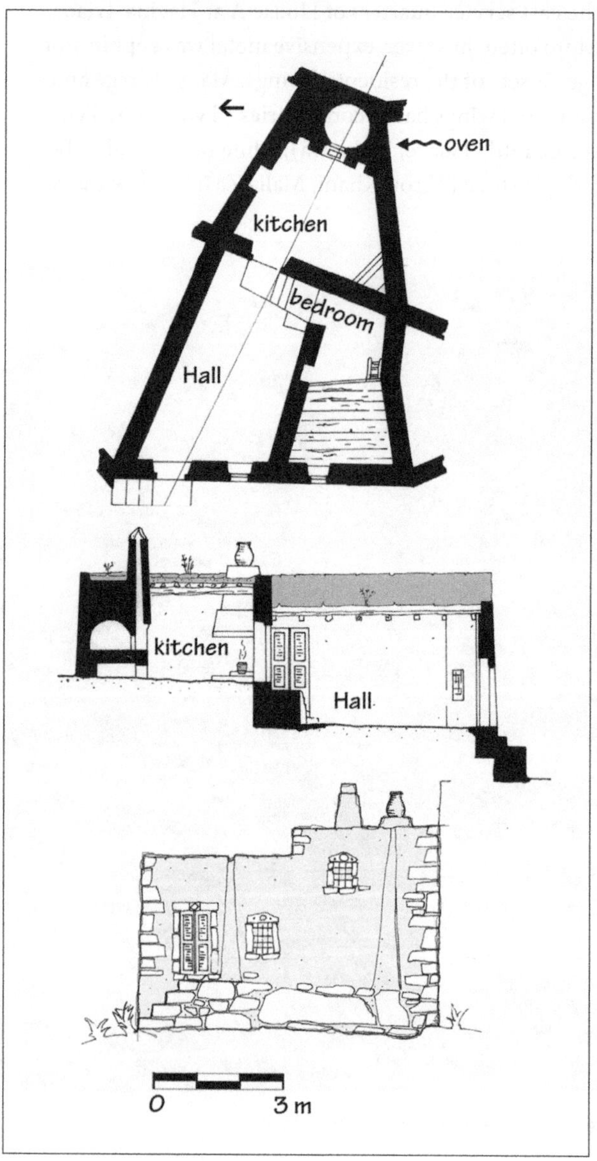

9.28. Plan, section, and elevation. Modern traditional house, Achladia. After Vasileidades 1976, fig. 148.

56 m^2 and in cities only 39 m^2.[38] The figure for the Minoan houses does not even take the second stories into consideration.

House Ck (see fig. 9.29) is a typical Gournia house.[39] It was one of the later structures on the east slope, built on ground that sloped gently down from southwest to northeast. Four steps led up to the door from the street. Inside the door was a vestibule, from which one could proceed to the other ground-story spaces. The largest of these was the hall, a central, multifunctional living space. The remaining ground-story rooms were used for storage and industry. The house had two stairways, one located next to the hall and providing almost direct access from the entrance to the upper-story residential rooms, the other near the southwest corner, just off the hall. The plans of the houses at Gournia vary according to the shape of the available lot, giving each house a unique exterior trace. Nevertheless most of the houses had more or less the same set of rooms (see fig. 9.31). Similar houses have been found throughout central and eastern Crete (fig. 9.30).[40]

Most of these houses had a second story. Although no example is preserved in Crete, there is abundant evidence concerning the general appearance and use of these upper stories from Thera. To some extent, the arrangement of the upper-story rooms can also be estimated from clues like the varying thickness of the ground-story walls, the location of the stairways and doorless spaces, objects or building materials fallen into the ground-floor rooms, and the locations of ground-story halls.

An MM III house model from Archanes gives another indication of how these houses might have originally looked (fig. 9.32). Its vestibule, lit by a large window, provides access to the ground floor rooms and to a stairway leading to the upper story. The house represented in the model is more elaborate than most of the houses at Gournia. On the ground floor it has a main room with a central column and, in addition, a version of the Minoan Hall that consists of hall, forehall, and light well.

9.29. House Ck, Gournia. After *Gournia*, plan.

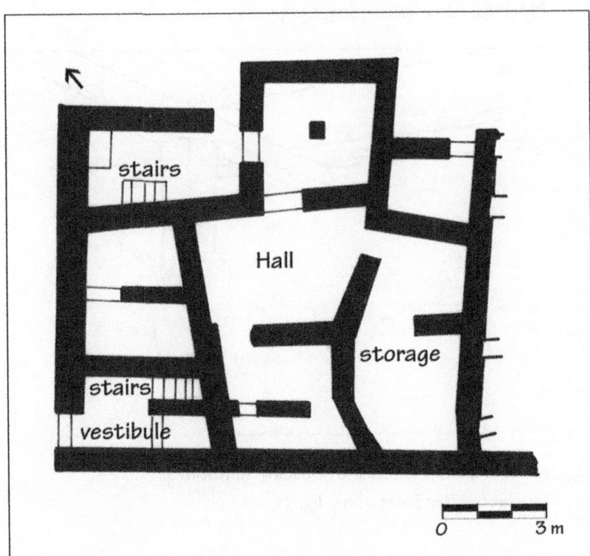

9.30. Plan. House P 7–16, Palaikastro. After Dawkins, 1904–1905, pl. 13.

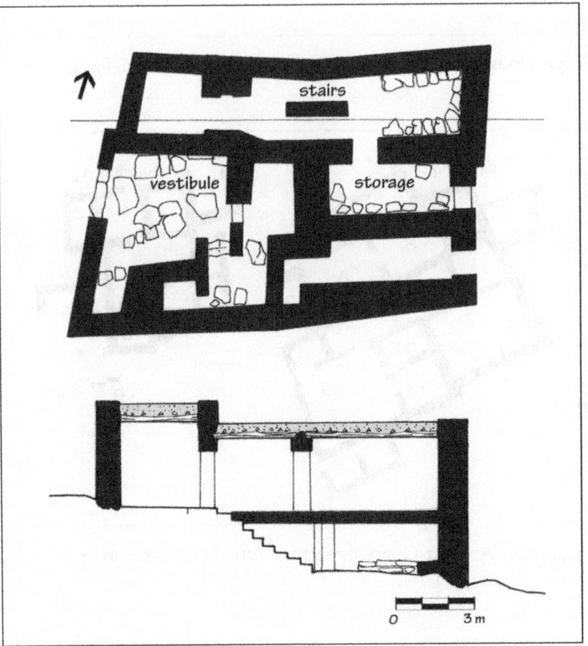

9.31. Plan and section. House Ad, Gournia. After *Gournia*, plan.

Nearly all the people who lived in the houses at Gournia were farmers, and many also worked at least part-time in various specialized crafts. The families in Houses Ac and Dd had wine presses. Metalsmiths lived in Houses Ea and Fh. The village carpenter lived in House Fa.[41] Most of the people in the village, however, were probably involved in a broad range of activities. From the House with the Snake Tube at Kommos, for example, there is evidence that the family farmed, raised animals, fished, prepared food, dined, wove fabrics, and made use of tools of bone, ground stone, and chipped stone.[42]

The best example of Neopalatial home workshops is the Artisans' Quarter at Mochlos (figs. 9.33–9.35).[43] The houses served as both residences and workshops for several crafts. Stone vase making was done in both houses (Building A, Room 1; Building B, Rooms 2 and 10). The resident of Building A also worked in bronze, while there were probably at least three looms for weaving in Building B. In addition, kilns and clay pits indicate that both households were engaged in pottery making. The Artisans' Quarter at Mochlos is somewhat reminiscent of the Protopalatial artisans' buildings in Quartier Mu at Malia (see fig. 6.15) but, unlike the earlier crafts makers,

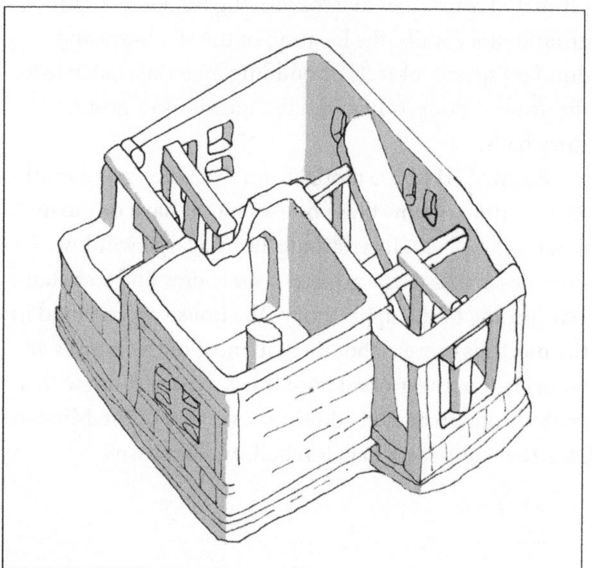

9.32. House model from Archanes. After Lembessi 1976, fig. 3.

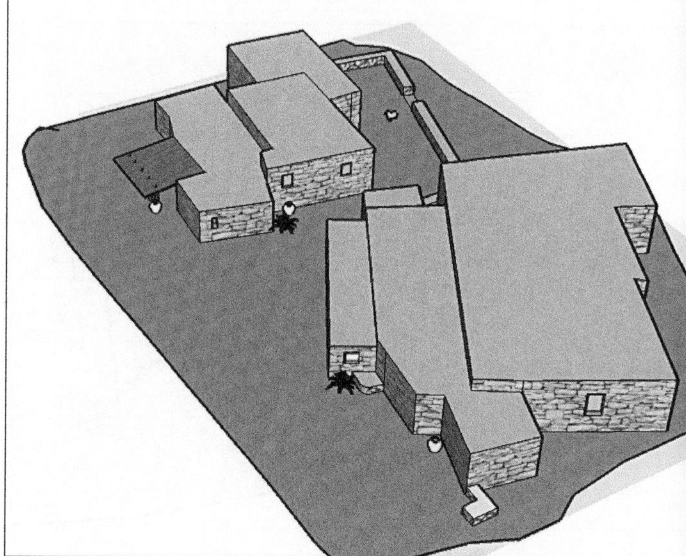

9.34. Reconstruction. Artisans' Quarter, Mochlos. After Soles 2003, fig. 5.

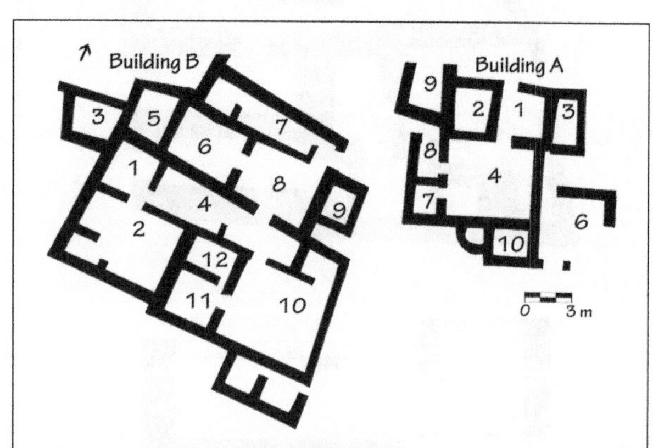

9.33. Plan. Artisans' Quarter, Mochlos. After Soles 2003, fig. 4.

9.35. Reconstruction. Interior of Building A, Room 4, Mochlos. After Soles 2003, fig. 13.

who apparently made luxury goods for the residents of the main buildings of Quartier Mu, the Mochlos artisans were freelancers employed in making utilitarian objects.[44]

House building was also a major industry. Even relatively small houses would have required the cooperation of several workers, as labor estimates for the small House AM at Pseira (fig. 9.36) suggest (see table 9.2).

Assuming a six-hour workday, four people could have built the house in slightly over three months, working, one assumes, during the part of the year when they were relatively free from agricultural duties.[45] The cost of this building was, in other words, about a tenth the cost of the South House at Knossos.

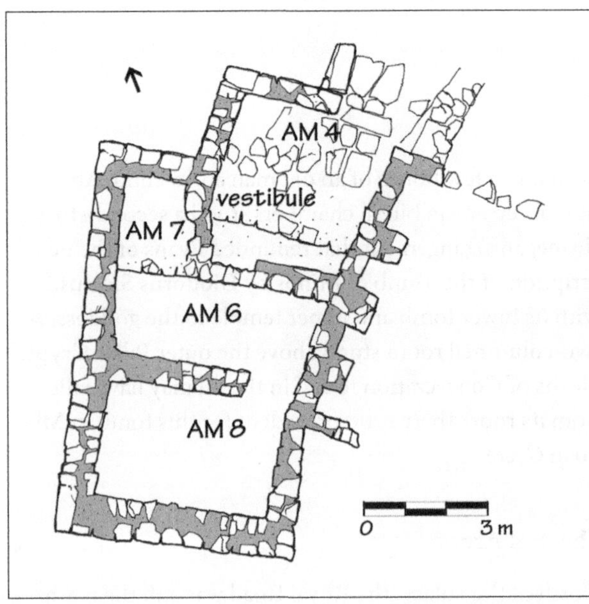

9.36. Plan. House AM, Pseira. After McEnroe 2001, fig. 46.

Towns and Cities: Knossos

Widespread archaeological surveys show that there was a significant increase in the population of the island in the Neopalatial period. New settlements were founded, and old settlements were expanded. Knossos, already large in the Protopalatial period, reached a peak of fourteen to eighteen thousand people.[46] The basic fabric of the city, however, did not change much from the Protopalatial period. The main public courts and the street system that had been laid out in the Protopalatial period remained in use.

There were a few new urban constructions. For example, a remarkable building that A. Evans named the Caravanserai was built near the Viaduct in the gulley formed by the Vlychia stream (fig. 9.37).[47] Evans pictured weary travelers pausing here to use the footbath, dining room, and stables before proceeding to the Palace. To the northwest the tiny, elegant Spring Chamber (a fountain house) was arranged at an angle to the main axis of the Caravanserai. Fresh water rises through the pebble floor to fill the central reservoir. The back wall, with its fine gypsum masonry forming a symmetrical composition with two ledges flanking a central recess with a niche for a lamp, was as refined as any of the most polished architectural elements of the Royal Villa or Palace. The specific combination of features in the Caravanserai has no precise parallel in Minoan architecture. Its use of several sorts of pools, tubs, fountains, and springs is paralleled only by the extravagances at Zakros, where a well, a spring chamber, and a circular pool were built in the Residential Quarter of the Palace (see fig. 8.6).

Table 9.2.
Labor Hours Required for House AM at Pseira

Excavating terrace	100 m^3 earth	@ .25 m^3/hr	= 400 hours
Quarrying	120 m^3 @ 4 hr/m^3		= 480 hours
Transporting materials			= 450 hours
Building walls	120 m^3 @ 10 hr/m^3		= 1,200 hours
Laying roof			= 40 hours
Total			= 2,570 labor hours

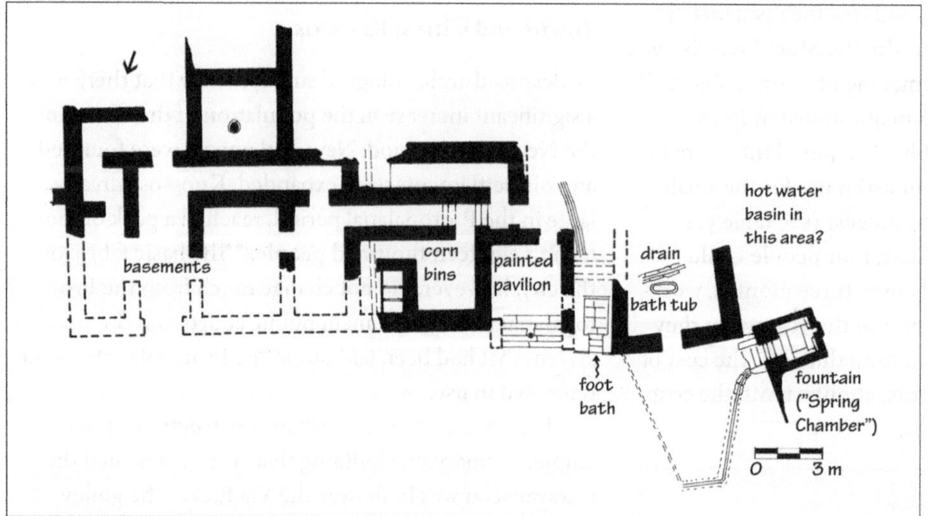

9.37. Plan. Caravanserai, Knossos. After *PM II*. fig. 48.

South of the Caravanserai, a group of Knossian architects constructed the Temple Tomb, the only monumental tomb known from the Neopalatial period (fig. 9.38).[48] The Temple Tomb was located along the road just south of the Palace at Knossos and would have been visible to all who approached the Palace from this direction. It seems to have been both private tomb and public monument. In general form, the Temple Tomb imitates on a tiny scale the layout of colossal Middle Kingdom tombs of Egypt that featured a series of symmetrical elements arranged sequentially along a central axis. Here the Egyptianizing form has been reinterpreted and combined with a series of uniquely Knossian architectural features and techniques, in the same way that the Egyptianizing Chancel Screen was adopted for a few of the houses at the site.

The Temple Tomb was set into the slope of Gypsades Hill. A narrow entrance passage led down to a two-columned portico. Beyond that was a paved court and the entrance to the inner chambers. The central passage led to a door that was fitted with a lock of the type used in the basement of the South House. Through the door was the Outer Pillar Crypt. As early as the LM IA period, this had been subdivided into a series of enclosures that contained, amidst the rubble fill, the bones of some twenty people. The central passage through the room was kept clear. At its west end, a third door led to an inner Pillar Crypt, which contained an LM IIIA deposit and a few bones of an old man and a child. Above the subterranean burial chambers stood a second-story shrine, an arrangement that reminded Evans of the description of the Tomb of Minos by Diodorus Siculus, with its lower tomb and upper temple to the goddess. A two-columned room stood above the outer Pillar Crypt. Horns of Consecration found in the fill may have fallen from its roof. There is no precedent for this tomb in Minoan Crete.

Theatral Areas

North of the Palace, the Royal Road was still the main street, now connecting the Palace with the Little Palace and the Unexplored Mansion. In the Neopalatial period the eastern end of the Royal Road was cut off by the construction of an additional bank of seats to the Theatral Area (fig. 9.39).[49] Eighteen risers, shallower than those of the southern bank, were supported on an artificial fill. The fill was held in place by retaining walls on the north and east. In the narrow space at the top of the eastern bank, between the top seat and the back retaining wall, Evans envisioned a stoa. Such a stoa might have served as a replacement for the MM portico at the top of the southern flight that was destroyed by the new walkway that cut obliquely through the seats. The junction of the new bank of seats with the old was somewhat awkward. The builders attempted to knit the seats together by overlapping the second through fifth risers of the eastern flight with the first riser of the southern bank. The leftover rectangular gap between the two banks of seats was filled with a raised platform that Evans named the Royal Box.

At Phaistos, the Neopalatial changes to the Theatral Area were different. Here, the Theatral Area was reduced in size by raising the level of the Theatral Area courtyard, which covered the lowest courses of the Old Palace facade and the first five risers of the Theatral Area. Seating capacity was reduced by half. As if in compensation, the back (north) wall was moved back about a meter, increasing the space at the top of the seats (see fig. 6.4).

Just as many houses of the Neopalatial period followed the forms of the Palaces, in a few towns residents of the largest residential structures built miniature Theatral Areas. At Gournia, a small Theatral Area was built along the south facade of the so-called Palace overlooking the north end of the Public Court (fig. 9.41).[50] Like the Theatral Area at Knossos, it consists of two banks of

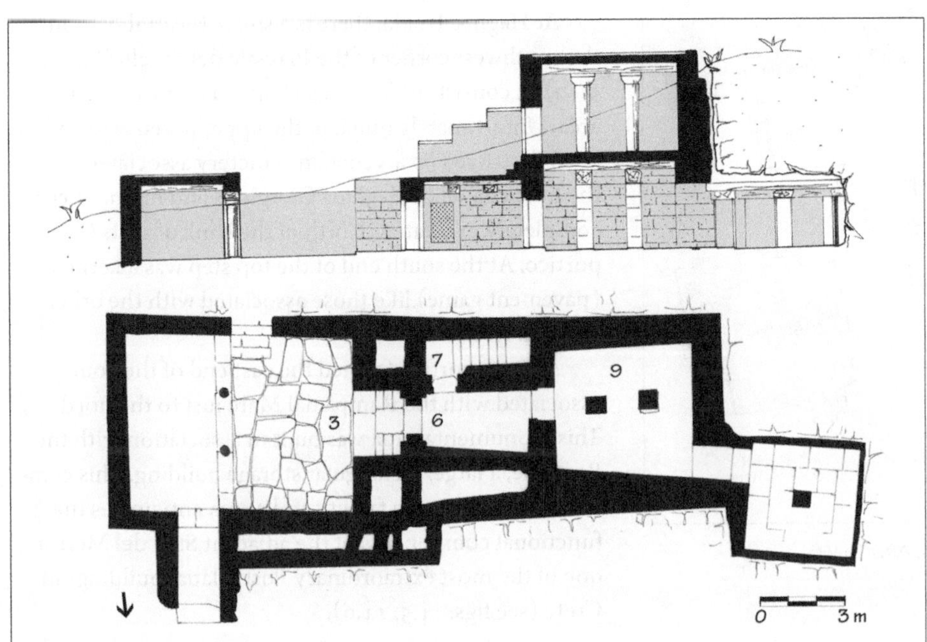

9.38. Plan and restored section. Temple Tomb, Knossos. After *PM IV*, plan.

9.39. Theatral Area, Knossos, from west. Photo by author.

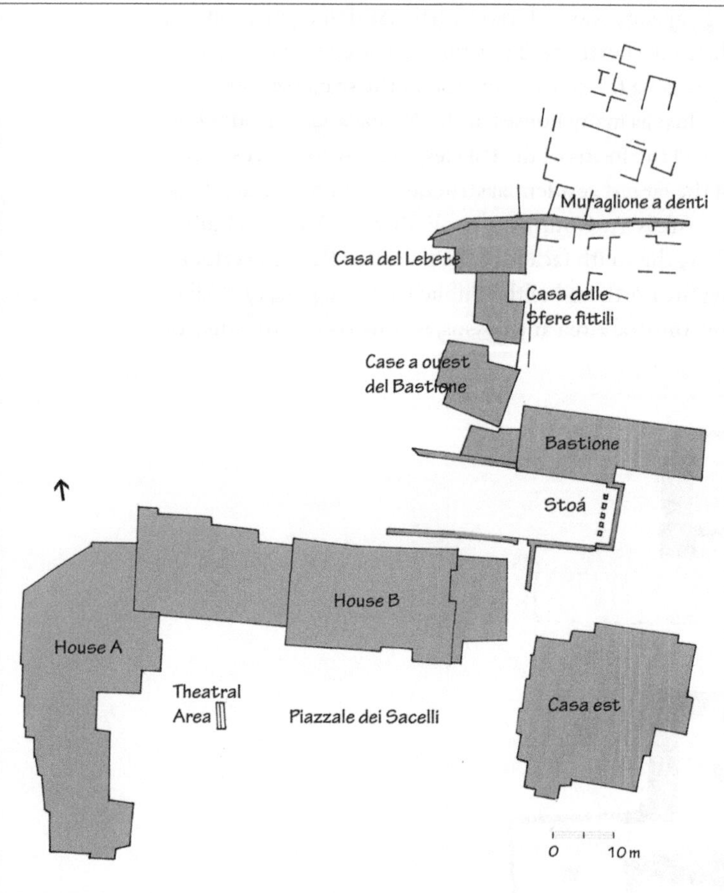

9.40. Plan. Neopalatial Haghia Triada. After Di Vita and La Regina 1984, p. 163, fig. 230.

seats that meet at a right angle. At the top of the eastern bank is a narrow pavilion whose roof was supported on three pillars, the bases of which were found tumbled into the Public Court. A pair of Horns of Consecration, also found in the court, may have belonged to the entablature of the pavilion. At the southwest corner of the Theatral Area, a second pavilion with one pillar in antis framed the northwestern edge of the Public Court. These small pavilions recall the porticoes that had been associated with the Theatral Areas since their origins in the First Palatial period.

At Haghia Triada, there is a small Theatral Area in the southwest corner of the Piazzale dei Sacelli (fig. 9.40). It consists of four steps that led up to a paved area. Unfortunately much of the upper paved area had been destroyed by a Venetian cemetery associated with the little chapel of Haghios Giorghios and has not been completely excavated. North of the bank of seats is a portico. At the south end of the top step was a kernos (pavement game) like those associated with the other Theatral Areas.

A larger portico formed the east end of the court associated with the Rampa dal Mare just to the north. This monumental stoa was built in association with the Bastione, a large, rectangular storage building. This combination of a storage facility and a stoa anticipates the functional components of the adjacent Stoà del Mercato, one of the most extraordinary Postpalatial buildings in Crete (see figs. 11.5, 11.6).

9.41. Theatral Area, Gournia, from south. Photo by author.

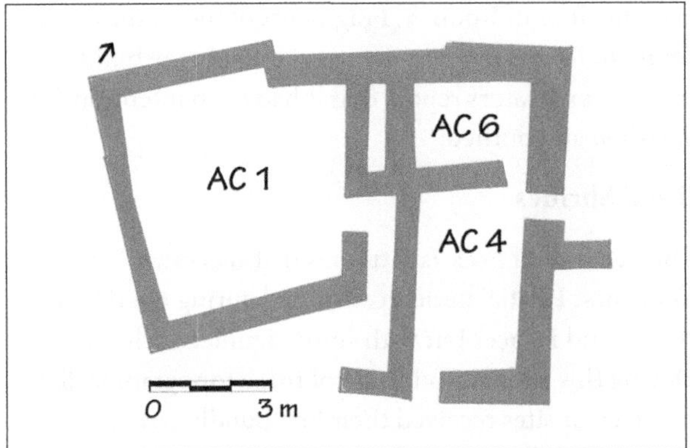

9.42. Plan. Building AC, Pseira. After McEnroe 2001, fig. 15.

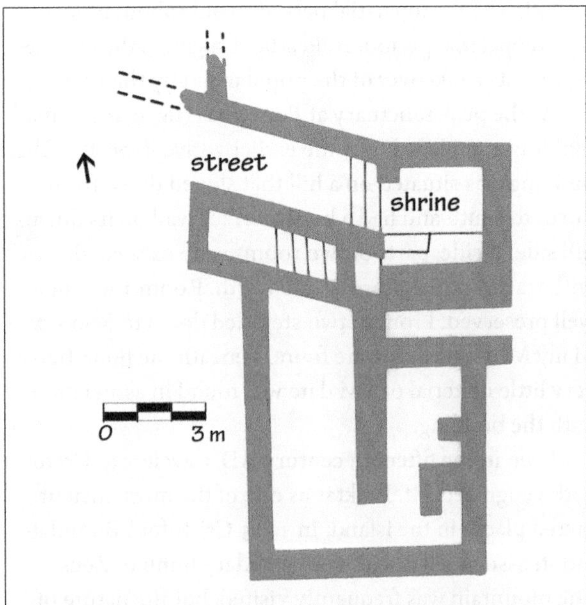

9.43. Plan. Civic Shrine, Gournia 1904. After Boyd 1904, fig. 23.

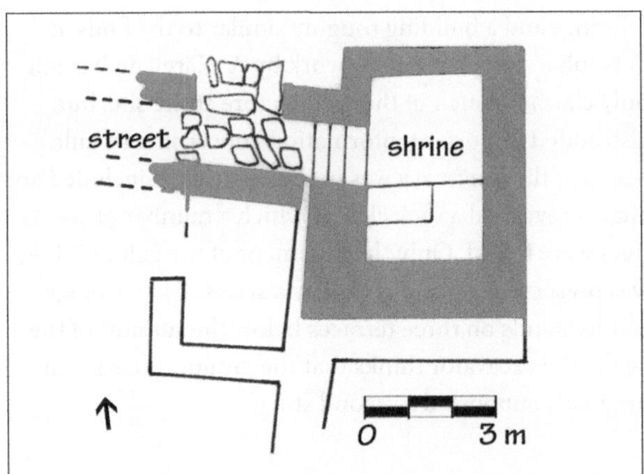

9.44. Plan. Civic Shrine, Gournia, 1908. After *Gournia*, Plan.

Urban Shrines

The evidence for independent Neopalatial shrines is sparse. The so-called Shrine (Building AC) at Pseira was almost barren of finds; only fragments of two seated women in plaster relief were found (fig. 9.42).[51] Those frescoes are the only reason for regarding the building as a shrine, and one wonders if they are sufficient evidence.

Cult equipment was found in the Civic Shrine at Gournia, but all of it dates to the LM IIIB period.[52] In LM IIIB the shrine was a single, square room with a bench against its south wall. Originally there was more to the building. Several earlier walls, still visible at the site, are shown on a plan published in 1904 but not on the final plan of 1908, in which the building is shown as a single, isolated room (figs. 9.43, 9.44).

Parts of a magnificent ivory statue of a young boy were found in the Shrine at Palaikastro in 1987 (fig. 9.45).[53] The shrine was part of a reconstruction of an existing Neopalatial building. By LM IB, however, access from the rest of the building was cut off, and the entrance to the main room (Room 2) was through a 1.60-m-wide door from the small courtyard on the north. At the same time a slab-covered pit was dug

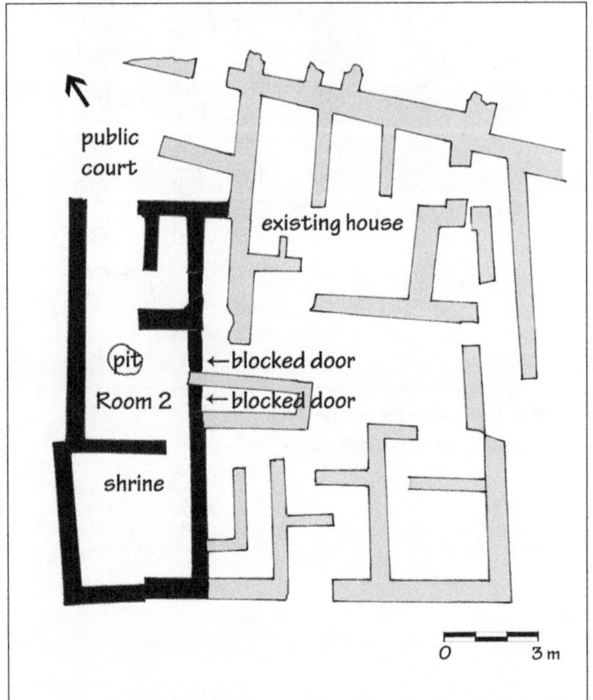

9.45. Plan. Building V, Palaikastro. After Macgillivray, Sackett et al. 1991, p. 124, fig. 2.

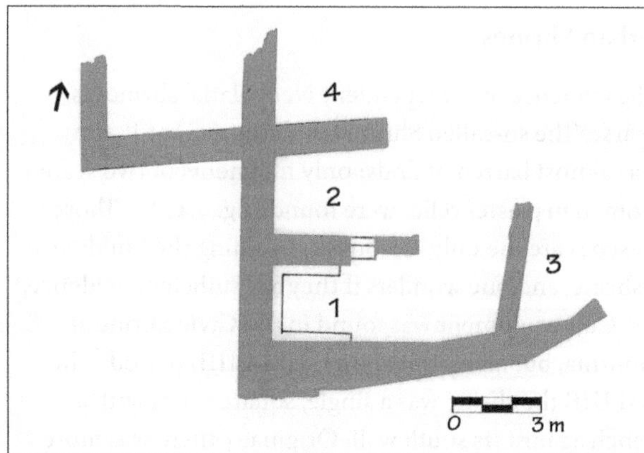

9.46. Plan. Peak sanctuary, Petsophas. After Myres 1902–1903, Pl. 7.

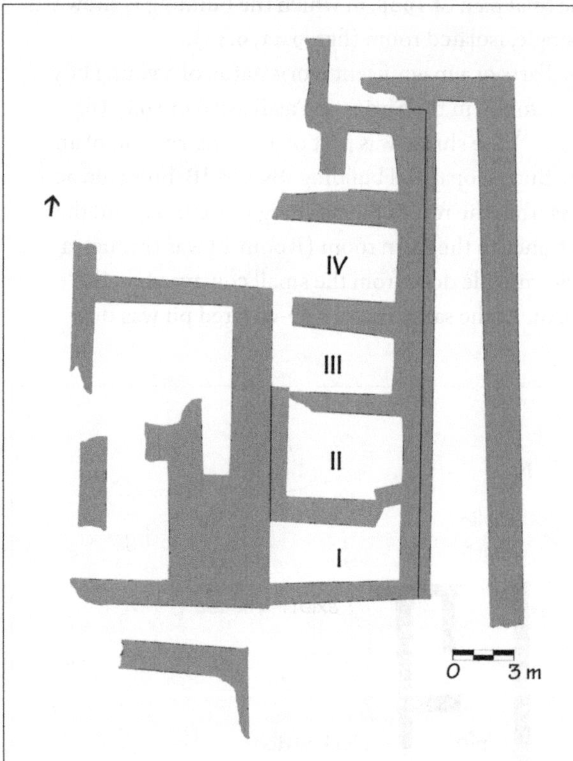

9.47. Plan. Peak sanctuary, Iouktas. After Ioannidou-Karetsou 1985, pl. IG.

into the floor of Room 2. Fragments of the statues were found in Room 2 and in the court outside the building. The excavators report that it had been intentionally smashed and burned.

Rural Shrines

The network of peak sanctuaries that was established in the first Palatial period continued during the time of the second Palaces but with some significant changes. During this later period some of these topographically spectacular sites received their first buildings, monumentalizing the popular rural cult. At the same time the number of peak sanctuaries was reduced from around thirty in the Protopalatial period to only about nine in the Neopalatial period. A. Peatfield suggests the change represents a takeover of the popular cult by the Palaces.[54]

At the peak sanctuary at Petsophas (fig. 9.46) a small building was placed over the earlier votive deposit.[55] The building was situated on a hill that sloped down from north to south and had a heavy terrace wall on its downhill side. Inside, parts of two rooms were excavated, with traces of two more on the north. Room 1 was not well preserved. From it, two steps led down to Room 2. Many MM figurines were found beneath the floor, but very little material of LM date was found in association with the building.

Even in the fifteenth century AD, travelers to Crete had recognized Mt. Iouktas as one of the most ancient sacred places in the island. In 1415 Cristoforo Buondelmonti associated it with the legendary tomb of Zeus. The mountain was frequently visited, but the nature of the ancient remains started to become clear only with the excavations of A. Evans in 1909. Evans found votive offerings and a building roughly similar to the finds at Petsophas. Supplementary work by A. Karetsou has not only clarified much of the architecture at the site, but also added important information concerning its cult. Much of the sanctuary was in the open air. It included an altar, a cave, and a rock cleft in which a number of votives were found. Only the basement of the cult building was preserved (fig. 9.47). Today a series of five storage rooms stands on three terraces below the summit of the peak. The excavator thinks that the ground-floor rooms originally supported a second story.

Gournia and Minoan Town Planning

Like most Minoan settlements, the town of Gournia was built on a hill. The narrow cobblestone streets either followed the contours like the circular Ridge Road and the East Valley Road, or they ran at right angles to the contours as did the three major ascents on the east. Streets that cut across the contours were stepped. Remarkably few Minoan streets were suitable for wheeled traffic, and none bear the telltale ruts that would have resulted from routine use of vehicles with wheels. As at many sites, the streets at Gournia had been originally built in the Protopalatial period during the great era of civic architecture. The Neopalatial streets followed the established routes.[56] As the population grew over the course of the period, every available space was filled in, sometimes resulting in oddly shaped houses.

The houses at Gournia were well suited to the compactness of the community. They shared materials, techniques, features, and plans with neighboring houses. They were arranged contiguously so that the town resembled a honeycomb of spaces. Walls between the houses were either party walls of a single thickness or double walls, as the occasion required. Builders paid special attention to the facades facing the streets. These were always the best-built walls of the houses, and they joined the street walls of the neighboring houses to form a continuous facade lining the street (fig. 9.48). Visitors to the town were routed through a maze of narrow streets lined with massive walls, unable to see beyond the buildings that were constantly at arm's length. The arrangement was well suited to defense.

9.48. Street wall, Gournia. Photo by author.

Eventually all the major routes through the town found their way into the Public Court that fills the level saddle of land near the center of the excavated area (see fig. 9.27). The contrast between the compressed streets and the broad, open expanse of the Public Court would have been dramatic as visitors stepped into the Public Court. The space suddenly expanded, and the light and heat of the sun replaced the shade of the narrow lanes. Visitors got their first view of the ashlar facade of the Palace through the screen of pillars behind the small Theatral Area.

Houses, Towns, and History

In *The Troubled Island*, Driessen and Macdonald tried to demonstrate that the effects of the eruption of Thera in the late seventeenth century BC had a more serious impact on Crete than is generally assumed.[57] In their view, the island had been devastated by earthquake damage, a tsunami, ash fall, crop failure, and economic and political confusion from which it never fully recovered. Rather than one of the high points of Minoan history, they described the LM IB period as the twilight of Evans's New Era.

Some sites—Galatas and Kommos are good examples—fit the *Troubled Island* pattern, but many others do not. As we have seen, most of the construction of the Palaces at Zakros and Phaistos dates to late LM IA and LM IB. In addition, monumental ashlar facades were built at Gournia, Mochlos, Haghia Triada, and Palaikastro in LM IB.[58] Following the Thera eruption a period of recovery lasted for about a century until around 1490 BC, when every village and city on the island, with a single exception, was destroyed, burned, and abandoned.[59] Towns like Gournia were left as empty as they are today.

Some propose that the destructions were caused by another earthquake, but the scenario looks more like war. Specific buildings were targeted, particularly administrative buildings. Unburied bodies left in the ruins

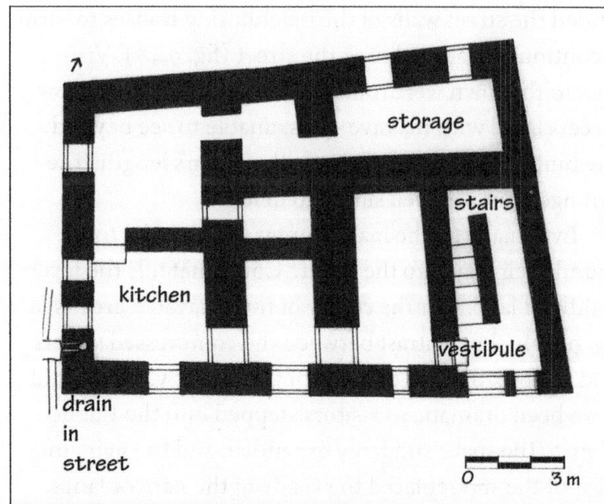

9.49. Ground story, West House, Akrotiri, Thera. After Marinatos 1984, p.13.

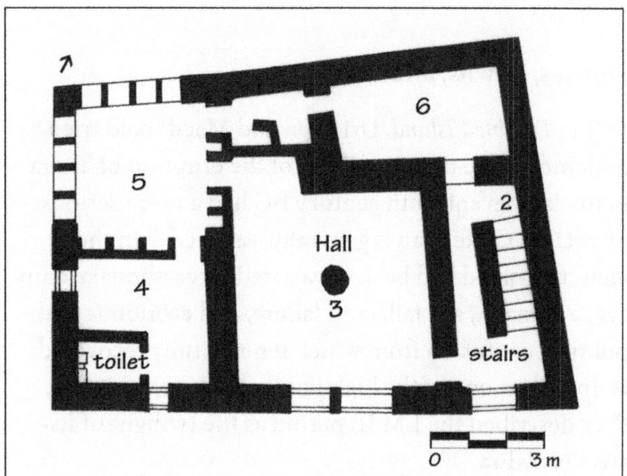

9.50. Plan. Second story, West House, Akrotiri, Thera. After Marinatos 1984, p. 13.

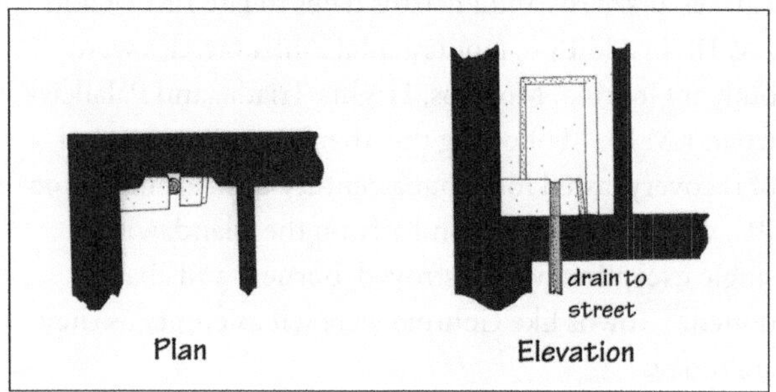

9.51. Restored plan and section. Toilet in Room 4a, West House, Akrotiri, Thera. After Palyvou 1986, fig. 6.

of the village of Mochlos and the bodies of butchered children at Knossos offer glimpses of extraordinary violence.[60] Only Knossos was spared, and its Palace would soon be occupied by a new regime of Mycenaeans and their Minoan collaborators.

Postscript: The West House at Akrotiri, Thera

The West House at Akrotiri is not on Crete, but its remarkable preservation and its similarity to a number of Minoan houses are instructive (figs. 9.49–9.53).[61] Among other things, it gives us a much better understanding of construction techniques that are similar to those used on Crete.[62]

The visitor to Thera today can make out the large ashlar blocks that were used as quoins at the angles of the building and to border the window and door frames. The timbers of these frames have now been restored in concrete. The bulk of the building was not ashlar, but rubble masonry coated with a thick layer of reddish brown stucco. In the West House carefully trimmed ashlar blocks were used only where they would be structurally useful, to frame the openings and to provide strength at the angles of the building. The builders apparently cared little for the appearance of the meticulously cut blocks themselves—they were covered with stucco—but they may have appreciated the sharp angles and straight lines they were able to create with them.[63]

Carpentry was simple on the ground floor, where small, horizontal timbers were used within the walls to help consolidate the rubble masonry.[64] Much larger timbers were used for framing the doors and the surprising number of windows, which afford every room its own source of light.[65] On the upper story, where the walls did not have to support as much weight as those of the ground floor, an extensive series of timbers was used to form the pier-and-door partitions and elaborate series of windows that extended around two walls of the northwestern room. These windows allowed this corner of the house to be as open or as closed as the residents liked. Mud brick partition walls were common on the upper floor. These light, flexible walls were used to screen off spaces like the toilet and, in the northwest room, to form a series of niches along the inner walls of the room.

The West House was moderate in size (ca. 150 m^2 on the ground floor), but its situation within the settlement was imposing. It was arranged at an angle to most of the other known buildings in the village, its impressive front (south) facade forming one side of a triangular courtyard. In overall proportions the building was a low, rectangular block. The house had two main stories with perhaps a third-story room covering the stairwell and providing access to the roof. From the outside, however, the division between the stories was partly obscured by the inconsistent positioning and shapes of the windows.

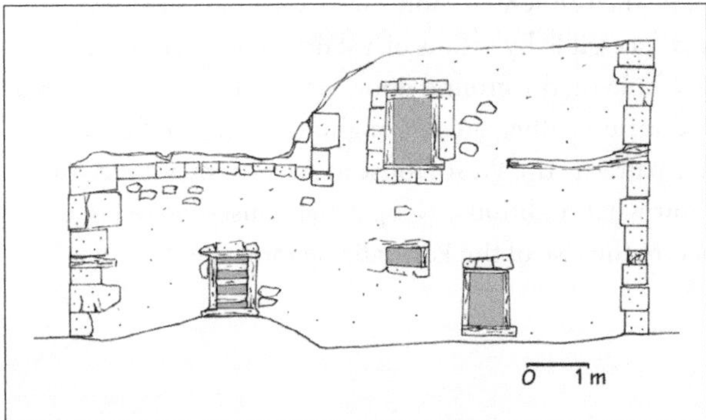

9.52. Elevation. West facade, West House, Thera. After Palyvou 1986, fig. 7.

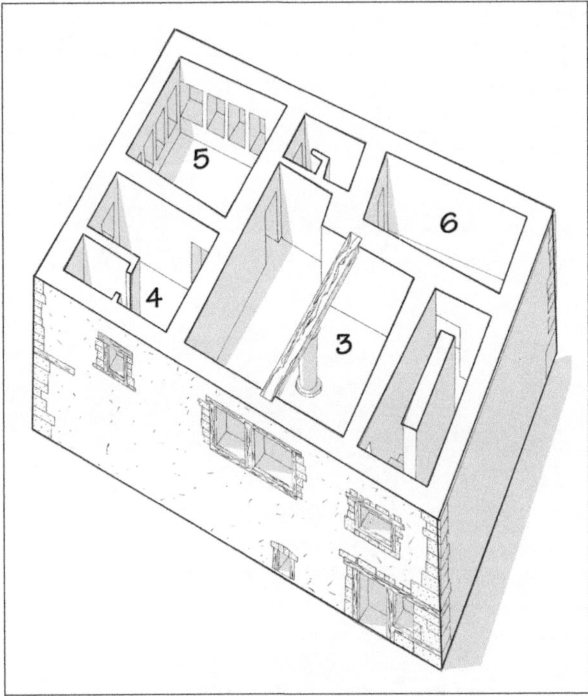

9.53. Reconstruction. West House, Akrotiri, Thera. Based on Palyvou 1986, fig. 4.

The entrance to the building was in the southeast corner. A single door with adjacent window led to a vestibule. As in the smaller houses at Gournia, the vestibule was the key to communication within the house. It was intermediary between the public space of the street and the private space of the house. From it the visitor could either go to the other ground-story rooms through the door on the left or proceed upstairs. Seven other rooms were located on the ground floor. They formed the service quarters of the house and were used for the storage of food, household goods, and raw materials. The room in the southwest corner was used partly as a kitchen and partly for bronze working. With the exception of two small rooms near the center of the house, each of the rooms was windowed.

The West House is one of the very few Bronze Age buildings in which two stories have been excavated, and it thus offers a rare opportunity to see how the ground-floor plan actually relates to the plan of the upper story.[66] The two floors differ slightly. Most of the upper-story walls were thinner than those of the ground floor. Some of the upper rooms were larger than the lower rooms. For example, a single large room with a central column stands above three ground-floor rooms, using the thick wall between them as support for its column. In other cases, such as the toilet, thin mud brick or *pisé* partitions could be used to define upper-story spaces without following the lines of the ground-floor walls. In conversation, J. Shaw suggested that the house might have had a partial third story, a single room covering the stairwell and providing access to the roof. The Archanes model and the Miniature Fresco from the West House depict a similar arrangement. A large window lit the landing above the vestibule. From the landing, a single door led to a hall with a central column and broad window overlooking the court below. The room was used, among other things, for weaving. From the inside, the reason the central support for the window was placed slightly to the west of the middle of the sill becomes obvious: the support had to align with the central column to support the main roof beam. The hall intervened between the stair landing and the more secluded rooms on the western side of the house.

In the northwest corner of the hall, a door led to an inner Room 5. Its north and west walls were made almost entirely of windows, and the shapes of the windows were reiterated in the series of pisé niches that formed the south and east walls. Frescoed friezes, including the famous Miniature Fresco and a Nilotic scene, ran around the tops of the walls. Frescoes of nude boys holding fish stood in the southwest and northeast corners of the room. Two other doors led out of Room 5. One in the northeast corner led, via a corridor with a closet, to Room 6. This room, to judge from the abundant pottery found in it, was a pantry. The other door from Room 5 led to Room 4. This room was painted with the images of eight *ikria*, the cabins seen on Aegean ships. Painted flowerpots holding lilies were painted on the jambs of the window.[67] C. Kopaka has suggested that the room was a bedroom.[68] A clay partition wall separated this room from the small space 4a in the southwest corner of the house. This room had a bathtub and bronze cauldron for bathing and a toilet (see fig. 9.51). The toilet was connected with a drain that led down through the wall to a collection pit and drain in the alley west of the house.

Several houses in Crete, including House G at Zakros (see fig. 9.25), resemble the West House at Akrotiri in significant ways. They incorporate ashlar masonry sparingly but lack most other Palatializing features such as pier-and-door partitions, light wells, and ground-story Minoan Halls. In these houses, most of the ground-floor rooms were used for storage and home industries, while the residential rooms were on an upper story that was accessible by means of a stairway adjacent to the vestibule on the ground floor. Smaller houses at Gournia and various other sites throughout Crete also follow this pattern. The West House at Akrotiri may, therefore, show what traditional Neopalatial houses looked like before the rise of the Palatializing movement.

Buildings, Frescoes, and the Language of Power in the Final Palatial Period

CA. 1490–1360 BC

A NEW REGIME at Knossos took advantage of the devastation caused by the LM IB destructions. This administration introduced the Linear B script to manage a newly centralized bureaucracy, completely rebuilt the Palace, and erected a series of exotic monumental tombs to advertise their power. The rest of the island, with the notable exception of several extraordinary buildings at Haghia Triada, remained eerily quiet.

The Linear B Tablets at Knossos

The study of Linear B has blossomed into a sizeable academic industry. Here I will limit the discussion to a handful of observations concerning the general nature and some of the historical and architectural implications of the Linear B tablets. A. Evans recovered thousands of them at Knossos. While they were found throughout the Palace, there were four main concentrations: the southern part of the West Wing, in most of the West Magazines, near the North Entrance Passage, and just north of the Residential Quarter near the Hall of the Double Axes (fig. 10.2). Several parts of the Palace, mostly on the upper story, were involved in administrative record keeping. At least seventy-five scribes—they should probably be regarded as administrative bureaucrats—can be distinguished on the basis of their handwriting. This inflated bureaucracy in itself marked a major change in the general nature of the Palace.

The tablets tell us a great deal about the relationship between Knossos and the rest of the island. Although a few Linear B tablets have recently been found in LM IIIB contexts at Khania, in the Final Palatial period economic administration was channeled through Knossos. This is very different from the Neopalatial Linear A administrations that had been spread throughout the island. The Linear B tablets mention over one hundred place names that were apparently economically tied to Knossos. The tablets also record massive quantities of agricultural produce.[1] One tablet, for instance, refers to 10,000 units of grain (about 960,000 liters) from a place named *da-wo*, which was located near Phaistos and may be either Kommos or Haghia Triada.[2] The largest recorded numbers concern sheep: over 100,000 are mentioned. In fact, unlike the Linear B bureaucracy at Pylos in the mainland, the tablets at Knossos are overwhelmingly concerned with sheep raising and the production of textiles.[3] Such numbers go far beyond anything needed for day-to-day subsistence and are grounded in an economy geared toward export. The wealth of Knossos during this period depended almost exclusively on the textile industry, which in turn depended largely on the labor of women and children working in various towns around the island.[4]

The date of the tablets has been the subject of heated debate for half a century. The controversy began in 1952 when Michael Ventris finally deciphered the Linear B script and found that the tablets were written in a form of Greek, the language of the Mycenaean mainland. Did this mean that Mycenaeans were running the Palace at Knossos and, through it, the rest of the island? Evans had insisted that non-Greek-speaking Minoans ruled until the final destruction of the Palace about 1400 BC. Was he wrong? Or did the tablets postdate Evans's "final destruction"? Did they date to a time when Evans thought the Palace site was partially reoccupied by squatters? Currently there are three main positions in the debate, and each has problematic ramifications.

One position is a slight modification of the final views of Evans. It assumes that all the tablets belong to the same period—the so-called unity of the archives—since they were only accidentally preserved by the fire that destroyed the Final Palace. The destruction took place a little later than Evans thought, at the end of LM IIIA1 or early in LM IIIA2, and in the Postpalatial LM IIIB period the Palace site was only partly reoccupied. As an administrative center, the Final Palace went out in a literal blaze of glory in the conflagration of early LM IIIA2. This position is supported by J. Boardman, M. Popham, D. Doxey, and most recently in two important articles by E. Hatzaki.[5] One of the problematic consequences of this position is that it envisions a vast Knossian bureaucracy overseeing an island that was otherwise nearly empty, having not recovered from the LM IB destructions.

L. Palmer, S. Hood, N. Momigliano and M. S. F. Hood, E. Hallager, and W.-D. Niemeier hold an opposing view.[6] They too assume the unity of the archives but date the tablets to LM IIIB. The main problem with this position is that in LM IIIB the Palace was vastly different from the elegant building it had been since its initial construction in the Protopalatial period, and most of the formerly magnificent houses were essentially burned-out shells in which a few people cleared out corners in which to live. Could this be the Knossos whose scribes administered the economics of most of the island?

A third position, originally proposed by J. Driessen and taken up by R. Firth, questions the unity of the archives and proposes that the tablets range in date from LM II to LM IIIB and had been preserved by several fires rather than a single conflagration.[7] This view offers greater flexibility but does not clarify the relations between Knossos and the rest of Crete.

In this chapter and the next I take the view that while some of the tablets might be considerably earlier than the LM IIIA2 destruction, few if any belong to LM IIIB. While it will not greatly affect the discussion of specific buildings, the date I assign to the bulk of the tablets will have a significant impact on how we understand the larger political and economic context, and readers should bear in mind the alternative views. Whatever their date, when considered as artifacts the masses of tablets and their distribution across the site marked a major change in the general nature of the Palace. Popham suggested an apt parallel situation from the time of World War II:

> The picture is . . . curious—scribes and archives spread over large areas of the Palace and in unexpected places. It is somewhat reminiscent of, say, the Ministry of Supply, evacuated from London during the last war and accommodated in one of the stately country houses of Britain, with clerks sitting in the ballroom (with its tapestries still hanging on the walls) and in alcoves along the corridors, filing cabinets and all, amid the ancestral possessions of the owners; the cellars firmly locked against intruders (I am thinking of the oil magazines of the Palace) and the family chapel available at hand for religious attendance."[8]

Material Culture and Ethnic Identity

After the discovery that the Linear B tablets were written in a nonalphabetic form of Greek, several scholars began to look for other evidence that Mycenaeans were living in Crete. They began to interpret such things as new tomb types and grave assemblages—the so-called Warrior Graves at Knossos—new pottery shapes like the Ephyraean goblet, and house forms like the so-called megaron as direct evidence of an invasion from the mainland.[9] Some newcomers did arrive on the island, but what did this mean in terms of the larger population? Through the mid-1990s, as we learned more about the Final Palatial and Postpalatial periods at sites outside Knossos, the question continued to be asked: was Crete in LM III Mycenaean?[10]

In the 1990s, other scholars began to take a more sophisticated approach to the issue of ethnicity.[11] As we saw in Chapter 3, ethnicity is not genetically or geographically fixed, but it is a social construction that can vary in degrees and change over time. Furthermore it is not possible to make a direct connection between an object and the genetic identity of the person who used it. Material culture does not equate directly with DNA but provides a repertoire of symbolic forms among which an individual may choose in order to project a desired image. In much of the world, for example, people become Irish on St. Patrick's Day.

For Knossos, much of the theoretical groundwork on this topic was laid out by L. Preston in three articles dealing with mortuary practices. She showed that Knossians sometimes chose to employ "Mycenaeanizing" forms that would emphasize their affinity with the new warrior elite and at other times chose "Minoanizing" forms rooted in the Neopalatial tradition that would underscore their political legitimacy. On occasion both forms can appear in a single monument (see fig. 10.13).[12] How might Preston's approach to the tombs be applied to other forms of architecture?

The Final Palace at Knossos

What might an allegedly Mycenaean Palace at Knossos look like? Would it be different from the earlier versions of the building? Would it incorporate recognizably mainland-style features? Over the course of the past several years much of the Final Palace has been thoroughly reexamined, and at least a general picture is settled: S. Mirié investigated the Throne Room Complex; Driessen studied the southeast part of the West Wing in the area of the Room of the Chariot tablets; Momigliano and Hood conducted excavations on the South Front of the Palace; M. Panagiotaki published a detailed study of the Central Palace Sanctuary; D. J. I. Begg and, more recently, K. Christakis reexamined the West Magazines and the Long Corridor. In addition, J. Overbeck and C. McDonald published a summary of the soundings A. Evans made in 1913 below the floors of the Residential Quarter.[13] The results from all these areas were clear and consistent. They show that, while most of the island still lay in ruins from the LM IB destructions, the Palace at Knossos was rebuilt from one end to the other.

10.1. Throne Room, Knossos. © Gail Mooney/Corbis.

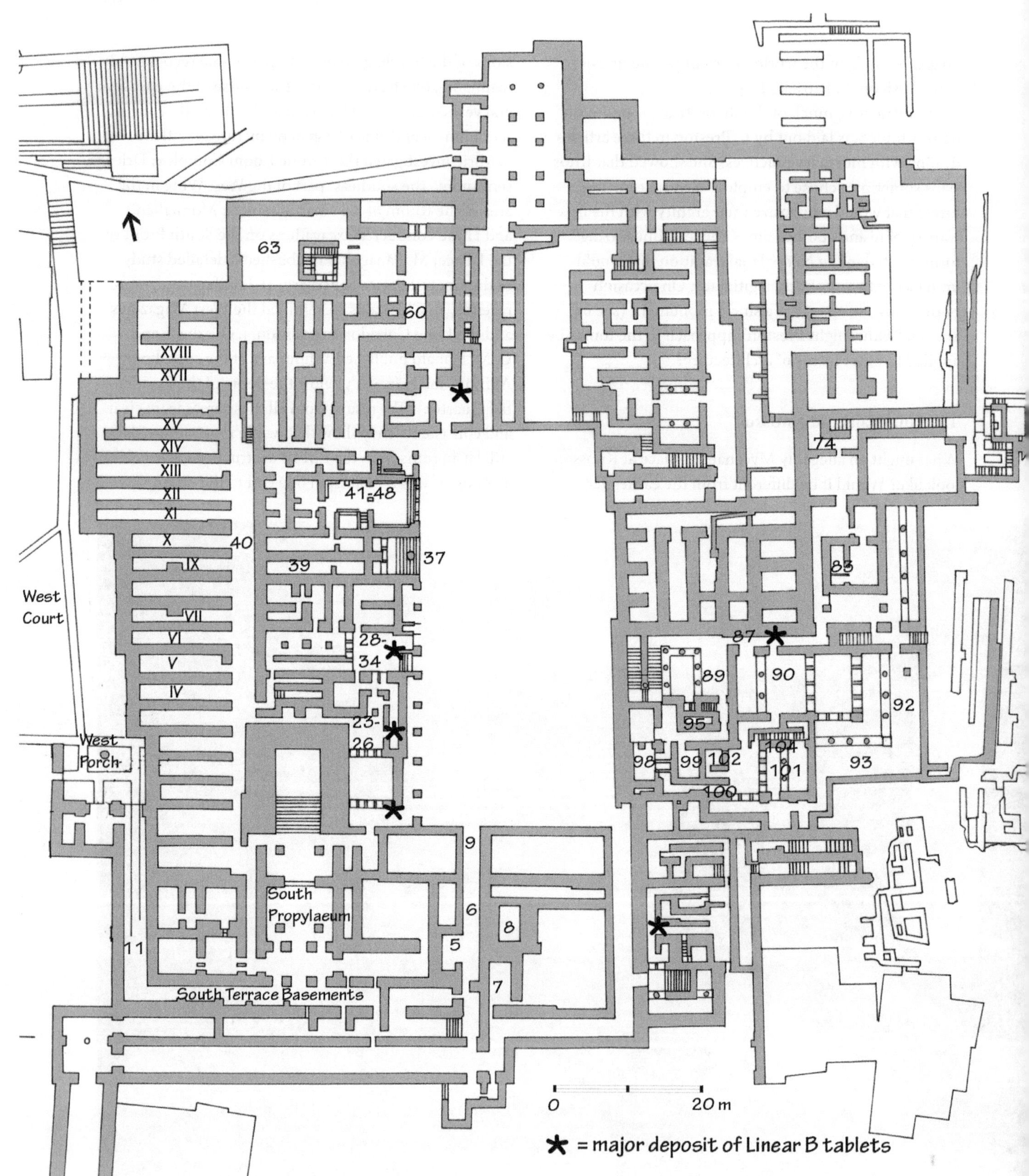

10.2. Plan. Palace at Knossos in the Final Palatial Period. After Pendlebury 1954, Plan. Keys appear on pages 121 and 125.

Key 1 to Figure 10.2
Final Palace LM II–LM IIIA Building Program

Room #		
5	Room of the Seal Impressions	Built LM II–LM IIIA[14]
6	Room of the Clay Signet	Built LM II–LM IIIA[15]
7	Room of the Egyptian Beans	Built LM II–LM IIIA[16]
8	Room of the Wheat	Built LM II–LM IIIA[17]
x	South Terrace Basements	Built LM II–LM IIIA[18]
23–26	Southeast part of West Wing	LM II–LM IIIA1[19]
28	Corridor to Magazines	Probably LM II–LM IIIA[20]
29–34	Central Palace Sanctuary	LM II–LM IIIA[21]
37	Stepped Porch and Central Staircase	LM IIIA[22]
39	Magazine of the Jewel Fresco	Door blocked LM IIIA[23]
40	Long Corridor	LM II–LM IIIA2 floor[24]
IV–VI	Magazine S. Cist	LM IIIA2 floor[25]
VII	Magazine	LM IIIA2 floor Buttress wall[26]
IV–VII	Magazine	LM IIIA2 floor[27]
IX–XIII	Magazines	LM IIIA2 floor[28]
XIV	Magazine	Buttress wall LM IIIA[29]
XV	Magazine	Door blocked LM IIIA[30]
XVII	Long Corridor	Stairway built LM IIIA[31]
41–48	Throne Room Complex	Paving LM IIIA[32]
Central Court		Paving outside the Throne Room Complex. LM IIIA[33]
89	Hall of the Colonnades	LM III floor[34]
92	Eastern light area	LM III floor[35]
93	Southern light area	LM III floor[36]
95	Service stairs	LM III floor[37]
98	Room of the Plaster Couch	LM II floor. Drain blocked LM IIIA?[38]
99	Treasure/Treasury/Lair	LM III floor[39]
104	Private staircase	LM III floor[40]

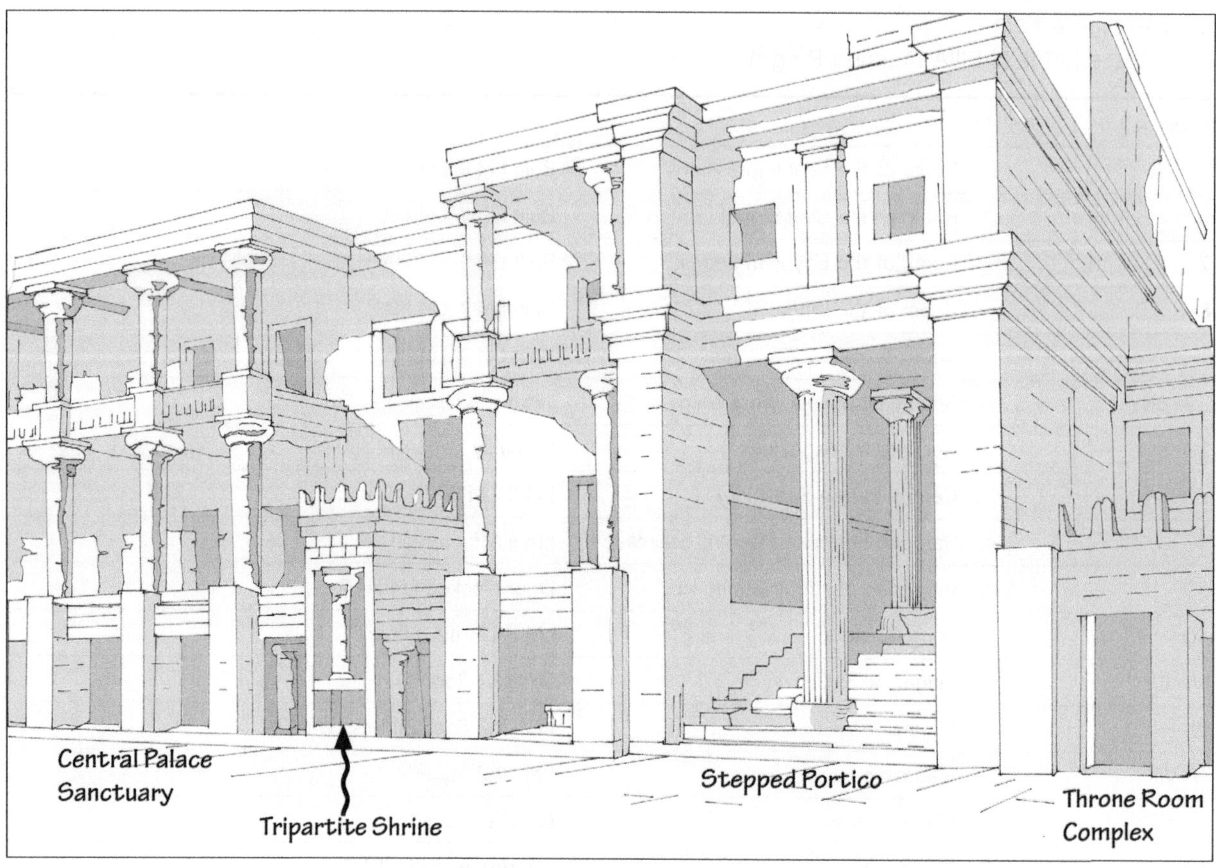

10.3. Restoration. Facade of the West Wing onto the Central Court, Knossos. After *PM III*, p. 526.

Most of what we see now of the central part of the West Wing that opens onto the Central Court also belongs to the Final Palatial period. The famous Throne Room, which so excited A. Evans during his first season of excavation, received its final form in LM IIIA (fig. 10.1). This involved a repaving of at least part of the Central Court outside the Anteroom and the building of two new stairs leading down into the room.

Just to the south, the grand Stepped Portico to the Piano Nobile may have been a new construction supported on the thickened south wall of the Throne Room Complex.[41] There were also several changes in the area of the Central Palace Sanctuary, including the moving of the pillars in the Pillar Crypts into their present positions. During this period the East Pillar Crypt and possibly the West Pillar Crypt were crowded with storage pithoi.[42] In fact, if one looks at Evans's reconstruction of the west facade on the Central Court (fig. 10.3) with these changes in mind, it quickly becomes apparent that the entire facade, with the exception of the Tripartite Shrine, was built in the Final Palatial period.

The area around the Room of the Chariot Tablets (Rooms 23–26 in fig. 10.2) underwent a series of architectural modifications from the Protopalatial period through the Postpalatial period into classical times. Driessen has tried to unravel this complex history. He dates a major rebuilding to the early part of the Final Palatial period.[43]

In work carried out further to the south, Momigliano and Hood showed that most of the rooms of the South Terrace Basements date to LM II–LM IIIA1.[44] Much of the material found in the area represented a broad range of domestic activities, prompting the excavators to propose that the area served as slave quarters.[45]

The West Magazines and the Long Corridor were modified slightly later in LM IIIA2 (fig. 10.4). While some of these modifications, such as the buttress walls built in Magazines VII and XIV, were relatively minor attempts to provide additional support for the upper story, most of them reflect a continuation of the new building program. Most of the fine stone pavements in the West Magazines and the Long Corridor were laid at this time. Above the West Magazines, many of the rooms of the Piano Nobile were renovated. The date of these alterations constitutes a *terminus post quem* of LM IIIA2 for the masses of Linear B tablets that were found fallen into the magazines. In fact, this is one of the few dates that is generally agreed upon by both factions involved in the debate over the date of the tablets.[46]

There have been fewer recent studies in the east wing of the Palace. C. Macdonald and J. Driessen came up with some useful information during their reinvestigation of the Palace's drainage system.[47] More important, Evans's soundings below the latest floors showed that most of the Residential Quarter had been rebuilt in LM II–LM IIIA.[48] Many famous rooms in the Palace were reconstructed, including the Queen's Megaron (fig. 10.5), the grand light well Evans named the Hall of the Colonnades (fig. 10.6), and the Hall of the Double Axes, the largest Minoan Hall ever built (fig. 10.7). There is only scattered information about what was actually constructed in the areas north and south of the Residential Quarter. Yet both areas saw extensive occupation in the Postpalatial period and were almost certainly occupied during the preceding Final Palatial period.

10.4. West Magazines, Knossos. © Atlantide Phototravel/Corbis.

10.5. Queen's Megaron, Knossos. © Roger Wood/Corbis.

10.6. Hall of Colonnades, Knossos. © Atlantide Phototravel/Corbis.

10.7. Hall of the Double Axes, Knossos. © Roger Wood/Corbis.

10.8. North Entrance Passage, Knossos from the east. Photo by author.

From such a sizeable body of evidence one deduces quite well what the so-called Mycenaean Palace at Knossos looked like. In fact, of all the phases of this building over the course of its seven-hundred-year history, this is the most familiar. It is the building at the heart of Evans's *Palace of Minos*. The Final Palace at Knossos was a total reworking of the two-hundred-year-old Neopalatial building into its quintessential form. In construction and in the design of its various elements—Magazines, Residential Quarter, Central Court, and the ceremonial rooms of the West Wing—it is the embodiment of architectural "Minoanness." In other words, in the architecture of the Palace the Mycenaean regime was presenting itself as the legitimate heir to Minoan tradition. As we shall see, the same regime built monumental tombs to convey a quite different message.

The Fresco Program of the Final Palace at Knossos

As part of the LM II–LM IIIA1 building program, much of the Palace was redecorated with a series of new frescoes whose iconography was geared to the tastes and ambitions of the new generation of Knossian elite (see fig. 10.2). Unlike the building program, which is clearly dated by pottery evidence, the frescoes are datable only by style, and the two most important studies of the frescoes, by S. Hood and S. Immerwahr, differ somewhat in the dates they assign. Hood tends to date many of them to LM II, whereas Immerwahr prefers LM IIIA1. With the possible exception of the Bull Relief in the North Entrance that Immerwahr dates to LM IB–LM II (fig. 10.8), however, they agree that the frescoes listed below were made for the Final Palace.

Key 2 to Figure 10.2
Fresco Program of the LM II–LM IIIA1 Palace at Knossos

Room #	
West Court	Campstool and "La Parisienne"[49]
West Porch	Bull-grappling scene, Dado imitating veined stone[50]
6	Palanquin[51]
11	Procession fresco and cupbearer[52]
37	Central staircase procession[53]
41	Bull in anteroom to Throne Room[54]
42	Throne Room griffins (see fig. 10.1)[55]
60	Bull Relief in North Entrance. LM I–LM II (see fig. 10.7)
74	Taureador fresco[56]
83	Palanquin-Chariot fresco[57]
87	Argonaut Frieze[58]
89	Shield fresco. Hall of the Colonnades[59]
90	Bull. Upper floor of Hall of the Double Axes[60]
90	Spiral Frieze. Hall of the Double Axes[61]
95	Bull Relief fragments. Service staircase[62]
100	Spiral Frieze. Corridor of the Painted Pithos[63]
102	Spiral Frieze. Queen's Bathroom[64]
101	Light well east of Queen's Megaron. Dancing Lady[65]

The subjects of the frescoes are noteworthy. First, compared with the frescoes of the Neopalatial Palace and houses, the range of motifs of the frescoes in the Final Palace is remarkably narrow. There are no fanciful nature scenes with exotic animals or scenes of fashionable women joyously participating in outdoor ceremonies. Instead, the fresco program was stripped down to a few bare essentials. Bulls, tribute-bearing processions, heraldic devices, and decorative friezes form the bulk of a thematically focused repertoire.

Second, most of the fresco motifs used in the Final Palace at Knossos would continue to have a long history in later mainland painting. The couchant griffins in the Throne Room and in Room 46 at Pylos owed something to those of the Throne Room at Knossos. Similarly, the processions of women in Minoan dress at Pylos, Tiryns, and Thebes are intentionally reminiscent of the processional scenes at Knossos. Figure-eight shields apparently appealed to the leaders of LH IIIB Tiryns and Thebes as much as they did to the new military elite in Final Palatial Knossos (see fig. 10.6). Even the smaller decorative works like the Argonaut Frieze at Pylos and the spiral friezes at Tiryns and Thebes were used in the Mycenaean Palaces.[66] What such imitation might say about how the later Mycenaeans wanted to present themselves is beyond my concern here, but it is important to keep the cross-cultural or hybrid nature of these motifs in mind.

Last, of all the motifs used in the Final Palace, only the image of the bull seems to have been specifically Knossian, where it had been long used for its propagandistic value.[67] The Bull in the West Porch, for example, was the third and final version painted in this room. The bull appears in about a third of the surviving Final Palace frescoes. These were placed at key points throughout the building: at the two major entrances, the West Porch and the North Entrance, in the Anteroom to the Throne Room, and in the Hall of the Double Axes. The image of the bull, like the almost neo-Neopalatial architectural form of the Final Palace, ostentatiously drew on powerful symbols from the past, associating the new regime with deeply engrained Minoan tradition.

The iconographic program of the Final Palace is thus pared down to a minimal core, focusing like a laser on the single concept of power.[68] The Campstool fresco from the Piano Nobile over the West Magazines portrays feasting, an activity closely tied to the notion of power in Mycenaean society.[69] Throughout the rest of the Palace, the emblematic power of the Knossian bull was reinforced by the supernatural power of the Throne Room griffins and the personal military prowess implied by the shield frescoes in the Hall of the Double Axes in the Residential Quarter. We cannot be certain of the genetic ethnicity of this new ruling elite, but how they wanted to be seen is unmistakable.

The Town of Knossos in the Final Palatial Period

In LM II–LM IIIA, Knossos had shrunk from its maximum Neopalatial population of around sixteen thousand to about eleven thousand.[70] Nevertheless it was a thriving and remarkably prosperous town. As Hatzaki remarked, "LM II Knossos began with an extensive building programme that was almost comparable in scale to A. Evans's 'Great Rebuilding' of the Neopalatial period."[71]

In the vicinity of the renovated Palace many prominent Neopalatial houses were repaired (if necessary) and occupied until the end of the Final Palatial period. These include the Little Palace, the Unexplored Mansion, the Southeast House, and the Royal Villa (see figs. 9.2, 9.7).[72]

In addition to the Neopalatial houses that continued in use, several more modest houses were newly constructed in LM II. A partly excavated house just to the south of the West Court included a well-made gypsum pier-and-door partition.[73] The extensive use of gypsum may have been a hallmark for the period, as it was used for floors, jamb bases, stairs, and cupboards in the appropriately named Gypsum House in the Stratigraphical Museum Extension Site. Just southeast of the Gypsum House, the smaller, less elaborate Stratigraphical Museum Extension Site South House was built in the same period.[74] These two houses were demolished at the end of LM II to make way for new public constructions.

A number of important public works projects were undertaken in the Final Palatial period.[75] The Royal Road, the most monumental street in Minoan Crete, was entirely repaved, and a new grandstand was built along its south side not far from where it crosses the modern highway. In LM IIIA1 three intriguing circular structures, respectively, 3 m, 3.22 m, and 8.38 m in diameter, were built in ashlar masonry over the LM II houses in the Stratigraphical Museum Extension Site.[76] The excavator describes these structures as Dancing Circles. Like most of the houses at Knossos the circular structures went out of use after much of the town was destroyed at some point in the early LM IIIA2 period.

Monumental Tombs

A fundamental shift in mortuary customs seems to have already begun in the Neopalatial cemetery at Poros, the port city of Knossos, and with the extraordinary Temple Tomb south of the Palace (see fig. 9.38), but a bigger change came at the beginning of the Final Palatial period.[77] New Mycenaeanizing tomb types, the shaft grave, the chamber tomb with dromos, and the tholos tomb were introduced along with a new set of grave goods that often included bronze weapons. Unlike the communal Prepalatial and Protopalatial tholoi and house tombs, these new tombs were intended for individuals or very small numbers of people. As in EM III–MM IA, tombs again became a medium for proclaiming personal status for the deceased individual and his descendants. For males such status depended on the display of personal weaponry to project a real or desired image of power, military prowess, and personal reputation.[78]

Three of the most interesting tombs built in LM II (figs. 10.9–10.11) were located in the same area north of the Palace, and were presumably built by people who knew one another. In recent studies, L. Preston determines that these tombs represent a wildly experimental group unique to the early part of the Final Palatial period. They had neither close predecessors nor did they inspire successors.[79]

The Royal Tomb at Isopata (see fig. 10.9) is the largest of the three, with a monumental ashlar chamber about 50 m². It is the larger of two rectangular corbelled, keel-vaulted tombs in the Isopata cemetery, an uncommon form in the island. Roughly similar tombs at Ugarit have been cited as parallels for its construction, and it also resembles the equally unique Tomb Rho in Grave Circle B at Mycenae.

The Kephala Tholos (fig. 10.10), on the other hand, at first looks like a canonical Mycenaean tholos tomb with a corbel-vaulted dome and a dromos. Yet this tomb, too, is unique. The only parallel for its elaborate forechamber is the forechamber in the Royal Tomb at Isopata.

Finally, the Tomb of the Double Axes is also unique (fig. 10.11). A double-chambered tomb with dromos, it features a burial cist cut into the shape of that traditional Neopalatial symbol, the Double Axe. Three bronze Double Axes and a Bull's Head rhyton, objects traditionally more closely associated with Cretan sanctuaries than with tombs, were included among the grave goods. To make the situation even more complex, included with these patently Minoanizing symbols were a number of Mycenaeanizing objects, including a set of bronze weapons. Like the architectural forms of these tombs, the grave goods juxtapose symbols from two traditions.

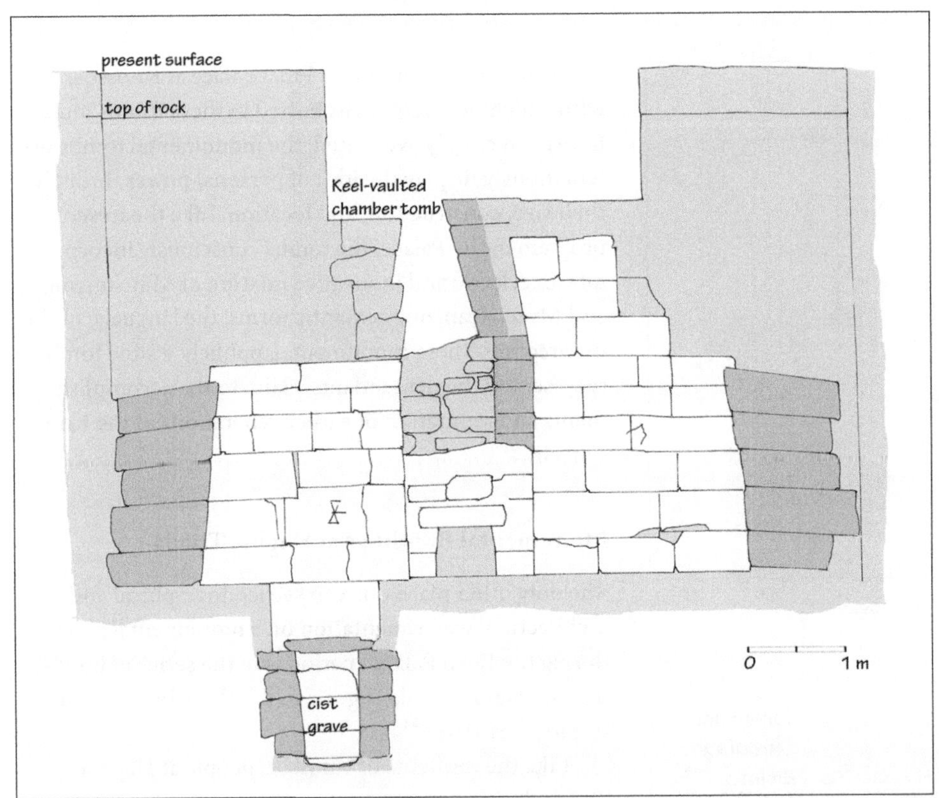

10.9. Section. Royal Tomb, Isopata (Knossos). After A. Evans 1906, pl. XLV.

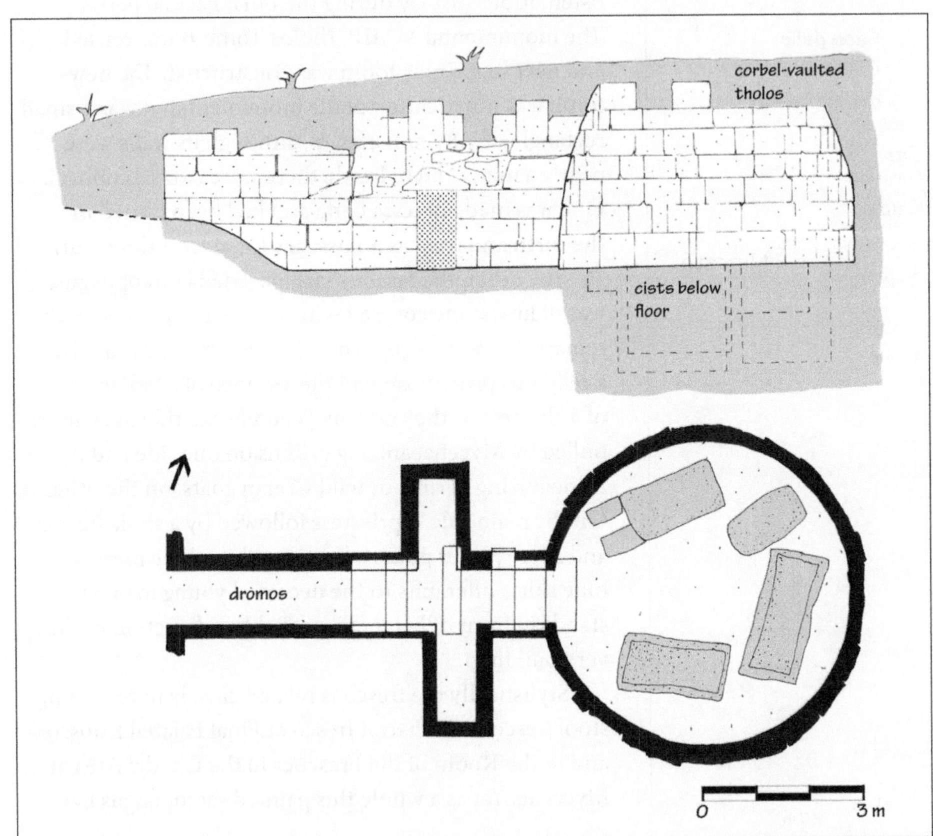

10.10. Plan and elevation. Kephala Tholos, Knossos. After Hutchinson 1962, fig. 58.

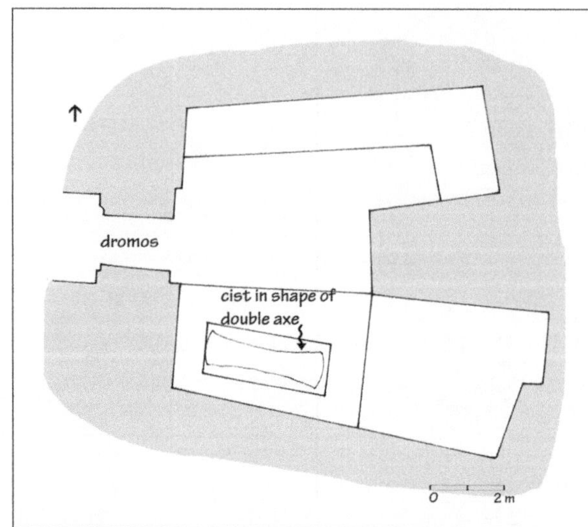

10.11. Plan. Tomb of the Double Axes, Knossos. After A. Evans 1914, plan.

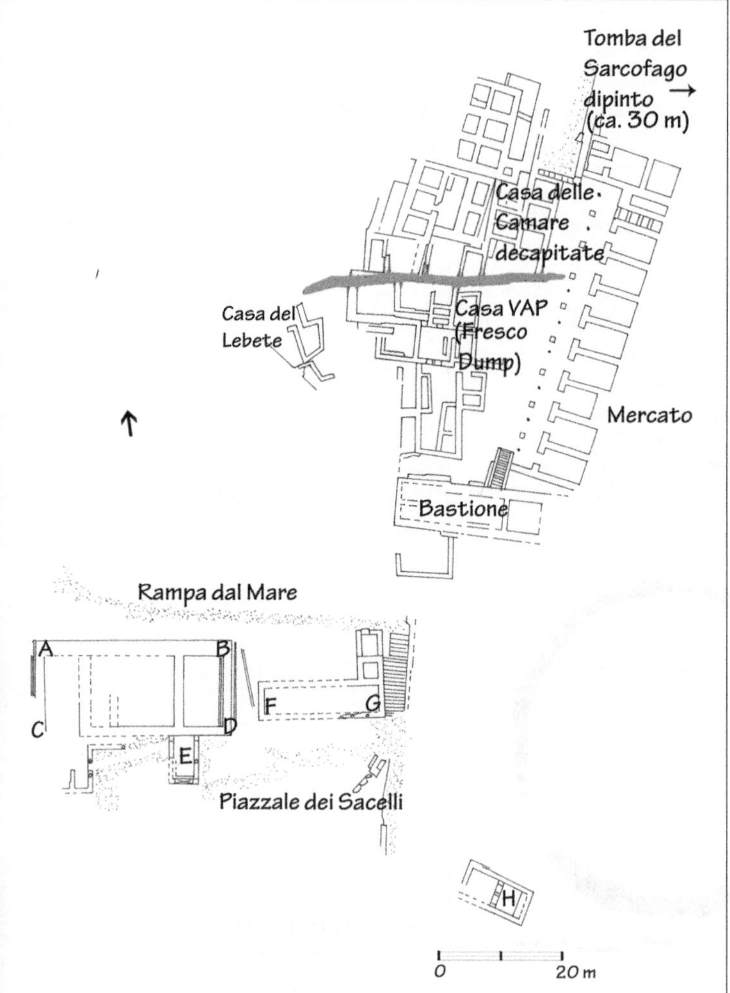

10.12. Plan. Haghia Triada in LM III. After Di Vita and La Regina 1984, p. 163, fig. 230.

As in the contemporary Final Palace at Knossos, with which the individuals buried in these tombs must have been closely associated, the monumental tombs ostentatiously display the idea of personal power through their size, construction, and location. Like the fresco program in the Palace, the tombs consciously incorporate an eclectic and innovative mixture of Minoanizing and Mycenaeanizing semantic forms, the language of the new regime. These monumental, publicly visible tombs represented the descendants' claim to the accomplishments and reputation of earlier generations of the Knossian elite.

Monumental Buildings at Haghia Triada

The only other place one can see iconographical and architectural experimentation on a monumental scale during the Final Palatial period is in the series of buildings at Haghia Triada (fig. 10.12).[80] These buildings date to early LM IIIA2.[81]

Like the residents of Knossos, people at Haghia Triada decided to use mortuary art as a medium for ostentatious display during the Final Palatial period. The monumental MMIB Tholos Tomb B was reused, and next to it a new tomb was constructed. The new tomb was not architecturally monumental: it was a small rectangle of 3.85 m × 4.25 m, although its walls were nearly a meter thick. Inside there were two sarcophagi. One was made of terra cotta and had been buried in the earth and used as an ossuary for at least three burials. The other, the famous Haghia Triada sarcophagus, was of limestone covered with stucco and painted with remarkable scenes (fig. 10.13).[82] On one side it depicts a religious procession and the sacrifice of a bull in front of a shrine. On the end panels goddesses ride in chariots pulled by Mycenaeanizing griffins on one side and by Minoanizing *agrimi*, or wild Cretan goats, on the other. On the main side, a priestess followed by a situla bearer and a lyre player pours a libation while three men in hide skirts offer gifts to the deceased young man who stands in front of his tomb, probably a depiction of this very building.

Stylistically the fresco is related closely to the Campstool fresco and Chariot fresco at Final Palatial Knossos and to the Room of the Frescoes in the Citadel Area at Mycenae. Yet as a whole this painted sarcophagus has

10.13. Haghia Triada Sarcophagus. © Gianni Dagli Orti/Corbis.

no close parallels anywhere. P. Militello summed up the new painting style at Haghia Triada: "The Mycenaean elite had sought to appropriate a local artistic language for the expression of a new politico-religious conception born of the fusion of a specifically Mycenaean ideology with the now age-old Minoan tradition."[83]

Sanctuary H at Haghia Triada

Sanctuary H at Haghia Triada (fig. 10.14) is an unusual free-standing building set into a cutting on the slope above the southeast corner of the Piazzale dei Sacelli. It opened to the west, sharing the orientation of the later Mercato and the slope that runs along the east sides of both buildings. Inside were two rooms, an anteroom and an inner room with a raised platform against its back wall. The floor of the inner room was originally painted with a marine scene representing an octopus symmetrically flanked by dolphins and fish, similar to the floor patterns at Pylos and Tiryns on the mainland and to the possibly earlier seascape floor in the Residential Quarter at Knossos. The edges of the plaster show that some rectangular fixture was installed against the south wall of the inner room, in a position similar to that of the throne in the Throne Room at Knossos and the Mycenaean Palaces. The building was identified as a shrine partly on the basis of its location in the Piazzale dei Sacelli and partly because inside it the excavators found a set of seven Snake Tubes.[84] There was no trace of a statuette of a goddess, which would be characteristic of later Minoan shrines.

The construction of Sanctuary H is different from that of the earlier buildings at the site. Its walls were made of ashlar blocks interspersed with rubble and held in place by a half-timber framework of the sort used in Building ABCD. The pier-and-door partition that divided the interior into two rooms was not of the form normal in earlier periods. Instead it was joined with the flanking thresholds formed of closely fitted stones. This type of threshold, found also in the Stoà del Mercato

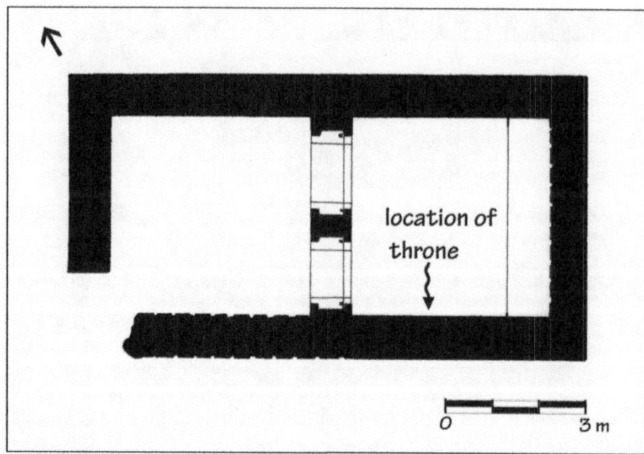

10.14. Plan. Sanctuary H, Haghia Triada. After Banti 1941–1943, fig. 27.

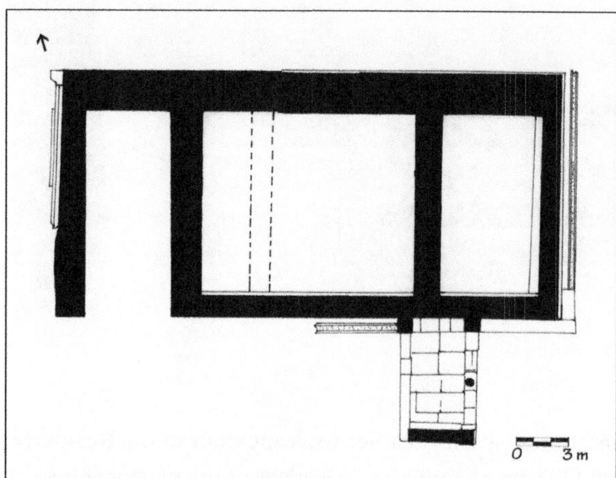

10.15. Plan. Building ABCD, Haghia Triada. After Di Vita and La Regina 1984, fig. 230.

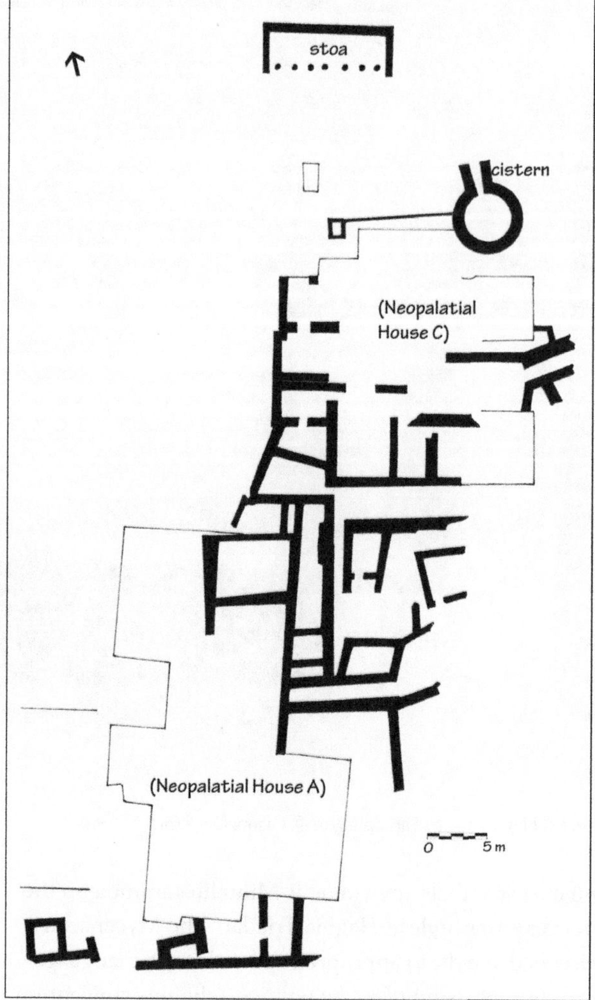

10.16. Plan. LM III Tylissos. After Hayden 1984, fig. 7.

(see fig. 11.6) and in an important LM III house at Gournia (see fig. 11.10), seems to have been characteristic of the LM III period. With its square mortices for the door pivots, the threshold also resembles the slightly later examples at Pylos.

Building ABCD

The large, rectangular Building ABCD at Haghia Triada (fig. 10.15) has been the subject of debate since 1905. So unusual was its plan for a Bronze Age building that W. Dörpfeld regarded it as the foundation of a Greek temple, while D. Mackenzie described it as a typical Mycenaean Megaron.[85] In fact it is neither. Now dated fairly specifically to early LM IIIA2 or slightly earlier, it has none of the features associated with large Mycenaeanizing houses (see Chapter 11).[86]

Building ABCD is preserved to only one course above the level of the Piazzale dei Sacelli, but on the north its foundations were sunk deep into the remains of the Neopalatial building below. Well-built stone channels were constructed along its south and east sides to drain water from the Piazzale. The main part of the building is a large (ca. 24 m × 15 m) rectangle divided into a series of four rooms. The western room was apparently a late addition, and the original entrance may have been in this corner. A small side porch, Chiostro E, opened to the east. It had a Neopalatial-style column (of the sort set into, rather than on top of, the stylobate) and a gypsum bench with a so-called triglyph pattern, and, like Sanctuary H, it was originally painted with frescoes. Fragments of painted rosettes, much like those on the Haghia Triada sarcophagus, and a fragment of a possible animal head were found in the original excavations.[87] This large ashlar building looks like a public rather than a private building, but its use remains unknown.

Stoa F-G

Stoa F-G was probably the last building to be added to this complex (see fig. 10.12).[88] Like ABCD, it was set into the fill in the destroyed Neopalatial buildings. Even part of the stepped street on the east—later restored by the excavators—was removed to make way for its foundations.[89] Measuring some 6 m × 21 m, F-G consists largely of a seven-columned portico, of which two bases remain *in situ*. The bases, like those of Chiosco E, are of the traditional Neopalatial type. A single doorless space was later added against the north side of the building.

A similar LM III stoa, though only about half the size of F-G, was found by L. Platon at Tylissos (fig. 10.16).[90] It too consisted of a portico of seven wooden columns resting on stone bases set into the stylobate. As at Haghia Triada, rubble walls, here incompletely excavated, butt against the back of the building. And here too the stoa overlooks an important paved courtyard that continued to serve as the center of religious ceremonies into the classical period.

Like Chiosco E, Stoa F-G at Haghia Triada was painted with frescoes. Militello reports that fresco fragments representing a bull's (or possibly horse's) leg were found inside the building. In addition, a series of stone bases for double axes, like the ones depicted on the Haghia Triada sarcophagus, were found nearby. One of the bases also was covered with stucco and painted with a griffin's head.[91] In his fanciful reconstruction of the area, E. Stefani restores the north room of F-G as an enclosure for a sacred tree and places the double axe bases between the columns of the colonnade.

The monumental buildings at Haghia Triada were clearly laid out as an organized group. Together they form a linked set of open facades into which people could see from the public piazza and from which people inside the porticos could view the activities in shelter and shade. The new generation at Haghia Triada chose to superimpose their monumental buildings over the ruins of the finest Neopalatial houses in the same way they placed the Tomb with the Painted Sarcophagus near the venerable Tholos B.

There was probably a sizeable LM II–LM IIIA1 town at Haghia Triada during this period, but in the northern part of the site the buildings are not well preserved. A partly excavated LM IIIA1 building was built over the LM IA Edificio Ciceplico and was in turn razed to make room for the later Stoà del Mercato. In addition the remains of the Casa delle Camere Decapitate were leveled by the construction of Edificio Nord-Ouest/P later in the LM IIIA2 period (see fig. 11.20).[92]

The Fresco Dump

The most important frescoes of Final Palatial Haghia Triada were in a dump below the later floor of Room A of Casa VAP. Recently published by Militello,[93] the fragments came from at least three main scenes, a Lady at the Altar, the Small Procession, and the Great Procession. The Great Procession is very close to the hybrid Minoanizing/Mycenaeanizing style of the Haghia Triada sarcophagus, and many of its details—situla bearers, animals, a lyre player, a flute player, and decorative triglyph and rosette border—are almost precisely the same.

What building was originally decorated with these frescoes? One possibility is the nearby Casa delle Camere Decapitate. However, given the fact that we are certain that both Stoa F-G and Chiostro E of ABCD were painted with figurative frescoes, it seems equally likely, as Militello points out, that these impressive frescoes were originally associated with the monumental buildings around the Piazzale dei Sacelli. As the painted sarcophagus portrayed the costly rituals accorded the deceased, so these frescoes lavishly displayed the rituals of the living that had probably been under the control of the same small group of individuals. In fact, V. La Rosa suggests that the young man who stands silently in front of his tomb (see fig. 10.13) might have been the actual sponsor of the monumental buildings in the southern part of the site.[94]

Conclusions

A. Evans had a clear understanding of the Final Palatial period at Knossos:

> It has been remarked that the last Palatial phase at Knossos presents a military and indeed militaristic aspect. Its most prominent feature, when the residential Quarter was still complete, must have been the great Shield Fresco winding down from story to story along the descending walls of its Grand Staircase and leading thus, we may conclude, to the material realization of its subject, the Shields themselves, namely, suspended along the similar dado frieze in the great Hall below. When, indeed, after the great catastrophe, the spirit and perhaps the actual persons of the Knossian lords transported themselves to the Mainland side, its psychological expression lived again in this respect in the closely imitative Shield frieze, less ambitious in its scale, on the walls of the later Palace at Tiryns.
>
> In Crete itself the appearance at Knossos of what there is every reason to believe to have been a new and aggressive dynasty about the beginning of the Fifteenth Century B.C. is marked not only by the break in continuity visible in the remains of the series of smaller sites along the Northern Coast from the neighboring Tylissos to Nirou Chani and Gournia, but by the eloquent cessation of the great rivals at Phaestos and Haghia Triada, bordering the Libyan Sea.
>
> The bureaucratic methods evidenced by the documents in the form of the linear script B, introduced by the new dynasty sufficiently declare the authoritative character of the new government.[95]

The monumental architecture and propagandistic fresco programs at Knossos and Haghia Triada also proclaim the "authoritative character" of the new regime. Like the new Linear B script, they were not merely the end product of that power. They were a large part of the means by which that power was generated and maintained.

After the Palaces

CA. 1360–1200 BC

AFTER THE EARLY LM IIIA2 fires, Knossos was drastically reduced in size. Throughout the island, Minoans found themselves in a grim new world. Utilitarian regional centers were established at several sites to administer an agricultural economy that, to judge from the industrial-scale storage and harbor facilities in the Mesara, was geared largely toward export (fig. 11.1).

The Palace Site at Knossos in LM IIIB

In the LM IIIB period, the Palace was very different from what it had been in the LM IIIA period. It was no longer the elegant, luxurious building of bright frescoes, dramatic lighting, clever construction, and imposing facades intended to pamper the royal residents and impress visitors. Builders did not trouble over dadoes and pavements. There were no new figural frescoes. And if some of the old colonnades, pillars, and pier-and-door partitions were in need of repair, they were replaced by the simplest means possible, with plain rubble walls. Superficial appearance mattered little in this relentlessly utilitarian building. Even the Shrine of the Double Axes (see fig. 11.3) smacks of the practicality of a business transaction in which offertory goods are exchanged for the beneficent, but frozen gesture of the goddess. The subtlety of Neopalatial religious sculpture had disappeared with the Palace that produced it.

The role of the building also changed. It was no longer concerned with the articulation of elaborate social ceremonies or even with the monumental expression of power. Much of the Palace was apparently focused on

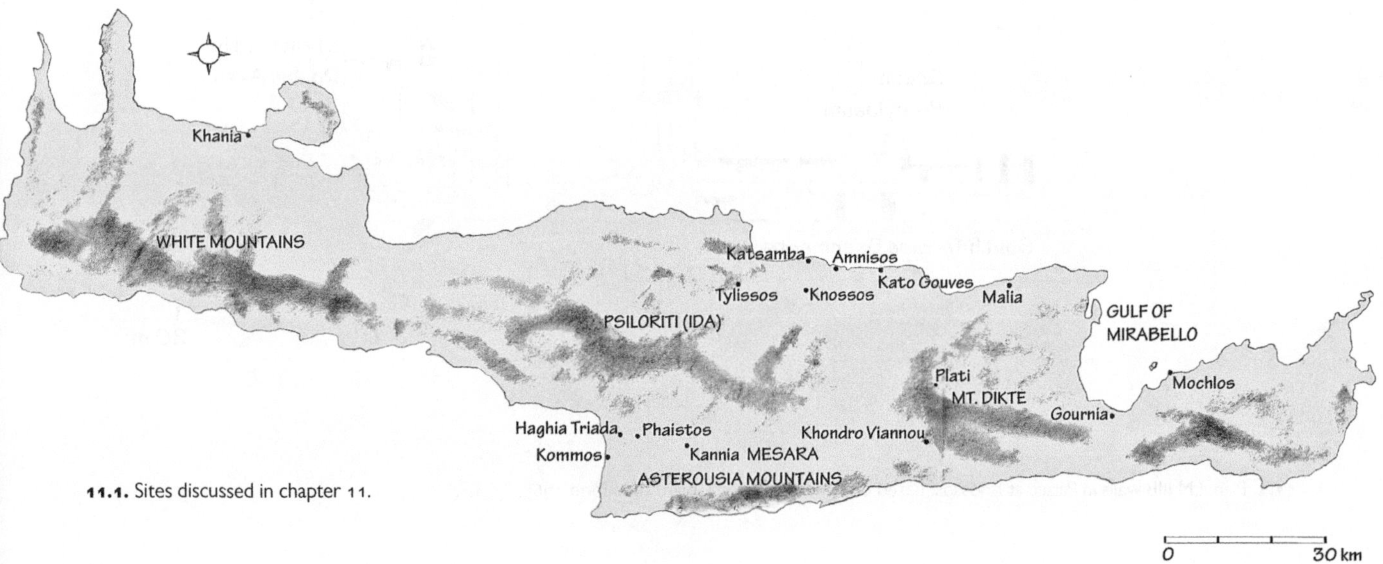

11.1. Sites discussed in chapter 11.

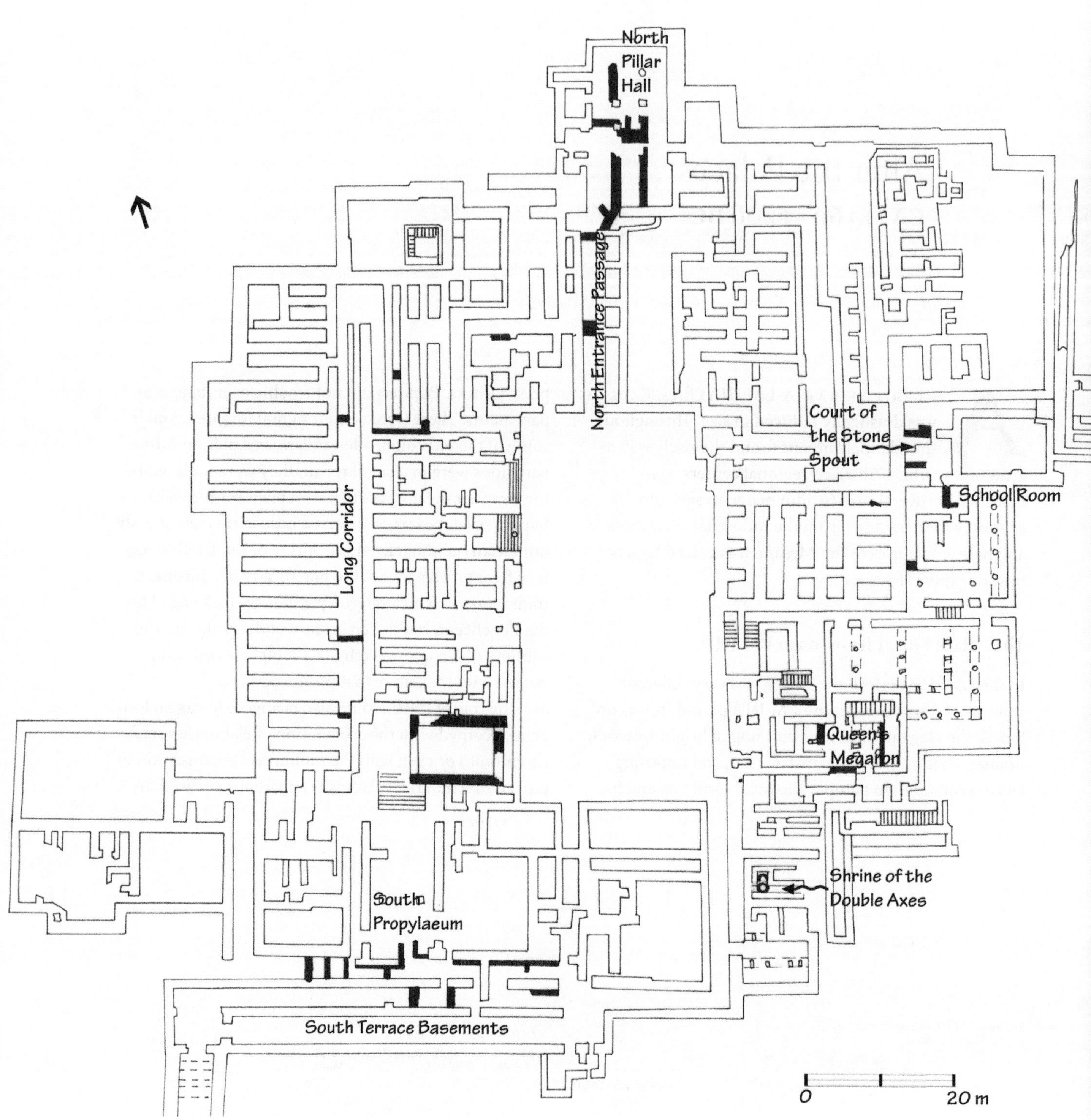

11.2. Plan. LM IIIB walls in Palace at Knossos. Based on Pendlebury 1954, plan, and Hood 1965, fig. 1.

mundane, day-to-day realities of keeping an aging building running at a time when, in the broader Aegean context, Crete was becoming increasingly irrelevant except as a source of agricultural produce. Elegant rooms with elaborate decorations would probably not have helped.

The Palace site at Knossos changed after it was rebuilt in LM II–LM IIIA1 (fig. 11.2). During the Postpalatial period, poorly built rubble walls were put up throughout the site. A number of the walls run directly counter to the earlier organization of the building. Corridors were blocked in several places: the South Terrace Basements, the South Propylaeum, the Long Corridor of the Magazines, the corridor north of the Throne Room, the North Entrance Passage, and the passageway on the west side of the School Room were all at least partly closed off. In other places, large rooms were divided into smaller spaces. The North Pillar Hall, the Court of the Stone Spout, the adjoining School Room, and the Queen's Megaron were all compartmentalized.

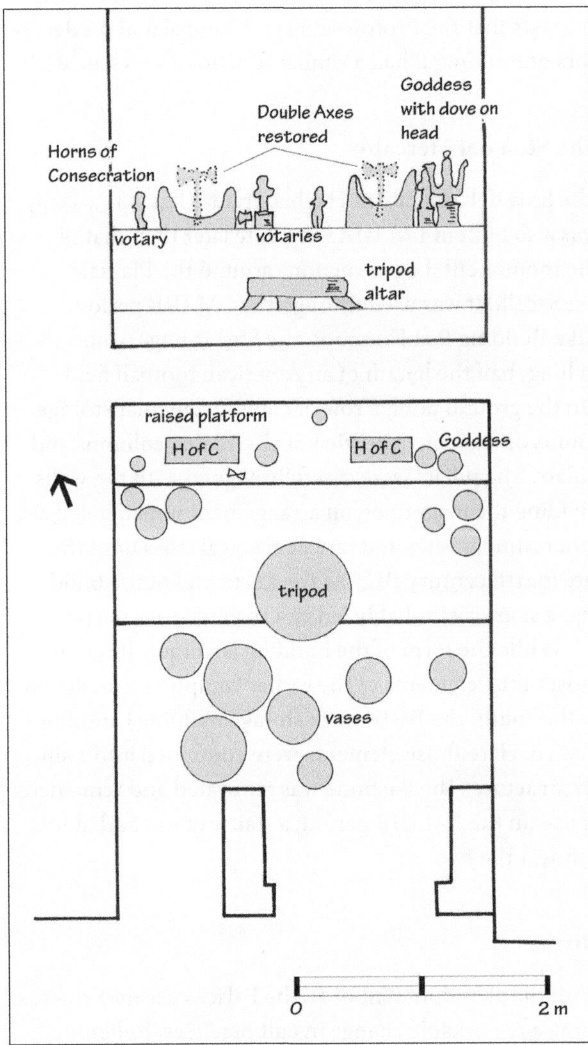

11.3. Plan and elevation. Shrine of the Double Axes, Knossos. After *PM II*, fig. 190.

Many of these late constructions not only resulted in changes to the form of the Palace, but also marked shifts of activities to areas of the Palace not originally intended for them. For example, the cult center, the Shrine of the Double Axes (fig. 11.3), was located on the east side of the Palace site, far from the earlier Palace cult center in the West Wing.

The Queen's Megaron was no longer the center of an elegant residential suite. The bathroom was used for storing lime produced in the kiln that had been installed in the room just to the east of the south light well. A number of other rooms were converted to storage rooms, including the room on the story above the Queen's Megaron, the South Propylaeum, the North Entrance Passage, the Room of the Stirrup Jars, and the corridor near the School Room. In addition, several parts of the Palace, including most of the West Magazines, with the earlier pithoi still in place, went out of use years before the final destruction.[1]

The Town of Knossos in LM IIIB

Like the Palace, much of the town was seriously damaged in the early LM IIIA2 fires. T. Whitelaw estimates that the population of Knossos plummeted from some nine to ten thousand people in LM II–LM IIIA1 to about one thousand in LM IIIB.[2] Whitelaw's calculations, based on his estimates of the area of the town, are supported by what we know from E. Hatzaki's recent studies of the architecture of the LM IIIB town.[3] There was some new construction, but it was very limited—a few scrappy walls built over the LM IIIA1 circular Dancing Floors, for example. The most common form of habitation outside the Palace was what A. Evans called squatter occupation—the partial reuse of small parts of some of the old mansions, while surrounding rooms remained in ruins from the early LM IIIA2 destructions.[4] Good examples include Room H of the Royal Villa (see fig. 9.7), Rooms F1, K1, and L1 of the Southeast House, a few rooms in the northern part of the Little Palace, and

Rooms A, B, C, D, E in the Unexplored Mansion (see fig. 9.2). Similarly, while there was basic continuity in tomb types and mortuary practices, no more ostentatious monumental tombs were built. At Knossos the entire range of trades that had been associated with monumental architecture—quarry workers, masons, skilled carpenters, fresco painters, etc.—ceased to exist.

The New Monumental Architecture

In contrast to Knossos, in the Mesara several new monumental buildings were constructed during LM IIIA2. These might have been connected with the Mesara's traditional role as the breadbasket of Crete and occasionally, as under the Romans, the food supplier for much of the Aegean. Two of the most interesting, Building P at Kommos and the Stoà del Mercato at Haghia Triada, are massive, well built but totally utilitarian warehouses.

Construction on Building P at Kommos (fig. 11.4) may have already begun in an early part of LM IIIA2, at about the same time as Building ABCD, Stoa FG, and Sanctuary H at Haghia Triada, but the building was still under construction long into the period.[5] By the time it was finished, it was one of the largest buildings of its time, measuring some 38.51 m by 39.60 m. The interior consisted of six galleries varying in width from 4.5 m to 5.88 m with a height of at least 4 m. Galleries P1 and P2 were the first part of the building to have been constructed. They employed a half-timber technique in which a horizontal beam was laid above a krepidoma. Vertical timbers were joined to the horizontal beam and the interstices filled with massive masonry. The technique is similar to that used for Building ABCD and Sanctuary H at Haghia Triada.

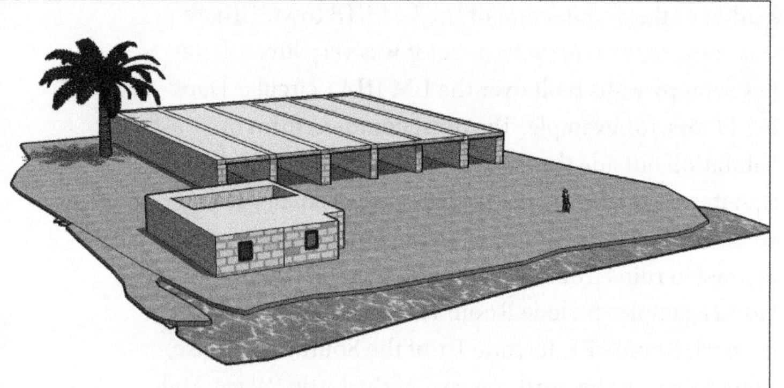

11.4. Reconstruction. Building P, Kommos. After J. Shaw and M. Shaw 2006, frontispiece.

The finds from the building are not of much help in figuring out its function. Building P contained many fragments of short-necked amphorae for transport but also domestic pottery and ovens. Building N had been used for metalworking and food preparation. Citing several Bronze Age and later classical parallels, the excavators propose that the building was a ship shed used for the winter storage of boats. The adjacent Building N would have been used by its overseer. The interpretation is appealing, given the location of the building on the beach and the fact that this monumental building is unlikely to have been commissioned and built by locals. It was probably a harbor facility tied to either Haghia Triada or Knossos or both. As we have seen, D. Puglisi suggests that the Protopalatial and Neopalatial predecessors of Building P had a similar function (see chap. 8).[6]

The Stoà del Mercato

The Stoà del Mercato at Haghia Triada (figs. 11.5, 11.6) was also built in LM IIIA2 at a date later than that of the monumental constructions around the Piazzale dei Sacelli. It was used through the LM IIIB period.[7] Like Building P at Kommos, the Stoà is huge, some 48 m long, half the length of an American football field. On the ground floor, a row of eight rectangular storage rooms opens onto a portico of alternating columns and pillars. The pillars were carefully aligned with the walls dividing the magazines, an arrangement unparalleled at other Minoan sites and rare in classical stoas until the late fourth century BC.[8] At the north end of the building, a stairway probably led to a second-story portico.

While the form of the building is unique, it retains most of the elements of the earlier complex immediately to the south, the Bastione (a storage building) and Portico 10. Here those elements were combined into a single structure. The Bastione was renovated and remained in use. In the LM IIIB period, a stairway was added to connect the two.

Shrines

With the abandonment of all the Palaces except Knossos came a remarkable change in cult practices. Religious ceremonies that had previously been conducted in the Palaces and in rural peak sanctuaries now shifted to the

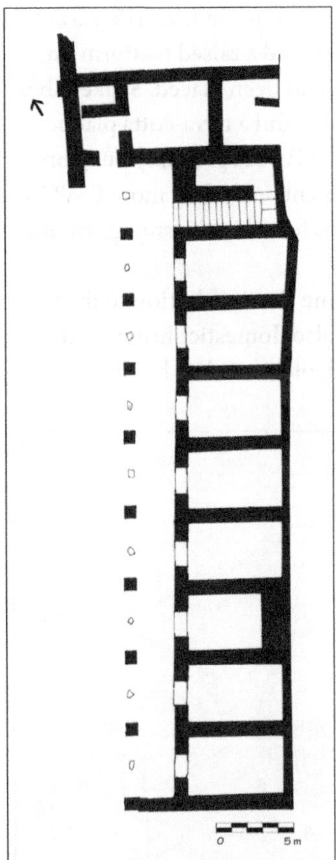

11.5. Plan. Stoà del Mercato. After Di Vita and La Regina 1984, fig. 230.

11.6. Stoà del Mercato from the south. Photo by author.

villages. Over the course of the LM IIIA2–LMIIIB period independent civic shrines became the major centers of worship, and for the first time a standard set of cult equipment was adopted. This included statues of the Goddess with the Upraised Arms (conventionally called the GWUA) and offertory cups supported on "snake tube" stands.[9]

The Shrine of the Double Axes at Knossos (see fig. 11.3) is the earliest of these shrines (probably LM IIIA2), and in some ways it is a transitional monument.[10] This small, rectangular structure was installed in a room just south of the Residential Quarter. Its floor was divided in three levels, rising from a low entrance level to a higher section in the center to a raised platform built against the north wall. On the platform were a statue of the GWUA, four statuettes of votaries, two sets of Horns of Consecration with sockets to hold Double Axes, and a small steatite Double Axe. This set of equipment is slightly different from the assemblage used in LM IIIB–LM IIIC. In addition several of the traditional symbolic objects here, including the Horns of Consecration and the Double Axes, would not be found in the later sanctuaries except as emblems attached to the GWUA's crown.[11]

Over the course of the LM IIIB period and continuing into LM IIIC, the cult equipment used in public shrines became increasingly standardized. Several GWUA figures were placed on a raised platform. Terracotta plaques, probably with painted images, were hung on the walls.[12] Nearby, snake tubes, stands with looping snakelike handles, held offertory vessels. The snake tubes were made of the same clay and apparently as a set with the GWUA figures, so that each goddess had her own stands.[13]

Outside Knossos the best example of this new kind of public shrine is the LM IIIB Civic Shrine at Gournia (see fig. 9.44).[14] The Civic Shrine was a small (ca. 3 m × 4 m), one-room building standing alone near the top of the site. It had been built within the remains of a Neopalatial building that, as mentioned in chapter 10, may also have been a shrine. A bench set into a recess in the south wall may have originally held the cult equipment, which included an offering table, statues of the GWUA, and five snake tubes.

Much less is known about what must have been a public shrine at Kannia, near Gortyn, because the building had been badly disturbed by plowing before its excavation (fig. 11.7).[15] Like the Civic Shrine at Gournia, this shrine had also been built into the remains of an earlier Neopalatial building. The main sanctuary room was Room I, which G. Gesell suggests may have been directly accessible from the exterior in LM IIIB. As at Gournia the sanctuary room had a raised platform on which four GWUA figures had been placed. Snake tubes stood in front of the platform and a terra-cotta plaque with a molded image of the GWUA probably hung on the wall. Other cult equipment, including more GWUA figures and snake tubes, was found in the storage rooms III, V, and XV.

Gesell and others assume that in addition to these public shrines, there were also domestic shrines in the LM IIIA2–LM IIIB period, often marked by the appear-

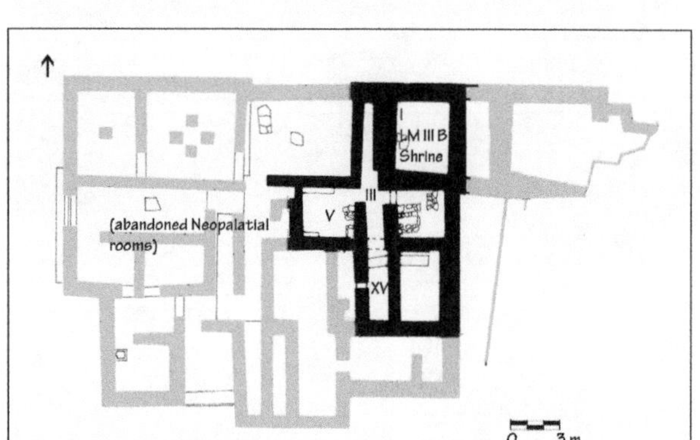

11.7. Plan. Kannia. After Levi 1959, p. fig. 4.

11.9. Reconstruction. House with the Snake Tube, Kommos. After McEnroe 1996, pl. 3.113.

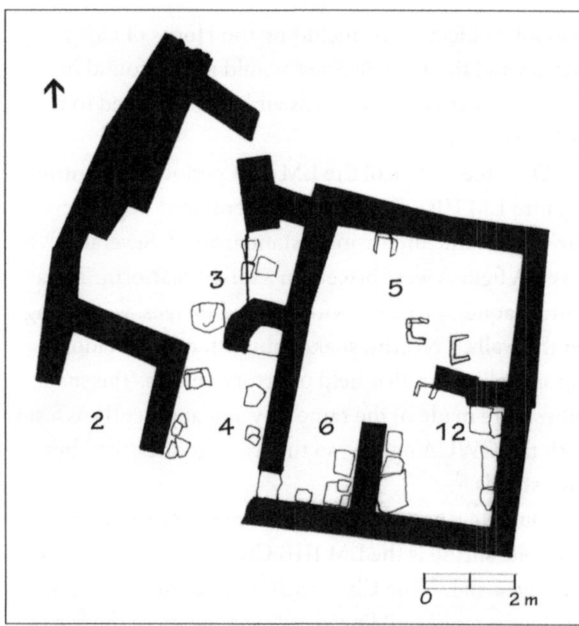

11.8. Plan. House with the Snake Tube, Knossos. After McEnroe 1996, pl. 3.112.

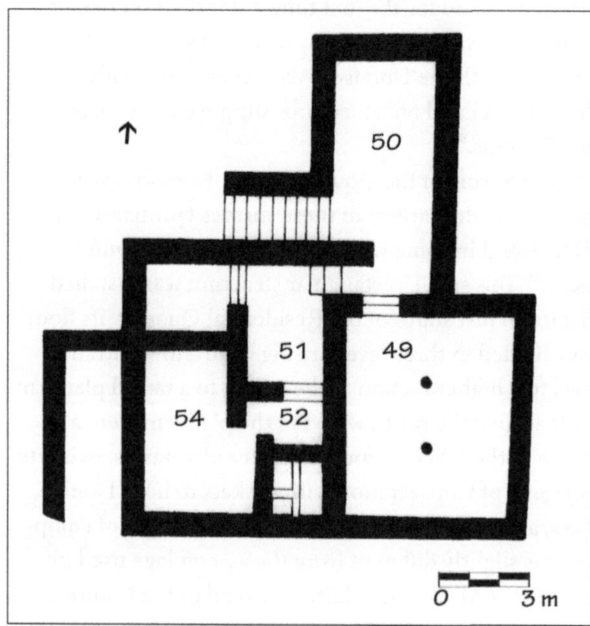

11.10. Plan. House Eh, Gournia. After *Gournia*, plan.

ance of snake tubes. Rooms in houses at Haghia Triada, Khondro Viannou, Kommos (fig. 11.9), and Katsamba had been identified as shrines on this basis.[16] However, if we define a shrine on the basis of a specific assemblage of cult equipment, of which the GWUA is the essential requirement, none of these rooms would qualify.[17] The picture is one of an emerging public cult conducted in specialized facilities.

The two shrines whose context we know best, those at Knossos and Gournia, present an intriguing picture of that new cult. Both are surrounded by the wreckage of the past: the Shrine of the Double Axes is in a largely abandoned Palace, while the Civic Shrine at Gournia stands in the midst of the ruins of the earlier town. Religion has a political dimension, and one wonders about the political implications of these shrines and who administered them. Did the cult proclaim continuity with the past? or did it represent the religion of resistance? In the following period, LM IIIC, this new cult of the GWUA would culminate in independent cult buildings that for the first time might properly be called temples.

Houses and Villages

The House with the Snake Tube at Kommos had been built originally in the LM IA period.[18] By the time it was finally abandoned some three hundred years later in LM IIIB it had undergone a number of changes (figs. 11.8, 11.9). A series of scrappy rubble walls blocked the door in the northwest corner, perhaps a result of someone's attempt to shore up the roof. The interior walls in the northwestern part of the house were leveled and covered with a new floor that turned this section of the house into a single room. The western part of the south wall had collapsed, and a wide gap in the wall opened from the room containing the snake tube toward the south. And while the eastern half of the house retained more of its original form, it was cluttered with a series of pot stands and slab-framed hearths whose distinctive form was studied by M. Shaw.[19] Most of the house had the appearance of a makeshift shelter, with crude furniture built of the rubble picked from the ruins.

Topographically only about fifty meters separate this building from the monumental LM III buildings to the south. In other respects, however, they are worlds apart. The House with the Snake Tube is not unusual: across the island more than half of the excavated dwellings of this period are reused Neopalatial buildings. People returned to the earlier settlements, and perhaps many had never left. Wherever possible the well-built houses of the earlier period were reinhabited. Repairs were made as necessary, often replacing costly wood construction with rubble. Little attention was paid to the earlier functions of the rooms: a stairway could become a storage room; a hall could become a kitchen; industries could be located in unlikely buildings.

Despite the fact that so many houses of the Second Palatial period continued to be used in LM III, surprisingly few buildings were actually built according to the traditional forms. House Eh at Gournia (fig. 11.10) is basically similar to the earlier houses at the site.[20] Save for the substitution of a court for the normal vestibule, it consists of the familiar set of rooms: the storage room, hall, industrial room, stairway, and doorless space, arranged as in the earlier houses. Only the thresholds, formed of a central slab of limestone with harder slabs closely fitted against either side, reflects a later style of construction. Buildings such as this were exceptions in the LM III A2–LM IIIB period. One might have expected more continuity at the local level. Instead, it appears that the link to the Neopalatial past had largely broken down.

At nearby Mochlos the Neopalatial buildings were apparently so badly damaged in the LM IB destructions that they were beyond repair and could not be reoccupied. Beginning in LM IIIA1 the new settlers started building a series of small houses (fig. 11.11). Six of the earliest were built by building short walls across the remains of the Neopalatial streets, incorporating the facades of the ruined houses into the new structures. The largest new house, House Alpha, was set apart from the other houses and had a large main room supported by two columns. The excavators identify this building as the house of the local ruler who was buried in Tomb 15 of the cemetery located across the bay.[21]

Several new villages or new neighborhoods in old settlements were established in this period. None has been completely published, and all of them are confusing. The tiny settlement at Khondro Viannou is typical (figs. 11.12, 11.13).[22] It was occupied from LM IIIA1 through the end of LM IIIA2, a period of about seventy years. Although the site has been the subject of two re-

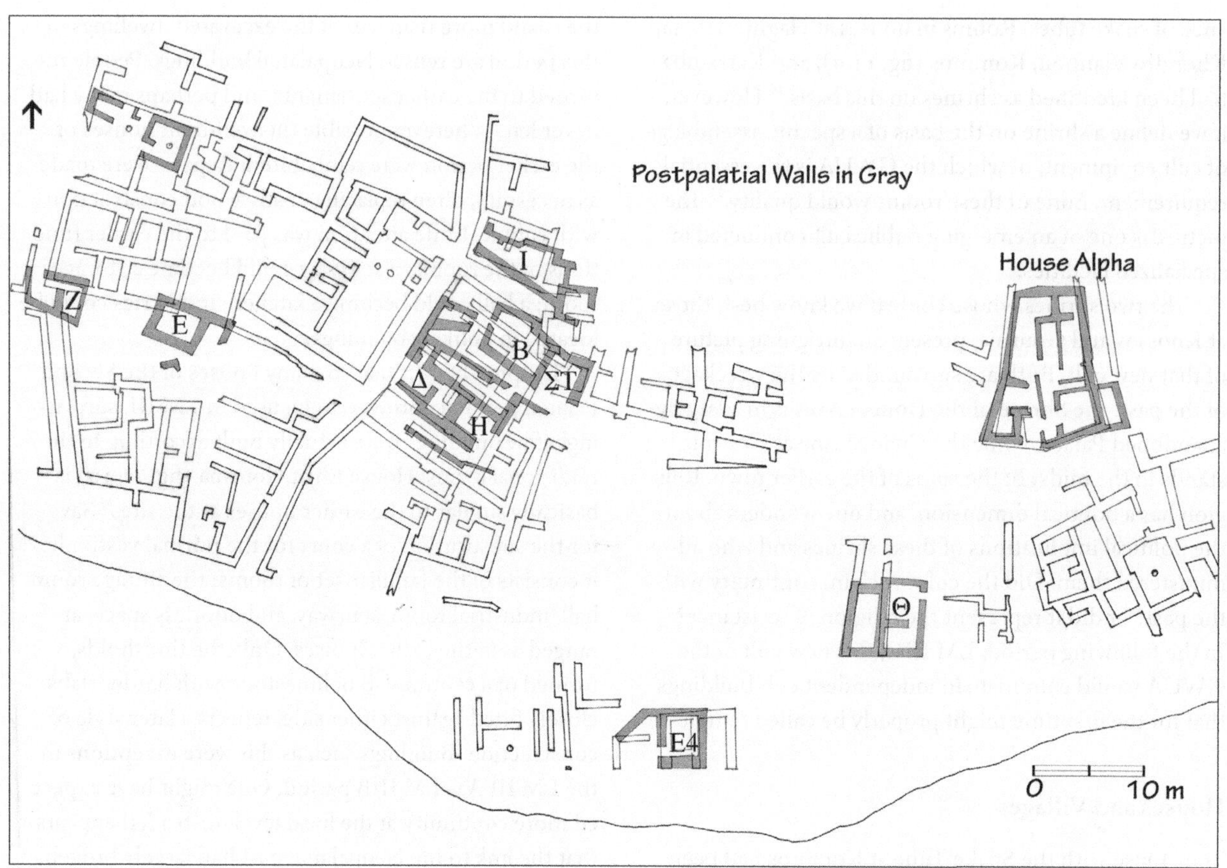

11.11. Plan. LM III buildings, Mochlos. After Brogan, Smith, and Soles 2002, fig. 4.

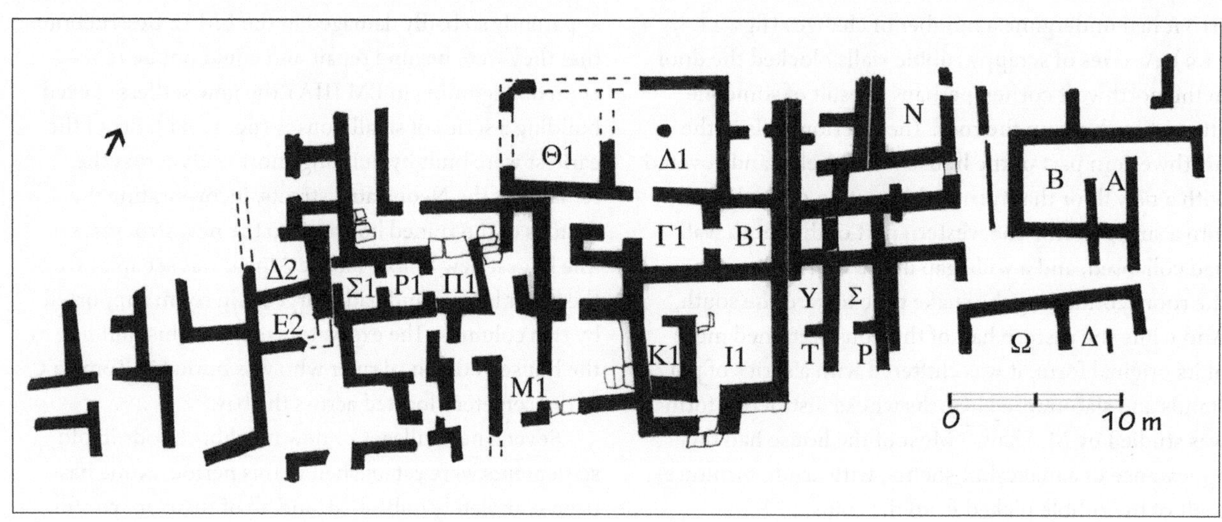

11.12. Plan. Khondro Viannou. After L. Platon 1997, fig. 4.

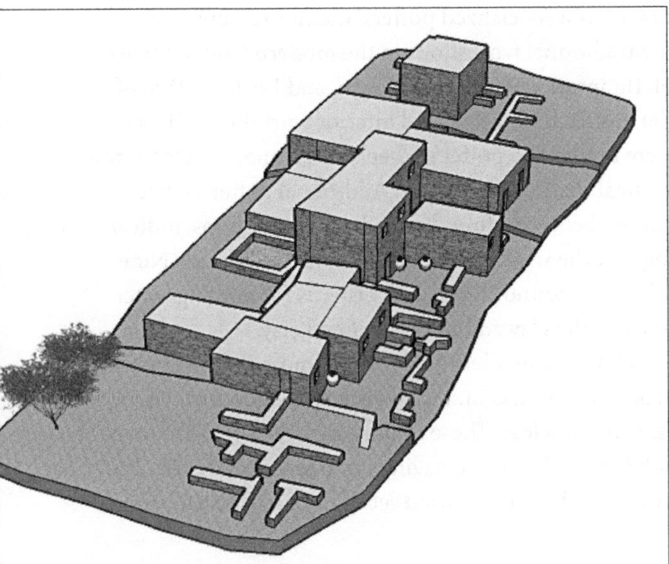

11.13. Isometric reconstruction. Khondro Viannou. After Hayden 1990, fig. 3.

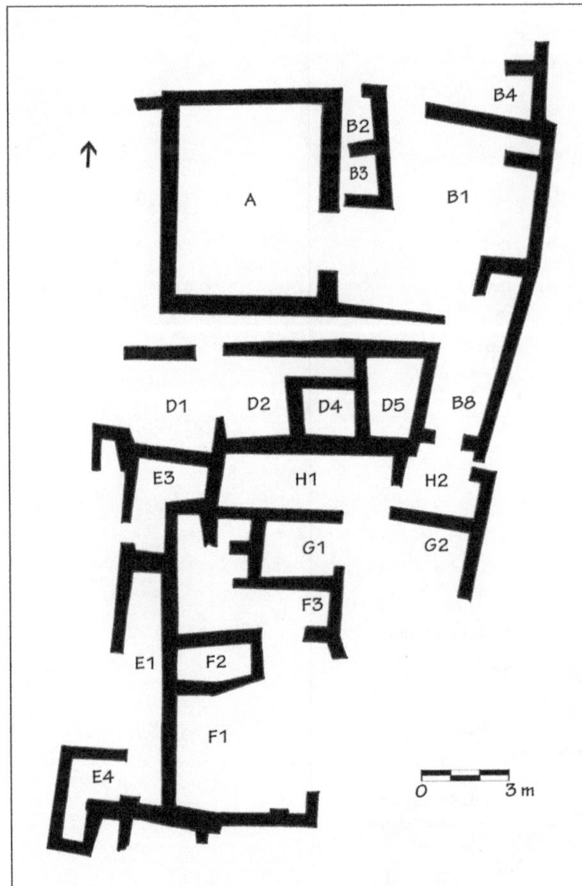

11.14. Plan. Amnisos. After Hayden 1990, fig. 4.

cent studies, there is still no general agreement on how to divide the complex into individual houses. One of the factors that makes the site difficult to understand is that it was not laid out all at the same time but accumulated over the course of its rather brief history. The earliest structures were those in the middle, Rooms Γ1, B1, K1, and I1. Gradually other structures were added to the east and the west.

Another new feature, characteristic of all the new LM III settlements, was the use of walled courtyards used for cooking or as work areas, supplementing the interior spaces of the tiny houses. B. Hayden observes that in this period these private walled courtyards seem to take the place of the public courtyards of the Neopalatial towns.[23] The hamlet at Khondro Viannou consists of a series of small, single-story houses, each having two to four rooms.[24] There was a degree of specialization within the settlement. For example, in the large room with the central column, D1, the number of drinking vessels found suggests a communal activity. The excavator and, more recently, L. Platon located a sanctuary someplace in the center of the site based on a snake tube found in Room Z1, but recently S. Privitera has challenged that proposal.[25]

Other settlements of this period similarly combine small houses and associated enclosed courtyards. The excavated portion of the LM III settlement at Amnisos (fig. 11.14) was built over the course of many years, beginning with the largest and best-built room, A, and gradually new houses were added in every direction as need arose. Unfortunately we know little about what was found in the houses.

Quartier Nu at Malia (fig. 11.15) appears to be essentially similar.[26] The excavators regard the entire area as a single building complex, but that seems unlikely.[27] For one thing, circulation patterns suggest a division into smaller units: access from one part of the site to the other is quite restricted. In addition, an examination of the butted joints indicates that the site had a more complex building history than the two broad phases that J. Driessen and A. Farnoux describe for the LM III period.[28] The final publication of the site may clarify the situation.

The LM IIIB settlement at Kato Gouves, located on the coast between Herakleion and Malia, is especially noteworthy (fig. 11.16).[29] The excavated portion of the

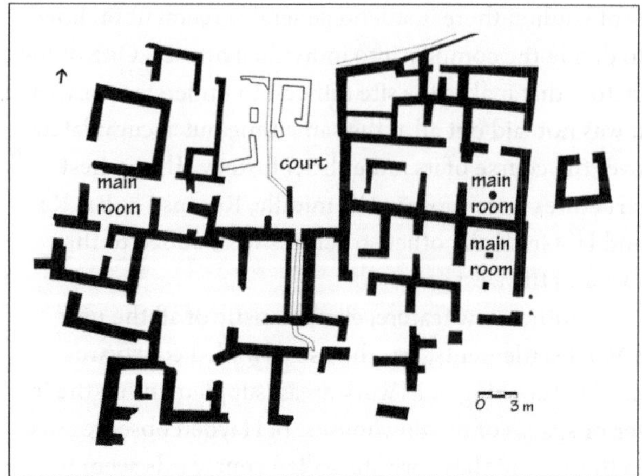

11.15. Plan. Quartier Nu, Malia. After Driessen and Farnoux 1994, fig. 4.

town was a specialized potters' quarter reminiscent of the traditional workshops in the modern Cretan towns of Thrapsano, Margarites, Kentri, and Lochria. Two of the houses had specialized interior workshops. These were marked by potter's wheels and stone sockets for the vertical shaft of the wheels. Additional potter's wheels and sockets were found outside the workshops, indicating that the work spilled out into the courtyards. Nine kilns were found, along with cisterns for holding water to clean the clay and piles of refined clay.

D. Vallianou identified parts of more than six houses, at least one in the southeast Area A and three in Area C. Area B is unclear. These houses are larger than the ones at Khondro Viannou, having up to ten rooms each. The houses had a standardized set of rooms. The main room

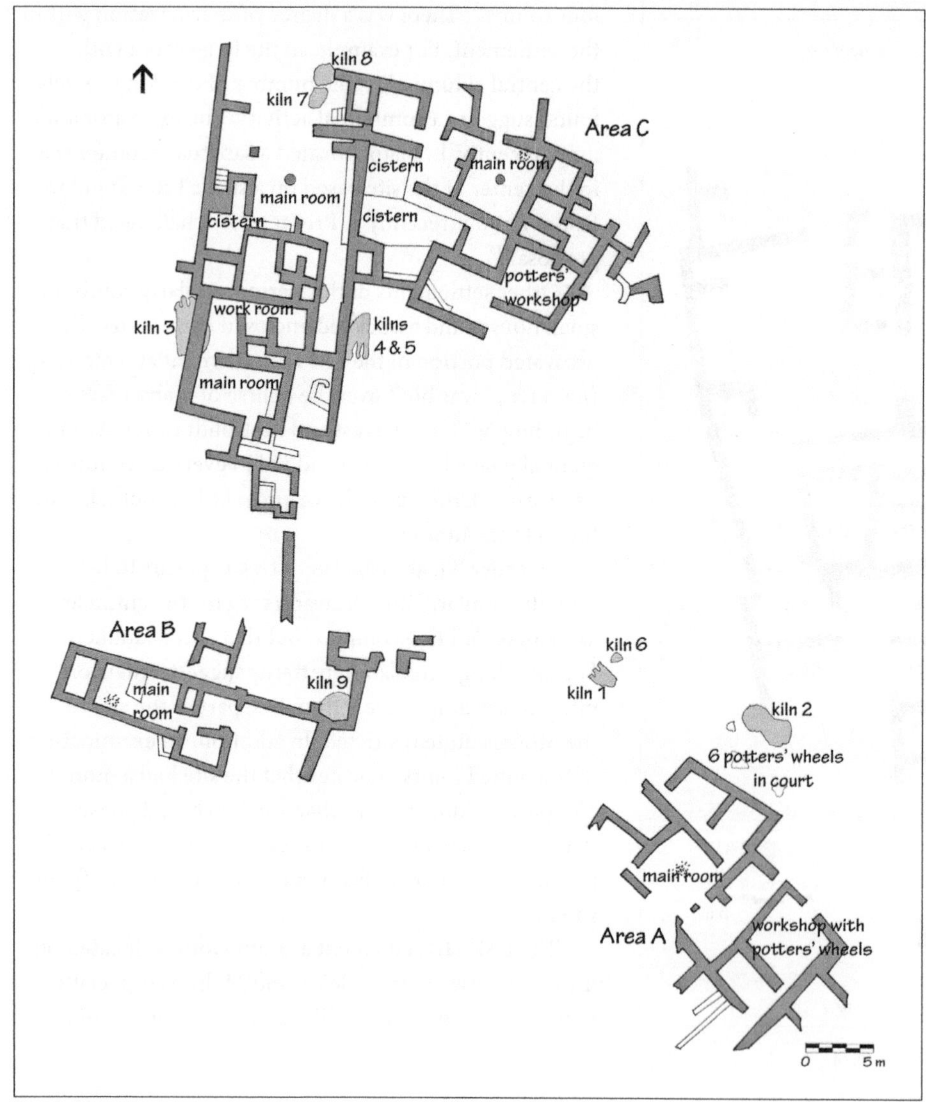

11.16. Plan. Kato Gouves. After Vallianou 1997, pl. CXXIV.

was approximately square with a central column and a hearth. Around the main rooms were supplementary storage rooms and work areas.

By the late LM IIIA2–LM IIIB period, house architecture had very little to do with the earlier architecture of the age of Palaces. Houses grounded in local traditions were again the norm. The Palatial veneer that once had so tentatively covered the island had cracked, and people were left to their own devices.

"Mycenaeanizing" Corridor Houses in Crete

There was, however, one form of LM IIIA2–LM IIIB house that followed an international model. Four well-built LM IIIA2–LM IIIB houses have been reasonably compared with a specific type of Mycenaean house on the mainland, a type G. Hiesel calls the Korridorhaus and I. Shear Type D1.[30] Shear writes that this type "consists of a main room with a hearth, preceded by a vestibule and frequently containing a rear chamber. This two- or three-roomed suite is arranged along a single axis behind a courtyard and it was entered from one of the narrow ends of the suite. Parallel to the main axis there is a corridor which leads to a series of secondary rooms arranged along an axis roughly parallel to the major axis of the building . . . it is usually the most elaborate type of private house to be found on LH sites, except at Mycenae."[31] Shear lists examples at Mycenae, Tiryns, the Menelaion at Sparta, Prosymna, Zygouries, Mouriatada, and Krisa. The form also appeared at Mycenaean-dominated sites outside the mainland, including Phylakopi and Miletus.[32]

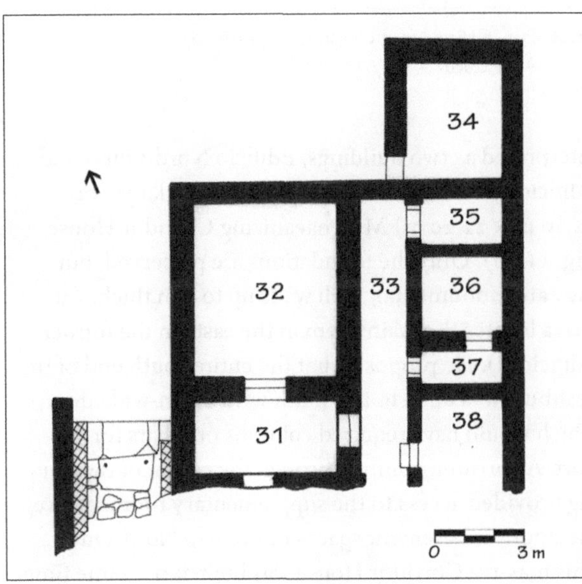

11.17. Plan. House He, Gournia. After *Gournia*, plan.

11.18. House He, Gournia, from south. Photo by author.

Shear's definition is useful because it does not rely on one or two simple characteristics—an axial plan or a central hearth, for example—but involves an entire set of rooms arranged in a specific way. When we see that same set of rooms and the same arrangement appear in LM IIIA2–LM IIIB Crete we can be reasonably confident they constitute a reference to mainland forms. This does not necessarily mean that the individuals who lived in these buildings were genetically Mycenaean (see chap. 10); it does, however, indicate that they intentionally chose to present a Mycenaeanizing image.

No two of these Cretan houses were precisely the same. Each was made of locally available materials and used some techniques specific to the site. Nevertheless their plans are similar to one another and similar to the examples on the mainland. The even distribution of the Corridor Houses across most of the island—one at Khania, one at Haghia Triada in the Mesara, one in the fertile Lasithi plain, and one at Gournia—is reminiscent of the "second-order" regional administrative hubs J. Bennet identified in the slightly earlier Linear B tablets.[33]

The idea that there might be mainland-style houses in Postpalatial Crete is not new. F. Oelmann recognized House He at Gournia (figs. 11.17, 11.18) as a Mycenaeanizing form in 1912.[34] The building consists of an anteroom, a main room, a side corridor, and supplementary rooms, all arranged along a single axis. It corresponds closely to Shear's Type D1 house, and in all these aspects differs from Cretan Neopalatial traditions.

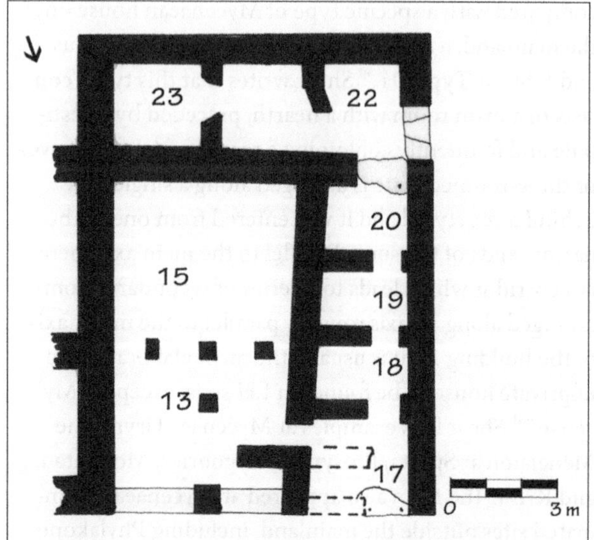

11.19. Plan. House A, Plati. After Dawkins 1913–1914, Pl. I.

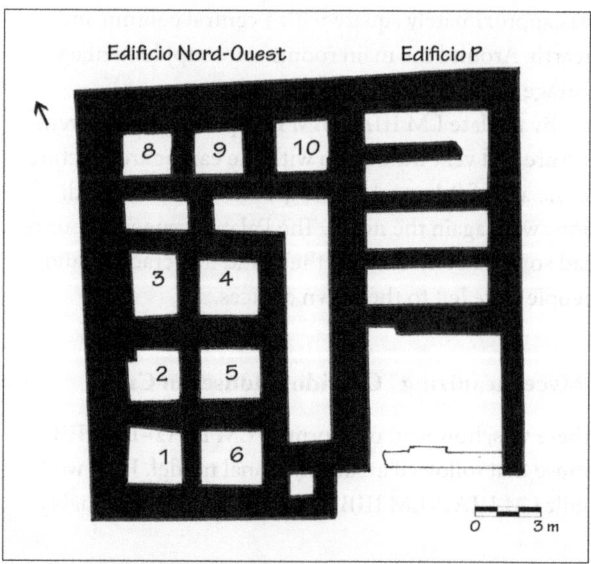

11.20. Plan. Edificio Nord-Ouest/P, Haghia Triada. After Cucuzza 1997, fig. 8.

In addition, the type of threshold used in the building, formed of several closely fitting slabs, may also reflect Mycenaean construction techniques.

Two buildings at Plati in the Lasithi Plain may belong to the same type.[35] Building A consists of an anteroom, a main room, and a side corridor leading to a set of back rooms (fig. 11.19). Its rooms as well as its axial arrangement and emphasis on the front facade are similar to House He at Gournia. Other features, such as the pier-and-door partition, the decorative paving, and the paved exterior court with a bench come from Neopalatial traditions.

Building B, though not preserved above its foundations, is similar. R. Dawkins, the excavator, insightfully compared the building with the Menelaion near Sparta on the mainland, which he had excavated three years earlier.[36] The arrangement of these two buildings in a right angle around a courtyard may be simply a continuation of the arrangement of the Neopalatial arrangement of the site. Yet the formality of the plan here contrasts with the tangled arrangements of the houses at Khondro Viannou, Amnisos, and Gouves.

A series of new buildings, including the Stoà del Mercato, was constructed in the northern part of Haghia Triada in the later part of LM IIIA2. Recently N. Cucuzza proposed that what the original excavators had interpreted as two buildings, Edificio Nord-Ouest and Edificio P, actually were parts of the same large (ca. 22.20 m × 22.20 m) Mycenaeanizing Corridor House (fig. 11.20). Only the foundations are preserved, but they are monumental, with walls up to 2 m thick. Cucuzza locates the main room in the east (in the former Edificio P). He proposes that the entire south end of the vestibule was open to the south with a 7-m-wide door, which would have required columns or pillars for support. A corridor running through the center of the building provided access to the supplementary rooms above the doorless basement spaces of Edificio Nord-Ouest.[37] This massive Corridor House was built at the same time as the Stoà del Mercato and, by the LM IIIB period, was physically joined to it. The Corridor House is likely to have been the residence of the chief administrator of Haghia Triada, who may also have controlled Kommos and much of the Mesara.

Excavations at Kastelli, Khania, in the middle of the modern city, have produced important information on Linear B, stratigraphy, and chronology.[38] Unfortunately the architecture has been seriously disturbed by later construction, and only the basic outlines of the buildings along with a few intriguing details with clear Mycenaean parallels are decipherable. The main room of each house had a circular hearth up to 1.5 m in diameter, built of clay and stones on a bedding of potsherds and clay. These hearths are strikingly similar to hearths excavated on the mainland at, for example, the Palace at Pylos.[39] In addition, several figurines, some of which appear to have been imported from the mainland, were inserted into or placed near the hearths in a way that is also reminiscent of Mycenaean practice. This evidence, along with several stirrup jars inscribed with Linear B, suggested to the excavators that Greeks from the mainland actually lived in at least one building at Kastelli, Khania.

Crete in the Postpalatial Period

During the long (ca. 1360–1200 BC), complex Postpalatial period, life in Crete was radically different from what it had been in the Neopalatial period. The Palaces and the elaborate houses were gone. In their place were villages like Khondro Viannou that were geared toward subsistence farming, villages of crafts makers such as Kato Gouves, large-scale export facilities in the Mesara, and a handful of regional centers with Mycenaean-style Corridor Houses. Knossos was no longer the major city on the island. Perhaps that role had been taken over by Khania; perhaps Cretan affairs were overseen directly by the mainland powers at Mycenae or Thebes; or perhaps there was no island-wide social and economic integration at all, just a set of independent regions.[40] Compared with the Neopalatial period, the picture is utilitarian and bleak. Yet it would soon get much worse.

At the end of this period, around 1200 BC, Crete experienced a new wave of destructions. This time the devastation was almost complete. Crete was caught up in a series of events that devastated the entire eastern Mediterranean: the palaces and cities of Mycenaean Greece were destroyed; the Hittite empire of Anatolia collapsed; waves of invaders and fleeing refugees swept the Aegean islands, Cyprus, Syria, and the Levantine coast; further east, the Kassite kingdom in Mesopotamia was overthrown; even Egypt suffered permanent damage. This was one of the most profound upheavals in history, and the forces behind it are still not fully understood. Later Greeks recalled the Dorian invasion, while Egyptian documents and letters found at Ugarit in Syria refer to invasions of the Sea Peoples. Several other factors, including the introduction of iron weapons, changes in military tactics, and drought, may have contributed. The damage was not only to people and property, but to the entire social and economic system. The sophisticated Bronze Age network of international trade broke down. In the Aegean, writing ceased. The few survivors in Crete retreated to remote villages to fend for themselves at a subsistence level. With this cataclysm, the Bronze Age ended and the Dark Age began.

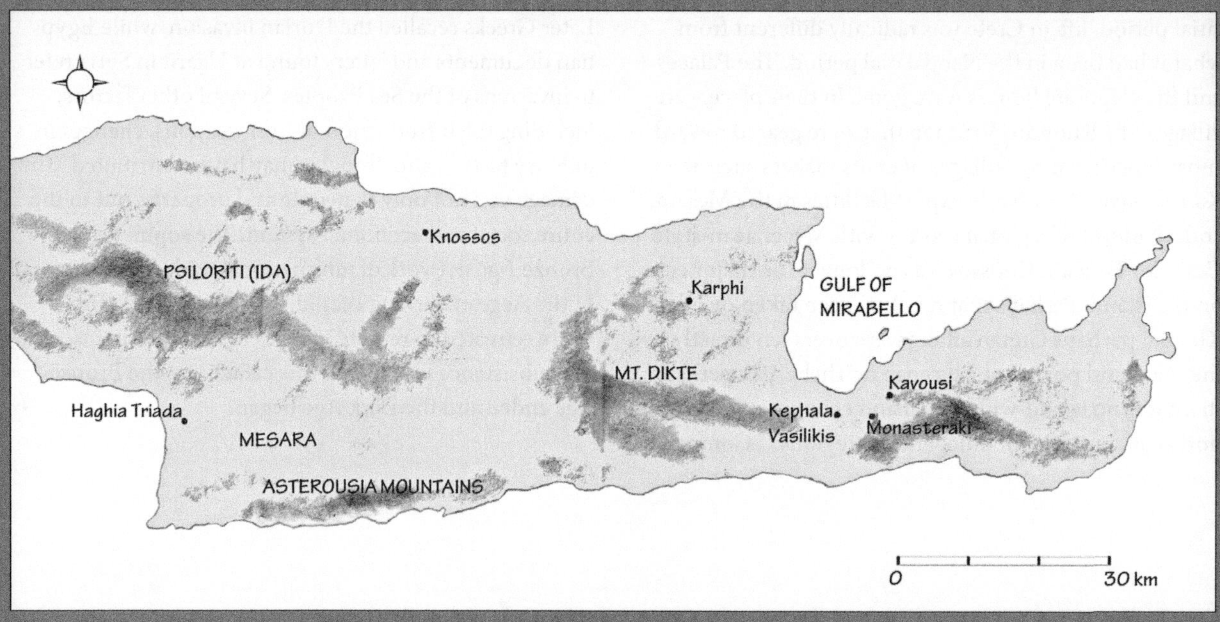

12.1. Sites discussed in chapter 12.

Survival and Memory in LM IIIC

CA. 1200–1100 BC

THE CATASTROPHES at the end of LM IIIB resulted in the abandonment of nearly all the Minoan settlements along the coasts and in low-lying inland areas (fig. 12.1). In LM IIIC, new hamlets were established in defensible upland areas. With this dramatic shift came changes in economy and religion, and the Bronze Age past began to take on the aura of myth.

Defensible Settlements

At traumatic moments in Cretan history—in Final Neolithic, under the Byzantines, the Venetians, and the Ottomans—islanders fled the threatened, accessible coastal areas and sought safety in the mountains. In LM IIIC, vast expanses of the lowlands were abandoned and at least 109 remote upland settlements were established.[1] Four of these new villages—Kavousi, Monasteraki, Kephala Vasilikis, and Karphi—have several characteristics in common:

1. The architecture of poverty. It embodies the struggles of three or four generations of refugees for survival.
2. Part of the survival strategy involved locating the new settlements in difficult-to-reach areas high on the slopes of mountains, at a safe distance from the sea, but with a clear view of it. A few LM IIIC sites were surrounded with fortification walls.[2]
3. Many of these sites were grouped in tight clusters. Kavousi Kastro is a high precipice overlooking Kavousi Vronda on the slopes below. Similarly Monasteraki is composed of the almost inaccessible Monasteraki Katalimata perched at the edge of Ha Gorge and the lower and larger site of Monasteraki Halasmenos. Karphi consists of a tight group of sites. In each case, the higher component was founded first as an impregnable defensive refuge and the lower, more sustainable component slightly later. D. Haggis found that a similar pattern of interdependent clusters of sites operated in the Kavousi region until World War II.[3]
4. Following the total collapse of the island-wide Linear B economy, the settlements had to be self-sustainable. All are small (under 40,000 m^2) and are located near sources of water and arable land.[4] To borrow two oxymoronic phrases from H. Glassie, over the long term in Crete there had been a dramatic change from the "individualistic dependence" of the Palatializing network to the "communal self-sufficiency" of the remote mountain hamlets.[5]

Reconstructing Houses and Households at Kavousi

H. Boyd (and later H. Hawes) excavated at Kavousi for a month in 1900, and from 1978 to the present G. Gesell, W. Coulson, and L. Day have continued the project.[6] In LM IIIC Kavousi was made up of two distinct sites, Kavousi Kastro and Kavousi Vronda, both of which were also linked with the important Iron Age site at Azoria to the northeast.

Kavousi Kastro, as the name Kastro ("castle") implies, is a towering citadel visible from miles away. It projects from the north face of the Kavousi-Thripti Mountains and overlooks the sea, the Kampos plain, and the transit routes that run along the coast and through the Isthmus of Hierapetra. Although this was the first part of the Kavousi complex to be established in LM IIIC, nearly all of its preserved architecture dates to the later Protogeometric and Geometric periods.

Kavousi Vronda (fig. 12.2) is located on the top of a hill about 300 m below and to the west of Kastro. Disrupted by a series of Geometric graves and later farming and erosion, the settlement in plan looks at first glance as confusing as any of the small LM IIIB villages discussed above (see chap. 10). However, here the excavators have managed to interpret the architecture so specifically that we can not only understand much about this site, but also use the conclusions drawn here as a starting point for examining other settlements of the period.

K. Glowacki's study of cluster I-O-N in the western part of the site gives a distinct picture of the typical Vronda house and a description of how the small clusters of buildings were formed over time (fig. 12.3).[7] Building I, the first part of the cluster to have been built, originally consisted of three axially arranged rooms, I3, I4, and I5. The main room, I3, was a rectangular room with a central hearth for cooking, light, and heat and a small, domed clay oven in the northeast corner. A bench ran along its east wall, and near the hearth there must have been a vertical post to support the ceiling. The room had a broad range of stone tools (for grinding, pounding, and chopping) and pots (for cooking, storage, and fine ware), indicating that it had been the center of several domestic activities. The other rooms were supplementary: Room I4 was an anteroom, and I1 and I2 were later additions. The walls were carried up in rubble. Chimney pots placed above the central hearths

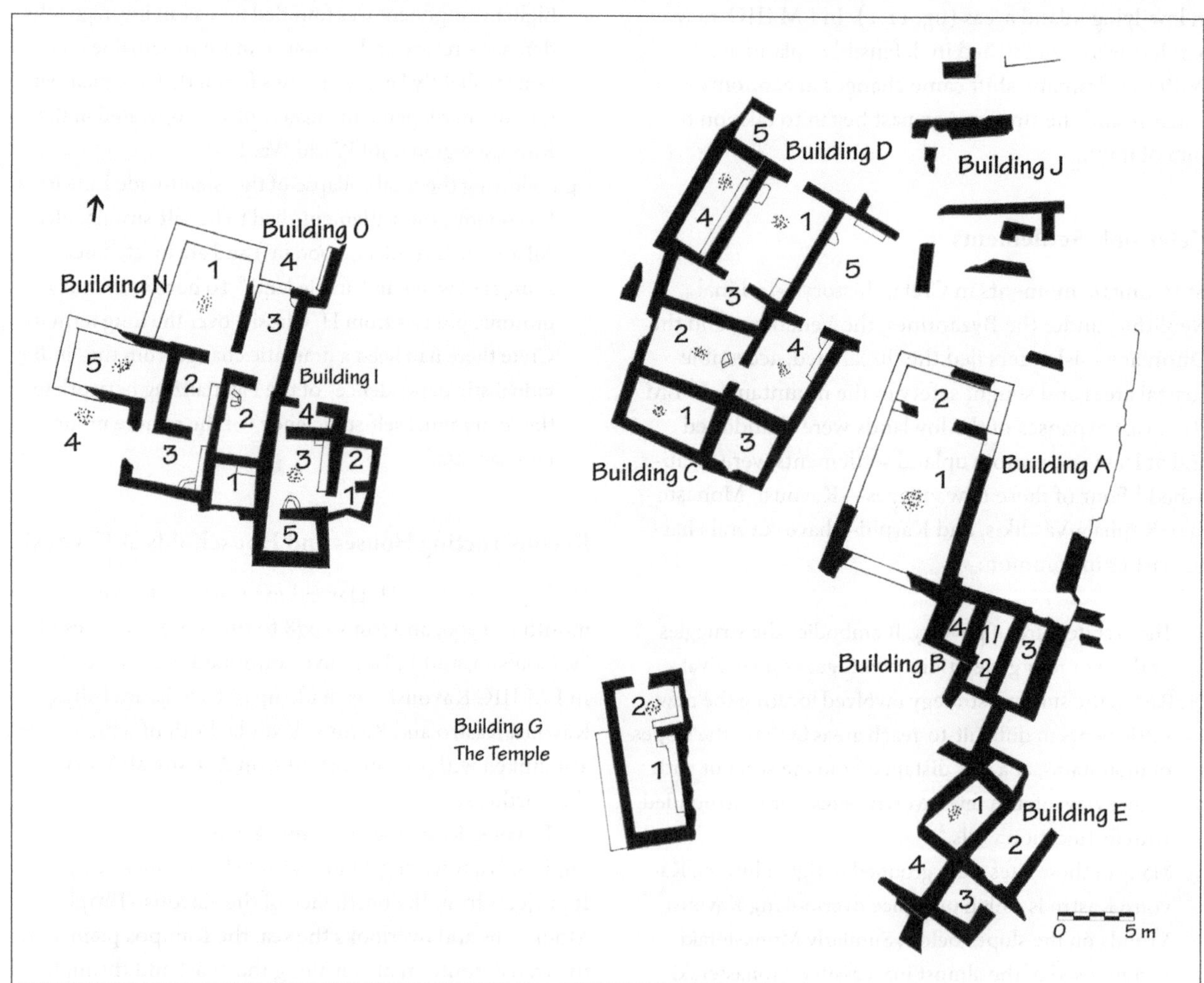

12.2. Plan. Kavousi Vronda. After Day and Snyder 2004, fig. 5.1.

allowed the smoke to escape.[8] This typical Vronda house would have been home to a family of about five people.

Applying the same crude calculations used to estimate the labor costs for the construction of the Neopalatial House AM at Pseira, one can come up with a rough idea of the amount of work that went into the construction of House I (see table 12.1). This is about a third of the labor cost of House AM at Pseira. Assuming once again a six-hour workday, four people could have built House I in about thirty-six work days.[9]

Building I, however, was never a completely finished project. As children became parents and the family grew, the building cluster grew with it, following the natural contours of the site downward toward the west. The axial Building O was built next, followed by Building N. Each new house had a large main room with a central

Table 12.1.
Labor Hours Required for House I at Vronda

Excavating terrace	40 m³ earth removed	@ .25 m³/hr = 160 hr
Quarrying	40 m³	@ 4 hr/m³ = 160 hr
Transporting materials		120 hr
Building walls	40 m³	@ 10 hr/m³ = 400 hr
Laying roof		20 hr
Total = 860 labor hours		

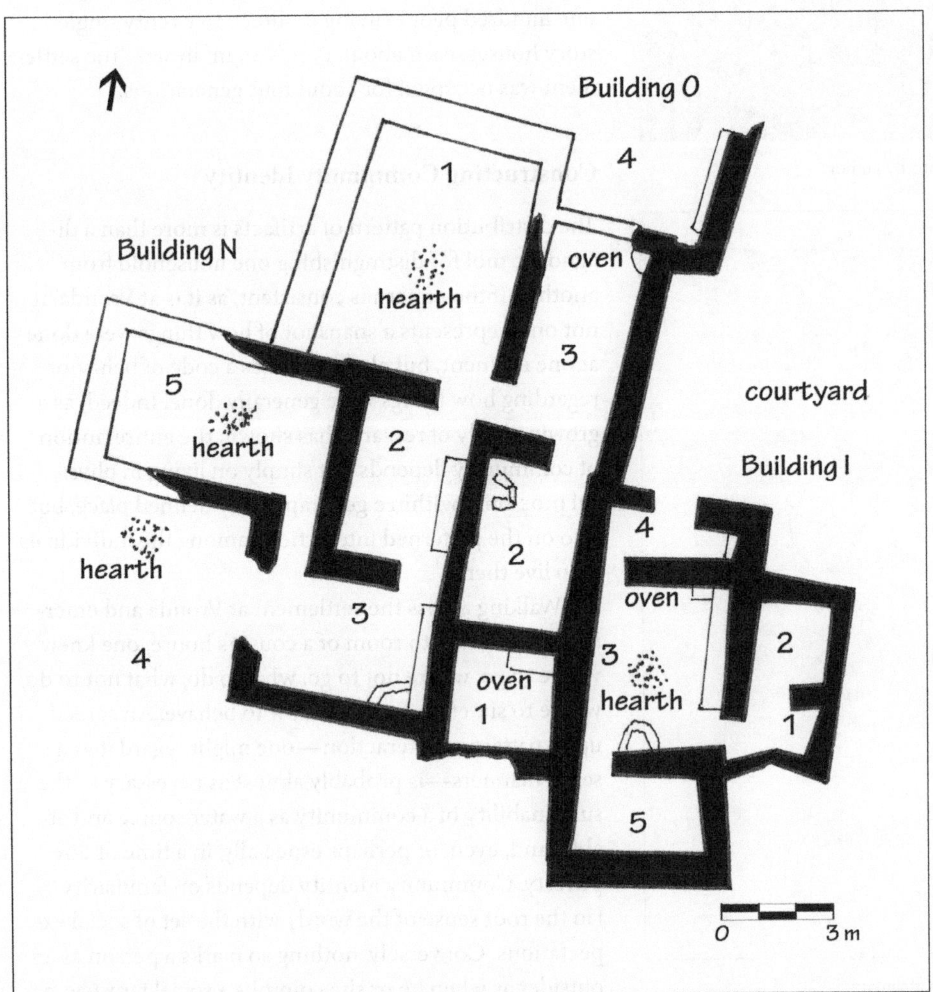

12.3. Plan. Houses I-O-N. After Glowacki 2004, fig. 9.3.

12.4. Ha Gorge from the west. Photo by author.

12.5. Reconstruction. Monasteraki Katalimata. After Haggis and Nowicki 1993, fig. 13.

hearth, vertical support for the roof, and the same assemblage of stone tools and pots. In fact, the relationship between central hearth and tool and pot assemblage is so standardized at Vronda that it is possible to divide the complicated site into a series of individual houses more or less on the basis of the large, rectangular room with the central hearth alone. Building N, then, might actually represent two households with main rooms in N1 and N5. (N4, which also has a large central hearth, is not well preserved.)

Using Glowacki's analysis of I-O-N as a template, one can relatively simply decipher the rest of the site. Each of the building clusters D, C, and E is probably the result of the changing makeup of specific families. Individual houses are recognizable by their main rooms with central hearths (in D1, D4, C1, C2, C4, E1, and N1. At its maximum size Vronda was a settlement of fewer than one hundred people living in fifteen to twenty single-story houses, each about 35 m^2–45 m^2 in size. The settlement was occupied for about four generations.[10]

Constructing Community Identity

The distribution pattern of artifacts is more than a diagnostic tool for distinguishing one household from another. If the pattern is consistent, as it is at Vronda, it not only represents a snapshot of how things were done at one moment, but also embodies a code of behavior regarding how things were generally done. Indeed, as a growing body of research has shown, the entire notion of community depends not simply on living in physical proximity within a geographically defined place, but also on the patterned interactions among the individuals who live there.[11]

Walking across the settlement at Vronda and entering, say, the hearth room of a cousin's house, one knew where to go, where not to go, what to do, what not to do, where to sit, etc.—in short, how to behave. An agreed-upon pattern of interaction—one might regard it as a set of manners—is probably almost as necessary to the sustainability of a community as a water source and arable land, even, or perhaps especially, in a time of dire poverty. Community identity depends on familiarity (in the root sense of the word) with the set of social expectations. Conversely, nothing so marks a person as an outsider as when he or she commits a social faux pas, a transgression of the unwritten code.

Monasteraki Katalimata and Halasmenos

Monasteraki is also a double site.[12] The lower, more extensive settlement at Halasmenos is similar in many ways to the hamlet at Vronda, while the upper group of buildings at Katalimata was probably only sporadically occupied for defensive purposes.

Katalimata (figs. 12.4, 12.5) is one of the most spectacularly situated sites in all of Greece. It consists of several buildings perched on individual narrow ledges of the sheer face of the cliff on the north flank of the Ha Gorge. Today the site is visited by goats, a few archaeologists, and a handful of thrill-seeking rock climbers equipped with ropes, pitons, and neoprene climbing suits. It is, in short, almost inaccessible. Under the direction of M. Tsipopoulou and Coulson, K. Nowicki single-handedly excavated the site, uncovering an LM IIIC building that by its final stage consisted of six rooms.[13]

The excavated portion of the lower site, Halasmenos (fig. 12.6), consists of a series of about fifteen houses. As at Vronda, the houses were built gradually over the course of the LM IIIC period. They were single-story buildings with a main room and one or two supplementary storage rooms. Hearths were built into the corners of some of the main rooms (Room B5, for example).

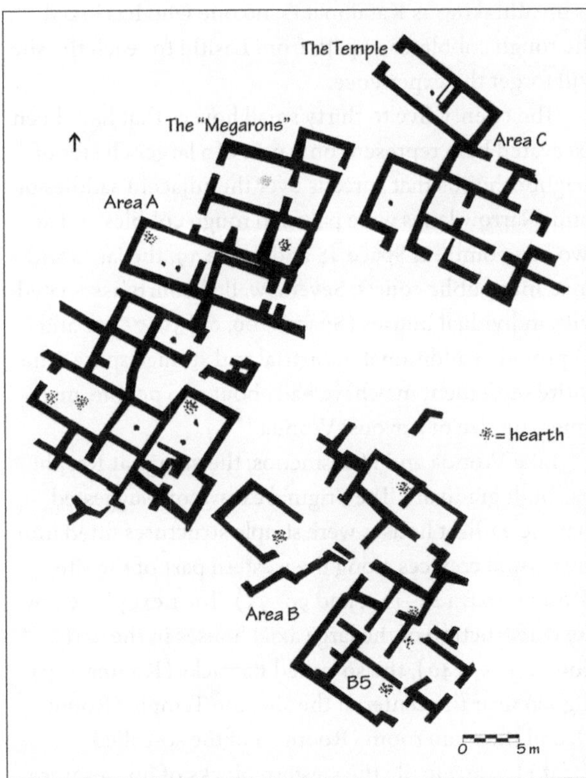

12.6. Plan. Monasteraki Halasmenos. After Tsipopoulou 2004, fig. 8.1.

The excavators divided the site into three areas, A, B, and C. Although built in phases, like the buildings of Vronda, the buildings here belong to the same general period. They were built in the middle part of LM IIIC and abandoned before the end of the period.

Tsipopoulou notes a distinct difference between the irregular plans of the houses and the axial plans of five buildings in area A, which she refers to as "megara of Mycenaean type."[14] There have been numerous calls to avoid the use of the term "megaron."[15] The term is problematic partly because it has been used so inconsistently (see chap. 10).[16] In addition, the term is loaded with assumptions about race and ethnicity. As early as 1908, D. Mackenzie warned against the already widespread tendency to interpret axial "megaron" plans as embodiments of the "Achaean" or "Nordic" race based on simplistic nineteenth-century stereotypes of fixed racial mentalities.[17] Nevertheless, the term "megaron" has been routinely used to contrast the logical, organized, axial, masculine "Mycenaeans" with the nature-loving, labyrinthine, feminine "Minoans."

Tsipopoulou's argument is more sophisticated than the usual ethnic stereotyping. She is concerned not directly with genetic identity but with cultural identity. Those two concepts are quite distinct (see chap. 10). Racial identity implies something fixed and essential, while cultural identity is a flexible social construction. Tsipopoulou describes Halasmenos as having a mixed population of "Mycenoans" whose most "Mycenaean" elements may have been several generations removed from the mainland. Within this complex community, different groups used architecture as one of the means of ascribing to themselves a particular cultural tradition.[18]

Kephala Vasilikis

Kephala Vasilikis is clearly visible from Halasmenos. It is located a short distance away, across the modern and ancient routes that run through the Isthmus of Hierapetra (fig. 12.7).[19] The site is on a steep-sided hill only about 200 m above sea level, but at a strategic point with a clear view of the sea both to the north and to the south.

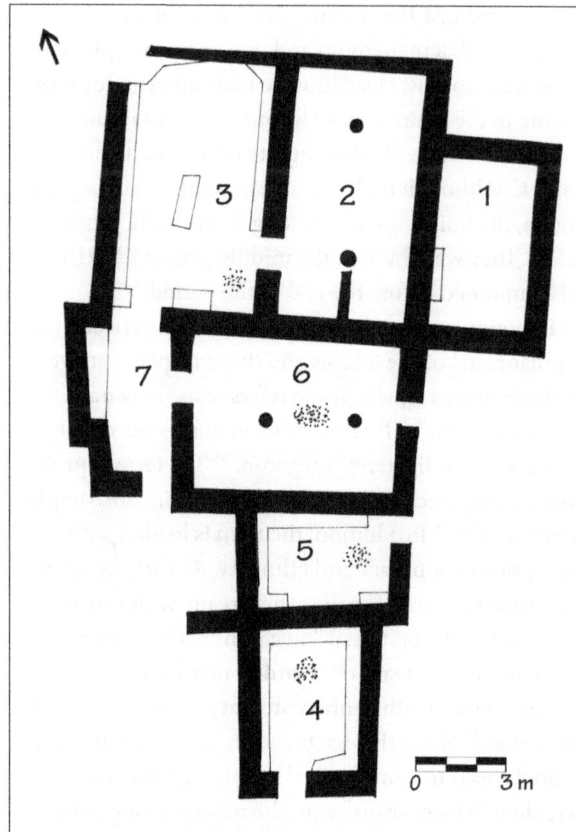

12.7. Plan. Kephala Vasilikis. After Eliopoulos 1998, fig. 9.

12.8. Karphi from the east. Photo by author.

The excavator described the Building E complex as a single, integrated eight-room temple complex, an interpretation to which I shall return. The complex was not, however, laid out at one time but was constructed over the course of many years from LM IIIC to Protogeometric (the construction of Room E1). Moreover, as both T. Eliopoulos and M. Prent note, objects specifically associated with the cult were found only in Room E4 and in the fill above E5, and E4 may have been the actual center of the cult.[20] Much of the rest of the complex may have been domestic. If the presence of a hearth indicates the location of the main room of a house, as it did at Vronda, the rooms at Kephala Vasilikis could represent three houses built over the course of two or more generations.

Karphi

"Karphi" means "nail," which describes this site perfectly: a rocky spike jutting out from the north face of the mountainous ridge that frames the upland Lasithi plain (figs. 12.8–12.11).[21] While its location is not nearly as breathtaking as Katalimata's, no one who has hiked the rough cobblestone path from Lasithi to reach the site will forget the experience.

The twenty-five to thirty small houses that have been excavated here represent only part of a larger cluster of neighborhoods that spreads over the adjacent saddles of land. Narrow lanes were paved in rough cobbles and at two key points, in Space 48 and Space 39, the lanes widened into public courts. Several walled courts associated with individual houses (Spaces 106, 61, 39, 75, 41 and 4) provided additional industrial and storage space. The entire settlement may have had about 750 people, many times the size of Kavousi Vronda.[22]

Like Vronda and Halasmenos, the village at Karphi was built gradually. The original excavators suggested that the earliest houses were simple structures fitted into the natural crevices along the western part of the site (Rooms 104, 123–125, and 90–95). The next phase saw the construction of the large axial houses in the east, Rooms 135–140), the so-called Barracks (Rooms 3–7), aligned near the center of the site, the Temple (Room 1), and the main room (Room 9) of the so-called Great House. Finally the western blocks of houses were squeezed into and occasionally over the existing street

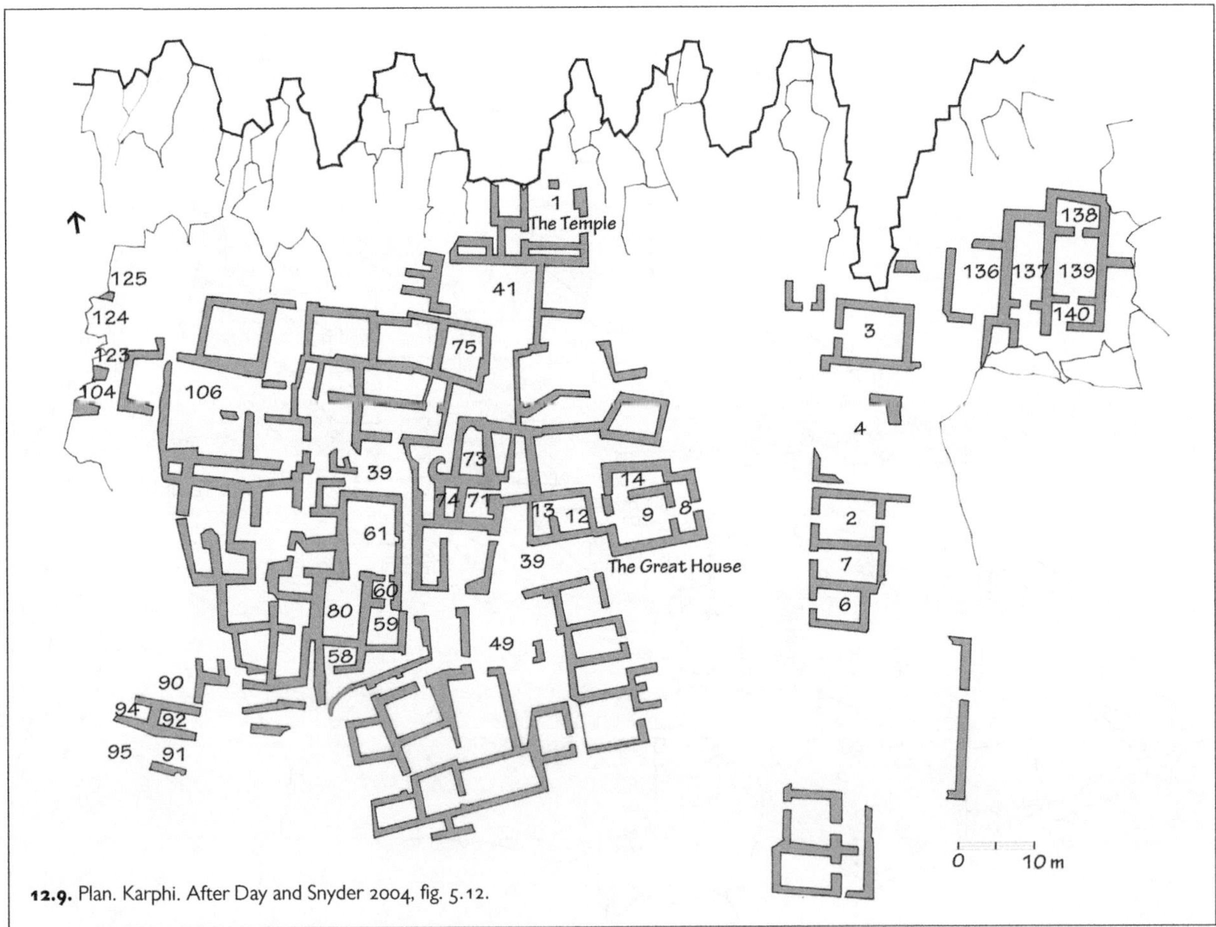

12.9. Plan. Karphi. After Day and Snyder 2004, fig. 5.12.

system. Nowicki is almost certainly right in suggesting that these phases are probably to be understood as part of an ongoing process rather than as discrete historical horizons.[23] As at Vronda and Halasmenos, the houses probably changed as families changed.

The houses are similar to those at Vronda and Halasmenos. The northeastern cluster can be read as three adjacent houses of one, two, and three rooms, each centered on a main room (Rooms 136, 137, and 139) with a central hearth. The Great House seems to have begun as a one-room house (Room 9) with a central hearth and, rather like House I at Vronda, was expanded with the addition of an anteroom (Room 8), a side supplementary room (Room 14), and storage rooms (Rooms 11–13). Several other houses, such as the Baker's House (Rooms 71, 73, and 74) and the Priest's House (Rooms 58–61) were nonaxial buildings that were laid out as the topography and existing buildings and streets allowed.

One set of buildings at Karphi stands out from the rest. Rooms 135–144, located on the eastern edge of the excavated area, are laid out on axial plans similar to the "megara" of area A at Halasmenos. Nowicki has interpreted the differences between this set of buildings and those on the saddle to the southwest as evidence that there were two different cultural groups in the town, a view that is consistent with Tsipopoulou's interpretation of the buildings at Halasmenos.[24]

Nowicki's reconstruction of House 138–140 (fig. 12.11) provides a vivid illustration of life in a refuge village: a family of perhaps five was squeezed into three rooms with a single hearth for light, warmth, and cooking; water was carried every day from the spring; the edges of the rooms and a loft offered limited space for the family possessions and the more than 2,000 kg of foodstuffs that moved through the house over the course of the year to keep the family alive.[25]

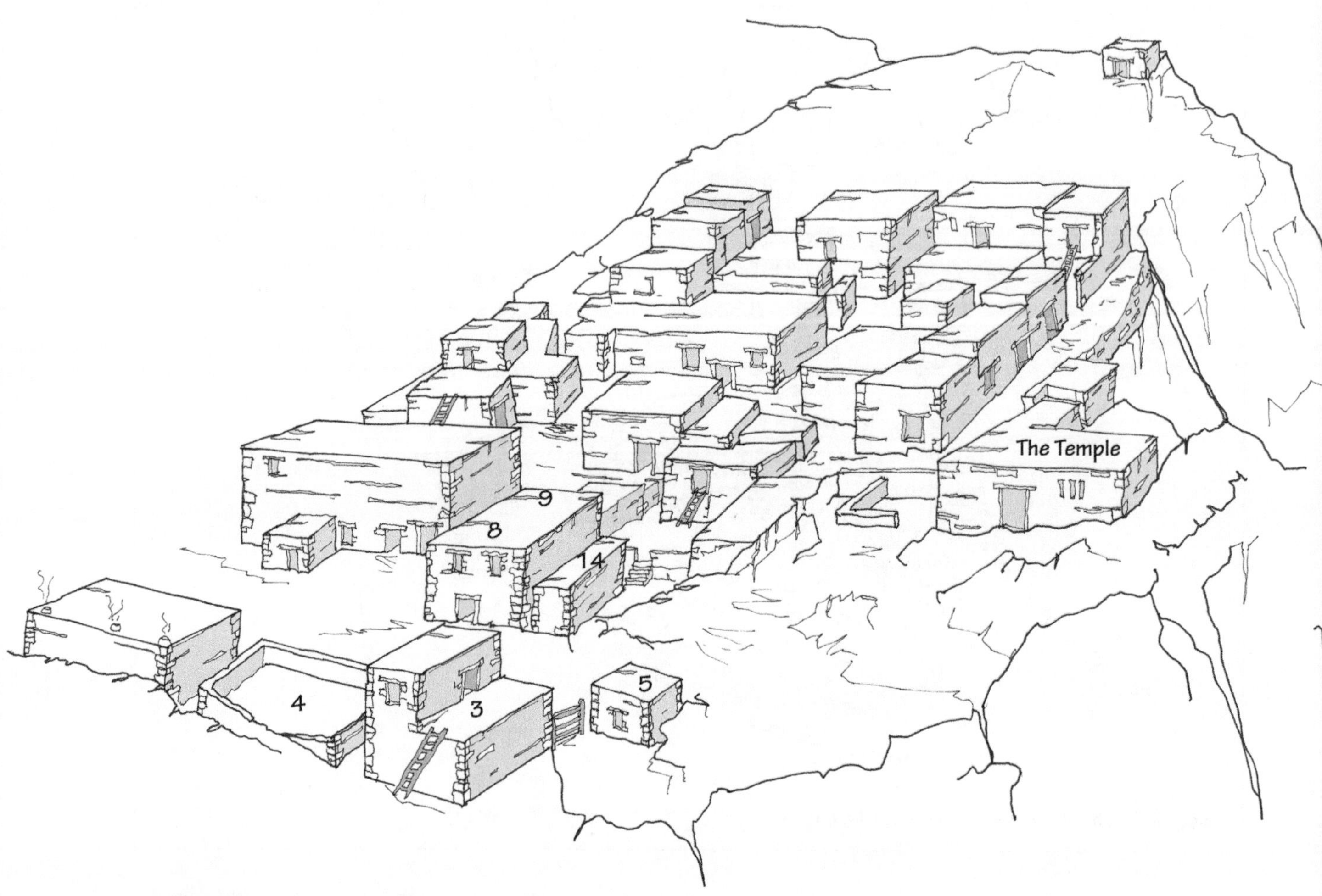

12.10. Reconstruction. Karphi. After Nowicki 1987, fig. 6.

Houses and Hierarchy

Two buildings at Vronda do not fit the model of the typical house. One of these is the Temple, Building G, which I shall consider later. The second is the Big House (Building A–B), which is often assumed to have been the house of the local ruler (see fig. 12.2). The building was originally excavated by H. Boyd at the beginning of the last century and has since badly eroded. Despite its poor preservation, several architectural features distinguish this building from others at the site. It is located on the highest part of the settlement. The building consists of two parts, a main room, A1, with an anteroom, A2, and a series of basement storerooms, B1–4 and B7, that supported the only second story at the site. The main room is extraordinarily large, ca. 7 m by 10 m, or 70 m^2. This makes it nearly twice the size of the next largest main room at the site and about twice the size of the average house. The size of a house has often been taken as a direct indication of the social status of the residents: the largest house, in this commonsense view, must be the house of the local ruler.[26] But is this direct equation between size and status supported by other evidence?

Size differentiation—whether or not one associates it with hierarchical social stratification—is less obvious at the other sites. At Karphi, for example, the excavators thought that the house they called the Great House

(Rooms 8–9 and 11–14) was the house of the local ruler. There are, however, other possibilities. Nowicki pointed out that, in its original state, the Great House had been much smaller and that both House 138–140 and the Priest's House (Rooms 58–61 and 80) were at least as large. What should we make of the differences between Vronda and Karphi? L. Day and L. Snyder suggest some possibilities: perhaps Karphi was not as centralized as Vronda; perhaps the role of the leader shifted from one person and one house to another; perhaps the "Big House" has not been found yet.[27] What is clear, however, is that in the broader context of Minoan Crete there was much less hierarchical distance between the largest buildings and the smallest houses than at any time since the construction of the first Palaces eight hundred years earlier.

Communal Feasting

It is not only size that distinguishes Building A-B from the other houses at Vronda. The finds were also unusual. A unique large painted and fenestrated terra-cotta object may have hung on one of the walls. Agrimi horns and cattle skulls, probably from sacrificed animals, had been shaped into plaques intended for display. In addition, pithoi from B1–B3, cooking pots from B4, and numerous large *kylikes* (stemmed drinking cups) from B3 led the excavators to propose that this building was used for communal feasting and drinking.[28]

Only recently have we begun to understand that feasting in the Bronze Age and Early Iron Age was a crucial means of integrating society. It tied celebrations with the agricultural calendar; marked most major life events (births, deaths, celebrations); and, through social reciprocity and competition, bound people with each other.[29] Although the occurrence of feasting might seem ironic in a village like Vronda, where people struggled to get by and lived on the economic edge, it is precisely in these circumstances that it would have been especially important. To be meaningful, in other words, the feast had to offer something quite distinct from ordinary activities.

In a recent article, S. Wallace takes the discussion of LM IIIC feasting in a new direction.[30] She suggests that Building A-B at Vronda was not necessarily the residence of the local leader but primarily a building set aside for secular public feasting. She also proposes that the largest "megaron" in area A at Halasmenos and

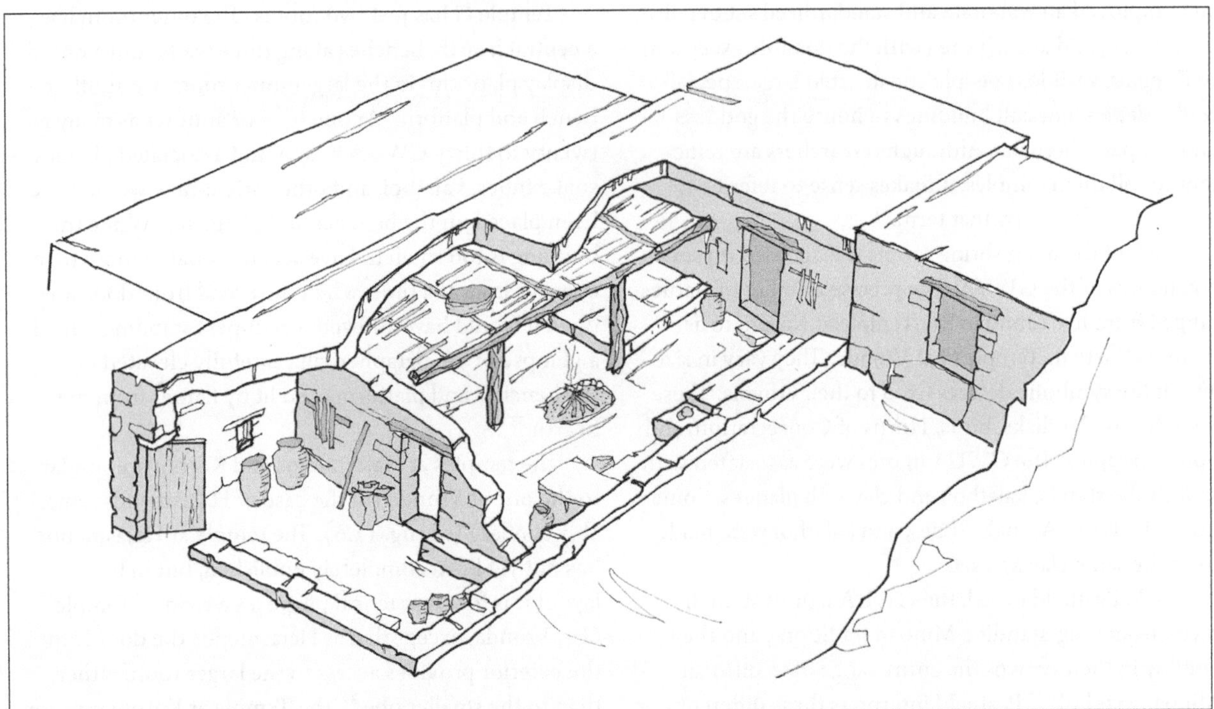

12.11. Reconstruction. House 138–140, Karphi. After Nowicki, 1999, fig. 3.

Building 138–140 at Karphi served the same functions at those sites. In her view, these buildings were the ancestors of the *andreion,* a communal dining room for men that was a standard part of Cretan towns in the Archaic and classical periods. There are problems with some details of her proposal: there is more artifactual evidence for cooking and feasting in Area B at Halasmenos and in the Priest's House at Karphi than in either of the buildings Wallace identifies as communal dining facilities. Room 61 of the Priest's House even contained horns of oxen, deer, and goats like the material found in Vronda Building A-B.[31] Nevertheless Wallace sees two distinctive and complementary institutions of later Cretan society already taking root in LM IIIC: the secular *andreion* and the sacred temple.

Public Shrines and Temples

The differences among the houses and hamlets at Vronda, Halasmenos, Karphi, and Kephala Vasilikis probably had to do with variations in immediate historical, social, and topographical conditions at each of the sites. At the same time, the sites were tied together by means of a common form of public cult centered on the Goddess with the Upraised Arms (GWUA) (fig. 12.12).[32] The cult employed an elaborate and standardized set of cult equipment, and at each site (with the possible exception of Kephala Vasilikis) people constructed large, specialized independent cult buildings to house the goddess and her paraphernalia. Although researchers are reluctant to call them temples, it makes sense to refer to at least some of them by that term.[33]

Each of the main shrine rooms was focused on several figures of the GWUA. The precise number of statues ranged from five found in the Temple at Karphi to as many as thirty in Temple G at Vronda. They vary in size and in the symbolic devices fixed to their crowns. These include circular disks, birds, Horns of Consecration, and opium poppies. The GWUA figures were associated with snake tube stands, kalathoi, and clay wall plaques. Sometimes the GWUA, snake tubes, and kalathoi were made from the same clay as a set.

As A. Peatfield noted, the GWUA figures stem directly from long-standing Minoan traditions, and they employ in their crowns the entire range of traditional Minoan symbols.[34] Peatfield interprets these different emblems as the identifying marks of the individual goddesses represented in this polytheistic cult. M. Prent offers a different reading of the various emblems. She proposes that the costly sets of terra-cotta statues, plaques, and vessels had been placed in the temples by the heads of leading families. Their public display signaled the donor's piety and generosity.[35] In this scenario the temple was an arena for social competition.

Temple G at Vronda (see fig. 12.2) is the best example of the new temple architecture. At first glance, it appears to be an unremarkable two-room structure. However, as N. Klein and K. Glowacki propose in a forthcoming article, every element in this building was carefully conceived to manipulate and intensify the worshiper's experience.[36] Like the temples at Karphi and Halasmenos, Temple G was set apart from the nearby houses and located near an open area where worshipers could gather. A bench used by spectators or for the occasional exhibition of cult objects or both ran along its south wall, visible from the adjacent open court. In addition to the practicality of the location in terms of accommodating crowds, the building's isolation from other structures may have helped to signal that this was a special domain of spiritual experience, a place distinct from the mundane world that surrounded it.[37]

Temple G has just two rooms. The outer room has a central hearth, benches along three walls, and a raised display platform. In the larger inner room are another bench and platform. At one time or another as many as twenty to thirty GWUA figures and associated plaques, snake tubes, kalathoi, and other bric-a-brac would have been placed on the benches and platforms. While the building is too small to have accommodated more than a few visitors at a time, when the broad front door was open it would have allowed worshipers standing outside a glimpse of the paraphernalia carefully elevated on the benches and platforms and lit by flames from the hearth.[38]

The temples at Halasmenos and Karphi are similar to the one at Vronda (in the case of Halasmenos remarkably similar) (see fig. 12.6). The temple at Halasmenos has not yet been completely published, but in basic layout it is for all practical purposes a twin of Temple G at Vronda, except that at Halasmenos the door from the exterior provides access to the larger room rather than to the smaller one.[39] The Temple at Karphi is more

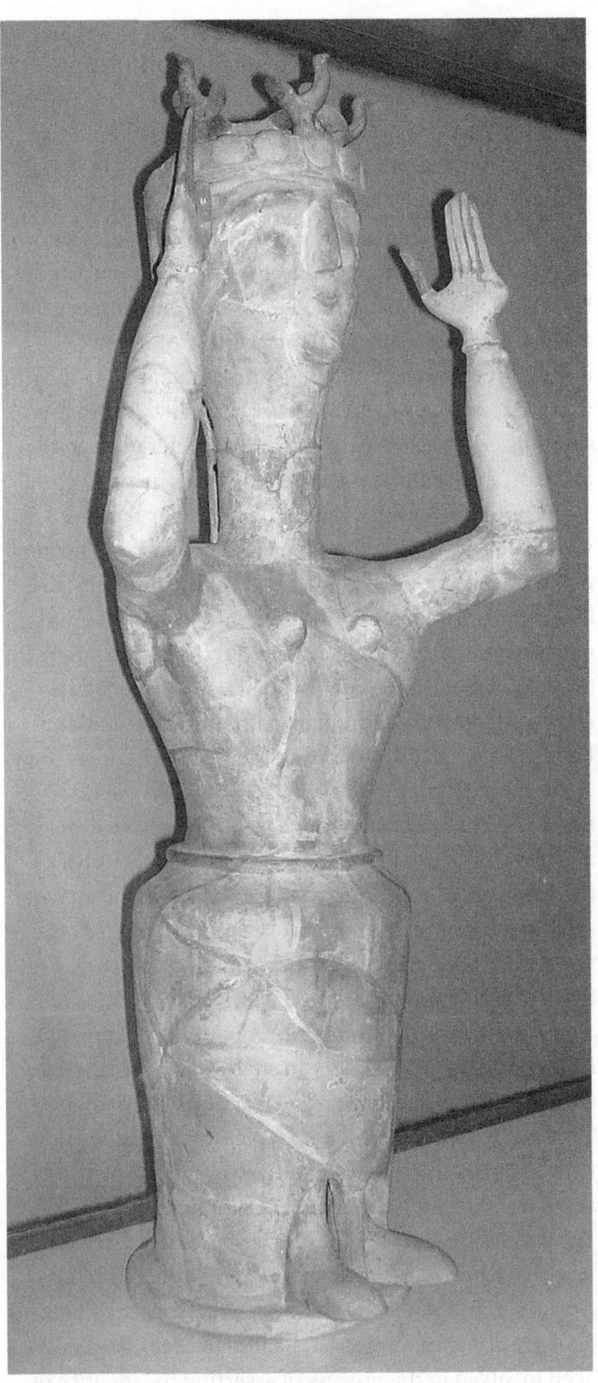

12.12. Goddess with Upraised Arms, Karphi. Herakleion Museum. Photo by author.

complex, in part because of its more complicated building history. The north wall of the building is missing, and the south side of the building was at one point expanded, the remains of the earlier south wall being left to form a bench. There was a free-standing platform (an altar?) on the north and another platform on the east wall. On the west were two storage rooms. The cult equipment was the same as that in the temple at Vronda (see fig. 12.9).

Building E at Kephala Vasilikis is generally grouped with the three buildings at Vronda, Halasmenos, and Karphi,[40] but it is not the same sort of free-standing temple. As mentioned above, all the cult equipment associated with the building—which was essentially identical to that at the other three sites—was found in Room E4 or in the fill above E5. Very little is known about the other rooms. The excavator interprets all eight rooms as a single, sprawling temple complex, while Prent suggests that most of the rooms belonged to the house of the community leader and that E4 was a small, attached semipublic sanctuary.[41] In either case, the building is architecturally different from the others.

Were LM IIIC Temples Purely Regional?

Because of the consistency of the cult assemblages at these four sites and the scarcity of comparable material elsewhere, Prent proposes that the sanctuaries of the GWUA at Vronda, Halasmenos, Kephala Vasilikis, and Karphi represent a purely regional development, restricted to the newly established defensible LM IIIC settlements in eastern Crete.[42]

There is, however, some evidence that this cult was practiced in other parts of the island. At Prinias, near Phaistos, at least five GWUA figures, numerous snake tubes, and kalathoi were found near the later Temple A.[43] So far, the building they were originally associated with has not been discovered. Similarly, cult material from Gazi, just west of modern Herakleion, dated by G. Rethemiotakis to his Late Phase (LM IIIC), might also be reconsidered on the basis of what we now know from Vronda and the other LM IIIC temples. The single room S. Marinatos excavated at Gazi may just as well belong to a free-standing, independent religious building as to the traditionally assumed domestic shrine.[44]

Prent's proposal that the GWUA cult was largely regional is nevertheless important. The island probably did not operate as a monolithic whole in the LM IIIC period, and the possibility of distinct regional variations cautions that one ought not view these buildings as representing an undifferentiated stage in a unilinear cultural evolution from the Minoan shrine to classical temple or, as a widely used undergraduate course title phrases it, "from palace to polis." As the idiosyncratic complex at Kephala Vasilikis vividly demonstrates, history is messier than that.

Constructing Memory

Much of this book has been concerned with constructing various sorts of social identities: the identity of the family, the identity of community, of authority, of status, and of ethnicities. Here I want to talk about the ancient construction of the identity of the past, or memory.[45] Humans' memories—the stories we tell ourselves about the past—are necessarily selective: we choose from among the infinite body of undifferentiated data those instances that, for the moment, suit us. A similar process operated in the past. R. Van Dyke and S. Alcock write, "Past peoples knowingly inhabited landscapes that were palimpsests of previous occupations. Sites were built on sites; landscapes were occupied and reoccupied time and again. Rarely was this a meaningless or innocent reuse. Like us, past peoples observed and interpreted traces of more distant pasts to serve the needs and the purposes of their present lives."[46]

We have already seen several examples of Minoans staking claims to particular aspects of the past: the fresco program and reconstruction of the Final Palace at Knossos by the new military regime; the reuse in LM IIIA of Tholos B at Haghia Triada; the deliberate decision to locate monumental LM III buildings directly over the Neopalatial ruins at Haghia Triada, Tylissos, and Archanes, etc. In these cases, authority was legitimated through overt references to the past.

Not surprisingly, the situation was similar in LM IIIC. As Wallace has pointed out, the catastrophes that devastated Crete in the very beginning of the period, around 1200 BC, had constituted a watershed in the history of the island and served as the major frame of chronological reference for those who survived. In this era of almost total discontinuity, many people sought to associate themselves with the time before the apocalypse—with the lost "golden age."[47]

The yearning for continuity took several forms, often—as seems so common in times and places of abject poverty—having to do with radical (in the literal sense) religion. Thus in the new LM IIIC village temples the GWUA wore the entire range of symbols remembered from the palatial past: birds, Horns of Consecration, and snakes. Originally used on a variety of monuments, they were here distilled into emblems adorning the goddesses' crowns. Whatever else they might have symbolized—identities of the deities? references to the donors?—the emblems were a bridge to the past.

At more or less the same time new civic temples were being constructed for the GWUA, a second form of cult was developing in places far from the newly established upland villages.[48] This extra-urban cult involved not the veneration of cult statues but the presentation of large, elaborate votives—wheel-made terra-cotta animals, fantastic half-human, half-animal figures, and Horns of Consecration were the standard offerings. They were presented not in new village shrines but in traditionally hallowed places on the island. The sacred caves at Patsos, Psychro, Phaneromeni, Archalochori, and the Idean cave received new offerings as did the ancient sanctuaries at Syme, Kophinas, and Mt. Iouktas. At the same time, the Spring Chamber in the Caravanserai (see fig. 9.37) at Knossos was filled with votive vessels and, after a period of abandonment, worshipers bearing LM IIIC votives made their way to a new open-air sanctuary in the ancient Piazzale dei Sacelli at Haghia Triada (see fig. 9.40). On a more intimate scale, some individuals at Knossos placed offerings of pottery in the Royal Tomb at Isopata (see fig. 10.9) and at the monumental Kephala Tholos (see fig. 10.10). These offerings, as Wallace notes, "may have been ways of asserting an identity with the glorious, mythological past."[49] The practice seems particularly fitting in tombs that had themselves originally been involved in the process of asserting the identity of the owner and his descendents.

Over the course of the next few generations, such annexation of the past occurred in many parts of the island. Early Iron Age "ruin cults" were established over the partly visible Bronze Age remains at Knossos, Phaistos, Haghia Triada, Kommos, Amnisos, Tylissos, and

Palaikastro. In most cases this phenomenon was not a simple matter of continuity but part of a much broader appropriation of the imagined heroic past by an emerging aristocracy.[50]

The modest Temple G at Vronda (see fig. 12.2) tells its own multilayered version of the story. As one of the new temples established by the refugee generation, the building displayed the symbol-clad goddesses who offered a connection with the Palatial age that had preceded the catastrophes. By the end of LM IIIC, perhaps because the village was too small to subsist on its own, the people of Vronda moved again, this time probably to Kavousi Kastro or to the nearby village of Azoria. But Vronda was not entirely forgotten. Several generations later, in the Late Geometric period, a family dug a tomb in the temple and cremated three bodies. This was one of dozens of Geometric tombs at the site, built perhaps by descendants (real or imagined) using the ruins of Vronda as evidence of their own past.[51] In its turn, this part of the story faded from memory for centuries. In 1988, archaeologists excavated the small grave (Grave 19) and are now writing their final report.[52]

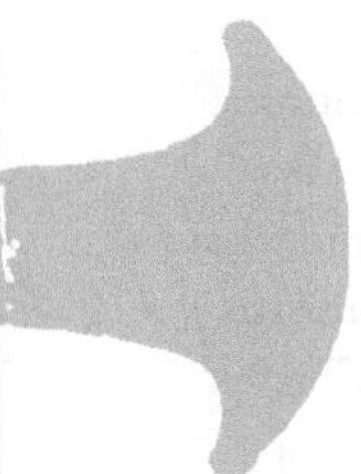

Conclusion
ARCHITECTURE AND IDENTITY

I ENDED CHAPTER 12 by mentioning two acts associated with the small temple at Vronda: the constructing of a Late Geometric tomb and the writing of a modern excavation report. The implication is that these two acts are in some way parallel—that both have to do with communicating meaning. Writing an excavation report is certainly a communicative act. But what of the tomb? How do buildings (mere *things*) convey meanings?

In the words of C. Tilley, "Things are meaningful and significant not only because they are necessary to sustain life and society, to reproduce or transform social relations and mediate differential interests and values, but because they provide essential tools for thought. Material forms are essential vehicles for the (conscious or unconscious) self-realization of the identities of individuals or groups because they provide a fundamental non-discursive mode of communication. We 'talk' and 'think' about ourselves through things."[1]

Architecture affords people a unique opportunity to understand, if only imperfectly, how Minoans talked and thought about themselves. Minoan buildings and towns continually changed: rooms were added or removed; roofs were damaged and repaired; doors were blocked; walls were removed; materials from old buildings were incorporated in newer buildings. A Minoan village like Gournia (see fig. 9.26) is like a giant game of pick-up sticks. Because walls were built over one another or against one another, we can determine which wall was built before another and, given enough time, we can unravel the building sequence of the entire settlement.[2] All these changes were the results of significant choices. Significant choices involve meanings.

For example, during the Neopalatial period, the residents of House Zb at Malia chose to modify their house by adding a Minoan Hall (see fig. 9.15). Seen in the context of the wider Palatializing movement in the LM I period, we read that choice as the proclamation of a different social status within the community. The builders or sponsors or both chose to present themselves as members of the group whose houses were distinguished by that characteristic feature.

Significant choices and architectural changes are dynamic processes. In Minoan architecture, meanings were not fixed but were created through the active processes of becoming and of emulating. (This has led to the frequent use in this book of awkward present participles such as Cycladicizing, Palatializing, and Mycenaeanizing.) While these processes were almost infinitely complex, the broad, diachronic narrative I have constructed from them can be reduced to a simple outline:

a. During the Prepalatial period each settlement had a distinct style of architecture, giving each village an individual physical presence and a specifically local identity (see figs. 3.2, 3.5, 3.6). At the same time, the people of Crete chose to build tombs that were tied to regional, rather than local, traditions.
b. During the Protopalatial period, the construction of the first Palaces at Malia, Knossos, and Phaistos were the embodiments of an island-wide (or at least transregional) style that, perhaps for the first time, proclaimed a distinctively Minoan identity.
c. Eventually elements of those Palaces would get caught up in the competitive Palatializing movement of the Neopalatial period, when Palaces and houses became

the major means of proclaiming status identity.

d. During LM IIIA–LM IIIB, architecture became an arena for playing out complex relationships between Minoanizing and Mycenaeanizing constituencies.
e. Finally, after the widespread destructions that devastated Crete around 1200, people of the Dark Age laid claim to the ruins as evidence of their heroic past. Fragments of the past, such as the ruins of the little temple at Vronda, became part of a new identity in the present.

Yet there is a serious problem with this outline. By focusing mainly on building types and epochal shifts, the broad sketch risks overlooking the key role of the individual people of Crete—the family that built the tomb in the Vronda temple or the people who renovated House Zb at Malia, for example. Their individual choices provided the basis for the broader outline: without the individuals, no pattern exists; without the pattern, no social identity for the individuals exists. One of the aims of this book has been to focus attention on the interdependent relationships between individuals, the social context the individuals belong to and shape, and the language of material culture.

In 1989, Tilley wrote, "The individual does not so much construct material culture or language, but is rather constructed through them."[3] To understand what he meant, let us return finally to the Palace at Knossos (see fig. 7.1) and to a set of questions posed in Chapter 1. What did it mean to be a Bronze Age Knossian, a Herakleiot, or a Minoan? To a large extent, the Palace *is* the answer to the questions. To be a Minoan was not primarily a matter of birthplace, language, or genetics. To be a Minoan was to be an active participant in and product of the social, cultural, economic, and ideological networks that made and used Minoan buildings and the assemblages of meaningful things in them. As the Minoans constructed the buildings, they constructed also themselves.

APPENDIX
Useful Websites

The American School of Classical Studies at Athens. News and information about programs. Provides a link to *Ambrosia*, the Union Catalogue of the Blegen and Gennadius Libraries of the American School of Classical Studies at Athens and the Libraries of the British School of Archaeology at Athens. http://www.ascsa.edu.gr/

The BSA at Knossos, British School of Archaeology. Includes a virtual tour. http://www.bsa.ac.uk/knosos

Digital Crete, FORTH Institute for Mediterranean Studies. A massive archaeological atlas of Crete and numerous associated databases. Complete bibliographical references. http://digitalcrete.ims.forth.gr/

Greek Ministry of Culture. With links to sites and museums. http://www.culture.gr/

INSTAP Study Center for East Crete, Institute for Aegean Prehistory. Information and links. http://www.instapstudycenter.net

Kommos Excavations, Crete, University of Toronto. Description and photos of the Bronze Age and classical site. http://www.fineart.utoronto.ca/kommos/

Mediterranean Archaeology Resources, Ioannis Georganas. Links to online professional journals, bibliographies, online resources, services, online courses, organizations, schools, and institutes. An indispensable address book. http://www.geocities.com/i_georganas/main.html

Minoan Crete, Ian Swindale. Photos and brief discussions of all major Minoan sites. http://www.uk.digiserve.com/mentor/minoan/

Mochlos Archaeological Excavations. Written by students in the Archaeology Program at the University of North Carolina, Greensboro. http://www.uncg.edu/%7Ejssoles/Mochlos/first.html

Prehistoric Archaeology of the Aegean. Jeremy Rutter. An online course with extensive coverage of Minoan Crete. Illustrations, extensive bibliography, and links. The most informative and useful general source on Aegean prehistory. http://projectsx.dartmouth.edu/history/bronze_age

NOTES

CHAPTER 1

1. Rackham and Moody 1997, 12–14.
2. Watrous et al. 1993, 194.
3. Pendlebury 1939, 20–21.
4. Bosanquet 1914, 15–17.
5. *Odyssey* 19:186–191 (Lombardo, trans.).
6. McEnroe 1995, 6–8.
7. Carter, King, and Underhill 2007.
8. McKee 2000; Green 2000.
9. Herzfeld 1991, 62–66.
10. McKee 2000, 2.
11. Diaz-Andreu, Lucy, Babić, and Edwards 2005.
12. Diaz-Andreu and Lucy 2005, 1–2.
13. Herzfeld 1985, xii.
14. Herzfeld 1985, 36.
15. Pashley [1837] 1970, 272–273.
16. McGlade 1999, 144.
17. Hodder 1993, 275.
18. McEnroe 1995.
19. For a brief overview of this complex issue, see Rehak and Younger 1998, 97–100.
20. Warren and Hankey 1989.
21. Manning 1995.
22. Alexiou and Warren 2004, 195.
23. Dinsmoor's standard study of classical Greek architecture is a remarkable example of the grand evolutionary/biological vision: "Works of architecture in themselves are material, perishable, incomplete; but a style of architecture is one of the higher manifestations of Nature, reaching in through the human spirit. Should we try to grasp as a whole one great period of architecture, one great style of art, like that of ancient Greece, our study is simplified in finding that it presents all the features of natural growth. Art is a flower and, like the flower of the field, is sown in obscurity, nourished by the decay of pre-existing organisms and, though refined and perfected by high culture, buds and blooms at its own time. It is in large measure what the soil and the sunshine make it; it repays the care and toil that human hands bestow upon it; yet its form and color are its own. And so we might not know all the causes which produce the phenomenon, but we may at least watch it grow, enjoy its full beauty and follow it in its withering; for, like the plant, it is beautiful not only when in full flower, but at every stage of progress and even in decline." Dinsmoor 1950, xv.

CHAPTER 2

1. Recent surface finds apparently attest to people arriving in Crete as early as the Mesolithic and even Paleolithic eras. C. Runnels and T. Strasser (pers. comm.).
2. Broodbank 1992, 39; Tomkins 2004.
3. Tomkins 2004, 39–41.
4. Tomkins, Day, and Kilikoglou 2004.
5. Halstead 1995; Tomkins 2004, 41–52.
6. Broodbank 1992; Whitelaw 1992; Efstratiou, Karetsou, Banou, and Margomenou 2004, 46.
7. In 1940 half the communities in Crete had fewer than five hundred residents while only 2 percent had more than twenty-five hundred. Both farming families and nonfarming families lived in communities. Allbaugh 1953, 58, 73. For the organizational characteristics of the village as a settlement type, see K. Flannery 1972.
8. McEnroe 1990.

9. *MA:MAT*.
10. *MA:MAT*, 11.
11. For the relation between house types and climate within Greece, see Creutzberg 1933; Wagstaff, 1965, 1982.
12. *MA:MAT*, 77–83; Mook 1998, 49–51.
13. *MA:MAT*, 187–198.
14. J. Shaw 1977; Mook 2000, 1998, 51–55; Bozineki-Didonis 1985, 59–61; For the distribution of flat and pitched roofs in Greece, see Wagstaff 1965, 58–64.
15. Oliver 1987, 64–66.
16. Bozineki-Didonis, 1985, 59–61.
17. *PM II*, 1–21; J. Evans 1964, 1971, 1994.
18. Efstratiou, Karetsou, Banou, and Margomenou, 2004.
19. Broodbank 1992, 43, table 1.
20. Schmandt-Besserat 1977.
21. The excavator refers to many of these walls as "pisé." As J. Shaw points out, pisé architecture depends on pouring mud into an exterior form, the way concrete walls are poured today. There is no evidence that an exterior form was used in Minoan architecture. *MA:MAT*, 79 note 1.
22. Broodbank 1992, 43, table 1. Whitelaw thinks this estimate may be too high. Whitelaw (pers. comm.).
23. Allbaugh 1953, 8, 73.
24. Treuil 1983, 324.
25. Broodbank 1992, 43, table 1. Whitelaw thinks the lower figure is probably more reasonable. Whitelaw (pers. comm.).
26. Treuil 1983, 288–292.
27. Driessen (pers. comm.).
28. Alexiou 1954; Strasser 1992, 262.
29. A. Evans, PM II, 1–21; J. Evans 1964, 188.
30. Watrous 1994, 700–701.
31. Nowicki, 2000, 30.
32. Vagnetti 1972–1973, 50–53; Treuil 1983, 299, 328, suggests that the building is a granary.
33. Dawkins 1904–1905, 263–268; Strasser 1992, 254.
34. Mackenzie 1907–1908, 360–398.
35. Lawrence 1973, 18.
36. McEnroe 2007.
37. Du Boulay 1974, 38.
38. McEnroe 1990.
39. Allbaugh 1953.
40. J. Evans 1964, 140–142.

CHAPTER 3

1. Warren 1972.
2. Whitelaw 1983. In 1992 Tenwolde revived Warren's notion of Myrtos as a communal settlement, one not divided into individual households (Tenwolde 1992). Whitelaw argues convincingly in favor of his own interpretation of the settlement as a gradually constructed hamlet of five or six houses used by nuclear families. Whitelaw 2007. I am grateful to Todd Whitelaw for allowing me to read this article in advance of its publication.
3. This is a crude estimation. One could come up with a much more accurate estimate by building a duplicate house. For the kind of estimate used here, see Erasmus 1977, 52–78; Walsh 1980; Kramer 1982. Even if this approach is not particularly accurate, it can at least serve as a means of comparing the relative costs of one house to another. I shall make use of the same criteria in later chapters.
4. Rykwert 1976, 135.
5. Seager 1904–1905, 1907; Zois 1976, 1979.
6. Watrous 1994, 707–709.
7. Shaw 1973, 139–140.
8. Shaw 1973, 208.
9. Vasilakis 1989, 1990, 1995. I am grateful to Todd Whitelaw for information concerning the date of the tholos tomb.
10. Wilson and Day 1994; Day, Wilson, and Kiriatzi, 1997, 1998.
11. Hillbom 2005. See also Whittaker 2002 for a similar conclusion based on sixty-two examples.
12. Hillbom 2005, 122.
13. Dawkins 1904–1905, fig. 10.
14. Daux 1966; Pelon 1993.
15. Schoep 1999 argues that these buildings, even if they differ in form from the later Palaces, might well have had a palatial function.
16. Driessen 2007.
17. Two tholoi have been identified at Trypiti, one of which was excavated by Vasilakis. Alexiou, 1967, 484; Vasilakis 1989, 56. Branigan estimates that the settlement excavated by Vasilakis had eight or nine households, which would put the number of associated tholoi at about four. Branigan 1993, 110. For tholos tombs in general, see Blackman and Branigan 1982; Branigan 1993, 1998; Murphy 1998; Alexiou and Warren 2004.

18. Murphy 1998, 30.
19. Blackman and Branigan 1975, 1977.
20. Branigan 1993, 33–38, with references.
21. Blackman and Branigan 1982, 45–46; Alexiou and Warren 2004, 15.
22. Alexiou and Warren 2004.
23. Ibid., 180.
24. Branigan 1993, 93; Bintliff 1977, 635–641.
25. Murphy 1998; Danforth and Tsiarias 1982.
26. Murphy 1998; Yaeger and Canuto 2000; Canuto and Yaeger 2000.
27. Soles 1992.
28. Ibid., 51–62.
29. Ibid., 243–247.
30. Ibid., 251-255; Branigan 1993, 93; Bintliff 1977, 635–641.
31. Davaras and Betancourt 2004.
32. Ibid., 238–239.
33. Ibid., 200–201.
34. Ibid., 241.
35. Day, Wilson, and Kiriatzi 1998, 138–139.
36. Hall 1997, 182.
37. Shennan 1989a, 1989b; Renfrew 1996; Jones 1997; Hall 1997.
38. Hall 1997, 19–26.
39. Ibid., 25.
40. Day, Wilson, and Kiriatzi, 1998.
41. Ibid., 137.

CHAPTER 4

1. Zois 1968.
2. Watrous 1994, 752.
3. Momigliano 1991; Manning 1995, 63–65; Haggis 1999; Whitelaw 2004a.
4. Walberg 1983.
5. Soles 1992, 41; Whitelaw 2004b, 236–246.
6. Branigan 1993, 65; Maggidis 1998, 95–100; Relaki 2004.
7. Murphy 1998, 38.
8. Relaki, 2004, 180–184.
9. Ibid.
10. Sakellarakis and Sapouna-Sakellaraki 1997, 152–267.
11. Maggidis 1998.
12. Peatfield 1987, 1990, 1994; Rutkowski 1986; Haggis 1999.
13. Peatfield 1987, 89.
14. Cherry 1986, 31.
15. While it is not clear that the few EM sherds found at Iouktas were related to a peak sanctuary, the Final Neolithic and EM material found at Atsipadhes was connected with the cult. Whitelaw (pers. comm.). Driessen also notes EM II material at Petsophas. Driessen (pers. comm.). I am indebted to Jan Driessen and Todd Whitelaw for this information.
16. Haggis 1999.
17. Driessen and Macdonald 1997, 55.
18. Tsipopoulou 1999a.
19. Davaras and Betancourt 2004, 2.
20. Isipopoulou 1999a.
21. Davaras 1972; Driessen and Macgillivray 1989, 102; Tsipopoulou 1999a, 185–189. For a historiographical review of Chamaizi, see McEnroe 2007.
22. Tsipopoulou 1999a.
23. Van Effenterre 1980, 32–35; Poursat 1988, 65.
24. Chapouthier and Demargne 1942, 13–17; van Effenterre 1980, 168–171.
25. Muhly 1984.
26. Connected with looms: Pelon 1966; feeding animals: J. Shaw 1978b, 247–248.
27. Demargne and Gallet de Santerre 1953, 23–39.
28. Van Effenterre 1980, 447.
29. Demargne and Gallet de Santerre 1953, 19–21.
30. Van Effenterre 1980, 246–247; Soles 1992, 205.
31. Demargne and Gallet de Santerre 1953, 11–18.
32. Soles 1992, 205.
33. Watrous 1994, 278; Stürmer 1993, 123–187. Poursat prefers a date in MM IB. Poursat 1988, 73. Soles dates it to MM IB on the basis of architectural style. Soles 1992, 170–171.
34. J. Shaw 1973; *MA:MAT*, 83–92.
35. J. Shaw 1973, 320.
36. Demargne 1945, 25–69; van Effenterre 1980, 214–247; Soles 1992, 163–166.
37. Muhly 1984, 114–115.
38. Watrous 1994, 729.
39. *MA:MAT*, 79, figure 72.
40. Whitelaw 2001, 27–28. Whitelaw puts the area of the Neopalatial city at Malia at 36 ha. An estimate of 200–225 people per hectare gives a population of 7,200. Even half that number would mean that EM III–MM IA Malia was categorically different from anything we have seen so far in Bronze Age Crete. Whitelaw sees no reason to doubt that Malia had a population of around 7000. Whitelaw (pers. comm.).

41. Momigliano 1992, 167, 171, 175 pl. 8a; Wilson 1994, 38.
42. *MA:MAT*, 79, figure 73.
43. Macgillivray 1998, 34.
44. *PM I*, 104; Macgillivray 1994, 49–51.
45. Momigliano 1991, 163–167; Macgillivray 1994, 51.
46. Farnoux 1989, 770.
47. Schoep 2002a, 2002b, 2004, 2006; Schoep and Knappett 2004.
48. Van Effenterre 1980, 36.
49. Pelon 1982, 1983, 1984, 1986, 1992, 1993, 1999; Schoep 2004, 2006.
50. Poursat, 1988.
51. Pelon 1982, 1983.
52. McEnroe 1995, 5–8.
53. Renfrew 1972; Branigan 1970; Warren 1987.
54. Watrous 1987; Weingarten 1990; Dabney 1995.
55. Cherry 1983.
56. Dabney 1995; Schoep 2002a, 2002b, 2004, 2006; Schoep and Knappett 2004; Whitelaw 2004a.

CHAPTER 5

1. Pernier 1935; Levi 1976.
2. Driessen and Schoep 1995, 651.
3. *MA:MAT*, 42.
4. *MA:MAT*, 135–185.
5. For the development of Minoan orthostates, see J. Shaw 1973, 319–331. For Minoan ashlar, see *MA:MAT*, 83–111; for the issue of the monumentality of the west facades, see van Effenterre 1987.
6. Graham 1960a.
7. *MA:MAT*, 44–75.
8. *MA:MAT*, 109–110; Hood 1987; Begg 2004a, 2004b.
9. Graham 1960a.
10. Since it was built over several phases and stands on different levels (see fig. 5.4), Todd Whitelaw doubts that the west facade of the Palace at Phaistos formed a unified whole. Whitelaw (pers. comm.). The careful alignment of all parts of the west facade and (eventually) the straight line of the west facade of the Central Court (see fig. 5.5), however, suggest that the final form of the first Palace at Phaistos constituted a coherent, rectilinear whole. In two recent articles Schoep insists that there are no "palatial features" in what I am here referring to as the first Palace at Phaistos. Schoep 2004, 2006.
11. Driessen 2004, 77.
12. For a concise summary of the objects found in the first Palace at Phaistos and the activities they imply, see Branigan 1987, 245–249.
13. Gesell 1985, 120.
14. Muhly 1984, 114–119.
15. For the history of the excavations at Knossos, see Brown 1983.
16. *PM I*, 359.
17. Heller 1961.
18. For a summary of Evans's views, see Pendlebury 1939, 94–100, 126–132.
19. Momigliano 1992.
20. MacGillivray 1998.
21. *MA:MAT*, 109–110; Hood 1987; Begg 2004.
22. *MA:MAT*, 111–125.
23. Van Effenterre 1980.
24. Poursat 1987.
25. Pelon 1982, 1983, 1984, 1986, 1992, 1993, 1999.
26. Schoep questions the palatial character of the Protopalatial Palace at Malia as well as at Phaistos (Schoep 2004, 2006). Her disagreement with the scenario I present here centers on what one means by "palatial."
27. Chapouthier and Charbonneaux 1928, 38; Chapouthier and Demargne 1942, 75; Pelon 1992, 46.
28. Driessen 2002.
29. See the various essays in *The Function of the Minoan Palaces*. Hägg and Marinatos 1987.
30. Schoep 2002b, 18.
31. Cherry 1983a, 1986. The phrases "quantum leap" and "critical moment of transformation" are from Cherry 1986, 21.
32. Haggis 1999; Knappet 1999; Schoep and Knappett 2004, 2000; Schoep 2000, 2002, 2006.
33. Dabney 1995.
34. Levi 1961–1962.
35. Rykwert 1982, 65.
36. For the traditional view that writing appeared suddenly as part of a cultural upheaval, see Weingarten 1990.
37. Schoep 1999.

CHAPTER 6

1. Driessen and Schoep 1995.
2. Palyvou 2004, 207.
3. Ibid., 214. Driessen 2004, 79–80, makes a similar point.

4. *PM II*, 578–587.
5. Pernier 1935, 185–190.
6. Hillbom 2005.
7. Graham *PoC*, 27–28; *PM II*, 585–586; McDonald 1943, 6–19; Damiani Indelicato 1982.
8. H. and M. van Effenterre 1969; van Effenterre 1980. For a detailed criticism of van Effenterre's interpretation, see Poursat 1988.
9. The fourth Kouloura at Knossos is under the Theatral Area, not technically in the West Court.
10. Carinci 2001 opts for sacred tree planters.
11. Halstead 1981, 1997.
12. Strasser 1997. Strasser agrees with Halstead that the Neopalatial silos at the southwest corner of the later Palace at Malia were granaries.
13. Jan Driessen is skeptical of this interpretation. He notes that at Pyrgos-Myrtos there is both a Kouloura and a cistern and prefers the sacred tree hypothesis. Driessen (pers. comm).
14. Niemeier 1994 shows that the easternmost Kouloura at Knossos remained open into LM IB. The other Koulouras in the West Court were paved over in MM III.
15. Chryssoulaki 1990; Warren notes that some streets at Knossos may be as early as EM III. Warren 1994. At least part of the street system at Malia had been laid out in MM IA. Farnoux 1989, 770.
16. Catling 1973–1974, 34.
17. Chryssoulaki 1999.
18. Watrous 1994, 736.
19. Nowicki 1999b.
20. Palyvou 2004, 207.
21. H and M. van Effenterre, 1969.
22. Halstead 1981.
23. For a parallel but slightly different view of the relation between the Palace at Malia and neighboring buildings, see Schoep 2002a, 2006.
24. Ibid.
25. Palyvou 2004, 207.
26. Gesell 1985, 112–113; Niemeier 1987a.
27. Muhly 1984, 116.
28. Poursat 1996.
29. Ibid., 149–153.
30. For example, Schoep 2006.
31. Nilsson 1950.
32. Poursat 1966.
33. Gesell 1985, 107.
34. Sakellarakis and Sapouna-Sakellaraki 1997, 268–311.
35. Levi 1976, Plan B; N. Platon 1973, plate Theta.
36. Civitillo and Greco 2003.
37. Palyvou 2004, 216.
38. Driessen and Schoep 1995, 659.
39. The relationship between the first Palace at Malia and the neighboring buildings has been interpreted in diverse ways. For the van Effenterres, the public buildings of the city took precedence, and the Palace coalesced only in the Neopalatial period. H. van Effenterre 1980. Schoep located the generating authority in the elite citizens who lived in Quartier Mu. Schoep 2002a, 2006. Here, I have emphasized the role of the Palace, but, along with Schoep, would also stress the interaction of all three components of the city, the Palace, Quartier Mu, and the buildings in the area of the Agora.
40. Schoep 2002a.

CHAPTER 7

1. The west facade is now firmly dated to MM III. Niemeier 1994, 76. For the windows of the upper story, see Graham 1960 and Hägg 1987.
2. H. Frankfurt 1951.
3. *MA:MAT*, 146 note 1 says that the average column height in Minoan architecture ranges from five to eight times the base diameter.
4. Driessen 2004, 79.
5. Niemeier, on the other hand, holds that there is little evidence for the South-North Corridor as proposed by Evans; Niemeier suggested that the fresco fragments Evans restored as the Priest King Fresco actually belonged to three separate figures that originally decorated the wall of a cult room he hypothetically restores over the South Terrace Basements. Niemeier 1987; Momigliano and Hood 1994, 142–146.
6. Driessen 2004, 75.
7. Evans originally thought that the Throne Room was built only in the Final palatial period. Mirié showed that elements of the architecture go back to the Protopalatial Palace. Mirié 1979; Niemeier 1987, 163–168.
8. Mirié 1979, 51–59.
9. J. Shaw 1978a.
10. Panagiotaki 1999.
11. Ibid., 247–257.
12. For example, *PoC*, 30; Gesell 1985, 85–88.

13. Rutkowski 1986, 21–47, with references.
14. Begg 2004a, 2004b.
15. Panagiotaki 1999, 240; Christakis 2004, 305.
16. Panagiotaki 1999, 241.
17. Rehak and Younger 1998, 128–129.
18. Begg 1987, 183; Hallager 1987.
19. Driessen 1990.
20. J. Shaw with Lowe 2002.
21. Macdonald 2002, 43.
22. Graham 1979.
23. *PoC*, 130–131; Christakis 2004. Christakis estimates the total capacity to have been around 231,000 liters.
24. Graham, 1956; *PoC*, 114–124.
25. Begg 1987.
26. Christakis 2004, 301–302.
27. Graham 1959.
28. Nordfeldt 1987.
29. *PoC*, 20.
30. MacGillivray 1998, 97–98.
31. Macdonald 2002, 36–38.
32. Niemeier 1994, 71–72; Walberg 1992.
33. Macdonald 2002.
34. Macdonald 2002, 38–43.
35. *MA:MAT*, 111–134.
36. *MA:MAT*, 144–151.
37. *MA:MAT*, 211–218.
38. Brown 1983; Papadopoulos 1997; Hitchcock and Koudounaris 2002; Karetsou 2004.
39. Evans 1927, 262.
40. McEnroe 2002.
41. Harcourt-Smith 1933, 71.
42. Karetsou 2004.

CHAPTER 8

1. Several other Neopalatial buildings have been described as Palaces, including the large, partially excavated building at Archanes, Building T at Kommos, Petras, Makrygiallos, and Zominthos. In this book I use the term "Palace" to refer to a reasonably consistent architectural form. That form includes the components and structural features described in the text below. By this definition only Knossos, Phaistos, Malia, Zakros, and Galatas meet the criteria.
2. Driessen and Macdonald 1997. Driessen and Macdonald use the Warren and Hankey chronology. For consistency their absolute dates have been altered in the text to correspond with the chronology I am using in this book.
3. Carinci 1989; La Rosa 2002.
4. Pelon 1984, fig. 1.
5. Driessen and Macdonald 1997, 182–193; van Effenterre 1980, 336–337.
6. Poursat 1988, 76; Farnoux 1989–1990, 25.
7. Rethemiotakis 2002.
8. Driessen and Macdonald 1997, 237–238; L. Platon, 2002; and L. Platon 2004, 390.
9. *PoC*. In her recent book, Hitchcock also compares a set of types of rooms (e.g., Lustral Basins, Hypostyle halls, etc.), spaces (e.g., West Courts, Theatral Areas, etc.) and features (e.g., the *auge*) in each of the Palaces and some of the Villas. Hitchcock 2000.
10. *PoC*, 73.
11. Palyvou 2002, 171.
12. J. Shaw 1977b.
13. Lawrence 1973, 23.
14. J. Shaw 1977b.
15. Rethemiotakis 2002, 58.
16. Palyvou 2002, 171–172.
17. Halstead 1981.
18. *PoC*, 140–141.
19. Hallager 1987.
20. Graham 1956, 1960, 1979.
21. N. Platon 1971, 155–173.
22. Rethemiotakis 1999, 2002, 58–59.
23. Graham 1961; *PoC*, 125–128.
24. Graham 1959.
25. Rehak and Younger recently doubted the existence of toilets in the Palaces. Rehak and Younger 1998, 129 note 266. In fact, there are toilets in most, if not all, of the Palaces: Knossos (Room 98, next to the Queen's Megaron, fig. 7.2), Malia (Room III2, next to the "Queen's Megaron," fig. 8.3), Phaistos (Room 63e, next to the "Queen's Megaron" and 82, fig. 8.2), Zakros (Rooms XXVII and XVIII, fig. 8.6). *PoC*, 108–110. There are also toilets in houses at Malia, Knossos, Sklavokambos, Tylissos, and Thera.
26. Graham 1960b.
27. Cherry 1985.
28. Preziosi 1983. For a critical review, see McEnroe 1984.
29. Preziosi 2003, 236.
30. For a recent discussion of the term "Palace," see Rehak and Younger 1998, 102–103; Driessen 2002.

31. Soles recently tried to show that the Palace at Gournia did have a Central Court. His restoration, however, involves, among other things, carrying a second story over part of a steeply sloping street. Soles 2002.
32. Davaras 1997.
33. Sakellarakis 1983.
34. Sakellarakis and Sapouna-Sakellaraki 1997, 63–136.
35. Tsipopoulou 2002, 133. See also Tsipopoulou 1999b.
36. Tsipopoulou 1999a.
37. Tsipopoulou 1999a, 186.
38. J. Shaw and M. Shaw 2006; J. Shaw 2000, 2002, 2003.
39. J. Shaw 2002.
40. Puglisi 2001.
41. J. Shaw and M. Shaw 2006, 850–853.
42. Ibid. 1985.
43. J. Shaw 2002, 2003.
44. J. Shaw 2003, 242.
45. Prent 2003.
46. *PoC*, vi.

CHAPTER 9

1. The figures are estimates based on information in the "Gazetteer of Neopalatial Sites," in Driessen and Macdonald 1997, 120–258.
2. Ibid.
3. Hägg 1997; *Oxford English Dictionary* s.v. "villa."
4. Hatzaki 2005a.
5. Popham 1984.
6. Poblome and Dumon, 1987–1988. Hitchcock and Preziosi 1997; Hitchcock 2000, 187–188; Hatzaki 2005a.
7. Schoep 2006.
8. *PM II*, 373–390; Lloyd 1998, 1999; Driessen 2003.
9. Driessen 1982.
10. Mountjoy 2003, 22–25.
11. Erasmus 1977; Walsh 1980. For ethnographic analogies, see Kramer 1982.
12. Lloyd 1998; Driessen 2003, 28.
13. *PM II*, 396–413; Fotou 1990, 1997.
14. Hiller 2000; Betancourt and Marinatos 1997, 97–98.
15. Driessen 1999a; Tzedakis and Chryssoulaki 1987; Chryssoulaki 1997; Hallager 1990.
16. Wiener 1984, 17. For the influence of Knossos at Haghia Triada, see Cucuzza 1991.
17. Driessen 1982.
18. Driessen and Macdonald 1997.
19. Soles 2004.
20. Driessen and Macdonald 1997, 42.
21. Betancourt 2002; Warren 2002.
22. Day and Relaki 2002; Schoep 2002a, 2004; Schoep and Knappett 2004.
23. Day and Relaki 2002; Hamilakis 2002b.
24. Cherry 1986.
25. LaRosa 2002, 2004; J. Shaw 2002, 2003.
26. Driessen 1982, 1999a.
27. McEnroe 1979, 92.
28. Driessen 1999a.
29. McEnroe 1979, 92; for the Little Palace see Hatzaki 2005, 52.
30. McEnroe 1979, 92.
31. The term "Villa," used to describe certain monumental Minoan houses, goes back to Evans. Despite a number of attempts to define it (see several articles in Hägg 1997), the term is still used loosely and inconsistently. Like other conventional terms ("Lustral Basin," "Pillar Crypt," and "Palace"), the term is too deeply rooted in the discipline to be eliminated. In American English, a "villa" is a country estate (*Websters' Seventh New Collegiate Dictionary*, s.v. "villa"). Most, if not all, of the buildings I am concerned with here were not country estates but belonged to settlements of various sizes.
32. Begg 1975; for industries in the Service Quarters, Demargne and Gallet de Santerre 1953, 70; Hazzidakis 1934, 10.
33. Driessen and MacGillivray 1989; Driessen 1999a.
34. L. Platon 2000; Chryssoulaki and L. Platon 1987.
35. Chryssoulaki and L. Platon 1987; L. Platon 2004.
36. *Gournia*.
37. Watrous 2000, 129, gives the size of the settlement. Whitelaw gives an estimate of ca. 450 people per hectare for the section of the site that has been excavated. Whitelaw 2001. Because the settlement is likely to have been less dense toward the fringes of the site, I am guessing roughly 350 people per hectare.
38. Allbaugh 1953, 89–91; note that a considerable amount of the apparent discrepancy between the sizes of the Minoan houses and modern houses is due to a difference in what they measure. The figures for the Minoan houses refer to the total area within the exterior borders of the house, whereas Allbaugh's figures refer only to the amount of floor space, not including the thickness of the walls.

39. *Gournia*, 24.
40. These houses are what I called Type 3 houses in an article published in 1982. The main purpose of that article was to provide a vocabulary that could be used to describe and compare modest houses of the sort found at Gournia that had been largely ignored in the literature. The "typology" also proposed that researchers examine houses on the basis of a broad range of specific criteria rather than just a few. McEnroe 1982. That article is often cited and provoked split reactions, particularly at the International Symposium at the Swedish Institute in 1992. Hägg 1997. I agree with much of the criticism that suggested it is better to see the relationships among what I labeled types as a continuum rather than hard and fast hierarchical categories. Hamilakis 2002b, 189. I also agree that it now seems at least as important to approach Neopalatial houses from a local and regional perspective as from an island-wide perspective. McEnroe 1990; Adams 2006, 6, note 52. I do, however, maintain that it is important to compare buildings on the basis of a consistent set of observable criteria.
41. *Gournia*, 21–26.
42. McEnroe 1996.
43. Soles 2003.
44. Soles 2003, 91–99.
45. This very rough estimate is based on the methods used by Erasmus 1977, 52–78; Walsh 1980; and Kramer 1982.
46. Whitelaw 2004b.
47. *PM II*, 414–421.
48. *PM IV*, 964–1018.
49. *PM II*, 578–587.
50. *Gournia*, 25; Russell 1979.
51. Betancourt and Davaras 1998, 1–76.
52. *Gournia*, 41–42.
53. MacGillivray, Driessen, and Sackett, 2000.
54. Peatfield, 1987, 1990, 1994.
55. Myres 1902–1903.
56. The same is true at Knossos, Phaistos, Malia, Zakros, Palaikastro, and Kommos.
57. Driessen and Macdonald 1997. In their study Driessen and Macdonald used the lower chronology. The date used here, 1628 BC, comes from the higher chronology.
58. Rehak and Younger 1998, 129–130; Watrous 2004, 145–147.
59. Driessen and Macdonald 1997.
60. Rehak and Younger 1998, 148.
61. Televantou 1994; Michailidou 1990, 2001; Palyvou 1999, 2005.
62. J. Shaw 1978c.
63. Palyvou 1999, 75–76.
64. Ibid., 71–75.
65. Palyvou 1990, 1999, 375–420.
66. Michailidou 2001.
67. Televantou 1994.
68. Kopaka 1990.

CHAPTER 10

1. The few Linear B tablets recently discovered at Khania date to the Postpalatial period, as do the inscribed stirrup jars. For differences between the Linear A and Linear B administrations, see Palaima 1987 and Driessen and Schoep 1999.
2. Bennet 1987; Driessen and Schoep 1999.
3. Bennet 1987; Driessen and Schoep 1999; Driessen 2001.
4. Hallager 1977, 72.
5. Boardman 1963; Popham 1964, 1970, 1994, 1997; Doxey 1987; Hatzaki 2004, 2005b.
6. Palmer 1963; Hood 1965; Momigliano and Hood 1994; Hallager 1977; Niemeier 1982; Bennet 1990.
7. Driessen 1990, 1997a; Firth 2000–2001.
8. Popham 1987, 298.
9. "Megaron" is a term still widely but inconsistently used to refer to an axial building form that somehow embodied the mainland Greek (or Achaean) mentality in contrast to the non-Greek Minoan mentality. As we shall see in Chapter 12, this notion is grounded in nineteenth-century racial stereotypes. Here I am arguing for a more complex view of race and ethnicity. As we shall see below, while buildings do have the power to call up a rich variety of cultural associations, they are not direct indicators of the builders' DNA. For a recent review of the use of race as an explanatory tool in Late Bronze Age/Early Iron Age Crete, see Prent 2005, 88–92.
10. Many of the papers delivered at the Table Ronde in 1991, *La Crète mycénienne*, addressed this issue. See Driessen and Farnoux 1997. In addition, for Malia, see Driessen and Farnoux 1994, 2000; for Haghia Triada, see D'Agata 1999; for Mochlos, see Brogan, Smith, and Soles 2002.

11. Shennan 1989a, 1989b; Renfrew 1996; Jones 1997; Hall 1997; Bennet 1999; D'Agata and Moody, 2005.
12. Preston 1999, 2004, 2005.
13. Mirié 1979; Driessen 1990, 1997; Momigliano and Hood 1994; Panagiotaki 1999; Begg, 1975, 166–75; Christakis 2004, 299–309; Overbeck and McDonald 1976, 160–164.
14. Momigliano and Hood 1994, 128–150.
15. Ibid.
16. Ibid.
17. Ibid.
18. Ibid.
19. Driessen 1990, 108–110.
20. Panagiotaki 1999, 251; Christakis 2004, 299.
21. Panagiotaki 1999, 239–240, 271–272.
22. Mirié 1979, 51–59; Niemeier 1987, 163.
23. Christakis 2004, 301.
24. Begg 1975, 166–175; Hallager 1977m 17–50; Driessen 1990, 117–123; Raison 1993, 154–161; Christakis 2004, 299–309.
25. Christakis 2004, 299–309.
26. Ibid.
27. Ibid.
28. Ibid.
29. Ibid.
30. Ibid.
31. Ibid.
32. Popham 1970, 55–56; Mirié 1979, 56–60; Niemeier 1987, 163.
33. Ibid.
34. Overbeck and McDonald 1976, 160–164.
35. Ibid.
36. Ibid.
37. Ibid.
38. Ibid.; Macdonald and Driessen 1988, 258.
39. Overbeck and McDonald 1976, 160–164.
40. Ibid.
41. Mirié 1979, 51–59, plate 35; Niemeier, 1987, 163. This would seem to confirm the date that Marcar proposes on the basis of the textile patterns for the Procession frescoes that were originally on the walls of the Central Staircase. I think it is likely, however, that a predecessor of the Central Staircase already existed in the Neopalatial period, although it clearly postdates the initial MM III construction phase. Marcar 2004.
42. Hallager 1987; Panagiotaki 1999, 239, 271–272.
43. Driessen 1990.
44. Momigliano and Hood 1994.
45. Ibid., 150.
46. Popham 1970, 85; Hallager 1977, 50.
47. Macdonald and Driessen 1988, 1990.
48. Overbeck and McDonald 1976, 160–164.
49. Immerwahr 1990, 84–89; Hood 2000.
50. Immerwahr 1990, 176.
51. Ibid., 84–89.
52. Ibid.; Hood 2000.
53. Marcar 2004, 234. See note 33 above.
54. Immerwahr 1990, 76; Hood 2000.
55. Immerwahr 1990, 84–89; Hood 2000.
56. Ibid.
57. Ibid.
58. Hood 2000.
59. Immerwahr 1990, 84–89; Hood 2000.
60. Hood 2000.
61. Ibid.
62. Immerwahr 1999, 177; Hood 2000.
63. Hood 2000.
64. Ibid.
65. Immerwahr 1990, 84–89; Hood 2000.
66. Immerwahr 1990, 105–146. The Chariot scene, known from fragments at Knossos, also has mainland parallels.
67. B. Hallager and E. Hallager 1995. The bull does appear in mainland painting, particularly in early frescoes at Pylos, but it is rare. Immerwahr 1990, 110.
68. The Campstool Fresco, to which the Parisienne belongs, came from an upper story room in the west wing. Its fragments were found on both sides of the west wall of Magazines XIII–XV. It should probably be understood as a feasting scene. For feasting as a politically charged social practice in the Aegean Bronze Age, see the special issue of *Hesperia* 2004, 119–337.
69. Wright 2004a, 2004b.
70. Whitelaw 2004a.
71. Hatzaki 2004, 124. Much of my description of the town of Knossos in the Final Palatial period is based on Hatzaki's important article.
72. Hatzaki 2004. Other important Neopalatial houses did not continue in use in the Final Palatial period. These include the South House, the House of the Frescoes, and the House of the Chancel Screen.
73. Coldstream and Macdonald 1997, 192–193; Driessen and Macdonald 1997, 148–149; Hatzaki 2004, 122.

74. Warren 1983.
75. Driessen 1990, 121; Driessen and Schoep 1995.
76. Warren 1984.
77. Dimopoulou 1999.
78. Driessen and Schoep 1999.
79. Preston 1999, 2004.
80. For many years LM II pottery was so rarely found outside Knossos that many scholars doubted its existence as a chronological phase, regarding it instead as a pottery style restricted to Knossos. Popham compiled a list of excavated sites at which LM II–LM IIIA1 material had been found. See Popham 1981. It included partial reoccupation of Neopalatial houses at ten settlements: Zakros, Palaikastro, Malia, Khondros Viannou, Katsamba, Archanes, Tylissos, Phaistos, and Pyrgos. Since then many of these sites have been studied, reexcavated, and studied again in greater detail. To these we can now add Kommos, Haghia Triada (which Popham had listed only as a tomb site) and Khania. All these sites continued to be occupied into LM IIIB and will be considered in the next chapter. The colossal LMIIIA2 harbor building at Kommos, Building P, might belong to this period, but it might equally be contemporary with the later LM IIIA2 phase at Haghia Triada. See J. Shaw and M. Shaw 1993, 2006, and Chapter 12 below. In short, Knossos appears to have been a thriving town in the midst of a Crete that had not yet recovered from the almost universal LM IB destructions.
81. La Rosa 1997; Cucuzza 2001, 2003; D'Agata 2005, 111.
82. Long 1974; Immerwahr 1990, 100–102; Militello 1998, 86–87, 154–167, 283–309, 346–355.
83. Militello 1998, 335.
84. Gesell 1985, 74–75; Militello 1998, 148–153, 321–335; Cucuzza 2001.
85. Dörpfeld 1905, 271–280; Mackenzie 1904–1905, 220–222.
86. Cucuzza 2001, 2003.
87. Militello 1998, 80.
88. Cucuzza 2001.
89. Halbherr, Stefani, and Banti 1977, 192, figure 118.
90. Hayden 1982, 1984.
91. Militello 1998, 80.
92. Cucuzza 2003, 220.
93. Militello 1998, 81–85, 132–148.
94. La Rosa 1999, 2000.
95. *PM IV*, 785–786.

CHAPTER 11

1. Driessen 1990, 126 figure 17.
2. Whitelaw 2004b, 156 figures 10.7, 10.8.
3. Hatzaki 2004, 2005b.
4. Popham relied heavily on the pottery from the LM IIIA1–early LM IIIA2 destruction debris in the houses—particularly the Royal Villa—to support his date for the destruction of the Palace. There was little pottery of this date in the Palace and much more LM IIIB material including many whole pots found on datable LM IIIB floors along with Linear B tablets. Popham 1970. For datable LM IIIB floors inside the Palace with whole pots and tablets, see, for example, Firth 2000–2001, 215–226.
5. J. Shaw and M. Shaw 2006, 845–854.
6. Puglisi 2001.
7. La Rosa 1997; Cucuzza 1997, 2003.
8. Coulton 1976, 19.
9. Gesell 1985, 69–75; Peatfield 1994, 28–35; Privitera 2004; B. Hallager 2006.
10. *PM II*, 335–344; Rethemiotakis dates the goddess and votary figures to LM II–LM IIIA1 on stylistic grounds. Rethemiotakis 2001, 10–18. The pottery in the room is later.
11. Alexiou 1958; Gesell 1985, 41; Peatfield 1994, 33.
12. Gesell 2001.
13. Gesell 1976.
14. *Gournia*, 47–48; Russell 1979, 27–33; Gesell 1985, 72.
15. Gesell 1985, 76–79.
16. Ibid., 41–56.
17. Privitera 2004; B. Hallager 2006.
18. McEnroe 1996, 223–232.
19. M. Shaw 1990.
20. *Gournia*, 23.
21. Soles and Davaras 1996, 218–222; Brogan, Smith, and Soles 2002.
22. Hayden 1990; L. Platon 1997.
23. Hayden 1990, 209.
24. L. Platon, on the other hand, regards the central section as a single public building intended for use by more than one household. The fact that it was built over the course of several construction phases argues against his interpretation. L. Platon 1997.
25. Privitera 2004.
26. Farnoux 1989–1990, 1992, 1997; Driessen and Farnoux 1997, 54–64.

27. Driessen and Farnoux 1997, 56–60.
28. The excavators have described two main phases within the LM III period but note that earlier walls (MM, LM I, and LM II–IIIA1) had been incorporated into the later building. This process was partly responsible for the irregular layout of the building. Driessen (pers. comm.).
29. Vallianou 1997.
30. Hiesel 1990, 111–144, 205–209; Shear 1968, 459–460. The LM IIIB buildings in the Greek-Swedish excavations at Khania are also Mycenaeanizing; they have central hearths in the main rooms and Mycenaean figurines placed near the hearths and the entrances. It is not clear, however, whether or not these buildings are Corridor Houses.
31. Shear 1968, 459–460.
32. Ibid., 459–464.
33. Bennet 1990, 208–209.
34. Oelman 1912.
35. Dawkins 1913–1914; Hayden 1987, 111–113.
36. Dawkins 1909–1910, 1913–1914, 9.
37. Cucuzza 1997.
38. E. Hallager and B. Hallager, 2000, 2003.
39. M. Shaw 1990.
40. I am grateful to Todd Whitelaw for his comments on this topic.

CHAPTER 12

1. For general background on defensible settlements in Crete, see Nowicki 2000 and Wallace 2003.
2. The fortified sites are Rogdia Kastrokefala, Iouktas, Kofinas, and Kato Kastello in the Zakros Gorge. Nowicki 2000, 41–48.
3. Haggis 1993, 138–143.
4. Wallace 2003, 256–257.
5. Glassie 1982, 423.
6. Boyd 1901; Gessell, L. Day, and Coulson 1983, 1985, 1988, 1995; Gesell, Coulson, L. Day 1991; L. Day 1997.
7. Glowacki 2004.
8. L. Day, Glowacki, and Klein 2000, 116–117.
9. As noted in Chapter 3, it would be possible to get a reasonably accurate estimate of the labor hours required by building a duplicate house. For the kind of cruder estimate used here, see Erasmus 1977, 52–78; Walsh 1980; Kramer 1982.
10. L. Day and Snyder 2004, 65.
11. Knapp 2003, 566–568; Cohen 1985; Anderson 1991; Isbell 2000; Canuto and Yeager 2000.
12. Haggis and Nowicki 1993; Coulson and Tsipopoulou, 1994, 1994–1996; Tsipopoulou 2001, 2004, 2005.
13. Nowicki in Coulson and Tsipopoulou 1994, 94–97.
14. Tsipopoulou 2005, 318.
15. For example, Darcque 1990.
16. See Chapter 10, note 9. Wallace 2005, 222–225.
17. Mackenzie 1907–1908.
18. Tsipopoulou 2005, 324.
19. Eliopoulos 1998, 2004; Klein 2004; Prent 2005, 148–149, 194, 470; Klein and Glowacki, forthcoming.
20. Eliopoulos 1998, 310 and note 20; Prent 2005, 470.
21. Pendlebury, Pendlebury, and Money-Coutts 1937–1938; Nowicki 1987, 2000, 157–164; Wallace 2005.
22. This number is based on an estimate of five people per house, and Nowicki's estimate of a total of 120–150 houses. Nowicki 1987, 246. The figure is much lower than the 3,500 estimated by Pendlebury, Pendlebury, and Money-Coutts, 1937–1938, 65.
23. Nowicki 1987, 239.
24. Nowicki 1999, 147–148.
25. Nowicki estimates food requirements on the basis of data collected by Allbaugh in the years just after World War II. Nowicki 1999, 153, table 1. Wallace has recently proposed that this building was not an ordinary house, but a specialized building intended mainly for public feasting. Wallace 2005. I shall return to this topic below.
26. For example, Whitley assumes that building A at Vronda was the residence of the local "Big Man." Whitley 1991, 184–186; Prent 2005, 120.
27. L. Day and Snyder 2004, 76–79.
28. Gesell, L. Day, and Coulson 1986, 365–366 note 2; L. Day 1999; L. Day, Glowacki, and Klein 200, 121–122; L. Day and Snyder 2004; Prent 2005, 152–153.
29. Wright 2004a, 2004b, and the rest of the special edition of *Hesperia* 73, 121–337.
30. Wallace 2005.
31. L. Day and Snyder 2004; Nowicki 1999a.
32. Gesell 1985, 41–54; Rutkowski 1987; Whittaker 1997; Albers 2001; Gesell 2001; Eliopoulos 1998, 2004; Klein 2004; Klein and Glowaki, forthcoming; Prent 2005, 103–154, 614–623.
33. Prent 2005, 126–154, 614–622; Klein and Glowacki, forthcoming. The term "temple" is controversial when

applied to this period. Albers warns against using it to refer to Minoan and Mycenaean buildings primarily because, in her view, these buildings lack the requisite monumentality (even though they are literally as big as a house). Prent notes that the word may too simplistically imply a direct unilinear development from Bronze Age shrines to the canonical classical form. See Albers 2001; Prent 2005, 62 note 133; Klein and Glowacki, forthcoming. The term is useful, however, because it signals the fact that the LM IIIC shrines/temples considered in this chapter represent a fundamentally new form of independent building intended specifically to house the deity and associated cult equipment, and that this new form of building was one of the key components of the LM IIIC village in this part of the island.

34. Peatfield 1994, 33–35.
35. Prent 2005.
36. Klein 2004; Klein and Glowacki, forthcoming. I am grateful to Nancy Klein for allowing me to read this article in advance of its publication.
37. Prent 2005, 12–26.
38. Klein and Glowacki, forthcoming.
39. Tsipopoulou 2001.
40. Eliopoulos 1998, 2004; Prent 2005, 147–149 and 619–620.
41. Prent 2005, 620.
42. Ibid., 614–620.
43. Ibid., 132–133.
44. Gesell 1985, 69–71; Rethemiotakis 2001, 28–52.
45. Van Dyke and Alcock 2003; Prent 2003; Wallace 2003.
46. Van Dyke and Alcock 2003a, 1.
47. Wallace 2003, 273.
48. Prent 2005, 154–174 and 200–211.
49. Wallace 2003, 269.
50. Prent 2003.
51. Wallace 2003, 269.
52. Gesell, Coulson, and L. Day 1991, 163.

CONCLUSION

1. Tilley 2006, 7.
2. For an example of this process, see McEnroe 2001, 1–30.
3. Tilley 1989, 189.

GLOSSARY

Central Court. A large, unroofed area in the center of a monumental Minoan Palace. It is roughly 2:1 in L:W proportion and is typically oriented approximately north-south.

forehall. A room in the Minoan Hall complex located between the light well and the Minoan Hall. It is separated from the light well by one or more columns and from the Minoan Hall by a pier-and-door partition.

Kouloura. A circular, stone-lined pit found in the West Courts of the first palaces at Knossos and Phaistos. Koulouras have been variously interpreted as cisterns, dry wells, granaries, and pits for sacred trees.

Lustral Basin. Initially the Lustral Basin was a small, square room with a floor at a lower level than that of the surrounding floors. It was entered by a small flight of stairs. At some time during the course of the Neopalatial period, the floors of many Lustral Basins were raised to the level of the surrounding rooms. Lustral Basins have been interpreted as baths or cult rooms.

Minoan Hall. The largest room in the Residential Quarters of the Palaces and of Palatializing houses. It is part of a set of rooms that includes the forehall and light well. The Minoan Hall is separated from the forehall by a pier-and-door partition.

Palace. A Minoan Palace is a monumental architectural form characterized by a standard set of quarters (including a Residential Quarter, storage magazines, and rooms for bureaucracy and cult) arranged around a Central Court. The five known Minoan Palaces are at Knossos, Phaistos, Malia, Zakros, and Galatas.

peak sanctuary. A rural sanctuary located on or near a prominent peak. It is typically marked by votive offerings, particularly terra-cotta figurines.

Piano Nobile. A term A. Evans borrowed from Italian Renaissance architecture to refer to grand, upper-story rooms, particularly those in the west wing of the Palace at Knossos.

pier-and-door partition. A partition formed by a series of doors that could be closed (creating a barrier), open (merging two spaces), or partly opened (separating the spaces but allowing communication and admitting light). The pier-and-door partition is typically associated with the Minoan Hall. The pier-and-door partition is sometimes called a Polythyron.

Pillar Crypt. A ground-floor room with one or more central pillars. Since the time of A. Evans, they have been interpreted as cult spaces. Most were used for storage.

Residential Quarter. A set of rooms found in the Minoan Palaces and Palatializing houses. It usually consists of a Minoan Hall, forehall, light well, Lustral Basin, and a private room that A. Evans called the Queen's Megaron in the Palace at Knossos.

WORKS CITED

ABBREVIATIONS

In addition to the standard abbreviations employed by the *American Journal of Archaeology* (http://www.ajaonline.org), the following are used:

ÉtCrét	*Études crétoises.*
Gournia	Hawes, H., B. Williams, R. Seager, and E. Hall, 1908. *Gournia, Vasilike, and Other Prehistoric Sites on the Isthmus of Hierapetra, Crete.* Philadelphia.
MA:MAT	Shaw, J. 1971. *Minoan Architecture: Materials and Techniques (ASAtene 44)*. Rome.
PM I–IV	Evans, A. 1921–1936. *The Palace of Minos at Knossos.* 4 volumes.
PoC	Graham, J. W. 1962. *The Palaces of Crete,* Princeton.
SIMA	*Studies in Mediterranean Archaeology.*
TUAS	*Temple University Aegean Symposium.*

Adams, E. 2006. "Social Strategies and Spatial Dynamics in Neopalatial Crete: An Analysis of the North-Central Area." *AJA* 110:1–36.

Albers, G. 2001. "Rethinking Mycenaean Sanctuaries." In *POTNIA: Deities and Religion in the Aegean Bronze Age* (*Aegaeum* 22), ed. R. Laffineur and R. Hägg, 131–141. Liège.

Alexiou, S. 1958. Η μινωϊκή Θεά μεθ' υψωμένων χειρών. *KrChron* 12:179–299.

———. 1967. Αρχαιότητες και Μνημεία Κεντρικής και Ανατολικής Κρήτης. *ArchDelt* 22:480–488.

———. 1979. Τείχη και ακροπόλεις στη Μινωϊκή Κρήτη. *Cretologia* 8:41–56.

Alexiou, S., and P. Warren. 2004. *The Early Minoan Tombs of Lebena, Southern Crete* (*SIMA* 30). Sävedalen, Sweden.

Allbaugh, L. 1953. *Crete: A Case Study of an Underdeveloped Area.* Princeton.

Amouretti, M.-Cl. 1970. *Le centre politique II: la crypte hypostyle (1957–1962) Fouilles exécutées à Mallia.* (*ÉtCrét* 18). Paris.

Anderson, B. 1991. *Imagined Communities: Reflections on the Origin and Spread of Nationalism.* 2d ed. London.

Banti, L. 1941–1943. "I culti minoici e greci di Haghia Triada." *ASAtene,* n.s. 3-5:9-74.

Begg, D. J. I. 1975. "Minoan Storerooms in the Late Bronze Age." Ph.D. diss. University of Toronto.

———. 1987. "Continuity in the West Wing at Knossos." In *The Function of the Minoan Palaces* (Skrifter Utgivna av Svenska Institutet i Athen, 40, 46), ed. R. Hägg and N. Marinatos, 179–184. Stockholm.

———. 2004a. "An Interpretation of Mason's Marks at Knossos." In *Knossos: Palace, City, State* (British School at Athens Studies 12), ed. G. Cadogan, E. Hatzaki, and A. Vasilakis, 219–223. London.

———. 2004b. "An Archaeology of Palatial Mason's Marks on Crete." In *ΧΑΡΙΣ: Essays in Honor of Sara Immerwahr* (*Hesperia* Supp. 33), ed. A. Chapin, 1–25. Princeton.

Bennet, J. 1987. "Knossos and LM III Crete: A Post-Palatial Palace?" In *The Function of the Minoan Palaces* (Skrifter Utgivna av Svenska Institutet i Athen, 40, 35), ed. R. Hägg and N. Marinatos, 307–312. Stockholm.

———. 1990. "Knossos in Context: Comparative Perspectives on the Linear B Administration of LM II–III Crete." *AJA* 94:193–211.

Betancourt, P. 2002. "Who Was in Charge of the Palaces?" In *Monuments of Minos: Rethinking the Minoan Palaces*

(*Aegaeum* 23), ed. J. Driessen, I. Schoep, and R. Laffineur, 207–211. Liège.

Betancourt, P., and C. Davaras, eds. 1998. *Pseira II: Building AC ("The Shrine") and Other Buildings in Area A.* Philadelphia.

Betancourt, P., V. Karageorghis, R. Laffineur, and W.-D. Niemeier, eds. 1999. *MELETEMATA: Studies in Aegean Archaeology Presented to Malcolm H. Wiener as He Enters His 65th Year (Aegaeum* 20). Liège.

Betancourt, P., and N. Marinatos. 1997. "The Minoan Villa." In *The Function of the "Minoan Villa"* (Skrifter Utgivna av Svenska Institutet i Athen, 40, 46), ed. R. Hägg, 91–98. Stockholm.

Bintliff, J. 1977. *Natural Environment and Human Settlement in Prehistoric Greece* (*BAR* Supp. 28). Oxford.

Blackman, D., and K. Branigan. 1975. "An Archaeological Survey of the South Coast of Crete between the Ayiofarango and Chrysostomos." *BSA* 70:17–36.

———. 1977. "An Archaeological Survey of the Lower Catchment of the Ayiofarango Valley." *BSA* 72:13–83.

———. 1982. "An Early Minoan Tholos Tomb at Ayia Kyriaki, Ayiofarango, Southern Crete." *BSA* 77:1–57.

Boardman, J. 1963. "The Date of the Knossos Tablets." In *On the Knossos Tablets*. Oxford.

Bosanquet, E. 1914. *Days in Attica*. New York.

Boyd, H. 1901. "Excavations at Kavousi, Crete in 1900." *AJA* 5:125–158.

Bozineki-Didonis, P. 1985. *Crete (Greek Traditional Architecture)*. Athens.

Branigan, K. 1970. *The Foundations of Palatial Crete*. London.

———. 1987. "The Economic Role of the First Palaces." In *The Function of the Minoan Palaces* (Skrifter Utgivna av Svenska Institutet i Athen, 40, 35), ed. R. Hägg and N. Marinatos, 245–249. Stockholm.

———. 1993. *Dancing with Death: Life and Death in Southern Crete 3000–2000 B.C.* Amsterdam.

———. 1998. "The Nearness of You: Proximity and Distance in Early Minoan Funerary Behavior." In *Cemetery and Society in the Aegean Bronze Age* (Sheffield Studies in Aegean Archaeology, 1), ed. K. Branigan, 13–26. Sheffield.

Bretschneider, J., J. Driessen, and K. Van Lerberghe, eds. 2007. *Power and Architecture in the Ancient near East and the Aegean: Proceedings of an International Conference Held at Leuven in 2002*. Leuven.

Brogan, T., R. Smith, and J. Soles. 2002. "Mycenaeans at Mochlos? Exploring Culture and Identity in the Late Minoan IB to IIIA1 Transition." *Aegaean Archaeology* 6:89–118.

Broodbank, C. 1992. "The Neolithic Labyrinth: Social Changes at Knossos Before the Bronze Age." *JMA* 5:39–75.

Brown, A. 1983. *Arthur Evans and the Palace of Minos*. Oxford.

Canuto, M., and J. Yaeger, eds. 2000. *Archaeology of Communities: A New World Perspective*. London.

Carinci, F. 1989. "The 'III fase protopalaziale' at Phaestos: Some Observations." In *Transition. Le monde égéen du bronze moyen au bronze récent* (*Aegaeum* 3), ed. R. Laffineur, 73–80. Liège.

———. 2001. "Per una diversa interpretazione delle 'kulure' nei cortili dei palazzi minoici." *Creta Antica* 2:53–62.

Carter, T., R. King, and P. Underhill. 2007. "The Origin of the Minoans: New Genetic Data on the Populations of Prehistoric Crete." *Archaeological Institute of America. 108th Annual Meeting. Abstracts*, 92 (abstract).

Catling, H. 1973–1974. "Archaeology in Greece." *AR* 20:3–41.

Chapouthier, F., and J. Charbonneaux. 1928. *Fouilles exécutées à Mallia: Premier rapport* (*ÉtCrét* 1). Paris.

Chapouthier, F., and P. Demargne. 1942. *Fouilles exécutées à Mallia: Quatrième rapport* (*ÉtCrét* 12). Paris.

Chapouthier, F., and R. Joly. 1934. *Fouilles exécutées à Mallia: Troisième rapport* (*ÉtCrét* 6). Paris.

Cherry, J. 1983. "Evolution, Revolution, and the Origins of Complex Society in Minoan Crete." In *Minoan Society*, ed. O. Krzyszkowska and L. Nixon, 33–45. Bristol.

———. 1985. "Putting the Best Foot Forward." *Antiquity* 57:52–56.

———. 1986. "Polities and Palaces: Some Problems in Minoan State Formation." In *Peer Polity Interaction and Socio-Political Change*, ed. C. Renfrew and J. Cherry, 19–45. Cambridge.

Christakis, K. 2004. "Palatial Economy and Storage in Late Bronze Age Knossos." In *Knossos: Palace, City, State* (British School at Athens Studies 12), ed. G. Cadogan, E. Hatzaki, and A. Vasilakis, 299–309. London.

Chryssoulaki, S. 1990. "L'urbanism minoen: A. Le réseau routier urbain." In *L'habitat égéen préhistorique* (*BCH* Supp. 19), ed. P. Darcque and R. Treuil, 371–378. Paris.

———. 1997. "Neroukourou I Building and Its Place in Neopalatial Crete." In *The Function of the "Minoan Villa"*

(Skrifter Utgivna av Svenska Institutet i Athen, 40, 46), ed. R. Hägg, 27–32. Stockholm.

———. 1999. "Minoan Roads and Guard Houses—War Regained." In *POLEMOS: Le contexte guerrier in Egée à l'âge du Bronze* (*Aegaeum* 19), ed. R. Laffineur, 75–86. Liége.

Chryssoulaki, S., and L. Platon. 1987. "Relations between the Town and Palace of Zakros." In *The Function of the Minoan Palaces* (Skrifter Utgivna av Svenska Institutet i Athen, 40, 35), ed. R. Hägg and N. Marinatos, 77–84. Stockholm.

Civitillo, M., and B. Greco. 2003. "Il complesso protopaziale di Apodoulou Amariou: riflessione preliminari." *ASAtene* 81:767–796.

Cohen, A. 1985. *The Symbolic Construction of Community*. London.

Coulson, W., and M. Tsipopoulou. 1994. "Preliminary Investigations at Halasmenos, East Crete, 1992–1993." *Aegean Archaeology* 1:65–97.

———. 1994–1996. Χαλασμένος. *Κρητική Εστιlα* 5:166–378.

Coulton, J. 1976. *The Architectural Development of the Greek Stoa*. Oxford.

Creutzburg, N. 1933. "Die ländliche Seidlungen der Insel Creta." In *Die ländliches Seidlungen in verscheidenen Klimatzonen*. Breslau.

Cucuzza, N. 1991. "Mason's Marks at Haghia Triada." *Sileno* 17:53–65.

———. 1997. "The North Sector Buildings of Haghia Triada." In *La Crète mycénienne* (*BCH* Supp. 30), ed. J. Driessen and A. Farnoux, 73–84. Paris.

———. 2001. "Religion and Architecture: Early LM IIIA2 Buildings in the Southern Area of Haghia Triada." In *POTNIA: Deities and Religion in the Aegean Bronze Age* (*Aegaeum* 22), ed. R. Laffineur and R. Hägg, 169–174. Liège.

———. 2003. "Il Volo del Grifo: Osservazione sulla Haghia Triada 'micenea.'" *Creta Antica* 4:199–272.

Dabney, M. 1995. "The Later Stages of State Formation in Palatial Crete." In *POLITEIA: Society and State in the Aegean Bronze Age* (*Aegaeum* 12), ed. R. Laffineur and W.-D. Niemeier, 43–47. Liège.

D'Agata, A. L. 1999. "Hidden Wars: Minoan and Myceneans at Haghia Triada in the LM III Period: The Evidence from Pottery." In *POLEMOS: Le contexte guerrier in Egée à l'âge du Bronze* (*Aegaeum* 19), ed. R. Laffineur, 47–55. Liège.

———. 2005. "Central Southern Crete and Its Relations with the Greek Mainland in the Postpalatial Period." In *Ariadne's Threads: Connections between Crete and the Mainland in Late Minoan III (LM IIIA2 to LM IIIC)*, ed. A. L. D'Agata, J. Moody, with E. Williams, 109–130. Athens.

D'Agata, A. L., and J. Moody. 2005. "Ariadne's Threads and Late Minoan III Crete: Old Questions and New Problems and More Sensible Approaches." In *Ariadne's Threads: Connections between Crete and the Mainland in Late Minoan III (LM IIIA2 to LM IIIC)*, ed. A. L. D'Agata, J. Moody, with E. Williams, 9–15. Athens.

D'Agata, A. L., J. Moody, with E. Williams, eds. 2005. *Ariadne's Threads: Connections between Crete and the Mainland in Late Minoan III (LM IIIA2 to LM IIIC)*. Athens.

Damiani Indelicato, S. 1982. *Piazza pubblica e palazzo nella Creta Minoica*. Rome.

Danforth, L., and A. Tsiarias. 1982. *Death Rituals of Rural Greece*. Princeton.

Darcque, P. 1990. "Pour l'abandon du terme 'mégaron.'" In *L'habitat égéen préhistorique* (*BCH* Supp., 19), ed. P. Darcque and R. Treuil, 21–31. Paris.

Daux, G. 1957. "Chroniques des fouilles et découvertes archéologiques en Grèce en 1956. Mallia." *BCH* 81:687–705.

———. 1966. "Chronique des fouilles 1965, Mallia." *BCH* 90:1007–1014.

Davaras, C. 1997. "The 'Cult Villa' at Makrygialos." In *The Function of the Minoan Villa* (Skrifter Utgivna av Svenska Institutet i Athen, 40, 46), ed. R. Hägg, 117–135. Stockholm.

Davaras, C., and P. Betancourt. 2004. *The Haghia Photia Cemetery I: The Tomb Groups and Architecture*. Philadelphia.

Davaras, K. 1972. "The Oval House at Chamaizi Reconsidered." *AAA* 5:283–288.

Dawkins, R. 1904–1905. "Excavations at Palaikastro IV." *BSA* 11:258–308.

———. 1909–1910. "Excavations at Sparta 1910." *BSA* 16:1–11.

———. 1913–1914. "Excavations at Plati in Lasithi, Crete." *BSA* 20:1–17.

Day, L. 1997. "The Late Minoan IIIC Period at Vronda, Kavousi." In *La Crète mycénienne* (*BCH* Supp. 30), ed. J. Driessen and A. Farnoux, 391–406. Paris.

———. 1999. "A Late Minoan IIIC Window Frame from Vronda, Kavousi." *MELETEMATA: Studies in Aegean*

Archaeology Presented to Malcolm H. Wiener as He Enters His 65th Year (*Aegaeum* 20), ed. P. Betancourt, V. Karageorghis, R. Laffineur, and W.-D. Niemeier, 185–190. Liège.

Day, L., K. Glowacki, and N. Klein. 2000. "Cooking and Dining in LM IIIC Vronda, Kavousi." *Πεπραγμένα του Η' Διεθηνούς Κρητολογικού Συνεδρίου*, 115–125.

Day, L., M. Mook, and J. Muhly, eds. 2004. *Crete Beyond the Palaces: Proceedings of the Crete 2000 Conference.* Philadelphia.

Day, L., and L. Snyder. 2004. "The 'Big House' at Vronda and the 'Great House' at Karphi: Evidence for Social Structure in LM IIIC Crete." In *Crete Beyond the Palaces: Proceedings of the Crete 2000 Conference*, ed. L. Day, M. Mook, and J. Muhly, 63–79. Philadelphia.

Day, P., and M. Relaki. 2002. "Past Factions and Present Fictions: Palaces in the Study of Minoan Crete." In *Monuments of Minos: Rethinking the Minoan Palaces* (*Aegaeum* 23), ed. J. Driessen, I. Schoep, and R. Laffineur, 217–234. Liège.

Day, P., D. Wilson, and E. Kiriatzi. 1997. "Reassessing Specialization in Prepalatial Cretan Ceramic Production." In *TEXNH: Craftsmen, Craftswomen, and Craftsmanship in the Aegean Bronze Age* (*Aegaeum* 16), ed. R. Laffineur and P. Betancourt, 275–289. Liège.

Day, P., D. Wilson, and E. Kiriatzi. 1998. "Pots, Labels and People: Burying Ethnicity in the Cemetery at Aghia Photia, Siteias." In *Cemetery and Society in the Aegean Bronze Age* (Sheffield Studies in Aegean Archaeology, 1), ed. K. Branigan, 133–149. Sheffield.

Demargne, P. 1945. *Exploration des nécropoles, I* (*ÉtCrét* 7). Paris.

Demargne, P., and H. Gallet de Santerre. 1953. *Mallia, Maisons I* (*ÉtCrét* 9). Paris.

Deshayes, J., and A. Dessenne. 1959. *Fouilles exécutées à Mallia: Exploration des maisons et quartiers d'habitation (1948–1954) II* (*ÉtCrét* 11). Paris.

Diaz-Andreu, M., S. Lucy, A. Babić, and D. Edwards, eds. 2005. *The Archaeology of Identity.* London.

Diaz-Andreu, M., and S. Lucy. 2005. "Introduction." In *The Archaeology of Identity*, ed. M. Diaz-Andreu, S. Lucy, A. Babić, and D. Edwards, 1–12. London.

Dimopoulou, N. 1999. "The Neopalatial Cemetery of the Knossian Harbour-town at Poros: Mortuary Behavior and Social Ranking." *Eliten in der Bronzeit* (Monographien des Römisch-Germanishes Zentralmuseum 43), 27–36. Mainz.

Dinsmoor, W. 1950. *The Architecture of Ancient Greece.* 3d ed. London.

Di Vita, A., and A. La Regina, eds. 1984. *Creta Antica: Cento anni di archaeologia italiana (1884–1984).* Rome.

Dörpfeld, W. 1905. "Die kretischen, mykenischen und homerischen Paläste." *AM* 30:257–297.

Doxey, D. 1987. "Causes and Effects of the Fall of Knossos in 1375 B.C." *OJA* 6:301–324.

Driessen, J. 1982. "The Minoan Hall in Domestic Architecture on Crete: To Be in Vogue in Late Minoan IA?" *ActaArchLov* 21:27–92.

———. 1990. *An Early Destruction in the Mycenaean Palace at Knossos* (*ActaArchLov* Monographie 2). Leuven.

———. 1997a. "Le Palais de Knossos au MR II–III: combien de destructions?" In *La Crète mycénienne* (*BCH* Supp. 30), ed. J. Driessen and A. Farnoux, 113–134. Paris.

———. 1997b. "Some Observations on the Access Systems of Minoan Palaces." *Aegean Archaeology* 2 (1995): 67–85.

———. 1999a. "The Dismantling of a Minoan Hall at Palaikastro." In *MELETEMATA: Studies in Aegean Archaeology Presented to Malcolm H. Wiener as He Enters His 65th Year* (*Aegaeum* 20), ed. P. Betancourt, V. Karageorghis, R. Laffineur, and W.-D. Niemeier, 227–237. Liège.

———. 1999b. "The Archaeology of a Dream: The Reconstruction of Minoan Public Architecture." *JMA* 12.1:121–127.

———. 2001. "Center and Periphery: Some Observations on the Administration of the Kingdom of Knossos." In *Economy and Politics in the Mycenaean Palace States* (Cambridge Philological Society Supp. 27), ed. S. Voutsaki and J. Killen, 96–112. Cambridge.

———. 2002. "'The King Must Die': Some Observations on the Use of Minoan Court Compounds." In *Monuments of Minos: Rethinking the Minoan Palaces* (*Aegaeum* 23), ed. J. Driessen, I. Schoep, and R. Laffineur, 1–15. Liège.

———. 2003. "An Architectural Overview." In *Knossos: The South House* (British School at Athens Supp. 34), ed. P. Mountjoy et al., 27–37. London.

———. 2004. "The Central Court of the Palace at Knossos." In *Knossos: Palace, City, State* (British School at Athens Studies 12), ed. G. Cadogan, E. Hatzaki, and A. Vasilakis, 75–82. London.

———. 2007. "IIB or not IIB? On the Beginning of Minoan Monument Building." In *Power and Architecture in the Ancient Near East and the Aegean: Proceedings of an International Conference Held at Leuven in 2002*, ed. J. Bretschneider, J. Driessen, and K. Van Lerberghe. Leuven.

Driessen, J., and A. Farnoux. 1994. "Mycenaeans at Malia?" *Aegean Archaeology* 1:54–64.

———, eds. 1997. *La Crète mycénienne* (*BCH* Supp. 30). Paris.

———. 2000. "'La Crète vaut bien un messe': Domination and 'Collaboration' on Mycenaean Crete." *Πεπραγμένα του Η' Διεθηνούς Κρητολογικού Συνεδρίου*, 431–438.

Driessen, J., and C. Macdonald. 1997. *The Troubled Island: Minoan Crete Before and After the Santorini Eruption* (*Aegaeum* 17). Liège.

Driessen, J., and J. A. MacGillivray. 1989. "The Neopalatial Period in East Crete." In *TRANSITION: Le monde égéen du Bronze moyen et Bronze recent* (*Aegeaum* 3), ed. R. Laffineur, 99–111. Liège.

Driessen, J., and I. Schoep. 1995. "The Architect and the Scribe: Political Implications of Architectural and Administrative Changes on MM II–LM IIIA Crete." In *POLITEIA: Society and State in the Aegean Bronze Age* (*Aegaeum* 12), ed. R. Laffineur and W.-D. Niemeier, 649–664. Liège.

———. 1999. "The Stylus and the Sword: The Role of Scribes and Warriors in the Conquest of Crete." In *POLEMOS: Le contexte guerrier en Égée à l'Age du Bronze* (*Aegaeum* 19), ed. R. Laffineur, 389–397. Liège.

Driessen, J., I. Schoep, and R. Laffineur, eds. 2002. *Monuments of Minos: Rethinking the Minoan Palaces* (*Aegaeum* 23). Liège.

Du Boulay, J. 1974. *Portrait of a Greek Mountain Village*. Oxford.

Efstratiou, N., A. Karetsiou, E. Banou, and D. Margomenou. 2004. "The Neolithic Settlement at Knossos: New Light on an Old Picture." In *Knossos: Palace, City* (British School at Athens Studies 12), ed. G. Cadogan, E. Hatzaki, and A. Vasilakis, 39–49. London.

Eliopoulos, T. 1998. "A Preliminary Report on the Discovery of a Temple Complex of the Dark Ages at Kephala, Vasilikis." In *Eastern Mediterranean: Cyprus-Dodecanese-Crete 16th–6th Century B.C.*, ed. V. Karageorghis and N. Stampolidis, 301–313. Athens.

———. 2004. "Gournia, Vronda Kavousi, Kephala Vasilikis: A Triad of Interrelated Shrines of the Expiring Minoan Age on the Isthmus of Ierapetra." In *Crete Beyond the Palaces: Proceedings of the Crete 2000 Conference*, ed. L. Day, M. Mook and J. Muhly, 81–90. Philadelphia.

Erasmus, C. 1977. "Monument Building: Some Field Experiments." In *Experimental Archaeology*, ed. P. Ingersoll, J. Yellen, and W. Macdonald, 52–78. New York.

Evans, A. 1906. "The Prehistoric Tombs of Knossos." *Archaeologia* 6:391–562.

———. 1914. "The 'Tomb of the Double Axes' and Associated Group and Pillar Rooms with Ritual Vessels of the 'Little Palace' at Knossos." *Archaeologia* 65:1–94.

———. 1921–1935. *The Palace of Minos at Knossos*. 4 vols. London.

Evans, J. 1964. "Excavations in the Neolithic Settlement of Knossos 1957–1960." *BSA* 59:132–240.

———. 1971. "Neolithic Knossos: The Growth of a Settlement." *Proceedings of the Prehistoric Society*, n.s. 37:95–117.

———. 1994. "The Early Millennia: Continuity and Change in a Farming Settlement." In *Knossos: A Labyrinth of History. Papers presented in Honour of Sinclair Hood*, ed. D. Evely, H. Hughes-Brock, and N. Momigliano, 1–20. London.

Farnoux, A. 1989. "La Crypte Hypostyle." *BCH* 113:768–771.

———. 1989–1990. "Malia à fin du Bronze Récent." *ActaArchLov* 28–29:25–34.

———. "Quartier Gamma at Malia Reconsidered." In *Late Minoan III Pottery* (Monographs of the Danish Institute at Athens, 1), ed. E. Hallager and B. Hallager, 259–271. Athens.

Firth, R. 2000–2001. "A Review of the Find-places of the Linear B Tablets from the Palace of Knossos." *Minos* 35–36:63–290.

Flannery, K. 1972. "The Origins of the Village as a Settlement Type in Mesoamerica and the Near East: A Comparative Study." In *Man, Settlement, and Urbanism*, ed. P. Ucko, R. Tringham, and G. Dimbleby, 23–53. London.

Fotou, V. 1990. "L'implantation des bâtiments en Crète à l'époque neopalatial: aménagement du terrain et mode d'occupation du sol." In *L'habitat égéen préhistorique* (*BCH* Supp. 19), ed. P. Darque and R. Treuil, 45–73. Paris.

———. 1997. "Elements d'analyse architecturale et la question des functions de trois bâtiments-'villas:" la Royal Villa, Le "Megaron" du Nirou et la "Megaron" de Sklavokambos." In *The Function of the Minoan Villa* (Skrifter Utgivna av Svenska Institutet i Athen, 40, 46), ed. R. Hägg, 33–50. Stockholm.

Frankfurt, H. 1951. *Arrest and Movement: An Essay on Space and Time in the Representational Art of the Near East.* London.

Gesell, G. 1976. "The Minoan Snake Tube: A Survey and Catalogue." *AJA* 80:247–259.

———. 1985. *Town, Palace and House Cult in Minoan Crete.* Göteborg.

———. 2001. "The Function of the Plaque in the Shrines of the Goddess with U-Raised Hands." In *POTNIA: Deities and Religion in the Aegean Bronze Age (Aegaeum* 22), ed. R. Laffineur and R. Hägg, 253–258. Liège.

Gesell, G., W. Coulson, and L. Day. 1991. "Excavations at Kavousi, Crete, 1988." *Hesperia* 60:145–178.

———. 1995. "Excavations at Kavousi, Crete, 1989 and 1990." *Hesperia* 64:67–120.

———. 1983. "Excavations and Survey at Kavousi 1978–1981." *Hesperia* 52:389–420.

———. 1985. "Kavousi, 1982–1983: The Kastro." *Hesperia* 54:327–355.

———. 1988. "Excavations at Kavousi, Crete, 1987." *Hesperia* 57:279–301.

Glassie, H. 1982. *Passing Time in Balleymenone.* New York.

Glowacki, K. 2004. "Household Analysis in Dark Age Crete." In *Crete Beyond the Palaces: Proceedings of the Crete 2000 Conference,* ed. L. Day, M. Mook, and J. Muhly, 125–136. Philadelphia.

Graham, J. W. 1956. "The Phaistos 'Piano Nobile.'" *AJA* 60:255–262.

———. 1959. "The Residential Quarter of the Minoan Palace." *AJA* 63:47–52.

———. 1960a. "Windows, Recesses, and the Piano Nobile in the Minoan Palaces." *AJA* 64:329–333.

———. 1960b. "The Minoan Unit of Measurement and Minoan Palace Planning." *AJA* 64:335–341.

———. 1961. "The Minoan Banquet Hall." *AJA* 65:165–172.

———. 1962. *The Palaces of Crete.* Princeton.

———. 1979. "Further Notes on Minoan Palace Architecture: 1. West Magazine and Upper Halls at Knossos and Mallia, 2. Access to, and Use of, Minoan Palace Roofs." *AJA* 83:49–69.

Green, M. 2000. *A Shared World: Christians and Muslims in the Early Modern Mediterranean.* Princeton.

Hägg, R. 1987. "On the Reconstruction of the West Façade of the Palace at Knossos." In *The Function of the Minoan Palaces* (Skrifter Utgivna av Svenska Institutet i Athen, 40, 35), ed. R. Hägg and N. Marinatos, 129–134. Stockholm.

———, ed. 1997. *The Function of the "Minoan Villa"* (Skrifter Utgivna av Svenska Institutet i Athen, 40, 46). Stockholm.

Hägg, R., and N. Marinatos, eds. 1987. *The Function of the Minoan Palaces* (Skrifter Utgivna av Svenska Institutet i Athen, 40, 35), Stockholm.

Haggis, D. 1993. "Intensive Survey, Traditional Settlement Patterns and Dark Age Crete: The Case of Early Iron Age Kavousi." *JMA* 6:131–174.

———. 1999. "Staple Finance, Peak Sanctuaries, and Economic Complexity in Late Prepalatial Crete." In *From Minoan Farmers to Roman Traders,* ed. A. Chaniotis, 53–85. Stuttgart.

Haggis, D., and K. Nowicki. 1993. "Khalasmeno and Kataleimata: Two Early Iron Age Settlements in Monasteraki, East Crete." *Hesperia* 62:303–337.

Halbherr, F., E. Stefani, and L. Banti. 1980. "Haghia Triada nel periodo tardo palaziale." *ASAtene,* n.s. 39 (1977), 13–296.

Hall, J. M. 1997. *Ethnic Identity in Greek Antiquity.* Cambridge.

Hallager, B. 2006. "Domestic Shrines in LM IIIA:2–IIIC Crete: Fact or Fiction?" (Paper, Athens 2006).

Hallager, B., and E. Hallager. 1995. "The Knossian Bull: Political Propaganda in Neo-palatial Crete?" In *POLITEIA: Society and State in the Aegean Bronze Age (Aegaeum* 12), ed. R. Laffineur and W.-D. Niemeier, 547–554. Liège.

Hallager, E. 1977. *The Mycenaean Palace at Knossos: Evidence for Final Destruction in the IIIB Period.* Stockholm.

———. 1987. "A 'Harvest Festival Room' in the Minoan Palaces? An Architectural Study of the Pillar Crypt Area at Knossos." In *The Function of the Minoan Palaces* (Skrifter Utgivna av Svenska Institutet i Athen, 40, 35), ed. R. Hägg and N. Marinatos, 169–176. Stockholm.

———. 1990. "Upper Floors in LM I Houses." In *L'habitat égéen préhistorique.* (*BCH Supp.* 19), ed. P. Darcque and R. Treuil, 281–292. Paris.

———. 2000. "The Architecture." In *The Late Minoan IIIC Settlement (The Greek-Swedish Excavations at the Aghia Aikaterini Square: Kastelli Khania 1970–1987,* vol. 2), ed. E. Hallager and B. Hallager, 127–134. Stockholm.

Hallager, E., and B. Hallager, eds. 2000. *The Late Minoan IIIC Settlement. (The Greek-Swedish Excavations at the Aghia Aikaterini Square: Kastelli Khania 1970–1987,* vol. 2), ed. E. Hallager and B. Hallager, 127–134. Stockholm.

———. 2003. *The Late Minoan IIIB:2 Settlement. (The Greek-Swedish Excavations at the Aghia Aikaterini Square: Kastelli Khania 1970–1987 and 2001).* Stockholm.

Halstead, P. 1981. "From Determinism to Uncertainty: Social Storage and the Rise of the Minoan Palace." In *Economic Archaeology*, ed. A. Sheridan and G. Bailey, 187–213. Oxford.

———. 1995. "The Neolithic Foundations of Aegean Bronze Age Society?" In *POLITEIA: Society and State in the Aegean Bronze Age* (*Aegaeum* 12), ed. R. Laffineur and W.-D. Niemeier, 11–21. Liège.

Hamilakis, Y. 2002a. *Labyrinth Revisited: Rethinking Minoan Archaeology.* Oxford.

———. 2002b. "Too Many Chiefs? Factional Competition in Neopalatial Crete." In *Monuments of Minos: Rethinking the Minoan Palaces* (*Aegaeum* 23), ed. J. Driessen, I. Schoep, and R. Laffineur, 179–199. Liège.

Harcourt-Smith, C. 1933. "L'aménagement des champs des fouilles et l'education du public." *Mouseion* 1–2:71–74.

Hatzaki, E. 2004. "From Final Palatial to Postpalatial Knossos: A View from the Late Minoan II to Late Minoan IIIB Town." In *Knossos: Palace, City, State* (British School at Athens Studies 12), ed. G. Cadogan, E. Hatzaki, and A. Vasilakis, 121–126. London.

———. 2005a. *Knossos. The Little Palace.* London.

———. 2005b. "Postpalatial Knossos: Town and Cemeteries from LM IIIA2 to LM IIIC." In *Ariadne's Threads: Connections between Crete and the Mainland in Late Minoan III (LM IIIA2 to LM IIIC)*, ed. A. L. D'Agata, J. Moody, with E. Williams, 65–95. Athens.

Hawes, H., B. Williams, R. Seager, and E. Hall. 1908. *Gournia, Vasilike, and Other Prehistoric Sites on the Isthmus of Hierapetra, Crete.* Philadelphia.

Hayden, B. 1982. "The Derivation and Architectural Context of Cretan Bronze Age Stoas." *Archaeological News* 11:1–7.

———. 1984. "Late Bronze Age Tylissos: House Plans and Cult Centers." *Expedition* 26, no. 3:37–46.

———. 1990. "Aspects of Village Architecture in the Cretan Postpalatial Period." In *L'habitat égéen préhistorique* (*BCH* Supp. 19) ed. P. Darcque and R. Treuil, 203–213. Paris.

Hazzidakis, J. 1934. *Les villas minoennes de Tylissos* (*ÉtCrét* 3). Paris.

Heller, J. 1961. "A Labyrinth from Pylos." *AJA* 65:57–62.

Herzfeld, M. 1985. *The Poetics of Manhood: Contest and Identity in a Cretan Mountain Village.* Princeton.

———. 1991. *A Place in Time: Social and Monumental Time in a Cretan Town.* Princeton.

Hiesel, G. 1990. *Späthelladischehausarchitektur.* Mainz am Rhein.

Hillbom, N. 2005. *Minoan Games and Game Boards.* Lund.

Hiller, S. 2000. "Egyptian Features at Knossos." *Πεπραγμένα του Η' Διεθηνούς Κρητολογικού Συνεδρίου*, 577–591.

Hitchcock, L. 2000. *Minoan Architecture: A Contextual Analysis.* Jonserad, Sweden.

Hitchcock, L., and D. Preziosi. 1997. "The Knossos Unexplored Mansion and the Villa-Annex Complex." In *The Function of the "Minoan Villa"* (Skrifter Utgivna av Svenska Institutet i Athen, 40, 46), ed. R. Hägg, 51–62. Stockholm.

Hitchcock, L., and P. Koudounaris. 2002. "Virtual Discourse: Arthur Evans and the Reconstructions of the Minoan Palace at Knossos." In *Labyrinth Revisited: Rethinking Minoan Archaeology*, ed. Y. Hamilakis, 40–58. Oxford.

Hodder, I. 1993. "The Narrative and Rhetoric of Material Culture Sequences." *World Archaeology* 25:268–269.

———, ed. 1989. *The Meanings of Things.* London.

Hood, S. 1965. "'Last Palace' and 'Reoccupation' at Knossos." *Kadmos* 4:16–44.

———. 1987. "Mason's Marks in the Palaces." In *The Function of the Minoan Palaces* (Skrifter Utgivna av Svenska Institutet i Athen, 40, 35), ed. R. Hägg and N. Marinatos, 205–211. Stockholm.

———. 2000. "Cretan Fresco Dates." In *The Wall Painting of Thera* I, ed. S. Sherrat, 191–208. Athens.

Hood, S., and W. Taylor. 1981. *The Bronze Age Palace at Knossos: Plan and Sections.* London.

Immerwahr, S. 1990. *Aegean Painting in the Bronze Age.* University Park.

Ioannidou-Karetsou, A. 1985. Το ιερό κορυφής Γιούχτα. *Prakt* 1985:277–288.

Isbell, W. H. 2000. "What We Should Be Studying: The 'Imagined Community' and the 'Natural Community.'" In *Archaeology of Communities: A New World Perspective*, ed. M. Canuto and J. Jaeger, 243–266. London.

Jones, S. 1997. *The Archaeology of Ethnicity: Constructing Identities in the Past and Present.* London.

Karetsou, A. 2004. "Knossos After Evans: Past Interventions, Present State and Future Solutions." In *Knossos: Palace, City, State* (British School at Athens Studies 12), ed. G. Cadogan, E. Hatzaki, and A. Vasilakis, 547–555. London.

Klein, N. 2004. "The Architecture of the Late Minoan IIIC Shrine (Building G) at Vronda, Kavousi." In *Crete Beyond the Palaces: Proceedings of the Crete 2000 Conference*, ed. L. Day, M. Mook, and J. Muhly, 91–101. Philadelphia.

Klein N., and K. Glowacki. Forthcoming. "From Vronda to Dreros: Architecture and Display in Cretan Cult Buildings 1200–700 B.C."

Knapp, A. B. 2003. "The Archaeology of Community on Bronze Age Cyprus: Politiko Phorades in Context." *AJA* 107:559–580.

Knappett, C. 1999. "Assessing a Polity in Protopalatial Crete: The Malia-Lasithi State." *AJA* 103:615–639.

———. 2005. *Thinking Through Material Culture.* Philadelphia.

Kopaka, C. 1990. "Des pieces de repos dans l'habitat minoen du IIe millénaire avant J.C.?" In *L'habitat égéen préhistorique* (*BCH* Supp. 19), ed. P. Darcque and R. Treuil, 217–230. Paris.

Kramer, C. 1982. *Village Ethnoarchaeology: Rural Iran in Archaeological Perspective.* New York.

Kryzyszkowska, O., and L. Nixon, eds. 1983. *Minoan Society.* Bristol.

Laffineur, R., ed. 1999. *POLEMOS: La contexte guerrier in Égée à l'Age du Bronze* (*Aegaeum* 19), 179–190. Liège.

Laffineur, R., and P. Betancourt, eds. 1997. *TEXNH: Craftsmen, Craftswomen, and Craftsmanship in the Aegean Bronze Age* (*Aegaeum* 16). Liège.

Laffineur, R., and R. Hägg, eds. 2001. *POTNIA: Deities and Religion in the Aegean Bronze Age* (*Aegaeum* 22). Liège.

La Rosa, V. 1997. "Haghia Triada à l'époque mycénienne: l'utopie d'une ville capitale." In *La crète mycénienne* (*BCH* Supp. 30), ed. J. Driessen and A. Farnoux, 249–266. Paris.

———. 2002. "Pour une révision préliminaire du second palais de Phaistos." In *Monuments of Minos: Rethinking the Minoan Palaces* (*Aegaeum* 23), ed. J. Driessen, I. Schoep, and R. Laffineur, 71–98. Liège.

———. 2004. "Perché il Palazzo a Festós?" *Creta Antica* 5:43–51.

Lawrence, A. 1973. *Greek Architecture.* Harmondsworth.

Levi, D. 1959. "La villa rurale minoica di Gortina." *BdA* 44:237–266.

———. 1961–1962. "La tomba a tholos di Kamilari presso a Festòs." *ASAtene*, n.s. 23–24:7–148.

———. 1976. *Festòs e la civilità minoica.* Rome.

Lloyd, J. 1998. "The Minoan Hall System and the Problem of the Entrance to the South House at Knossos." *OpAth* 22–23:117–140.

———. 1999. "The Three-Dimensional Form of the Light Area of the Minoan Hall System and the Southeast Corner of the South House at Knossos." *OpAth* 24:51–77.

Long, C. 1974. *The Ayia Triada Sarcophagus: A Study of Late Minoan and Mycenaean Funerary Practices and Beliefs* (*SIMA* 41). Göteborg.

Macdonald, C. 2002. "The Neopalatial Palaces at Knossos." In *Monuments of Minos: Rethinking the Minoan Palaces* (*Aegaeum* 23), ed. J. Driessen, I. Schoep, and R. Laffineur, 35–54. Liège.

Macdonald, C., and J. Driessen. 1988. "The Drainage System of the Domestic Quarter in the Palace at Knossos." *BSA* 83:235–258.

MacGillivray, J. A. 1994. "The Early History of the Palace at Knossos (MM I–MM II)." In *Knossos: A Labyrinth of History. Papers Presented in Honour of Sinclair Hood*, ed. D. Evely, H. Hughes-Brock, and N. Momigliano, 45–55. London.

———. 1998. *Knossos: Pottery Groups of the Old Palace Period* (British School at Athens Studies 5). London.

MacGillivray, J. A., L. H. Sackett, et al. 1991. "Excavations at Palaikastro 1991." *BSA* 86:121–147.

MacGillivray, J. A., J. Driessen, and L. H. Sackett. 2000. *The Palaikastro Kouros: A Minoan Chryselephantine Statuette and Its Aegean Bronze Age Context* (British School at Athens Studies 6), London.

Mackenzie, D. 1904–1905. "Cretan Palaces and Aegean Civilization, I." *BSA* 11:181–223.

———. 1907–1908. "Cretan Palaces and Aegean Civilization, IV." *BSA* 14:343–422.

Maggidis, C. 1998. "From Polis to Necropolis: Social Ranking from Architectural and Mortuary Evidence in the Minoan Cemetery at Phourni, Archanes." In *Cemetery and Society in the Aegean Bronze Age* (Sheffield Studies in Aegean Archaeology 1), ed. K. Branigan, 87–102. Sheffield.

Manning, S. 1995. *The Absolute Chronology of the Aegean Early Bronze Age.* Sheffield.

Marcar, A. 2004. "Aegean Costume and the Dating of the Knossian Frescoes." In *Knossos: Palace, City, State* (British School at Athens Studies 12), ed. G. Cadogan, E. Hatzaki, and A. Vasilakis, 225–238. London.

Marinatos, N. 1984. *Art and Religion in Ancient Thera.* Athens.

McDonald, W. 1943. *Political Meeting Places of the Greeks.* Baltimore.

McEnroe, J. 1979. "Minoan House and Town Arrangement." Ph.D. diss., University of Toronto.

———. 1982. "A Typology of Minoan Neopalatial Houses." *AJA* 86:3–19.

———. 1984. Review of D. Preziosi, *Minoan Architectural Design. AJA* 88:600–601.

———. 1990. "The Significance of Local Styles in Minoan Vernacular Architecture." In *L'habitat égéen préhistorique* (*BCH* Supp. 19) ed. P. Darcque and R. Treuil, 195–202. Paris.

———. 1995. "Sir Arthur Evans and Edwardian Archaeology." *Classical Bulletin* 71:3–18.

———. 1996. "The Central Hillside at Kommos: The Late Bronze Age." In *Kommos I: The Kommos Region and the Houses of the Minoan Town.* 199–241. Princeton.

———. 2001. *Pseira V: The Architecture of Pseira* (University Museum Monograph 109). Philadelphia.

———. 2002. "Sir Arthur Evans and the Popular Press." *AJA* 106:246 (abstract).

———. 2007. "Minoan Archaeology and the Quest for the Primitive Hut." In *Krinoi kai Limenes: Studies in Honor of Joseph and Maria Shaw*, ed. P. Betancourt, M. Nelson, and H. Williams, 1–8. Philadelphia.

McGlade, J. 1999. "The Times of History." In *Time and Archaeology*, ed. T. Murray, 139–163. London.

McKee, S. 2000. *Uncommon Dominion, Venetian Crete and the Myth of Ethnic Purity.* Philadelphia.

Michailidou, A. 1990. "The Settlement of Akrotiri (Thera): A Theoretical Approach to the Function of the Upper Storey." In *L'habitat égéen préhistorique* (*BCH* Supp. 19), ed. P. Darcque and R. Treuil, 293–306. Paris.

———. 2001. *Ακρωτήρι Θήρας: Η Μελέτη των Όροφων στα Κτήρια του Οικισμού.* Athens.

Militello, P. 1998. *Haghia Triada I: Gli affreschi* (Monografie della Scuola Archeologica di Atene e delle Missioni Italiane in Oriente 9). Padova.

Mirié, S. 1979. *Das Tronraumareal des Palastes von Knossos. Versuch einer Neuinterpretation seiner Funktion* (Saarbrücker Beiträge zur Altertumswissenschaft 26). Bonn.

Momigliano, N. 1991. "MM IA Pottery from Evans' Excavations at Knossos: A Reassessment." *BSA* 86:185–191.

———. 1992. "The Protopalatial Façade at Knossos." *BSA* 87:165–175.

Momigliano, N., and M. S. F. Hood. 1994. "The Excavations of 1987 on the South Front of the Palace at Knossos." *BSA* 89:103–150.

Mook, M. 1998. "Early Iron Age Domestic Architecture: The Northwest Building on the Kastro at Kavousi." In *Post-Minoan Crete*, ed. W. Cavanaugh and M. Curtis, 45–57. London.

Mountjoy, P. A., with contributions by B. Burke, K. S. Christakis, J. M. Driessen, R. D. G. Evely, C. Knappett, and O. H. Krzyszkowska. 2003. *Knossos: The South House* (British School at Athens Suppl. 34). London.

Muhly, J., and E. Sikla, eds. 2000. *Crete 2000: A Centennial Celebration of American Archaeological Work in Crete.* Athens.

Muhly, P. 1984. "Minoan Hearths." *AJA* 88:107–122.

Murphy, J. 1998. "Ideology, Rites and Rituals: A View of Prepalatial Minoan Tholoi." In *Cemetery and Society in the Aegean Bronze Age* (Sheffield Studies in Aegean Archaeology 1), ed. K. Branigan, 27–40. Sheffield.

Myers, J. W. 1985. "An Aerial Atlas of Ancient Crete." *Archaeology* 38:15–25.

Myers, J. W., E. Myers, and G. Cadogan. 1992. *The Aerial Atlas of Ancient Crete.* Berkeley.

Myres, J. 1902–1903. "Excavations at Palaikastro II. The Sanctuary Site at Petsofa." *BSA* 9:356–387.

Niemeier, W.-D. 1982. "Mycenaean Knossos and the Age of Linear B." *SMEA* 23:219–287.

———. 1987. "On the Function of the 'Throne Room' in the Palace at Knossos." In *The Function of the Minoan Palaces* (Skrifter Utgivna av Svenska Institutet i Athen, 40, 35), ed. R. Hägg and N. Marinatos, 163–168. Stockholm.

———. 1994. "Knossos in the New Palace Period (MM III–LM IB)." In *Knossos: A Labyrinth of History. Papers presented in Honour of Sinclair Hood*, ed. D. Evely, H. Hughes-Brock, and N. Momigliano, 71–88. London.

Nilsson, M. 1950. *The Minoan-Mycenaean Religion and Its Survival in Greek Religion.* 2d ed. Lund.

Noack, F. 1907. *Ovalhaus und Palast in Kreta.* Leipzig.

Nordfeldt, A. 1987. "Residential Quarters and Lustral Basins." In *The Function of the Minoan Palaces* (Skrifter Utgivna av Svenska Institutet i Athen, 40, 35), ed. R. Hägg and N. Marinatos, 187–193. Stockholm.

Nowicki, K. 1987. "The History and the Setting of the Town at Karphi." *SMEA* 26:235–256.

———. 1999a. "Economy of Refugees: Life in the Cretan Mountains at the Turn of the Bronze and Iron Ages." In *From Minoan Farmers to Roman Traders*, ed. A. Chaniotios, 145–171. Stuttgart.

———. 1999b. "The Historical Background of Defensible Sites on Crete: Late Minoan IIIC versus Protopalatial." In *POLEMOS: Le context guerrier en égée à l'Age du Bronze* (*Aegaeum* 19), ed. R. Laffineur, 191–195. Liège.

———. 2000. *Defensible Sites in Crete ca. 1200–800 B.C.* (*Aegaeum* 21). Liége.

Oelmann, F. 1912. "Ein achäisches Herrenhaus auf Kreta," *JdI* 27:38–51.

Oliver, P. 1987. *Dwellings: The House across the World.* Austin.

Overbeck, J., and C. McDonald. 1976. "The Date of the Last Palace at Knossos." *AJA* 80:155–164.

Palaima, T. 1987. "Preliminary Comparative Textual Evidence for Palatial Control of Economic Activity in Minoan and Mycenaean Crete." In *The Function of the Minoan Palaces* (Skrifter Utgivna av Svenska Institutet i Athen, 40, XXXV), ed. R. Hägg and N. Marinatos, 301–306. Stockholm.

Palmer, L. 1963. "The Find-Places of the Knossos Tablets." *On the Knossos Tablets.* Oxford.

Palyvou, C. 1999. *Ακρωτήρι Θήρας: Η Οικοδομική Τέχνη.* Athens.

———. 2002. "Central Courts: The Supremacy of the Void." In *Monuments of Minos: Rethinking the Minoan Palaces* (*Aegaeum* 23), ed. J. Driessen, I. Schoep, and R. Laffineur, 167–178. Liège.

———. 2004. "Outdoor Space in Minoan Architecture: Community and Privacy." In *Knossos: Palace, City, State* (British School at Athens Studies 12), ed. G. Cadogan, E. Hatzaki, and A. Vasilakis, 207–217. London.

———. 2005. *Aktotiri Thera: An Architecture of Affluence 3,500 Years Old.* Philadelphia.

Panagiotaki, M. 1999. *The Central Palace Sanctuary at Knossos* (*BSA* Supp. 31). London.

Papadopoulos, J. 1997. "Knossos." In *The Conservation of Archaeological Sites in the Mediterranean Region*, ed. M. de la Torre, 93–125. Malibu.

Pashley, R. [1837] 1970. *Travels in Crete.* Amsterdam.

Peatfield, A. 1987. "Palace and Peak: The Political and Religious Relationship between Palaces and Peak Sanctuaries." In *The Function of the Minoan Palaces* (Skrifter Utgivna av Svenska Institutet i Athen, 40, 35), ed. R. Hägg and N. Marinatos, 89–93. Stockholm.

———. 1990. "Minoan Peak Sanctuaries: History and Society." *OpAth* 18:117–131.

———. 1994. "After the 'Big Bang' What?—Or Minoan Symbols and Shrines beyond the Palatial Collapse." In *Placing the Gods: Sanctuaries and Sacred Space in Ancient Greece*, ed. S. Alcock and R. Osbourne, 19–36. Oxford.

Pelon, O. 1966. "Maison d' Hagia Varvara et architecture domestique à Malia." *BCH* 90:552–585.

———. 1982. "L'epée à l'acrobate et la chronologie maliote." *BCH* 106:166–199.

———. 1983. "L'epée à l'acrobate et la chronologie maliote, (II)." *BCH* 107:679–703.

———. 1984. "Le palais." *BCH* 108:881–887.

———. 1986. "Un dépôt fondation au palais de Malia." *BCH* 110:3–19.

———. 1992. *Guide de Malia: Le palais et la nécropole de Chrysolakkos.* Paris.

———. 1993. "La Salle á pilier du palais de Malia et ses antecedents: recherché complémentaires" *BCH* 117:523–546.

———. 1999. "Travaux de l'école française à Athènes, Malia: Le palais." *BCH* 123:468–481.

Pendlebury, H., J. Pendlebury, and M. Money-Coutts. 1937–1938. "Karphi, a City of Refuge in the Early Iron Age in Crete: Excavations in the Plain of Lasithi, III." *BSA* 38:57–145.

Pendlebury, J. 1939. *The Archaeology of Crete.* London.

———. 1954. *A Handbook to the Palace of Minos at Knossos with Its Dependencies.* London.

Pernier, L. 1935. *Il Palazzo Minoico di Festós.* Rome.

Platon, L. 1997. "Caractère, morphologie et datation de la bourgade postpalatiale de Képhali Chondrou Viannou." In *La Crète mycénienne* (*BCH* Supp. 30), ed. J. Driessen and A. Farnoux, 357–373. Paris.

———. 2000. Ανακτορικά Χαρακτηριστικά στη Μινωική Αρχιτεκτονική. *Πεπραγμένα του Η' Διεθνούς Κρητηλογικού Συνεδρίου* (1996), 51–77.

———. 2002. "The Political and Cultural Influence of the Zakros Palace in Nearby Sites and in a Wider Context." In *Monuments of Minos: Rethinking the Minoan Palaces.* (*Aegaeum* 23), ed. J. Driessen, I. Schoep, and R. Laffineur, 145–155. Liège.

———. 2004. Το Υστεομινωικό Ανάκτορο της Ζάκρου: Μία "Κνοσός" έξο από την Κνοσό. In *Knossos: Palace, City, State* (British School at Athens Studies 12), ed. G. Cadogan, E. Hatzaki, and A. Vasilakis, 381–392. London.

Platon, N. 1971. *Zakros: The Discovery of a Lost Palace of Ancient Crete.* New York.

———. 1973. Ανασκαφή Ζάκρου. *Prakt* 1973:137–166.

Poblome, J., and C. Dumon. 1987–1988. "A Minoan Building Program? Some Comments on the Unexplored Mansion at Knossos." *AAL* 26–27:69–79.

Popham, M. 1964. *The Last Days of the Palace at Knossos: Complete Vases of the Late Minoan IIIB Period* (*SIMA* 5). Lund.

———. 1970. *The Destruction of the Palace at Knossos: Pottery of the Late Minoan IIIA Period* (*SIMA* 12). Göteborg.

———. 1981. "Cretan Sites Occupied Between the End of LM IB and the Destruction of the Palace at Knossos." *Πεπραγμένα του Δ' Διεθνούς Κρητηλογικού Συνεδρίου*, 454–460.

———. 1984. *Minoan Unexplored Mansion at Knossos*. London.

———. 1987. "The Use of the Palace at Knossos at the Time of Its Destruction." In *The Function of the Minoan Palaces* (Skrifter Utgivna av Svenska Institutet i Athen, 40, 35), ed. R. Hägg and N. Marinatos, 297–299. Stockholm.

———. 1994. "Late Minoan II to the End of the Bronze Age." In *Knossos: A Labyrinth of History. Papers presented in Honour of Sinclair Hood*, ed. D. Evely, H. Hughes-Brock, and N. Momigliano, 89–102. London.

———. 1997. "The Final Destruction of the Palace at Knossos: Seals, Sealings and Pottery. A Reconsideration." In *La Crète mycénienne* (*BCH* Supp. 30), ed. J. Driessen and A. Farnoux, 375–385. Paris.

Poursat, J.-Cl. 1966. "Un sanctuaire du Minoen moyen II à Mallia." *BCH* 90:514–551.

———. 1978. *Fouilles executeés à Mallia: le quartier Mu: Introduction general* (*ÉtCrét* 23). Paris.

———. 1987. "Town and Palace at Malia in the Protopalatial Period." In *The Function of the Minoan Palaces* (Skrifter Utgivna av Svenska Institutet i Athen, 40, 35), ed. R. Hägg and N. Marinatos, 75–76. Stockholm.

———. 1988. "La ville minoenne de Malia: recherches et publications récentes." *RA* 1988:61–82.

———. 1996. *Artisans minoens: Les maison-ateliers du Quartier Mu. Fouilles exécutées à Malia: Le Quartier Mu* (*ÉtCrét* 32). Paris.

Prent, M. 2003. "Glories of the Past in the Past: Ritual Activities at Palatial Ruins in Early Iron Age Crete." In *Archaeologies of Memory*, ed. R. Van Dyke and S. Alcock, 81–103. Malden, Mass.

———. 2005. *Cretan Sanctuaries and Cults: Continuity and Change from Late Minoan IIIC to the Archaic Period* (Religions in the Graeco-Roman World 154). Leiden.

Preston, L. 1999. "Mortuary Practices and the Negotiation of Social Identities at LM II Knossos." *BSA* 94:131–143.

———. 2004. "A Mortuary Perspective on Political Changes in Late Minoan II–III Crete." *AJA* 108:321–348.

———. 2005. "The Kephala Tholos at Knossos: A Study in the Reuse of the Past." *BSA* 100:61–123.

Preziosi, D. 1983. *Minoan Architectural Design: Formation and Signification*. Berlin.

———. 2003. "What Does a Module Mean?" In *METRON: Measuring the Aegean Bronze Age* (*Aegaeum* 24), ed. K. Foster and R. Laffineur, 233–237. Liège.

Privitera, S. 2004. "Culti domestici a Creta nel TM IIIA2–TM IIIB: Per un'analisi contestuale." *Creta Antica* 4:107–135.

Puglisi, D. 2001. "Un arsenale marittimo l'Edificio T di Kommos?" *Creta Antica* 2:113–123.

Rackham, O., and J. Moody. 1996. *The Making of the Cretan Landscape*. Manchester.

Rehak, P., and J. Younger. 1998. "Review of Aegean Prehistory 7: Neopalatial, Final Palatial and Postpalatial Crete." *AJA* 102:91–173.

Relaki, M. 2004. "Constructing a Region: The Contested Landscapes of Prepalatial Mesara." In *The Emergence of Civilization Revisited* (Sheffield Studies in Archaeology 6) ed. J. Barrett and P. Halstead, 170–188. Oxford.

Renfrew, C. 1972. *The Emergence of Civilisation*. London.

———. 1996. "Who Were the Minoans? Towards a Population History of Crete." *Cretan Studies* 5:1–21.

Rethemiotakis, G. 1999. "The Hearths of the Minoan Palace at Galatas." In *MELETEMATA: Studies in Aegean Archaeology Presented to Malcolm H. Wiener as He Enters His 65th Year* (*Aegaeum* 20), ed. P. Betancourt, V. Karageroghis, R. Laffineur, and W.-D. Niemeier, 721–728. Liège.

———. 2001. *Minoan Clay Figures and Figurines*. Athens.

———. 2002. "Evidence on Social and Economic Changes at Galatas and Pediadha in the New-Palace Period." In *Monuments of Minos: Rethinking the Minoan Palaces* (*Aegaeum* 23), ed. J. Driessen, I. Schoep, and R. Laffineur, 55–70. Liège.

Robertson, D. 1971. *Greek and Roman Architecture*. 2d ed. Cambridge.

Russell, P. 1979. "The Date of the Gournia Shrine." *TUAS* 4:27–33.

Rutkowski, B. 1986. *The Cult Places of the Aegean World*. New Haven.

———. 1987. "The Temple at Karphi." *SMEA* 26:257–279.

Rykwert, J. 1976. *The Idea of a Town: The Anthropology of Urban Form in Rome, Italy and the Ancient World.* Princeton.

———. 1982. *The Necessity of Artifice.* New York.

Sakellarakis, Y. 1983. Δοκιμαστική Ανασκαφή Ζώμινθου. *Prakt* 1983:488–498.

Sakellarakis, Y., and E. Sapouna-Sakellaraki. 1997. *Archanes: Minoan Crete in a New Light.* 2 vols. Athens.

Schmandt-Besserat, D. 1977. "The Beginnings of the Use of Clay in Turkey." *AnatStud* 27:133–150.

Schoep, I. 1999. "The Origins of Writing and Administration on Crete." *OJA* 18:265–276.

———. 2002a. "Social and Political Organization on Crete in the Protopalatial Period: The Case of MM II Malia." *JMA* 15:102–125.

———. 2002b. "The State of the Minoan Palaces or the Minoan Palace State?" In *Monuments of Minos: Rethinking the Minoan Palaces* (*Aegaeum* 23), ed. J. Driessen, I. Schoep, and R. Laffineur, 15–33. Liège.

———. 2004. "Assessing the Role of Architecture in Conspicuous Consumption in the Middle Minoan I–II Periods." *OJA* 23:243–269.

———. 2006. "Looking Beyond the First Palaces: Elites and the Agency of Power in EM II–MM II Crete. " *AJA* 110:37–64.

Schoep, I., and C. Knappett. 2004. "Dual Emergence: Evolving Hetarchy, Exploding Hierarchy." In *The Emergence of Civilization Revisited,* ed. J. Barrett and P. Halstead, 21–37. Oxford.

Seager, R. 1904–1905. *Report of Excavations at Vasilike, Crete, 1904: Transactions of the Free Museum of Science and Art, University of Pennsylvania, I (1904–1905),* 207–221. Philadelphia.

———. 1907. *Report of Excavations at Vasilike, Crete, in 1906: Transactions of the Free Museum of Science and Art, University of Pennsylvania, II (1906–1907),* 111–132. Philadelphia.

Shaw, J. 1971. *Minoan Architecture: Materials and Techniques* (*ASAtene* 44). Rome.

———. 1973. "The Chrysolakkos Facades." *Πεπραγμένα του Γ' Διεθνούς Κρητολογικού Συνεδρίου,* 319–331.

———. 1977b. "The Orientation of the Minoan Palaces." *AntCr* 1:47–59.

———. 1978a. "Evidence for the Minoan Tripartite Shrine." *AJA* 82:429–448.

———. 1978b. "Sliding Panels at Knossos." *BSA* 73:235–248.

———. 1978c. "Akrotiri as a Minoan Settlement." In *Thera and the Aegean World,* I, ed. C. Doumas, 429–436. London.

———. 2000. "Kommos: The Sea-Gate to Southern Crete." In *Crete Beyond the Palaces: Proceedings of the Crete 2000 Conference,* ed. L. Day, M. Mook, and J. Muhly, 43–51. Philadelphia.

———. 2002. "The Minoan Palatial Establishment at Kommos: An Anatomy of Its History, Function, and Interconnections." In *Monuments of Minos: Rethinking the Minoan Palaces* (*Aegaeum* 23), ed. J. Driessen, I. Schoep, and R. Laffineur, 99–111. Liège.

———. 2003. "Palatial Proportions: A Study of the Relative Proportions between Minoan Palaces and Their Settlements." In *METRON: Measuring the Aegean Bronze Age* (*Aegaeum* 24), ed. K. Foster and R. Laffineur, 239–245. Liège.

———. 2006. "The Architecture and Stratigraphy of the Civic Buildings." In *Kommos V: The Monumental Minoan Buildings at Kommos,* ed. J. Shaw and M. Shaw, 1–116. Princeton.

Shaw, J., with A. Lowe. 2002. "The 'Lost Portico' at Knossos: The Central Court Revisited." *AJA* 106:513–523.

Shaw, J., and M. Shaw. 1993. "Excavations at Kommos (Crete) during 1986–1992." *Hesperia* 62:129–190.

Shaw, J., and M. Shaw, eds. 1985. *A Great Minoan Triangle in South Central Crete: Kommos, Haghia Triada, Phaistos* (*Scripta Mediterranea* 6). Toronto.

———. 2006. *Kommos V: The Monumental Minoan Buildings at Kommos.* Princeton.

Shaw, M. 1990. "Late Minoan Hearths and Ovens at Kommos." In *L'habitat égéen préhistorique.* (*BCH* Supp. 19), ed. P. Darcque and R. Treuil, 231–254. Paris.

Shear, I. 1968. "Mycenaean Domestic Architecture." Ph.D. diss., Bryn Mawr College.

Shennan, S. 1989a. "Introduction: Archaeological Approaches to Cultural Identity." In *Archaeological Approaches to Cultural Identity,* ed. S. Shennan, 5–6. London.

———, ed. 1989b. *Archaeological Approaches to Cultural Identity.* London.

Soles, J. 1992. *The Prepalatial Cemeteries at Mochlos and Gournia and the House Tombs of Bronze Age Crete* (*Hesperia* Supp. 24). Princeton.

———. 1995. "The Functions of a Cosmological Center: Knossos in Palatial Crete." In *POLITEIA: Society and State in the Aegean Bronze Age* (*Aegaeum* 12), ed. R. Laffineur and W.-D. Niemeier, 405–414. Liége.

———. 2002. "A Central Court at Gournia?" In *Monuments of Minos: Rethinking the Minoan Palaces* (*Aegaeum* 23), ed. J. Driessen, I. Schoep, and R. Laffineur, 123–133. Liège.

———. 2003. *Mochlos IA, Period III: Neopalatial Settlement on the Coast: The Artisan's Quarter and the Farmhouse at Chalinomouri*. Philadelphia.

———. 2004. "New Construction at Mochlos in the LM IB Period." In *Crete Beyond the Palaces: Proceedings of the Crete 2000 Conference*, ed. L. Day, M. Mook, and J. Muhly, 153–162. Philadelphia.

Soles, J., and C. Davaras. 1996. "Excavations at Mochlos, 1992–1993." *Hesperia* 65:175–230.

Strasser, T. 1992. "Neolithic Settlement and Land-Use on Crete." Ph.D. diss., Indiana University.

———. 1997. "Storage and States on Prehistoric Crete: The Function of the *Koulouras* in the First Minoan Palaces." *JMA* 10:73–100.

Stürmer, V. 1993. "La céramique de Chrysolakkos." *BCH* 117:123–187.

Televantou, C. 1994. *Ακρωτήρι Θήρας: Οι Τοιχογραφίες της Δυτικής Οικίας*. Athens.

Tenwolde, C. 1992. "Myrtos Revisited: The Role of Relative Function Ceramic Typologies in Bronze Age Settlement Analysis." *OJA* 11:1–24.

Theocharis, D. 1973. *Neolithic Greece*. Athens.

Tilley, C. 1989. "Interpreting Material Culture." In *The Meanings of Things*, ed. I. Hodder, 185–194. London.

———. 2006. "Theoretical Perspectives in 2006." *Handbook of Material Culture*, ed. C. Tilley, W. Keane, S. Küchler, M. Rowlands, P. Spyer, 7–11. London.

Tilley, C., W. Keane, S. Küchler, M. Rowlands, P. Spyer, eds. 2006. *Handbook of Material Culture*. London.

Tomkins, P. 2004. "Filling in the 'Neolithic Background': Social Life and Social Transformation in the Aegean Before the Bronze Age." In *The Emergence of Civilization Revisited*, ed. J. Barrett and P. Halstead, 38–63. Oxford.

Tomkins, P., P. Day, and V. Kilikoglou. 2004. "Knossos and the Earlier Neolithic Landscape of the Herakleion Basin." In *Knossos: Palace, City, State* (British School at Athens Studies 12), ed. G. Cadogan, E. Hatzaki, and A. Vasilakis, 51–65. London.

Treuil, R. 1983. *Le neolithique et la Bronze ancien égéen*. Paris.

Tsipopoulou, M. 1999a. "From Local Center to Palace: The Role of Fortification in the Economic Transformation of the Siteia Bay Area, East Crete." In *POLEMOS: La contexte guerrier in égée à l'Age du Bronze* (*Aegaeum* 19), ed. R. Laffineur, 179–190. Liège.

———. 1999b. "Before, During and After: The Architectural Phases of the Palatial Building at Petras, Siteia." In *MELETEMATA: Studies in Aegean Archaeology Presented to Malcolm H. Wiener as He Enters His 65th Year* (*Aegaeum* 20), ed. P. Betancourt, V. Karageorghis, R. Laffineur, and W.-D. Niemeier, 847–855. Liège.

———. 2001. "A New Late Minoan IIIC Shrine at Halasmenos, East Crete." In *POTNIA: Deities and Religion in the Aegean Bronze Age* (*Aegaeum* 22), ed. R. Laffineur and R. Hägg, 99–103. Liège.

———. 2002. "Petras, Siteia: The Palace, the Town, the Hinterland and the Protopalatial Background." In *Monuments of Minos: Rethinking the Minoan Palaces* (*Aegaeum* 23), ed. J. Driessen, I. Schoep, and R. Laffineur, 133–143. Liège.

———. 2004. "Halasmenos, Destroyed But Not Invisible: New Insights on the LM IIIC Period in the Isthmus of Hierapetra. First Presentation of the Pottery from the 1992–1997 Campaigns." In *Crete Beyond the Palaces: Proceedings of the Crete 2000 Conference*, ed. L. Day, M. Mook, and J. Muhly, 103–123. Philadelphia.

———. 2005. "'Mycenoans' at the Isthmus of Ierapetra: Some Preliminary Thoughts on the Foundation of the (Eteo)cretan Cultural Identity." In *Ariadne's Threads: Connections between Crete and the Mainland in Late Minoan III (LM IIIA2 to LM IIIC)*, ed. L. D'Agata, L. Moody, with E. Williams, 303–333. Athens.

Tzedakis, Y., and S. Chryssoulaki. 1987. "Neopalatial Architectural Elements in the Area of Chania." In *The Function of the Minoan Palace* (Skrifter Utgivna av Svenska Institutet i Athen, 40, XXXV), ed. R. Hägg and N. Marinatos, 111–115. Stockholm.

Vagnetti, L. 1972–1973. "L'insediamento neolitico de Festòs." *ASAtene* 34–35:7–138.

Vallianou, D. 1997. "The Potters' Quarter in LM III Gouves." In *TEXNH: Craftsmen, Craftswomen, and Craftsmanship in the Aegean Bronze Age* (*Aegaeum* 16), ed. R. Laffineur and P. Betancourt, 333–344. Liège.

Van Dyke, R., and S. Alcock. 2003a. "Archaeologies of Memory: An Introduction." In *Archaeologies of Memory*, ed. S. Van Dyke and S. Alcock, 1–13. Malden, Mass.

———, eds. 2003b. *Archaeologies of Memory*. Malden, Mass.

Van Effenterre, H. 1980. *Le palais de Mallia et la cité minoenne. Étude de synthèse*, I and II. Rome.

———. 1987. "The Function of Monumentality in the Minoan Palaces." In *The Function of the Minoan Palaces* (Skrifter Utgivna av Svenska Institutet i Athen, 40, XXXV), ed. R. Hägg and N. Marinatos, 85–87. Stockholm.

Van Effenterre, H., and M. van Effenterre. 1969. *Fouilles exécutées a Mallia: La centre politique I. L'Agora* (*ÉtCrét* 17). Paris.

———. 1976. *Fouilles exécutées a Mallia: Exploration des maisons et des quartiers d'habitation (1956–1960), quatrième fascicule* (*ÉtCrét* 22). Paris.

Vasilakis, A. 1989. Ο Πρωτωμινωικός οικισμός Τρυπυτής, *Αρχαιολογία* 30:52–56.

———. 1990. Προιστορικές Θέσις στή Μόνι Οδιγίτρια/ Καλούς Λιμένες. *Kritiki Estia* 3:11–80.

———. 1995. Τρυπυτή 1986–1991: Ζητίματου προανακτορικού μινωικού πολιτισμού στή νότια κεντρική Κρήτη καί η ανασκαφή Τρυπθτής. *Πεπραγμένα του Θ' Διεθηνούς Κρητολογικού Συνεδρίου*, 69–73.

Vasileiades, D. 1976. *Το Κρητικό Σπίτι*. Athens.

Wagstaff, J. M. 1965. "Traditional Houses in Modern Greece." *Geography*, 50:58–64.

Walberg, G. 1983. *Provincial Middle Minoan Pottery*. Mainz am Rhein.

———. 1992. *Middle Minoan III: A Time of Transition* (*SIMA* 97). Jonserad.

Wallace, S. 2003. "The Perpetuated Past: Re-Use or Continuity in Material Culture and the Structuring of Identity in Early Iron Age Crete." *BSA* 98:251–277.

———. 2005. "Last Chance to See? Karphi (Crete) in the Twenty-First Century: Presentation of New Architectural Data and Their Analysis in the Current Context of Research." *BSA* 100:215–274.

Walsh, V. 1980. "A Computer Simulation of the House Construction Activity System at Nichoria in Southwest Greece." Ph.D. diss., University of Minnesota.

Warren, P. 1972. *Myrtos: An Early Bronze Age Settlement in Crete* (British School at Athens Supp. 7). Cambridge.

———. 1983. "Knossos: Stratigraphical Museum Excavations, 1978–1982: Part II." *AR* 29:63–87.

———. 1984. "Circular Platforms at Minoan Knossos." *BSA* 79:307–23.

———. 1987. "The Genesis of the Minoan Palace." In *The Function of the Minoan Palaces* (Skrifter Utgivna av Svenska Institutet i Athen, 40, XXXV), ed. R. Hägg and N. Marinatos, 47–55. Stockholm.

———. 1994. "The Minoan Roads of Knossos." In *Knossos: A Labyrinth of History: Papers Presented in Honour of Sinclair Hood*, ed. D. Evely, H. Hughes-Brock, and N. Momigliano, 189–210. London.

———. 2002. "Political Structure in Neopalatial Crete." In *Monuments of Minos: Rethinking the Minoan Palaces* (*Aegaeum* 23), ed. J. Driessen, I. Schoep, and R. Laffineur, 201–205. Liège.

Warren, P., and V. Hankey. 1989. *Aegean Bronze Age Chronology*. Bristol.

Watrous, L. V. 1987. "The Role of the Near East in the Rise of the Cretan Palaces." In *The Function of the Minoan Palaces* (Skrifter Utgivna av Svenska Institutet i Athen, 40, XXXV), ed. R. Hägg and N. Marinatos, 65–70. Stockholm.

———. 1994. "Review of Aegean Prehistory III: Crete from Earliest Prehistory through the Protopalatial Period." *AJA* 98:695–753.

———. 2000. "Gournia." In *Crete 2000: One Hundred Years of American Archaeological Work on Crete*, ed. J. Muhly and E. Sikla, 127–135. Athens.

———. 2004. "New Pottery from the Psychro Cave and Its Implications for Minoan Crete." *BSA* 99:129–147.

Watrous, L. V., D. Hadzi-Vallianou, K. Pope, N. Mourtzas, J. Shay, C. Shay, J. Bennet, T. Tsougarakis, E. Angelomati-Tsougaraki, C. Vallianos, and H. Blitzer. 1993. "A Survey of the Western Mesara Plain in Crete: Preliminary Report of the 1984–1987 Field Seasons." *Hesperia* 62:191–248.

Weingarten, J. 1990. "Three Upheavals in Minoan Sealing Administration." In *Aegean Seals, Sealings and Administration* (*Aegaeum* 5), ed. T. Palaima, 107–112. Liège.

Westgate, R., N. Fisher, and J. Whitley, eds. 2007. *Building Communities. House, Settlement and Society in the Aegean and Beyond*. London.

Whitelaw, T. 1983. "The Settlement at Fournou Korifi, Myrtos and Aspects of Early Minoan Social Organization." In *Minoan Society*, ed. O. Krzyszkowska and L. Nixon, 323–345. Bristol.

———. 1992. "Lost in the Labyrinth? Comments on Broodbank's 'Social Change at Knossos before the Bronze Age.'" *JMA* 5:229–243.

———. 2001. "From Site to Communities: Defining the Human Dimensions of Minoan Urbanism." In *Urbanism in the Aegean Bronze Age* (Sheffield Studies in Aegean Archaeology 1) ed. K. Branigan, 15–37. London.

———. 2004a. "Alternative Pathways to Complexity in the Southern Aegean." In *The Emergence of Civilization Revisited* (Sheffield Studies in Archaeology 6), ed. J. Barrett and P. Halstead, 232–256. Sheffield.

———. 2004b. "Estimating the Population of Neopalatial Knossos." In *Knossos: Palace, City, State* (British School at Athens Studies 12), ed. G. Cadogan, E. Hatzaki, and A. Vasilakis, 174–158. London.

———. 2007. "House, Household and Community at Early Minoan Fournou Korifi: Methods and Models for Interpretation." In *Building Communities: House, Settlement and Society in the Aegean and Beyond*, ed. R. Westgate, N. Fisher, and J. Whitley, 65–76.

Whitley, J. 1991. *Style and Society in Dark Age Greece.* Cambridge.

Whittaker, H. 1997. *Mycenaean Cult Buildings: A Study of Their Architecture and Function in the Context of the Aegean and the Eastern Mediterranean.* Bergen.

———. 2002. "Minoan Board Games: The Function and Meaning of Stones with Depressions (so-called 'Kernoi') from Bronze Age Crete." *Aegean Archaeology* 6:73–87.

Wiener, M. 1984. "Crete and the Cyclades in LM I: The Tale of the Conical Cups." In *Minoan Thalassocracy: Myth and Reality* (Skrifter utgivna av Svenska Institutet i Athen, 40, 35), ed. R. Hägg and N. Marinatos, 17–25. Stockholm.

Wilson, D. 1994. "Knossos before the Palaces: An Overview of the Early Bronze Age." In *Knossos: A Labyrinth of History. Papers Presented in Honour of Sinclair Hood*, ed. D. Evely, H. Hughes-Brock, and N. Momigliano, 23–44. London.

Wilson, D., and P. Day. 1994. "Ceramic Regionalism in Prepalatial Central Crete." *BSA* 98:1–87.

Wright, J. 2004a. "The Mycenaean Feast: An Introduction." *Hesperia* 73:121–132.

———. 2004b. "A Survey of Evidence for Feasting in Mycenaean Society." *Hesperia* 73:133–175.

Xanthoudides, S. 1906. Προιστορική Οικία εις Χαμαίζι Σητείας, *ArchEph* 1906, col. 117–156.

———. 1924. *The Vaulted Tombs of the Mesara.* London.

Yaeger, J., and M. Canuto. 2000. "Introducing an Archaeology of Communities." In *Archaeology of Communities: A New World Perspective*, ed. M. Canuto and J. Yaeger, 1–15. London.

Zois, A. 1968. Υπάρχει ΠΜ III Εποχή. *Πεπραγμένα του* Β' Διεθνούς Κρητολογικού Συνεδρίου, 141–156.

———. 1976. *Βασιλική I.* Athens.

———. 1979. "Gibt es Vortäufer der Minoishen Paläste auf Kreta? Ergibnisse neuer Untersuchungen." In *Palast und Hütte: Beiträge zum Bauen und Wohen in Altertum*, ed. D. Papenfuss and V. Strocka, 207–215. Mainz am Rhein.

INDEX

Page numbers in *italics* refer to figures.

Printed and bound by CPI Group (UK) Ltd, Croydon, CR0 4YY

09/06/2025

14685841-0001